GRAND CANYON

WITHDRAWN

KATHLEEN BRYANT

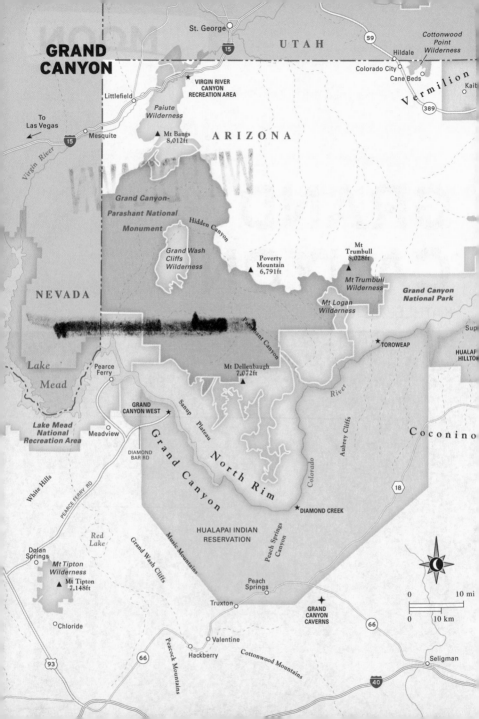

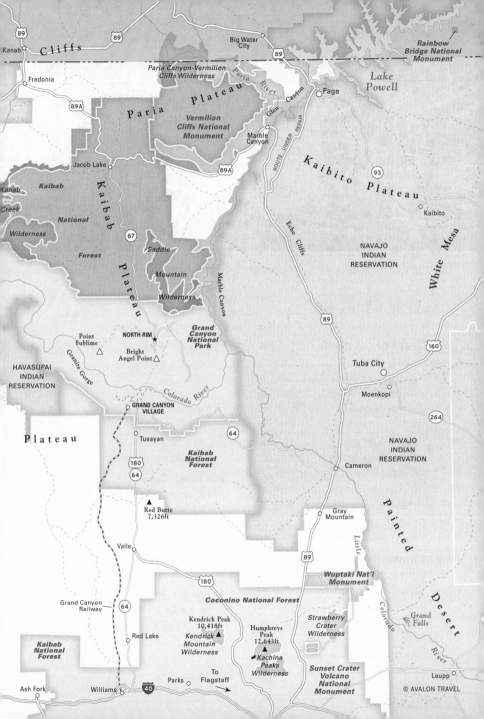

Contents

DISCOVER

Grand Canyon

I t's not hard to see why over 5 million people visit Grand Canyon each year. This UNESCO World Heritage Site is extraordinary in many ways.

It's old. Two billion years ago, rocks along the Colorado River were formed, and five to six million years ago, the river began cutting the canyon open, revealing one of the most complete geological histories on the planet. Today, layered cliffs of red, orange, gray, and tan record three eras of geological time.

It's big. The canyon isn't a single deep gorge; it's an entire collection of tributaries so vast and complex that it challenges the imagination. Dozens of landforms—such as Zoroaster, Shiva Temple, and Freya Castle—rise up from Grand Canyon's rocky folds. These features would be singularly remarkable anywhere else.

It's rich with biological diversity. From the North Rim's boreal forests to the inner canyon's river and desert landscape, Grand Canyon supports more than 2,000 species of plants, mammals, birds, reptiles, amphibians, and fish. Some of these species—like the tiny purple-and-white sentry milk-vetch—are found nowhere else on earth.

Clockwise from top left: Grand Canyon Lodge on the North Rim; Grand Canyon Railway in Williams; pack mule; painting during the Celebration of Art festival; aspens in autumn; Mather Point on the South Rim.

It's full of surprises. Though Grand Canyon appears stark and forbidding from the vantage point of its rims, hidden within are numerous springs, creeks, and waterfalls, such as Deer Creek or Ribbon Falls. For 10,000 years these oases have nourished people traveling through or sheltering in the canyon. Ancient people left their stories behind in the form of ruins, rock art, potsherds, and other artifacts.

Grand Canyon is a place not only of natural importance, but also of great significance to humanity. It's a place of grand drama and serene vistas, so vast and varied that each visitor will experience it from a different perspective.

Come and discover your own reasons to call Grand Canyon extraordinary.

Clockwise from top left: Angels Window from Cape Royal Road; deer in winter; hiking on the South Kaibab Trail; detail of Desert View Watchtower.

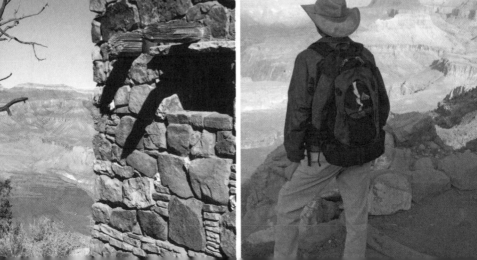

Planning Your Trip

Where to Go

The South Rim

The South Rim, the **most visited area** of Grand Canyon National Park, extends roughly 40 miles from **Hermits Rest** to **Desert View.** The Rim Trail and scenic overlooks such as **Mather Point** offer varying perspectives of the canyon and its maze of tributaries and monuments. **Grand Canyon Village** bustles with **lodging, dining, shopping,** and activities from mule riding to star gazing. Architect Mary Colter's eccentric buildings perch along the rim, and several hikes, including historic **Bright Angel Trail,** lead into the canyon's depths.

The North Rim

The North Rim, accessible **spring through fall,** is higher, cooler, and **more remote.** Only 1 in 10 park visitors travels to the North Rim, where **Grand Canyon Lodge** and the park's campground offer accommodations on **Bright Angel Point.** Scenic **Cape Royal Drive** leads to **Point Imperial** and **Angels Window,** with stops for picnicking and hiking along the way. **Jacob Lake,** the nearest town, is about 30 miles from the park entrance station.

The Inner Canyon

Accessible only **on foot, by mule, or by boat,**

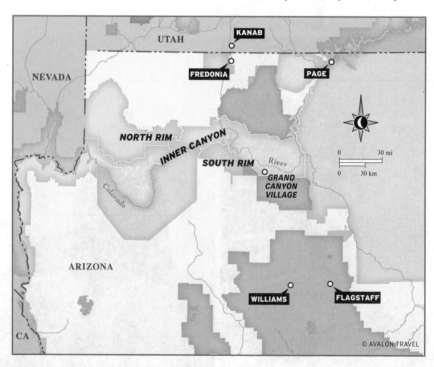

Mather Point

the inner canyon is a treasure of buttes and monuments, hidden waterfalls, and dozens of tributary canyons, all linked by the **Colorado River.** On its 277-mile journey from **Lees Ferry** to **Lake Mead,** the river churns over dozens of white-water rapids. The historic oasis of **Phantom Ranch** offers the only lodging and dining in the canyon's heart.

Beyond the Boundaries

Outside national park boundaries, such destinations as **Havasu Canyon, Grand Canyon Skywalk,** and historic **Lees Ferry** are part of Grand Canyon's story. Exploring may require a **high-clearance vehicle,** but those who want to **escape the crowds** will be rewarded with lonely vistas, rich cultural traditions, and landscapes from stark plateaus to dense forest.

Gateways to Grand Canyon

The mountain town of **Flagstaff** combines urban pleasures with a dazzling array of **outdoor activities. Williams** will delight **train buffs** and **Route 66** fans. **Page,** home to Lake Powell and its labyrinth of sandstone canyons, lures **boaters** and **backpackers. Kanab** makes an ideal

jumping-off point to the **North Rim** and also to Zion, Bryce Canyon, and other parklands on the Southwest's **Grand Circle.**

Williams

If You're Looking for...

- **Backpacking:** Secure your backcountry permit in advance for overnights in the inner canyon. Or sign up for a tour with the Grand Canyon Field Institute.

- **Bicycling:** Ride the Greenway Trail on the South Rim. Mountain bikers can tackle the North Rim's Point Sublime Road, a long up-and-down two-track with campsites for overnight (permit required).

- **Historic Sites:** Wander the Grand Canyon Village Historic District or climb Desert View Watchtower on the South Rim.

- **Horseback Riding:** Equines are allowed on the South Kaibab, Bright Angel, River, and Plateau Point Trails on the South Rim and on the North Kaibab, Uncle Jim, and Ken Patrick Trails on the North Rim.

- **Rafting:** Reserve a spot on a guided Colorado River trip through the inner canyon.

- **Driving Tours:** Cruise Desert View Drive and Hermits Road (Dec.-Feb.) on the South Rim or Cape Royal Drive on the North Rim.

- **Waterfalls:** Make advance reservations to hike into the Havasupai Nation's Havasu Canyon for a series of waterfalls.

riding the Greenway Trail

Havasu Falls

When to Go

Be ready for anything. Even on the South Rim, it can snow in June, and it isn't unheard of for temperatures to hit 90°F in October. Roads, trails, and buildings may close temporarily for needed maintenance, and the trans-canyon water pipeline is prone to breakdowns. Your phone may not get a signal, and the train could be late; however, the afternoon thundershower that spoils your hike to Indian Garden might yield a rainbow during a sunset viewed from Yaki Point.

High Season (Summer)

The South Rim's high season is **April to October** (with an early blip in March on the South Rim during spring break). At the **North Rim,** the season doesn't begin until **mid-May,** lasting until most visitor services close in mid-October.

During **summer,** hikers must strategize. Though mornings and evenings on both rims are relatively cool, the midday sun bakes trails and overlooks, and the inner canyon becomes a shadeless furnace. Time hikes for early or late in the day, choose trails with afternoon shade, and pack plenty of water.

Mid-Season (Spring and Fall)

Spring may arrive at the South Rim like a lamb or a lion, with blustery winds and late snow. Snow can blanket North Rim locations into May, just when inner canyon temperatures are climbing into the 90s. **Autumn** is a glorious time to visit—crowds have eased, and summer temperatures lose their grip. Expect dry, sunny days—**ideal hiking weather**—and clear dark nights, perfect for watching meteor showers. On the North Rim, aspens begin to turn gold in September, peaking in radiance the first week of October.

Low Season (Winter)

Don't let **winter** keep you from the canyon: The **South Rim** can be magical in winter months, and the **inner canyon** is temperate for hikers and backpackers, though commercial river trips don't run during this time. Guest services close October 15 on the North Rim, but day-trippers are welcome until December 1, weather permitting.

A snowstorm lifts from the South Rim.

Flagstaff Visitor Center

Before You Go

To make the most of your time, take advantage of trip-planning tools on the **National Park Service** (www.nps.gov/grca) website, including permit applications, trail descriptions, backpacking advice, and current weather forecasts.

Park Fees and Passes

The entrance fee for Grand Canyon National Park is **$30 per vehicle** ($25 per motorcycle). The fee is **$15 per person** when entering on foot, bicycle, or aboard the park shuttle, free for children under age 16.

To enter through the park's faster prepaid lanes, you can pay fees in advance at several locations:

- **National Geographic Visitor Center** (450 Hwy. 64, Tusayan, 928/638-2468, www.explorethecanyon.com, 8am-10pm daily Mar.-Oct., 9am-8pm daily Nov.-Feb.) and several other businesses in Tusayan and Valle
- **Williams Visitor Center** (200 W. Railroad Ave., Williams, 928/635-1418, www.experience williams.com, 8am-6:30pm daily summer, 8am-5pm daily fall-spring)
- **Flagstaff Visitor Center** (1 E. Route 66, Flagstaff, 928/213-2951 or 800/379-0065, www. flagstaffarizona.org, 8am-5pm Mon.-Sat., 9am-4pm Sun.)

Each year, Grand Canyon National Park offers several **fee-free days,** most on federal holidays or National Park Service occasions.

Discounts or free passes are available for seniors, military members, people with permanent disabilities, and federal lands volunteers with more than 250 hours of service. The "Every Kid in a Park" program (http://everykidinapark.gov) offers pass vouchers to U.S. fourth-graders from the beginning of the school year through the following summer. Other fee options include:

- **Grand Canyon Pass ($60):** Provides entrance to the park for one year.
- **Interagency Pass ($80):** Provides entrance

to all national parks, monuments, and recreation areas for one year.

Reservations

If you plan on backpacking or camping during your visit to the canyon, be sure to apply for a **backcountry permit** (up to four months in advance) and make campground reservations (up to a year in advance).

River trips and **mule tours** often fill up six months to a year in advance. **Rooms** and **campsites** may sell out during high season.

- For lodging and mule trips on the South Rim and inner canyon: **Xanterra Parks & Resorts** (888/297-2757 or 303/297-2757, www.grandcanyonlodges.com), except for Yavapai Lodge, operated by **Delaware North** (877/404-4611, www.visitgrandcanyon.com)

- For North Rim lodging: **Forever Resorts** (877/386-4383, http://grandcanyonforever.com)

- For North Rim mule rides: **Grand Canyon Trail Rides** (435/679-8665, http://canyon-rides.com)

- For campground reservations: **Recreation.gov** (877/444-6777, www.recreation.gov), except for the South Rim's Trailer Village RV Park, operated by **Delaware North** (877/404-4611, www.visitgrandcanyon.com)

Avoiding the Crowds

- Avoid spring break and weekends, especially holiday ones, or **visit during winter.**

- **Make reservations** 4-13 months in advance to secure a room, a camping spot, a backcountry permit, or a table at El Tovar.

- Buy your pass outside the park and enter via the **prepaid lane,** which requires only a brief stop to show your pass.

- Arrive **before 9am** or **after 2pm.**

- Park your car and hop on a **free shuttle.** Or bypass entry station queues altogether by **boarding the train** in Williams and arriving at the Grand Canyon depot in time for lunch.

- View the canyon from gorgeous **Yaki Point** (orange shuttle) or peaceful **Pima Point** (red shuttle).

Ride Grand Canyon's free shuttle buses.

In the Park

Entrance Stations

SOUTH RIM

Most visitors enter through the **South Entrance,** accessible from Flagstaff via U.S. 180 or Williams via Highway 64. The **East Entrance,** accessible from Flagstaff or Page via U.S. 89 and Highway 64, is smaller and receives far fewer visitors.

NORTH RIM

The **North Entrance Station** is on scenic Highway 67, and the road is open to travel **mid-May to early December,** or whenever winter snows close the road. Visitor services close for the season October 15.

Visitor Centers

Grand Canyon Visitor Center (8am-5pm daily spring-fall, 9am-5pm daily winter) is a couple of miles north of the South Entrance.

The **North Rim Visitor Center** (928/638-2481, 8am-6pm daily mid-May-Oct. 15) is at the end of Highway 67 at Bright Angel Point.

Where to Stay

SOUTH RIM

For **same-day reservations** at lodges inside the park, call 928/638-2631 or 928/638-4001. Accommodations outside the park can be found in nearby **Tusayan** (7 miles) or **Valle** (30 miles), or in the gateway cities of **Williams** (60 miles) or **Flagstaff** (80 miles).

The following campgrounds fill quickly during summer months:

- **Mather Campground** is usually fully booked during summer months, but December-February availability is first-come, first-served.

- **Desert View Campground** has 50 first-come, first-served sites (May-mid-Oct.), usually filled by early afternoon during summer.

- **Kaibab National Forest** (928/638-2443 or 928/643-7395, www.fs.usda.gov/kaibab) operates seasonal campgrounds near both rims that include some first-come, first-served sites. The forest also has at-large primitive camping.

North Rim Campground

In-Park Lodging

	Location	Rates	Season	Amenities
Mather Campground	South Rim	$18	year-round	tent sites
Trailer Village	South Rim	$44	year-round	RV sites
Bright Angel Lodge	South Rim	$97-217	year-round	hiker rooms, hotel rooms, cabins, restaurants
Maswik Lodge	South Rim	$107-205	year-round	motel rooms, cabins, restaurant
Yavapai Lodge	South Rim	$150-185	year-round	motel rooms, restaurant
Kachina Lodge	South Rim	$225-243	year-round	motel rooms
Thunderbird Lodge	South Rim	$225-243	year-round	motel rooms
El Tovar	South Rim	$217-354	year-round	hotel rooms, restaurant
Desert View Campground	East Rim	$12	May-mid-Oct	tent sites
North Rim Campground	North Rim	$18-25	May 15-Oct. 31	tent sites
Grand Canyon Lodge	North Rim	$13-205	May 15-Oct. 15	cabins, motel rooms, restaurant
Indian Garden Campground	inner canyon	permit required	year-round	hike-in tent sites
Bright Angel Campground	inner canyon	permit required	year-round	hike-in tent sites
Cottonwood Campground	inner canyon	permit required	year-round	hike-in tent sites
Phantom Ranch	inner canyon	$49-142	year-round	hike-in dorms, cabins, food

NORTH RIM

Lodging availability is limited during the North Rim's short season. Other options can be found in **Jacob Lake** (45 miles) and the gateway cities of **Page** (123 miles) and **Kanab,** Utah (80 miles).

The **North Rim Campground** has first-come, first-served sites October 15 to October 31, two weeks after North Rim services close.

Getting Around

The **South Rim's free shuttle** system covers Grand Canyon Village (year-round) and Hermit Road (Mar.-Nov.). Buses arrive every 10 to 30 minutes, running an hour before sunrise to an hour after sunset. The *South Rim Pocket Map and Services Guide,* available at entrance stations and visitor centers, includes routes and current schedules.

view from the Rim Trail

The Best of Grand Canyon

Even a lifetime isn't long enough to experience all of Grand Canyon, but with a well-planned week it's possible to sample some of the best the region has to offer. For a variety of scenery, history, and experiences, begin by touring the South Rim from Hermits Rest to Desert View, then travel through the Navajo Reservation and Marble Canyon area before winding up the Kaibab Plateau to Jacob Lake and the canyon's quiet North Rim.

Day 1

Begin at the South Rim's **Grand Canyon Village,** taking a day to get used to the elevation and acquaint yourself with the canyon during a ranger program or nature walk. If you plan to hike into the canyon, loosen up along the **Rim Trail.** The section from the village to **Mather Point** doubles as a sightseeing excursion, and trailside geology displays provide an overview of the layers you'll pass through when you make your descent into the canyon. Learn more at the **Yavapai Geology Museum** and peer through

its telescope at tomorrow's destination, the inner canyon oasis of Phantom Ranch. Walk or shuttle to the **Grand Canyon Visitor Center** to watch an introductory film and browse through the bookstore. Enjoy sunset colors on your way back to the village. If your journey to the inner canyon will be on a mule rather than on foot, remember to check in to confirm your tour reservations.

Day 2

Hiking into the canyon? Have an early breakfast before hopping a shuttle to Yaki Point, where the **South Kaibab Trail** begins its steep descent. The trail follows ridgelines for amazing views: Find a scenic spot for a pack lunch before continuing to **Bright Angel Campground** to unroll your sleeping bag. (Mule riders will descend via Bright Angel Trail to their destination, Phantom Ranch.) Stretch sore muscles with a stroll around the historic stone-and-wood cabins designed by architect Mary Colter, or relax on the sandy beach along the **Colorado River.** If you've reserved a

SOUTH RIM

Enter through the park's South Entrance and abandon your car in the parking lot at the **Grand Canyon Visitor Center.** Explore the visitor center, then walk a short distance to the jaw-dropping views at **Mather Point.** Follow the **Rim Trail** west to the **Yavapai Geology Museum** to learn how the canyon formed.

Board the shuttle bus to **Grand Canyon Village,** getting off at the train depot to explore the village's Historic District, including **El Tovar, Hopi House, Lookout Studio,** and **Kolb Studio.** Stop for lunch at Bright Angel Lodge or El Tovar.

Board the Hermits Rest shuttle route to take in the West Rim overlooks. The round-trip takes about 80 minutes (or more to stop and explore **Hermits Rest**).

For the grand finale, drive east along the park's Desert View Drive for 25 miles, stopping at **Tusayan Ruin** and ending with a flourish at **Desert View Watchtower.**

NORTH RIM

Scenic **Highway 67** crosses the Kaibab Plateau on its way to the North Rim entrance. Park near the visitor center and pick up a trail brochure for the 0.5-mile **Bright Angel Point Trail.** After you've soaked in the views, step into historic **Grand Canyon Lodge,** the center of North Rim activities and services. Have lunch in the stately dining room and relax on the sunny veranda.

Back in the car, head for **Cape Royal Drive,**

along Cape Royal Drive

a 23-mile (one-way) paved and winding road with spectacular overlooks. In five miles, follow a fork on the left to **Point Imperial** and descend the short path to the overlook and stunning views of Mt. Hayden.

Cape Royal Drive continues all the way to the edge of the Walhalla Plateau, ending at a large parking area. An easy 0.5-mile paved trail leads to **Cape Royal,** a rocky peninsula that curves dramatically into the canyon.

---

second night in the canyon, hike a mile or two up the **Clear Creek Trail** for fabulous views of **Phantom Ranch** and the **Inner Gorge.** Or spend your layover day drinking lemonade and writing postcards.

Day 3

In summer months, it's important to start hiking to the rim before dawn to beat the heat. On average, it takes six to nine hours to ascend

Bright Angel Trail, a route used for centuries by Havasupai people before it became a toll trail in the late 1800s. Today, the only toll is physical: About three miles up, the Devil's Corkscrew is a seemingly endless stretch of steep, sunbaked switchbacks. If you can't reach the rim before 10am, rest in the shade at **Indian Garden** (about 4.7 miles from camp) before continuing the second half of the hike later in the afternoon. (Mule riders will ascend the **South Kaibab Trail,**

sunset over Lake Powell

traversing colorful **Cedar Ridge** before topping out on **Yaki Point** at midday.)

After you've rewarded yourself with a rest and a cold drink upon emerging from the canyon, consider riding the shuttle to explore **West Rim** overlooks. Each offers a distinct perspective, from the wide panorama at **Hopi Point** to the sheer drop down at **The Abyss.** Find a perch to enjoy sunset before heading back to the village for dinner, or come prepared with selections from the General Store deli to eat at the best table in the house—the edge of the canyon.

Day 4

On your last morning in Grand Canyon Village, watch the sunrise, have a leisurely breakfast at historic **El Tovar Lodge,** or take in a ranger program. Pick up a box lunch or snacks from one of the lodges to take with you as you explore the **East Rim.** Beginning just south of Mather Point, Highway 64 travels 25 miles to **Desert View.** Stop en route at **Grandview Point** to gaze down at **Horseshoe Mesa** before continuing to **Tusayan Ruin,** where rangers lead daily tours in spring and summer. You'll want at least an hour at Desert View to explore Mary Colter's fabulous **Watchtower** and enjoy the sweeping **Marble Canyon** panoramas. If you haven't packed a picnic, save your appetite for a Navajo taco at the **Cameron Trading Post,** 30 miles away on the **Navajo Reservation.** En route, stop to peer into the **Little Colorado River Gorge,** a major canyon tributary. You can spend the night at the trading post's comfortable motel or drive up to **Page,** arriving in time to watch a **Lake Powell** sunset.

Day 5

Start your morning in Page with a smooth-water float from **Glen Canyon Dam** to **Lees Ferry,** a scenic half-day voyage below gorgeously colored sandstone cliffs. **Colorado River Discovery** will shuttle you back to Page, where you can begin the three-hour drive to the North Rim. Stop at the **Navajo Bridge Interpretive Center** and stroll across the **Colorado River**

Camping experiences in the canyon range from amenity-rich RV parks to lonely spots in the forest. Here's a sampling of the best:

SOUTH RIM

- **Desert View Campground** (page 83): Tucked into a juniper woodland near the park's east entrance, this seasonal campground is truly special. There are no showers or hookups, but civilization (food, gas, and flush toilets) is nearby. The 50 first-come, first-served sites are $12; the panorama of Desert View Watchtower and Marble Canyon—priceless.

- **Ten X Campground** (page 85): Only four miles from the park's South Entrance, some of the 70 sites ($10) can be reserved; the rest are first-come, first-served. There are no showers or hookups, but a nature trail and amphitheater make this seasonal forest service campground a pleasant spot.

- **Trailer Village** (page 83): Sidle up next to the South Rim's Mather Campground and general store for pull-through spaces ($44) accommodating RVs up to 50 feet long.

- **Spring Valley Cabin and Bunkhouse** (page 224): Located halfway between Williams and Flagstaff, about an hour away from the South Entrance, these historic U.S. Forest Service cabins (spring-fall, $100-150) make rustic but unique accommodations that can sleep up to 14 people.

NORTH RIM

- **North Rim Campground** (page 123): More than 80 sites ($18-25) come in a variety of shapes and sizes; some accommodate RVs up to 40 feet, though there are no hookups. For amazing views, reserve a walk-in site along the rim of Transept Canyon.

- **Jacob Lake Campground** (page 124): A half-hour from the North Rim's entrance station, this seasonal forest service campground ($18) has 53 sites, half of which can be reserved.

INNER CANYON

- **Bright Angel Campground** (page 160): Obtain a backcountry permit ($10, plus $8 pp per night) to stay at this inner canyon oasis of 30 tent sites along sparkling Bright Angel Creek.

Trailer Village

North Rim Campground in autumn

Best Day Hikes

SOUTH RIM

- **Rim Trail** (page 58): Although it's 13 miles long, the Rim Trail can be hiked in shorter sections for an easy scenic stroll. To avoid the crowds around Grand Canyon Village, start farther west. The section between **Monument Creek Vista and Hermits Rest** (2.8 miles one-way) is paved but quiet, alternating between woodland and rim for great views.

- **South Kaibab Trail** (page 63): This maintained corridor trail has wide-open panoramas. Make your first inner canyon hike to **Ooh Aah Point** (1.8 miles round-trip), suitable for beginners or families with children. Stronger hikers can try for **Cedar Ridge** (3 miles round-trip) or **Skeleton Point** (6 miles round-trip).

- **Hermit Trail** (page 63): For something off the beaten path, hike Hermit Trail to **Santa Maria Spring** (5 miles round-trip) or **Dripping Springs** (7 miles round-trip).

NORTH RIM

- **Widforss Trail** (page 112): This shady ramble is a rewarding day hike. Pick up the brochure at the trailhead that describes highlights on the trail's first 2.1 miles, and hike as long as you have the energy and time (up to 10 miles round-trip).

winter hiking on Bright Angel Point Trail

- **Bright Angel Point Trail** (page 106): Short but spectacular, this paved trail (0.5 miles round-trip) starts near Bright Angel Lodge and descends a limestone fin overlooking Roaring Springs.

Skeleton Point on the South Kaibab Trail

Walhalla Plateau

on the historic bridge, a favorite condor hangout. As you continue your journey along the base of the **Vermilion Cliffs,** look south for glimpses of the canyon, a dark gash across the broad **Marble Platform.** The road quickly ascends the **Kaibab Plateau** toward **Jacob Lake.** From here, Highway 67 leads through forest and meadows for 50 miles to the **North Rim.** Enjoy sunset from the tip of **Bright Angel Point** or, if you've made reservations, through the expansive dining-room windows at **Grand Canyon Lodge.**

Day 6

Get an early start to see the sun light up Mount Hayden at **Point Imperial** and then spend several hours exploring sights along the **Cape Royal Road** as it winds to the end of the **Walhalla Plateau.** Take time for a hike to **Cape Final** or the short-but-sweet **Cliff Springs Trail.** Stop at **Walhalla Overlook** to learn more about the Ancestral Puebloans who once called the canyon home. **Cape Royal,** where you can

gaze through **Angels Window** and look down on **Wotans Throne,** has lovely picnic spots. Return to the lodge for a ranger program or a stroll through the ponderosas on the **Transept Trail.** Toast your last canyon sunset from the lodge's veranda, watching as lights from Grand Canyon Village, 10 miles away as the raven flies, begin to twinkle across the canyon.

Day 7

If you don't need an early start for the long return back to civilization, you might begin your last day at Grand Canyon with a hike, heading partway down the **North Kaibab Trail** or getting a fresh canyon perspective from the rimside **Widforss Trail.** Or you could drive the back roads to **Jacob Lake,** exploring shady forest byways as you plan your next canyon sojourn. Because this is when it hits you: Even though you've toured the national park from rim to river, west to east, and north to south, there's so much more to explore.

Desert View Watchtower

A Romantic Winter Weekend

The most romantic time to visit the South Rim is during the winter, when crowds are lighter, sunrises are later, and frosty temperatures make snuggling by a fireplace even more fun.

Friday

Check into elegant **El Tovar** or a cozy cabin at **Bright Angel Lodge.** Some of the cabins have fireplaces or canyon views. If you want to impress your sweetie with a romantic dinner, make reservations in advance for El Tovar's candlelit dining room.

Saturday

After breakfast, pick up a picnic lunch at the General Store deli and spend a few hours exploring the overlooks along the West Rim's **Hermit Road.** Hike the **Rim Trail** from Pima Point to **Hermits Rest** (1.1 miles), where you can warm up with some hot chocolate. Rumor has it that

Mary Colter, the architect of this fanciful structure, liked to steal away for a few moments of solitude along the rim close by. See if you can find her special perch or, if it's not too icy, hike a short distance down nearby **Hermit Trail.**

Winter sunsets arrive early and paint the canyon walls in glowing orange, pink, and lavender. **Hopi Point** is popular at sunset; opt for **Pima** or **Mohave Points** if you'd prefer to avoid a crowd. After watching the celestial show, return to the village and warm up by your cabin's fireplace. No fireplace of your own? There's usually a blaze going in **El Tovar's Rendezvous Room,** and the lounge is a cozy spot for a warm drink.

The **Shrine of the Ages** hosts occasional evening programs in winter. But the most awe-inspiring show is outdoors: On dark, clear nights millions of diamond-bright stars will take your breath away. Pick up a star map at one of the park's shops or use a stargazing phone app. If you

The Wild Side

If outdoor adventure is your passion, there's no better way to get to know Grand Canyon than by taking the road—or trail—less traveled.

BACKPACKING

- Newbies should stick to corridor trails, like **Bright Angel, South Kaibab,** and **North Kaibab.**

- Day-hikers with more experience will leave the crowds behind after half a mile on **Hermit Trail** or **Grandview Trail.**

- For overnighters, there are even more options for solitude. The permit system limits the number of overnighters in any given area, and areas designated Wild or Primitive are especially quiet; for example, along the North Rim's **Ken Patrick Trail.**

BACK ROADS

- Miles of dirt roads for driving or mountain biking wind through **Kaibab National Forest.** On the North Rim, for example, bikes or cars can travel Forest Road 611 to the **East Rim Viewpoint.** Near the South Rim, a network of dirt roads lead to the single-track **Arizona Trail** south of Grandview Point.

- One of loneliest spots in Grand Canyon National Park is **Toroweap,** where a primitive campground waits at the end of 60 miles of dirt roads. Walk to the overlook where you'll see and hear roaring **Lava Falls** 3,000 feet below.

WHITE-WATER RAFTING

- Full-length **guided trips** put in at Lees Ferry and last **up to 18 days,** exploring side canyons and waterfalls en route to the takeout at Lake Mead. Meals, gear, and shuttle service are included. **Half-length trips** of 6 to 10 days begin or end at Phantom Ranch.

WINTER ACTIVITIES

- During the South Rim's off-season, you can ride a **fat-tire snow bike** along the rim or **snowshoe** near Grandview Point.

- Although North Rim roads and visitor services close seasonally, you can **ski or snowshoe** into the park and camp in the **winter yurt.**

boaters running the Colorado River

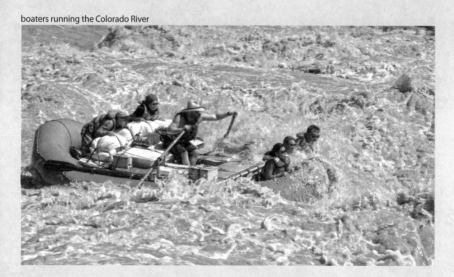

bundle up and bring a flashlight, you can view the night sky almost anywhere, but the amphitheater at **Mather Point** has front-row seats.

Sunday

Sunrise or sleep in? If you decide to greet the dawn from somewhere other than your window, grab a coffee at the **Canyon Coffee House** in Bright Angel Lodge, and then hop the shuttle to **Yaki Point.** Watch as buttery golden sunlight spreads over the canyon's inner peaks.

Return to the village for a hearty brunch, and then stroll along the rim to **Hopi House,** designed by architect Mary Colter in 1905. Inside this historic structure is the canyon's finest collection of Native American jewelry, perfect if you want a memento of your special weekend. ·

Spend the rest of the day exploring the **East Rim** by car. Watch the sunset from **Lipan Point** or **Desert View Watchtower,** another of Mary Colter's romanticized re-creations. To the west, inner canyon temples and buttes fade to layered silhouettes in blues and purples—a dramatic finale to the weekend.

Family Fun

The South Rim has so many activities and sights that it's easy for kids (and adults) to get overwhelmed. Set aside some quiet time, whether it's a shady rest in the ponderosa pine forest around the village or a nap in your room. If all else fails, take the kids to the **Grand Canyon IMAX movie** in nearby Tusayan, guaranteed to mesmerize them for 34 whole minutes.

Programs and Classes

For an expert introduction to the canyon's geology, ecology, and human history, join a one- or

Kids can learn about Grand Canyon by becoming a Junior Ranger.

Grand Canyon has provided food and shelter to people for thousands of years, and descendants of the canyon's first residents continue to live in the region today.

· **Hopi House** (page 50): Visit the upstairs gallery to see museum-quality pottery, jewelry, weavings, and other handiwork.

· **Desert View Watchtower** (page 57): Designed by architect Mary Colter in 1932, the interior of this observation tower is painted with colorful murals that offer a history of indigenous Southwestern cultures.

· **Tusayan Ruin** (page 57): Park rangers lead tours of these 800-year-old ruins summer-early fall. The adjacent museum has displays about prehistoric, historic, and contemporary Native American cultures.

· **Walhalla Glades** (page 102): Wander through the remains of this prehistoric village on the North Rim.

· **Havasu Canyon** (page 169): The home of the Havasupai (People of the Blue-Green Water) is famous for its waterfalls and travertine pools.

· **Grand Canyon West** (page 175): The Hualapai (People of the Tall Pines), historically known for their vast trade network, have translated those entrepreneurial skills into tour operations near the Skywalk.

· **Cameron Trading Post** (page 181): In the Navajo town of Cameron, this trading post has outstanding selections of jewelry, weavings, pottery, and other crafts.

· **Museum of Northern Arizona** (page

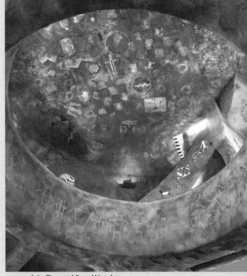

artwork in Desert View Watchtower

208): Flagstaff's excellent museum offers an introduction to the artistic traditions and culture of the Navajo, Hopi, and other Native American nations.

· **Wupatki National Monument** (page 209): Archaeology buffs will enjoy this side trip to Ancestral Puebloan ruins and a small but superb visitor center.

· **Pipe Spring National Monument** (page 237): Explore the history of Mormon pioneers and the Kaibab Paiute people via living history demonstrations and hands-on activities.

two-day program led by an instructor from the **Grand Canyon Field Institute.** The two-day program includes meals and lodging as well as a guided hike partway down **Bright Angel Trail** and a walking tour of historic **Grand Canyon Village.** Activities are suitable for adults and children age 10 and older.

Younger children can learn about the canyon by becoming a **Junior Ranger.** Kids ages 4 to 14 earn a certificate and badge when they participate in ranger-guided hikes or activities like critter chats and fossil walks.

Hikes

The **Rim Trail** is relatively level and easy to hike a section at a time, making it an ideal place to teach younger children about nature. Between **Verkamp's Visitor Center** and the **Yavapai Geology Museum,** the mile-long **Trail of Time** highlights touchable samples of the canyon's rock layers. Pick up a Rim Trail brochure to help identify plants or animals.

Mule Rides

The one-hour mule tour on the **North Rim** is suitable for children as young as age seven. There's no age limit for the two-hour **Canyon Vistas Mule Ride** on the South Rim, but riders need to be at least 4 feet 7 inches tall, and young children must be accompanied by an adult.

Bicycling

Bright Angel Bicycles rents bikes, helmets, and strollers. Ask for route suggestions or join one of their guided rides to **Hermits Rest** or **Yaki Point.** Younger children can ride in a pull-trailer behind an accompanying adult.

Train Spotting

If your youngster is crazy about trains, head for the depot and watch the **Grand Canyon Railway** arrive or depart. Serious train buffs will want to start their Grand Canyon visit on its vintage railcars, leaving **Williams** in the morning and arriving at Grand Canyon before noon.

History Lessons

Drive to **Desert View,** the South Rim's easternmost overlook, stopping en route to view 800-year-old **Tusayan Ruin** from the gentle loop trail. The grand finale for this 25-mile scenic journey along the East Rim is **Desert View Watchtower.** Kids love climbing the winding staircase to the top of the 70-foot tower.

Rafting

Hualapai River Runners guides the only one-day white-water trip in Grand Canyon. Tours launch from Diamond Creek on the **Hualapai Reservation,** and children must be at least eight years old to participate.

Colorado River Discovery leads motorized rafting tours (Mar.-Nov.) through Glen Canyon ending at Lees Ferry, a pleasant trip suitable for children as young as age four.

Picnicking

The park's general stores sell **picnic supplies and groceries.** Grab-and-go items are available at several South Rim locations, including Maswik Lodge, Yavapai Coffee Shop, and Canyon View Deli. You'll find **picnic tables** at most rim overlooks and several **picnic areas** along Desert View Drive.

Stargazing

Astronomers bring telescopes to the North and South Rims for the **annual Star Party** in June, but the night sky is amazing all year. Come prepared, or pick up star maps and red flashlights (to limit light pollution) at one of the park stores.

mules on the North Rim

The South Rim

Highlights

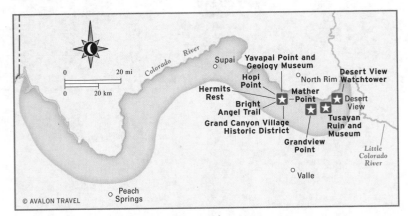

★ **Mather Point:** Get your first breathtaking views of the canyon from Mather Point, a short walk from the Grand Canyon Visitor Center, where you can listen to a ranger program, watch a film, and learn about tours and trails (page 46).

★ **Yavapai Point and Geology Museum:** Learn how Grand Canyon was formed and study its geological layers inside this historic pueblo-style building (page 46).

★ **Grand Canyon Village Historic District:** Learn the human stories behind the Grand Canyon. Meet Fred Harvey and the Harvey Girls, the Kolb brothers, sheriff and Rough Rider Buckey O'Neill, and architect Mary Elizabeth Jane Colter (page 50).

★ **Hopi Point:** You can see 30 miles or more in either direction from this West Rim overlook (page 54).

★ **Hermits Rest:** You'll feel like an early pioneer Inside this reimagining of a prospector's cave, designed in 1914 by Mary Colter (page 54).

★ **Grandview Point:** Look down on Horseshoe Mesa from this forested viewpoint, one of the highest on the South Rim (page 55).

★ **Tusayan Ruin and Museum:** Visit this 800-year-old village, where Ancestral Puebloans spent summers tending fields. The adjacent museum highlights how the canyon's resources were used to make arrowheads, pottery, and other necessities (page 57).

★ **Desert View Watchtower:** Climb this 70-foot-high masonry tower designed by Mary Colter for long views of the Painted Desert and Vermilion Cliffs (page 57).

★ **Bright Angel Trail:** Walking even a short distance down this trail gives you a sense of entering the canyon's embrace (page 61).

Welcome to Grand Canyon's most popular side, the South Rim.

Each year, six million people arrive here to gaze into the canyon's depths, hike its trails, or stay in one of the national park's historic lodges. From Hermits Rest to

Desert View, the South Rim stretches 40 miles to encompass more than a dozen overlooks, many linked by free shuttle buses and the 13-mile Rim Trail, where you can stop to smell the cliffroses or find a perch to watch ravens play.

The epicenter is Grand Canyon Village, with a historic district of over 250 structures, including architect Mary Colter's atmospheric Hopi House and Lookout Studio. Each morning, mule trips depart from the Old Stone Corral to descend the Bright Angel Trail. Every afternoon, the Grand Canyon Railway whistles its way into the depot, and visitors from around the world line up to buy ice cream cones at the Bright Angel Fountain, stroll the rim for views and selfies, or join a ranger program about fossils or condors.

Whether you're a science geek, a history buff, an art lover, or an adventurer, you'll find something to capture your imagination at the South Rim. In fact, there are so many ways to spend your time here that it's all too easy to skim the surface. Instead, go deeper. Step inside the canyon's rocky embrace, even if it's only for a short walk below the rim. Take time to watch a Navajo rug weaver at work or to learn more about the forces that formed the canyon. Venture out after dark to see the Milky Way and marvel at one of the starriest skies in the United States. Even on the busiest summer day, when you may be one of thousands of visitors, it's possible to escape the crowds and connect to the canyon on a personal level.

PLANNING YOUR TIME

You can sample the South Rim in **two days,** but allow more time for a hike or three, a mule trip, and a leisurely exploration of the overlooks east and west of Grand Canyon Village. Make a loop through Flagstaff, and you'll see more of the Grand Canyon region, including the Navajo Reservation, Wupatki and

Previous: mules at the Old Stone Corral; Lookout Studio. **Above:** Diana Sue Uqualla at the dedication of the renovated Bright Angel Trailhead.

South Rim

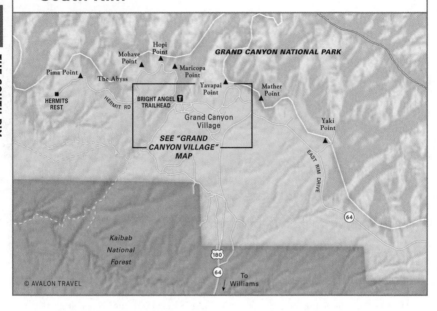

Sunset Volcano National Monuments, and the San Francisco Peaks. Park roads cover about 32 miles of the South Rim, which can be subdivided into three distinct areas: **Grand Canyon Village,** the **West Rim (Hermits Rest),** and the **East Rim (Desert View).**

Grand Canyon Village

Set aside at least **1-2 hours** to explore Grand Canyon Village. History and architecture buffs will want to spend even longer admiring the village's landmark structures, including **El Tovar,** the train depot, and **Lookout Studio.** Buildings and sidewalks are most crowded during the afternoon, when tour buses unload and the train pulls into the station, so consider taking your village **walking tour after breakfast or dinner.**

West Rim

You could easily spend **2-4 hours** exploring the views west of the village, taking the **Hermit Road** shuttle or walking along sections of the gentle **Rim Trail.** For the best

photos and fewest crowds, time your visit to the overlooks along Hermit Road for **early morning.** Sunsets are also dramatic, and crowds gather for the show like they would for an opening-night symphony performance.

East Rim

The East Rim is generally higher, cooler, and less visited than the West Rim, well worth the additional **2-6 hours** it takes to explore. You can visit overlooks on a guided bus tour or in your own vehicle. (The exception is **Yaki Point,** which is closed to private vehicles year-round; arrive here by shuttle, bike, or on foot.) Sunrise and sunset panoramas of the eastern canyon and the river's broad Unkar Delta are especially good from **Lipan Point** or **Desert View,** the easternmost overlook. Archaeology buffs will enjoy the short stroll through **Tusayan Ruin,** and kids love climbing the **Watchtower** at Desert View.

Inner Canyon

Walking below the rim, even a short distance,

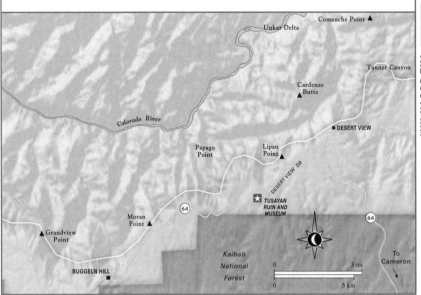

takes you into a different realm where your senses seem fresh and new and the world seems very, very old. Many South Rim trails offer inner canyon day-hike destinations that are scenic, historic, and—of course—geologic. For day hikes, you'll need to plan ahead to ensure you have adequate water, salty snacks, and sun protection. *Do not attempt to hike from the rim to the river and back in one day.*

To get from the rim to the bottom of the canyon and back on foot or by mule, you'll need at least **two days.** Backpackers must apply for a **backcountry permit.** Well-maintained corridor trails, such as **Bright Angel Trail** and **South Kaibab Trail,** are the best choice for those new to hiking or to the canyon. Wilderness trails require backcountry skills and are best attempted in three days or more. Advance planning is essential, and backcountry permits go quickly for popular spots like **Bright Angel Campground** or **Indian Garden.**

For more information on planning a trip to the Inner Canyon, see page 133.

Weather and Seasons

The South Rim is open year-round, and **spring** and **fall** are usually ideal for outdoor activities, though the weather can change quickly. Sudden wind gusts can catch you by surprise, especially along overlooks. Because of low humidity and high elevation, daytime and nighttime temperatures can vary 30 degrees or more: Wear layers and plan to shed them by midday.

In **summer,** temperatures along the rim are pleasant, topping out in the 80s. On summer afternoons, temperatures below the rim can rise above 100°F, so schedule your outdoor activities for early in the day. Afternoon thunderstorms—and dangerous lightning—are likely in July and August.

Most **winter** precipitation lands on the South Rim between December and March, but snowstorms can strike anytime from November through May, occasionally making travel difficult. Closed roads usually reopen within a day or two, giving you access to a wonderland of pines embellished by snow and icicles. Winter hikes into the canyon might start in ice and snow, making trails treacherous, before leading into pleasant, low-desert temperatures along the Colorado River.

Exploring the South Rim

When El Tovar opened in 1905, travelers would spend several weeks relaxing at the lodge and touring the South Rim. Today, when daily visitors number in the thousands, most with only a few hours to spend at the canyon, the pace can be far from relaxing. Plan ahead to avoid squandering precious time queuing up for meals or shuttles. If you find yourself feeling overwhelmed, focus on one or two experiences rather than checking off a long list of sights. And remember, it took millions of years to create this grand spectacle—slowing down is one of the most profound things the canyon can teach us.

VISITOR CENTERS

You'll find park information, maps, and exhibits on the canyon's natural and cultural history at many locations along the South Rim.

Grand Canyon Visitor Center

Grand Canyon Visitor Center (8am-5pm daily spring-fall, 9am-5pm daily winter) is located across from Mather Point, about five miles north of the South Entrance, the centerpiece of a plaza complex designed as an all-in-one stop. Facilities include parking, picnic pavilions, shuttle stops, pay phones, restrooms, a bike rental shop and café, and the Grand Canyon Association's **Park Store** (hours vary seasonally). The plaza's outdoor kiosks introduce canyon geology, hiking, and other topics and are open 24 hours daily, although the lights go out at 9pm. From the visitor center plaza, you can get on one of the park's free shuttle buses, walk the Rim Trail, or rent a bike and travel the paved Greenway Trail that connects to Grand Canyon Village.

The main building has exhibits on natural history and news about the latest weather forecast, road conditions, and trail closures. Rangers are on hand to answer questions, and interactive electronic kiosks are available to help choose a hike or guided tour, check program schedules, and more. A small theater to one side of the lobby projects an 8-minute video history of the earth onto a large sphere, highlighting geological processes. On the other side of the lobby, a large auditorium screens a 20-minute film, *Grand Canyon: A Journey of Wonder,* at every hour and half-hour.

Grand Canyon Village

Each of these smaller, focused visitor centers have retail areas with books and gifts, and all of them can be accessed from the Blue (Village) shuttle route, unless otherwise noted. The Yavapai Geology Museum, Verkamp's, and Kolb Studio are all open 8am-8pm daily in summer, 8am-7pm daily in spring and fall, and 8am-6pm daily in winter.

The **Yavapai Geology Museum** combines displays about the canyon's geology with afternoon ranger talks and telescopic views of the inner canyon. A hands-on outdoor geology experience, Trail of Time, follows the Rim Trail between the museum and Verkamp's. The Orange Route shuttle stops here.

Verkamp's hosts ranger talks on its shady veranda. Indoors you'll find displays about the history of Grand Canyon Village and its pioneer residents.

Kolb Studio, perched on the rim near Bright Angel Lodge, was built by brothers who filmed and photographed their canyon adventures. Their auditorium is now an art gallery with changing exhibits.

Park Headquarters (8am-5pm daily) houses the Grand Canyon's research library and the **Shrine of the Ages** auditorium, where evening ranger programs and special events are held. The **library,** a Wi-Fi hotspot, has computers for public use.

The **Backcountry Information Center** (928/638-7875, 8am-noon and 1pm-5pm daily), located on Center Road behind Maswik Lodge, is the best resource for serious hikers and backpackers. You can learn more about trails and campsites, pick up a *Trip Planner* or hiking map, or apply for a backcountry permit.

East Rim

The park's free shuttles don't travel the East Rim beyond Yaki Point; you'll need to make your own way here or sign up for the Desert View **bus tour** (928/638-2631, $50).

Tusayan Museum and Ruin (9am-5pm daily) highlights the region's Native American cultures. Located 22 miles east of the village on Desert View Drive, the museum has a retail area specializing in titles on archaeology and anthropology. Take a self-guided walk through the ruin or time your visit for a ranger-guided tour.

Desert View Watchtower (9am-5pm daily), one of architect Mary Colter's most fascinating structures, offers tours, books, and gifts with Native American themes, and

occasional cultural demonstrations. It is located 25 miles east of the village near the park's East Entrance Station.

Tusayan

Outside the national park boundaries in the town of Tusayan, the **National Geographic Visitor Center** (928/638-2206, www.explorethecanyon.com, 8am-10pm daily Mar.-Oct., 9am-8pm daily Nov.-Feb.) shows the most-watched IMAX film ever made: *Grand Canyon: The Hidden Secrets.* Millions of viewers have seen this 34-minute film, which screens every hour on the half-hour, with the last show starting at 8:30pm (6:30pm in winter). Bus tours often stop here, and for those who don't have the time or money for a whitewater adventure, the rafting scenes and fly-over views of the river offer a taste of the real thing. Tickets are $14 for "adults" (age 11 and older), with discounts for younger children, seniors, and groups that reserve in advance. The theater seats 500-plus, but if you have to wait for the next screening, you can pass the time browsing through the visitor center's gift shop and exhibits or grab a quick bite at the food court. Park passes can also be purchased here, allowing you to enter the park through the faster prepaid lanes. In summer months,

Yavapai Geology Museum

you can leave your vehicle here and take the shuttle's Purple Route into the park.

ENTRANCE STATIONS

The park's South Rim has two entrances, both located along Highway 64. When you enter the park, a ranger will hand you a *South Rim Pocket Map* with shuttle routes, parking areas, and other helpful information.

South Entrance

Most visitors arrive via the larger South Entrance, accessible from **Flagstaff** or **Williams.** During summer weekends and holidays, you might encounter lines of vehicles waiting to enter the park. To avoid idling in traffic on a sizzling summer afternoon, plan your arrival for the cooler, less busy morning or evening hours. You can skip the longest lines and use the faster prepaid lane if you pay your entry fee before arriving at the canyon. You'll find the nearest prepay location at the IMAX Theatre a mere two miles south of the entrance. You can also use the prepaid lane if you have a Grand Canyon annual pass or an interagency pass.

East Entrance

The East Entrance Station at Desert View is smaller than the South Entrance and receives far fewer visitors. About 30 miles east of Grand Canyon Village, the East Entrance Station is accessible via U.S. 89 and Highway 64. It adds a few miles to the drive from **Flagstaff,** but you can start off your visit to the canyon by exploring the East Rim overlooks on your way to Grand Canyon Village, arriving just in time to check into your room at the lodge.

TOURS

You can tour the Grand Canyon in many ways: on foot, bicycle, mule or horseback, by air, motor coach, or raft. In some cases, you'll need to plan ahead (four months to a year ahead for river expeditions, mule trips, or popular backpacking destinations), though cancellations and last-minute spots are possible. If you get the urge to take a tour after your bags are already unpacked, head for one of the **transportation desks** (928/638-2681, hours vary seasonally) in Maswik or Bright Angel Lodges, or see the concierge at El Tovar. At Yavapai Lodge and Grand Canyon Visitor Center, interactive **electronic kiosks** assist with tour reservations.

Travelers who stop en route to Grand Canyon will be greeted by racks of colorful brochures advertising Grand Canyon tours by Jeep, off-road vehicles, or passenger vans. Many of the companies that advertise outside of Grand Canyon National Park are not park-approved concessionaires, so inquire carefully about route locations and guide experience before making a decision. To learn more about park-approved guides and tours, visit the Guided Tours page on the park's website (nps.gov/grca).

West Rim Driving Tour
8 MILES

Personal vehicles are restricted from historic **Hermit Road** seasonally. From **March through November** free shuttle buses on the Hermits Rest Route leave every 15-30 minutes and stop at all the West Rim overlooks. You can get out and snap photos, then catch a later shuttle or walk the Rim Trail to the next shuttle stop.

From **December through February,** Hermit Road is open to passenger cars (weather permitting). The drive begins just west of Bright Angel Lodge, traveling between the canyon and the piñon-juniper woodland that characterizes much of the South Rim.

- For outstanding views of the historic village and Bright Angel Trail, make your first stop at either of the two Trailview Overlooks.

- Continuing on Hermit Road, about 1.5 miles from the village, Maricopa Point is marked by the tram tower that once served the Lost Orphan Mine, which yielded copper and later uranium. Far below, the Inner Gorge reveals the oldest rocks in Grand Canyon, Zoroaster granite (pink) and

West Rim and Hermit Road

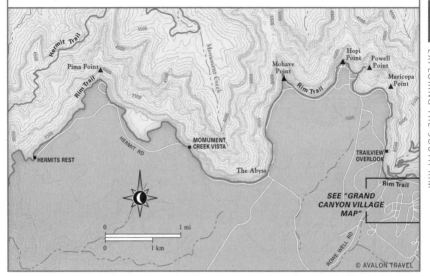

© AVALON TRAVEL

Vishnu schist (gray-black). The formation below the rim to the right is known as the Battleship.

- The memorial at Powell Point, two miles from the village, honors John Wesley Powell, the one-armed Civil War veteran who led the first expeditions down the Colorado River through Grand Canyon in 1869 and 1872.

- The views from Hopi Point, the northernmost point on the South Rim, stretch east from the Palisades of the Desert all the way west to Havasupai Point. It's a panorama nearly 100 miles wide, making this one of the most popular (and most crowded) overlooks for viewing sunrise or sunset.

- Look for the Colorado River far below Mohave Point, three miles west of the village. Three rapids—Hermit, Salt Creek, and Granite—are visible from this overlook. You might even be able to hear Hermit Rapids, the farthest west, formed by debris from Hermit Canyon.

- A mile farther down Hermit Road, The

Abyss marks one of the steepest drops from the canyon rim. The Great Mohave Wall, a sheer cliff of sandstone and limestone, plunges nearly 4,000 feet down to Monument Creek and Monument Canyon, named for the pillars found in its depth.

- Pima Point is farther off the main road than the other overlooks, making it a good place to pause and enjoy the natural quiet. In addition to a sweeping cross-canyon view that takes in the North Rim from Powell Plateau to Cape Royal, you can see the crumbling foundations of historic Hermit Camp below.

- Hermits Rest, a National Historic Landmark, was designed by architect Mary Colter and built in 1914. Inspired by Louis Boucher, a prospector who lived at Grand Canyon in the 1890s, Colter imagined the building as a cavern-like refuge carved out of the cliffs. The massive fireplace is a good spot for warming your feet in winter. There's a snack bar and a gift shop, and restrooms are south of the building. Nearby,

East Rim and Desert View Drive

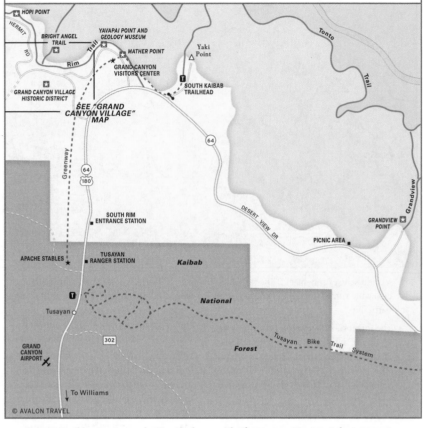

© AVALON TRAVEL

Hermit Trail begins its nearly 10-mile descent to the Colorado River.

East Rim Driving Tour
23 MILES

South of Grand Canyon Visitor Center, Highway 64 turns east for **Desert View Drive,** a scenic 23-mile stretch along the East Rim. This good paved road climbs through ponderosa forest to the South Rim's highest elevations, so snow sometimes forces road closures for brief periods in the winter. During peak season, parking can be limited at Grandview and Lipan points, but other overlooks are less visited. From west to east:

• The first turnout just past the intersection is Pipe Creek Vista. Stop for a good view of the central canyon, including Plateau Point and O'Neill Butte.

• Twelve miles east of the village, ponderosa-shaded Grandview Point once boasted a hotel, tent cabins, and a copper-mining operation centered on Horseshoe Mesa. The Grandview Trail starts at the east end of the stone barrier and leads to the mesa 3,000 feet below.

• About three miles past Grandview, you'll see the Buggeln picnic area, a shady (and often uncrowded) place for lunch.

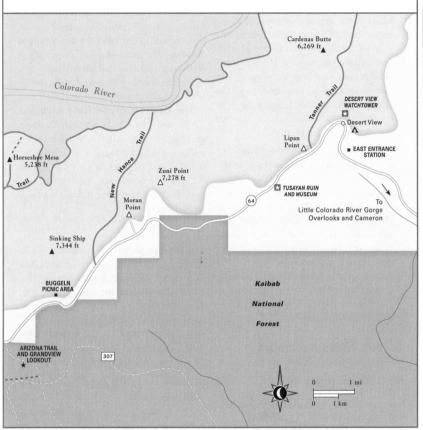

Although the rim is brushy here, you can walk through the forest for glimpses of the Sinking Ship, a tilted rock formation.

- Moran Point, overlooking Red Canyon, honors artist Thomas Moran, who captured the canyon's dramatic vistas in drawings and paintings, including Chasm of the Colorado, now part of the Smithsonian's art collection. Moran joined explorer John Wesley Powell on his third canyon expedition in 1873.

- Tusayan Ruin, 20 miles east of the village, was inhabited 800 years ago. This masonry complex of rooms sheltered about 30

people who farmed nearby in the summer, migrating to the canyon's floor in the winter. Rangers guide daily walks of the ruin in summer and early fall. The adjacent museum (9am-5pm daily) highlights regional Native American cultures.

- Lipan Point views take in the canyon from the undulating cliffs known as the Palisades of the Desert to the Inner Gorge. Across the canyon is the North Rim's Cape Royal, and below it, the rocks of the Grand Canyon Supergroup: soft, colorful layers carved into the hills and valleys above the river's Unkar Delta. Nearby, the challenging Tanner Trail leads to the river.

- Navajo Point also has fine views of the colorful Supergroup layers. In 1540, Hopi guides led a detachment from Francisco Vázquez de Coronado's expedition to the rim of Grand Canyon somewhere in this vicinity. Though the Hopis knew of trails leading into the canyon, we can imagine that the guides watched silently—and perhaps with some amusement—as the Spanish explorers tried to reach the river, a frustrating and failed endeavor they recorded in expedition journals.

- Desert View, the easternmost overlook inside the park, offers gorgeous views of the Colorado River as it exits Marble Canyon and bends west toward the Inner Gorge. The highlight is Mary Colter's fabulous Watchtower (9am-5pm daily), inspired by prehistoric structures built by the Ancestral Puebloans. From the top of the 70-foot tower, you'll have 360-degree views of the canyon and the Painted Desert. Nearby is the park's East Entrance Station, as well as a seasonal campground, a gas station, a general store, and a snack bar.

Guided Walks and Tours

Free **ranger-guided hikes** vary from gentle nature walks to a challenging four-hour hike to **Cedar Ridge.** Tours and talks focusing on fossils, geology, flora and fauna, archaeology, and other topics are scheduled throughout the day at various locations around the village, including **Lookout Studio, Yavapai Geology Museum,** or the shady veranda at **Verkamp's.** Check at lodges and visitor centers for the current program schedule; the list of programs is shortest in winter.

The **Grand Canyon Field Institute** (GCFI, 866/471-4435, 928/638-2485, www.grandcanyon.org/fieldinstitute) offers guided walking and hiking tours, some suitable for families with children as young as age 10. GCFI is a nonprofit park partner with the goal of educating visitors and helping them enjoy the canyon.

Bicycle Tours

Bright Angel Bicycles (928/638-3055, www.bikegrandcanyon.com) rents bikes and offers daily guided tours spring-fall; hours vary seasonally. The **Hermit Road Tour** ($60 adults, $45 under age 12) lasts three hours and includes gear and shuttle service for the 5.5-mile ride from Hopi Point to Hermits Rest. Guides stop at several overlooks, sharing their knowledge of history, geology, and other topics. The 7-mile round-trip **Yaki Point Ride**

Rent bikes or sign up for a tour at Bright Angel Bicycles.

($50 adults, $40 under age 12) also lasts three hours. During winter months, 3-hour **Fat Bike Tours** ($50 adults, $40 ages 13-17) venture through the pines and along the rim in rain, snow, or shine.

Air Tours

To see the canyon by helicopter or plane, you need to start outside the park. **Grand Canyon Airport** is in the town of Tusayan, although many tours originate from airports in the Las Vegas area and fly to the Hualapai Reservation (also known as Grand Canyon West). Be sure to clarify if you're seeking a flight *over* Grand Canyon versus *to* the canyon. Grand Canyon overflights are strictly regulated by the Federal Aviation Administration and are confined to particular areas and routes that exclude the central canyon. Even after being restricted to the western and eastern ends of the canyon, up to 100,000 flights are allowed to cross the canyon annually—plenty of options for those who want aerial views, and plenty of irritation for those who prefer natural quiet in national parks.

Keep in mind as you shop for a tour that canyon routes are limited, so your decision will factor in convenient scheduling, customer service, and what kinds of tour package features you'd like in addition to flights. Aircraft also vary in comfort, quiet, and visibility. Flights via helicopter, which fly slower and lower, are generally more expensive than fixed-wing flights. Air tours start at $160 pp, with combination tours topping out around $500-600. Most companies discount rates for children and provide tour narration in several languages in addition to English. Several offer charters for groups and special occasions like weddings.

- **Grand Canyon Airlines** (702/835-8484, 866/235-9422, www.grandcanyonairlines. com) offers options combining fixed-wing flights with helicopter flights, smooth-water rafting, and land tours.
- **Grand Canyon Helicopters** (702/835-8477, 855/326-9617, www.grandcanyonhelicopter.com) offers tours from Grand Canyon Airport and Las Vegas. Charter flights and custom itineraries are also available.
- **Papillon Grand Canyon Helicopters** (702/736-7243, 888/635-7272, www.papillon.com) has a wide selection of destinations and tours, including package tours with rafting, motorcycle, and Jeep options.
- **Maverick** (702/261-0007, 888/261-4414, www.maverick.com) offers the Canyon Spirit helicopter tour departing from the Grand Canyon Airport, as well as a wide range of plane tours and charters originating in Las Vegas and other locations. Destinations include the Hualapai Reservation, home of the Grand Canyon Skywalk.
- **Westwind Air Service** (480/991-5557, 888/869-0866, www.westwindairservice. com) has Grand Canyon plane tours and packages that combine flights with hiking, rafting, and 4WD excursions, originating from the South Rim, Page, Phoenix, and Sedona.

Bus Tours

Following a tradition established by the Fred Harvey Company, which offered stagecoach or limo tours during the early 1900s, **Xanterra** (303/297-2757 or 888/297-2757) offers year-round guided motor coach tours along the South Rim. For more information, call or visit one of the transportation desks (928/638-2631) in Bright Angel or Maswik Lodges, see the concierge at El Tovar, or consult the interactive kiosks at Yavapai Lodge and Grand Canyon Visitor Center. Times vary according to season, but options include sunrise or sunset tours as well as scenic drives along Hermit Road and Desert View Drive. Tours are free for children under age 17 with an accompanying adult.

Sunrise and **Sunset Tours** (90 minutes, $24 pp) take in nature's show from a rim-side location. The narrated, two-hour **Hermits Rest Tour** ($30 pp) travels 16 miles round-trip

Fred Harvey's Legacy

Harvey Girls near El Tovar, circa 1926

Fred Harvey, an Englishman, changed the face of the West. Appalled at the poor food and service he found at train stations, he convinced the Atchison, Topeka, and Santa Fe Railway that he could do better. The first Harvey House opened in 1876, and its success led to dozens of restaurants, hotels, and shops along Western rail lines.

Critical to the company's success were thousands of "Harvey Girls," hired to work in lunchrooms from Topeka to Los Angeles. They brought refinement and wholesomeness to rough-and-tumble communities settled by prospectors, ranchers, and lumbermen. They helped settle the West and advance women in the workforce.

Between 1896 and 1920, the Santa Fe built 17 hotels and more than a dozen train stations, most designed with regional flair. The railroad encouraged artists to visit locations and paint them, and then distributed lithographs of their work to popularize destinations. At Grand Canyon, the Santa Fe Railway's rustic but elegant El Tovar enticed guests with a chef from New York City and famously tender steak.

But arguably the most brilliant collaboration between Fred Harvey Company and the Santa Fe Railway was to hire architect Mary Elizabeth Jane Colter. Her fanciful constructions, including Hopi House and Lookout Studio, romanced canyon visitors with atmosphere and an air of authenticity.

Fred Harvey died in 1901 without seeing the company's marvelous Grand Canyon buildings, but several El Tovar staff members claim to have seen his ghost wandering about. You can see him too—his portrait hangs in the History Room at Bright Angel Lodge.

to visit overlooks along Hermit Road (the West Rim). The **Desert View Tour** ($50 pp) lasts nearly four hours, visiting East Rim overlooks that include Desert View and the Watchtower; for $65, it can be combined with any other tour, even on different days.

Train Tours

The Santa Fe Railway completed a spur line to Grand Canyon in 1901. The railroad partnered with the Fred Harvey Company to build and manage El Tovar, Hopi House, and other attractions, luring tourist services away from their original center near Grandview Point. Eventually, automobiles outpaced train travel, and the last train pulled out of Grand Canyon station in 1968. For more than 20 years, the tracks were silent. They were on the verge of being torn up by a salvage company when a retired couple wound up with 20 miles of track as repayment for a bad debt. Against the advice of business consultants, they determined to restore train service to the canyon.

Today, **Grand Canyon Railway** (800/843-8724, www.thetrain.com) offers six classes of passenger service from Williams to Grand Canyon's South Rim, plus packages that combine the train ride with lodging and guided rim tours. Vintage diesel-powered trains depart from Williams in the morning and arriving at the South Rim depot before noon. The route passes through ponderosa pine forest, piñon-juniper woodland, and open prairie.

Although you won't get any canyon views from the train, old-time musicians stroll through the refurbished railcars during the two-hour-plus ride. Round-trip ticket prices ($80-220 adults, $50-150 children) vary according to service level and railcar style, from a 1923 coach to a luxury observation dome. Group rates are available, and the railroad offers discounts and specials.

Special events include **Steam Saturdays** and the **Polar Express** ($35-50 adults, $25-40 children), a ride through the forest complete with hot chocolate, cookies, and a visit to Santa's workshop. Make reservations well in advance for this popular excursion, which has become a holiday tradition for many families.

Mule Trips

The Grand Canyon tradition of mule tours began more than 100 years ago, when prospectors discovered that guiding tourists into the canyon was more profitable than mining. Mule riders depicted in historic photos of the Bright Angel Trail include Teddy Roosevelt, William Jennings Bryan, and Arizona's indomitable Sharlot Hall.

There's nothing "soft" about getting to the bottom of the canyon on the back of a mule. Riding requires good strength, especially in your back and abdominal muscles—and after several hours in the saddle, your bottom might not be the only part that's sore. But it's a great way to see a lot of the canyon in a relatively short time.

Xanterra Parks & Resorts (303/297-2757 or 888/297-2757) offers a couple of options for mule rides from the South Rim: a three-hour ride along the East Rim, and two- or three-day rides with a layover at the inner canyon's Phantom Ranch. Although previous riding experience isn't necessary, height and weight restrictions are observed. Riders must be at least 4 feet 7 inches tall and weigh 200 pounds

A mule tour ascends South Kaibab Trail.

or less in full gear. Children under 15 must be accompanied by an adult. All riders must speak English, must be in good health, and cannot be pregnant. Xanterra's staff will provide you with a souvenir canteen and the loan of a rain poncho, but you'll need to bring appropriate garb (a wide-brimmed hat, a long-sleeved shirt, long pants, closed-toed shoes, etc.). Mule trip DVDs, useful as keepsakes or as preparation for a trip, are sold in lodges and on Xanterra's online shop (http://shop.grand-canyonlodges.com, $20).

PHANTOM RANCH

The **Phantom Ranch** mule trip (1 night $552, 2 nights $961, reduced rates for 2 or more people) begins in the morning at the corral near the Bright Angel Trail. After lunch at Indian Garden, riders continue to the bottom of the canyon and Phantom Ranch, a total of 10.5 miles (about 5.5 hours). The return trip, after breakfast on the second or third morning, is via the South Kaibab Trail, 7.3 miles (4.5 hours).

The cost includes meals and a stay at the Phantom Ranch cabins. A duffel service ($73 per duffel each way) is available for those who want to take more than the essentials. Those who make the wise choice to stay a second night, an option available November to March, can spend a day stretching sore muscles on inner canyon trails or resting in the pleasant oasis of Phantom Ranch before saddling up for the return trip.

Reservations for overnight rides to Phantom Ranch can be made up to 13 months in advance. The tours often fill up quickly. Last-minute cancellations are possible, however, and you can add your name to the "day-before waiting list" at one of the transportation desks (928/638-2631) when you arrive at the canyon. The waiting list is shortest in winter, when cancellations are most likely.

Confirm your reservations (928/638-3283) two to four days prior to your ride, not only to hold your place but also to learn about the latest weather and trail conditions. It's a good idea to check in at the Bright Angel Lodge transportation desk the day before your trip to attend an orientation and weigh-in session. If you fail to check in by 6:15am on the day of your ride, you risk losing your reservation and deposit.

CANYON VISTAS

Those who can't make the long journey into the canyon can get riding experience and views on the **Canyon Vistas** mule tour ($135 pp). The guided three-hour journey, departing twice daily (once daily in winter months), travels along the rim near Yaki Point. Reservations are required, and riders must check in at Bright Angel Lodge at least one hour prior to departure. The weight limit for the Canyon Vistas ride is 225 pounds.

Horseback Tours

Apache Stables (928/638-2891, www.apachestables.com) offers the only horseback tours near the South Rim. The rides ($53-93 pp) last one or two hours. On evening horseback ($63 pp) and wagon rides ($26 pp), guests gather around a campfire, where it's BYOHD—bring your own hot dogs and fixings to cook over the fire. Rates are discounted for children, who must be accompanied by an adult. None of the tours go below the rim but travel instead through National Forest lands that adjoin the park. The stables are located on Moqui Drive (Forest Rd. 328) between Tusayan and the park's South Entrance.

Geocaching Tour

It's illegal to place a cache on National Park lands without applying for a special use permit. However, tech-savvy Sherlocks can use their GPS devices in the park to seek out virtual caches and solve hidden clues along paved roads and established trails. Start by picking up **EarthCache** instructions at the Grand Canyon Visitor Center. The virtual geocaching tour takes four to six hours before arriving at the ultimate clue.

Audio Tours

If you have a cell phone, you can listen to

two-minute audio tours for selected sites from Yaki Point west to Hermits Road overlooks. Look for the numbered **Park Ranger Audio Tour** signs, dial 928/225-2907, enter the stop number, and listen to the narration. There are 26 audio-tour locations along the South Rim, linked to prerecorded narratives by park rangers. Cell coverage can be spotty along the rim, and not all service providers cover park locations. You can also listen to the narrations online (www.nps.gov/grca) or download text versions.

Virtual Tours

Preview your Grand Canyon visit through the park's online multimedia offerings (www.nps.gov/grca). Choose from ranger talks, hiking and river-running podcasts, or videos about the canyon's treasures, from hidden waterfalls to starry night skies. Even on your Mac or PC screen, the seven-minute animated flyover coproduced with NASA is an impressive orientation to the canyon's complex maze of tributaries.

Learning Adventures

Educational outings capture the spirit of the field trips undertaken by pioneering geologists, archaeologists, and others who made careers of studying the Grand Canyon. Even better, they're a good way to meet kindred spirits while learning new skills and gaining a deeper understanding of the canyon.

In 1993 the Grand Canyon Association (GCA), a longtime partner of the park, launched the **Grand Canyon Association Field Institute** (GCAFI, 928/638-2485 or 866/471-4435, www.grandcanyon.org/fieldinstitute) with the goal of offering expert canyon knowledge and skills. GCAFI leads more than 250 programs each year, many incorporating hiking, backpacking, or river-running. Programs (starting at $50 pp) focus on geology, photography, yoga, and other topics. Content is geared to the general public, though participants often include canyon residents and employees who want to expand their knowledge. Family classes

and women-only programs are also offered, with discounts available to groups and GCA members.

In coordination with Xanterra Parks & Resorts, GCAFI offers an introductory two-day program called **Learning & Lodging** (928/638-2525, www.grandcanyonlodges.com, from $794 pp). Fees include meals and two nights at Maswik Lodge, plus two full days of guided hiking and van tours. Children must be age eight or older to attend.

Road Scholar (800/454-5768, www.roadscholar.org) leads rafting trips and rim-to-river hiking expeditions (from $1,085 pp), as well as several milder canyon excursions. Formerly known as Elderhostel, Road Scholar no longer limits trips to seniors—options include several intergenerational trips destined to win the hearts of grandkids.

The park's Environmental Education staff provides teachers free **curriculum-based resources** designed for grades K to 7 and **field trips** for grades 3 to 12. Distance learning using video-conferencing equipment is also an option, and rangers may be able to arrange classroom visits. Teachers can attend free workshops to learn more about the program. For information, see the park's website (www.nps.gov/grca/learn/education) or call the park's education staff (928/638-7931).

Arizona middle-schoolers can join in summer hiking expeditions sponsored by the Tucson-based Udall Foundation's **Parks in Focus Program** (520/901-8500, www.udall.gov). Six-day Grand Canyon trips combine photography with nature education and are free for youth from underserved populations.

A trio of river-runners started **Grand Canyon Youth** (928/773-7921, http://gcyouth.org) to offer teens ages 15 to 19 the magical experience of being on the river. Programs combine learning, service, and canyon exploration with qualified guides at a lower cost than commercial trips. Participants are encouraged to earn part of their trip fees ($890-990), and financial assistance is available. Teens with impaired vision or hearing are welcome.

Northern Arizona University (928/523-3334, grandcanyonsemester@nau.edu, http://nau.edu/gcs) offers a Grand Canyon Semester, an interdisciplinary immersion experience for undergraduates. Up to 18 credit hours focusing on current issues in the American West can be earned in the classroom, on the river, or around a campfire. Financial aid is available to help offset the $8,950 cost, which includes tuition, housing, and other fees.

Sights

Most South Rim sights are located along Hermit Road's eight-mile length and Desert View Drive, covering about 32 miles. Between these two scenic routes is **Grand Canyon Village,** best explored on foot or by riding the park's free shuttle buses. Sights are described in order from the South Entrance Station.

GRAND CANYON VISITOR CENTER
★ Mather Point

Most visitors view Grand Canyon for the first time from **Mather Point,** the first canyon overlook inside the South Entrance Station, named in honor of Stephen T. Mather, the first director of the National Park Service. The overlook—a colorful canyon panorama anchored by a rocky foreground of pale Kaibab limestone—is easily reached by a paved path (or shuttle ride) from the Grand Canyon Visitor Center and plaza.

Hang around to enjoy the convivial atmosphere. Visitors from all over the world speak the shared language of photography as they swap cameras and phones back and forth to take portraits with canyon backdrops. Between saying "cheese," be sure to say "ah-h-h" and adjust to canyon time. Inhale the pure pine-scented air and take in the view, one of the canyon's loveliest perspectives.

★ Yavapai Point and Geology Museum

Via the Rim Trail, it's a pleasant 0.7-mile stroll to **Yavapai Point** from Mather Point. (You can also drive or catch the Orange Route's westbound shuttle to get here from Grand Canyon Visitor Center.) The **Yavapai**

Most visitors see Grand Canyon for the first time at Mather Point.

Yavapai Point

Geology Museum (8am-8pm daily summer, shorter hours fall-spring) is a must if you're interested in learning more about the canyon's colorful layers. Designed by architect Herbert Maier and opened in 1928, this pueblo-style structure of native limestone and wood blends into the rim. Displays include a three-dimensional map and a geological column that helps explain how the canyon was formed. Broad, canyon-facing windows frame panoramic views of the North Rim and Inner Gorge. Spotting scopes provide even closer views, and there's usually a ranger nearby who will help you focus the lens on **Phantom Ranch,** tucked among bright-green cottonwoods at the bottom of the canyon, or on the bridge that leads hikers across the river to **Bright Angel Campground.** The museum has daily ranger talks and a small bookstore.

Trail of Time

Walk through the canyon's geologic past along the 1.4-mile **Trail of Time** between the Yavapai Geology Museum and Verkamp's Visitor Center. Interpretive markers and rock samples from the canyon's depths line this section of the paved Rim Trail to form a geology timeline. Each meter of the timeline represents one million years of history, with viewing tubes and touchable rock samples

to help bring the canyon's geology closer to human understanding. Almost two billion years lie between the oldest rock, Elves Chasm gneiss (formed 1.8 billion years ago), and the newest, Kaibab limestone (270 million years old).

The Trail of Time leads to the Yavapai Geology Museum.

Grand Canyon Village

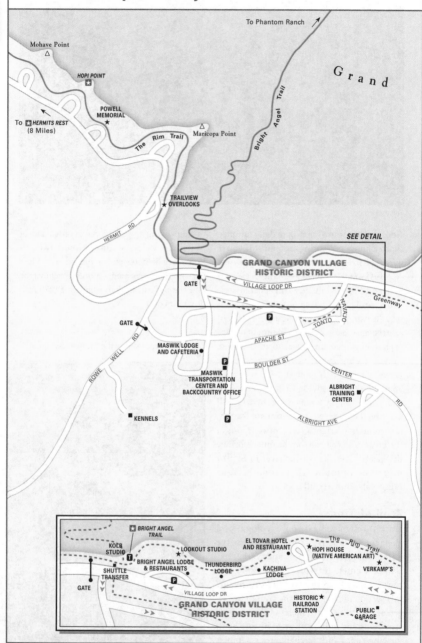

Mohave Point

HOPI POINT

POWELL MEMORIAL

To HERMITS REST (8 Miles)

The Rim Trail

Maricopa Point

TRAILVIEW OVERLOOKS

HERMIT RD.

Bright Angel Trail

To Phantom Ranch

Grand

SEE DETAIL

GATE

VILLAGE LOOP DR

GRAND CANYON VILLAGE HISTORIC DISTRICT

NAVAJO

Greenway

TONTO

GATE

ROWE WELL RD.

MASWIK LODGE AND CAFETERIA

MASWIK TRANSPORTATION CENTER AND BACKCOUNTRY OFFICE

APACHE ST

BOULDER ST

CENTER RD

ALBRIGHT TRAINING CENTER

KENNELS

ALBRIGHT AVE

GRAND CANYON VILLAGE HISTORIC DISTRICT

BRIGHT ANGEL TRAIL

KOLB STUDIO

LOOKOUT STUDIO

EL TOVAR HOTEL AND RESTAURANT

The Rim Trail

HOPI HOUSE (NATIVE AMERICAN ART)

SHUTTLE TRANSFER

Bright Angel Lodge & Restaurants

THUNDERBIRD LODGE

KACHINA LODGE

VERKAMP'S

GATE

VILLAGE LOOP DR

HISTORIC RAILROAD STATION

PUBLIC GARAGE

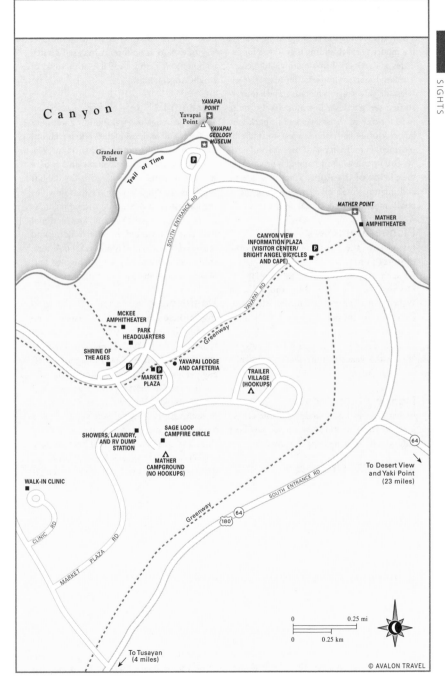

Canyon

YAVAPAI POINT
Yavapai Point
YAVAPAI GEOLOGY MUSEUM

Grandeur Point

Trail of Time

SOUTH ENTRANCE RD.

MATHER POINT
MATHER AMPHITHEATER

CANYON VIEW INFORMATION PLAZA (VISITOR CENTER/ BRIGHT ANGEL BICYCLES AND CAFE)

YAVAPAI RD.

Greenway

MCKEE AMPHITHEATER
PARK HEADQUARTERS

SHRINE OF THE AGES

YAVAPAI LODGE AND CAFETERIA

MARKET PLAZA

TRAILER VILLAGE (HOOKUPS)

SHOWERS, LAUNDRY, AND RV DUMP STATION

SAGE LOOP CAMPFIRE CIRCLE

MATHER CAMPGROUND (NO HOOKUPS)

WALK-IN CLINIC

CLINIC RD.

MARKET PLAZA RD.

64

To Desert View and Yaki Point (23 miles)

Greenway

180 64 SOUTH ENTRANCE RD.

0   0.25 mi
0   0.25 km

To Tusayan (4 miles)

© AVALON TRAVEL

Park Headquarters and the Shrine of the Ages

The **Park Headquarters** (8am-5pm daily) is a modern brick building that served for decades as the South Rim's main visitor center. The headquarters houses administrative offices, the park's research library, and a ranger-staffed service desk. But most likely you're here for one of three reasons: to park (the large lot often has open spaces), to find employment (a bulletin board lists current Park Service openings), or to attend a program at the **Shrine of the Ages,** a spacious nearby auditorium where many ranger programs, public meetings, and special events are held.

Pioneer Cemetery

Just west of the Shrine of the Ages is the **Pioneer Cemetery,** the final resting place for such canyon luminaries as John Hance, Ellsworth and Emery Kolb, and William Wallace Bass. There's also a memorial here for the victims of the horrific 1956 TWA-United collision over the canyon. Taphophiles (people who like tombstones) can easily while away an hour in this peaceful, pine-shaded spot while they visit the past.

McKee Amphitheater

Between park headquarters and the rim is **McKee Amphitheater,** where rangers host outdoor talks during temperate months.

MARKET PLAZA

Across the road from park headquarters is Market Plaza, home to the **general store,** a post office, and a bank with a 24-hour ATM. There's a large public parking lot here, and Yavapai Lodge, Trailer Village, and Mather Campground are nearby.

★ GRAND CANYON VILLAGE HISTORIC DISTRICT

Perched on the rim, Grand Canyon's town site is a registered National Historic Landmark District, with 257 contributing structures. Buildings designed by architect Mary Colter,

Craftsman-style offices and residences, log cabins, and Santa Fe Railway structures are all linked by the Village Loop Road, but the best way to explore is on foot. A free, self-guided walking tour map is available at El Tovar or Bright Angel Lodge.

Verkamp's

This large bungalow-style building was once the home and business of the Verkamp family. Before starting **Verkamp's Curios** in 1905, John Verkamp sold souvenirs and Native American crafts from a tent for the Babbitt Brothers. In 2008 Verkamp's shut down as the longest-running family-owned business in the national park system. The National Park Service acquired the 1906 building and reopened it as a visitor center and bookstore, with a timeline and displays that highlight pioneer life in Grand Canyon Village.

Hopi House

Hopi House was architect Mary Colter's first building at Grand Canyon. It opened shortly before El Tovar in 1905. Inspired by the Hopi village of Old Oraibi, Colter designed a rectangular masonry building of three stories, terraced to provide rooftop plazas where resident families, hired by the Fred Harvey Company to demonstrate crafts, could work and play. Look for authentic details like the stacked pottery chimneys ornamenting the building's corners.

Colter wanted visitors who stepped through the low doorway to feel as if they were entering another time and space, an effect enhanced by low lighting, log-and-brush ceilings, and roughly plastered walls. If you're interested in collector-quality jewelry, pottery, blankets, and baskets, head upstairs to the second-floor gallery.

El Tovar

Holding court just yards from the rim is **El Tovar,** the elegant "log palace" created from the partnership between the Fred Harvey Company and the Santa Fe Railway. The hotel was designed by Charles Whittlesey, an Illinois native who studied with Louis Sullivan (often credited as the father of modern architecture), before moving West to work for the Santa Fe.

When it opened in 1905, El Tovar was an eclectic mix of Victorian detail and rustic materials, from its rubble masonry foundation to its Queen Anne-style shingled turret. The first floor's log slab siding was given corner notching to create an illusion of log construction. Balustrades, indoors and out, were jigsawed in a Swiss chalet style. The original floor plan included a solarium, a ladies lounge, and a billiard room. The remote location required self-sufficiency: the hotel had its own kitchen garden, poultry barn, and dairy. The relative luxury targeted well-heeled travelers, among them Theodore Roosevelt, who established Grand Canyon as a national monument in 1908.

Despite modern updates and periodic refurbishments (the next scheduled for 2018), El Tovar retains its air of gracious hospitality. Even if you aren't a hotel guest, have a meal in the dining room, where murals depict Arizona's indigenous peoples, or sit by the fire in the Rendezvous Room, adorned with hunting trophies and paintings of the canyon.

To imagine what it must have been like to arrive as a guest during the early twentieth century, start downhill at the **train depot** (1909), one of three remaining log depots in the United States, and the only one still operating. Look for examples of the original copper hardware, just one fine detail on this building designed to complement El Tovar yet exude the spirit of the West.

Bright Angel Lodge

Bright Angel Lodge, which opened during the Great Depression, was meant to appeal to travelers on modest budgets. Mary Colter designed the lodge buildings to reflect the village's past as a pioneer settlement, with scattered structures in log cabin, clapboard, and Spanish Colonial themes. This approach allowed her to incorporate two existing buildings with long canyon histories: Buckey O'Neill's log cabin and Red Horse Station, a former stage stop. The main lodge entrance is west of El Tovar, on the other side of the mid-century Thunderbird and Kachina Lodges.

Across the lobby from the entrance, below the Fred Harvey Company's trademark thunderbird, an inglenook fireplace still warms hikers on cold winter days. A second fireplace, located down the west hall in what is now the **History Room,** replicates the canyon's rock layers. Park naturalist Edwin McKee worked with Colter to find geologic samples. Look closely, and you'll see that the base of the fireplace is made from Vishnu schist, the canyon's oldest and deepest layer. Around the fireplace's opening are the layers of the Grand Canyon Supergroup. Above that are narrow bands from the canyon's Paleozoic layers. The chimney is Kaibab limestone, the rock that forms the canyon's rim. History Room displays highlight the Fred Harvey Company and the Harvey Girls, the efficient white-aproned waitresses who worked in lunchrooms, train stations, and hotels on the Santa Fe lines.

Buckey O'Neill's Log Cabin

The dashing Buckey O'Neill helped shape Arizona Territory's frontier, serving as a newspaper editor, probate judge, supervisor of schools, and county sheriff. An investor in a mine south of the village, O'Neill was garnering support for a rail line to Grand Canyon when the Spanish-American War began. He was the first to volunteer for the regiment later known as Teddy Roosevelt's Rough Riders and was killed in Cuba in 1898. **Buckey O'Neill's log cabin,** built in the 1890s, still stands on the rim and is used today as suite accommodations.

Red Horse Station

Red Horse Station, built in the 1890s, once served as a station on the stagecoach line south of the village. It is the oldest building at Grand Canyon. In 1902, Ralph Cameron moved the station to the village, added a second story and veranda, and operated it as the Cameron Hotel. The building later served as the South Rim's post office. Mary Colter saved it from demolition and returned it to its single-story log structure, now one of the lodge's guest cabins.

Those Daring Young Men

Emery and Ellsworth Kolb arrived at Grand Canyon in 1902 and started a photographic business in a canvas tent. Because the rim's water supply was limited, the Kolbs developed their glass-plate negatives at Indian Garden, 4.5 miles down Bright Angel Trail. Each morning, they photographed mule riders starting down the toll trail, and then one (usually Emery) ran ahead to Indian Garden, returning in time to sell the riders their portraits.

The Kolbs also photographed their own hiking, climbing, and cliff-dangling exploits, often in the company of a Harvey Girl or two. They began building a permanent home and studio in 1904, so close to Bright Angel Trail that they could photograph mule riders from a window. After Emery married a former Harvey Girl, the studio expanded several times to accommodate the growing family.

To boost business, the brothers decided to do something daring: In 1911-1912, they ran the Colorado River through Grand Canyon, becoming the

Emery and Ellsworth Kolb

ninth successful canyon expedition, and the first to capture the experience on film.

Ellsworth moved to Los Angeles in 1924, but Emery stayed on with his wife and daughter. In later years, some people considered Kolb Studio an eyesore and lobbied the park service to oust Emery. But feisty Emery prevailed, showing his movie until his death at age 95. The park service acquired the studio after Emery's death and restored it with help from the Grand Canyon Association (GCA). Today visitors can once again watch Emery and Ellsworth's exploits: The studio's projection room features an interactive video with clips of the Kolbs running the Colorado River.

Lookout Studio

Low-roofed and with terraces constructed of the rim's Kaibab limestone, **Lookout Studio** blends almost seamlessly into the edge of the canyon. Designed by Mary Colter and completed in 1914, the studio displayed photographs of the canyon and featured a telescope for viewing the canyon from its balconies. Today it functions as a gift shop, and it still provides a sheltered perch—for humans and condors—from which to view mule riders and hikers descending Bright Angel Trail.

Kolb Studio

Multistoried **Kolb Studio** clings precipitously to the edge of the canyon. The wood-frame building was shaped and reshaped over 23 years as Ellsworth and Emery Kolb made room for a growing business selling souvenir photos and

screening the movie they made of their 1911-1912 run down the Colorado River. They took pictures of tourists on mules from one window, and from another sold the photos and tickets for their film. Today, Kolb Studio houses an excellent bookstore with an art gallery downstairs. Peek into the projection room to see the equipment the Kolbs used in the early 1900s.

The steep descent of **Bright Angel Trail** begins just west of Kolb Studio. Above the trail is the **old stone corral,** where mule parties still saddle up every morning to make the journey to Phantom Ranch.

Visitors who enjoy early-20th-century architecture can extend their self-guided history tour to take in the south half of Center Road. The impressive **Powerhouse** near the railroad tracks was built in Swiss chalet style in 1926. Past the **community building** (1935),

The Kolbs built their home and studio on the canyon's edge.

the **mule and horse barns** (circa 1907) are wood clapboard with massive rooftops broken by cupolas and small dormers. The road loops near the **garage,** built to maintain the Fred Harvey Company's fleet of touring cars, and the Craftsman-style **park operations building,** constructed in 1929.

WEST RIM

Eight-mile-long **Hermit Road** was once a stagecoach route linking the village with Hermits Rest, built in 1914 by the Santa Fe Railway and Fred Harvey Company. For $1.50, travelers could take the dusty but scenic trip by horse-drawn stage, relax and sip a lemonade at Mary Colter's curious Hermits Rest, then make the return journey. In later decades, the Fred Harvey Company's fleet of Harveycars (open touring cars) traveled the old stage route. Today, depending on the season, you can explore the sights along Hermit Road by car (winter), by free shuttle bus (spring-fall), by guided bus tour (year-round), or by bicycle.

Trailview Overlooks

The two **Trailview Overlooks** are named for their stellar views of Bright Angel Trail. From either overlook, you can watch hikers and mule tours descending the trail's switchbacks

into the canyon. Bright Angel Trail follows a long, straight fault line that stretches between the canyon's North and South Rims. During the summer, look for a patch of bright green roughly halfway down the canyon walls: These are the cottonwoods that mark **Indian Garden.** The gray-green Tonto Platform extends into the canyon, and you'll probably be able to make out the line of another trail snaking toward Plateau Point.

Eastward along the rim, you'll see the historic buildings of Grand Canyon Village. Look for El Tovar's distinctive roofline and the multiple levels of Kolb Studio perched above and below the rim. It's a pleasant walk to Trailview from the village along the Rim Trail. This mile-long section of the trail is paved and fairly level.

Maricopa Point

Along the Rim Trail near **Maricopa Point** you can see a headframe, shafts, cables, and other mining remnants. Daniel Hogan, who served under Theodore Roosevelt in the Spanish-American War, filed a copper claim here in 1893. Miners "commuted" by an open tramway bucket to the ore body below. The **Lost Orphan Mine** never yielded much, so Hogan opened a tourist camp along the rim in 1936, which was subsequently managed by

Will Rogers Jr. Years later, Hogan learned that his mine contained some of the richest uranium ore in the Southwest, earning millions of dollars for later owners and creating a noisy, dusty hazard for park residents and visitors. The 20-acre parcel became part of the park in 1987. Visitor access is restricted for safety reasons, but the views are unlimited.

Powell Point

At **Powell Point,** a memorial honors the members of John Wesley Powell's expedition down the Colorado River in 1869, when the area was still a blank spot on the national map. Four decades later, in 1920, the dedication ceremony for Grand Canyon National Park took place here. You can catch a glimpse of the river below, and to the south you can see the **San Francisco Peaks,** the jagged remnants of an extinct volcano. Mount Humphrey marks the highest point in Arizona at 12,633 feet.

★ Hopi Point

Hopi Point thrusts farther into the canyon than any other point on the South Rim, offering theatrical views. Across the canyon, below the North Rim, you can spot the rocky peaks known as **Osiris, Shiva, Isis,** and **Horus,** named by geologist Clarence Dutton in the 1880s. Dutton, a student of world history and philosophy, dubbed the inner canyon peaks "temples" and named many of them for mythological figures. A mile below, the Colorado River looks like a narrow blue-green band, or reddish-brown if it has been raining. Look for **Granite Rapid**—it helps to have binoculars—marked by flecks of white.

Mohave Point

Below **Mohave Point,** you can see three of the canyon's 160-plus rapids: From left to right are **Hermit, Granite,** and **Salt Creek Rapids.** Most rapids on the Colorado River through Grand Canyon were formed when boulders washed down tributary canyons after flash floods. A long, narrow formation, **the Alligator** stretches from the point into the canyon below. The cliffs to the east are known as the **Hopi Wall.**

The Abyss

From the **Abyss,** you can look down one of the rim's steepest drops to the river, nearly 4,500 feet. The drainage below the Abyss leads to Monument Canyon. With binoculars or sharp eyes, you might be able to spot the **Monument,** a pillar found in the depths of this tributary. If you enjoy the thrill of heights, walk west along the Rim Trail for especially vertiginous views. **Pima Point** is three miles farther; **Hermits Rest** is four miles.

Pima Point

Far below **Pima Point,** the remnants of historic **Hermit Camp** are reminders of a bygone attraction. The Santa Fe Railway established the tourist camp here in 1912 and built Hermit Trail to compete with Ralph Cameron's Indian Garden camp and Bright Angel Trail. During its glory days, Hermit Camp offered mule riders well-furnished tent cabins, a dining hall presided over by a Fred Harvey chef, stables, a blacksmith, restrooms, phones, and showers. Operating until 1930, the camp got its supplies via an aerial tramway leading 6,000 feet down from Pima Point, then the longest single-span cable system in the world. Today, this is one of the quietest spots along this part of the rim.

★ Hermits Rest

Designed by architect Mary Colter, **Hermits Rest** was completed in 1914 as another attraction to help the Santa Fe Railway entice tourists to the canyon. Drawing on the local history of miners who guided visitors to their inner canyon camps, she imagined the setting as a prospector's lair carved into the hillside, with a massive fireplace dominating the back wall. When Santa Fe employees kidded Colter that the building looked like it needed a good cleaning, she replied, "You can't imagine what it cost to make it look this old." (The price tag, about $185,000, was an impressive investment for the Santa Fe and Fred Harvey Company, which charged $1.50 pp to take the stage to Hermits Rest.) Just west is the start of **Hermit Trail.**

Pima Point is one of the quietest overlooks on the West Rim.

EAST RIM
Yaki Point

Yaki Point, about a mile past the turnoff on Desert View Drive, is accessible on foot or bicycle, or by shuttle or tour bus. Because private vehicles are banned, many people skip visiting one of the most beautiful overlooks on the South Rim. While Hopi Point get raves for sunset and sunrise snapshot opportunities, many photographers prefer Yaki Point for the gnarled piñon pines that lend foreground and framing to canyon scenes. Below, reddish-orange **Cedar Ridge** rises toward **O'Neill Butte.** Look closely and you'll see the **South Kaibab Trail** stretching across Cedar Ridge before descending in a steep zigzag below **Skeleton Point.** The trail starts 0.5 miles south of the rim.

★ Grandview Point

Grandview Point offers grand views of

Yaki Point

Mary Colter

Mary Colter designed intriguing Hermits Rest.

Mary Elizabeth Jane Colter was born in 1869 but was meant for the next century. One of a handful of women studying architecture in California, she learned the arts-and-crafts aesthetic of harmonizing structures with their natural settings. But family responsibilities called her back to St. Paul, Minnesota, where she supported her widowed mother and ailing sister by teaching mechanical drafting at a boys school.

Then, in 1902, Colter landed a life-changing opportunity: The Fred Harvey Company contacted her to decorate their "Indian building," a retail space in Albuquerque, New Mexico. Her keen appreciation for the culture of North American indigenous people suited the company's image-building efforts and, two years later, the Fred Harvey Company contacted her again, this time to design a store to complement El Tovar, then under construction on the South Rim. She designed Hopi House, drawing on the village of Oraibi for inspiration. It opened on January 1, 1905, to immediate acclaim. With Hopi House, Mary Colter didn't simply show visitors the West; she made it possible for them to experience it.

By 1910 Colter worked her way into a permanent full-time job styling the hotels, restaurants, and depots the Fred Harvey Company managed for the Santa Fe Railway. As for her personal style, well, "eccentric" describes it best. The chain-smoking Colter often wore riding breeches and a Stetson, knew how to shoot a pistol, and avidly collected books and Native American silver. Her jewelry collection numbered 1,000 pieces, and she wore rings on every finger.

Colter's buildings at Grand Canyon—including Lookout Studio (1914), Hermits Rest (1914), Phantom Ranch (1922), Desert View Watchtower (1932), and Bright Angel Lodge (1935)—influenced "parkitecture" throughout the West. Mary Colter died in 1958, but her Grand Canyon icons continue to fascinate visitors today.

the central canyon as well as a peek into the canyon's pioneer past. Today, it's the South Rim's most forested overlook, but in the early 20th century this was the heart of Grand Canyon's tourist operations, with hotels and a post office that used the cancellation mark of "Tourist, Arizona." The Grand Canyon's most successful copper mine was headquartered here, and its remnants can be seen on **Horseshoe Mesa** at the bottom of the challenging three-mile **Grandview Trail,** which starts just east of the overlook's stone barrier. After the Santa Fe Railway built tracks to present-day Grand Canyon Village, 12 miles west, traveling to Tourist fell out of favor. Mary Colter repurposed logs from the Grand View Hotel for the ceiling of her Watchtower, a few miles down the road. The Park Service removed the remaining buildings in the 1970s, and today, it takes imagination to paint a picture of the people and stories of Grandview; the overlook's interpretive signage helps.

★ Tusayan Ruin and Museum

Near the end of the 12th century, this small village was home to people who hunted game, tended corn and other crops, and gathered wild plants for food, fuel, and medicine. The multiroom pueblo had living spaces, a storage area, and two circular-shaped kivas, still visible in the outlines of ruined stone walls. The villagers lived within view of the San Francisco Peaks, mountains still considered sacred by many of the area's indigenous people.

In summer and early fall, rangers guide short tours of **Tusayan Ruin.** The self-guided loop trail is open year-round. Displays at nearby **Tusayan Museum** (9am-5pm daily) focus on prehistoric and contemporary Native American cultures, and artifacts include the enigmatic split-twig figurines found in a Grand Canyon cave. The bookstore has a fine selection of titles on archaeology and ethnology.

Lipan Point

From **Lipan Point** you can see **Unkar Delta,** a sinuous curve along the Colorado River where some of the canyon's Ancestral Puebloans had winter homes. In broad Unkar Valley, the colorful tilted layers of the Grand Canyon Supergroup have eroded into soft hills and folds. Above the valley is the North Rim's **Cape Royal,** surrounded by majestic temples and buttes. To the east are the cliffs known as the **Palisades of the Desert,** marking the end of Marble Canyon and the river's turn westward toward the Inner Gorge. From Lipan Point, the 10-mile **Tanner Trail** leads to the river, part of a trail once used by horse thieves.

★ Desert View Watchtower

Designed by Mary Colter, **Desert View Watchtower** is a masterpiece of atmosphere and ethnohistory. Rising 70 feet above the rim, the Watchtower combines prehistoric masonry style overlying a hidden steel frame

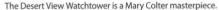
The Desert View Watchtower is a Mary Colter masterpiece.

built by railroad engineers. Colter's tower, built in 1932, reimagines the prehistoric towers built by Ancestral Puebloans in the Four Corners area, enigmatic structures that some archaeologists believe are observatories.

The tower's interior presents a visual and symbolic history of Southwestern cultures. At the base of the circular tower is a **mural** of Tiyo and the Hopi snake dance, painted by artist Fred Kabotie. Upper stories feature designs from the Mimbres culture and ancient cave paintings. Construction details include a log kiva-style ceiling. The second-story observation deck offers views of Comanche Point, the Colorado River, and the Little Colorado River Gorge. Eastern views encompass Navajo country, including Cedar Mountain, the Echo Cliffs, and the edge of the Painted Desert.

Recreation

DAY HIKES

The National Park Service warns, "There are no easy hikes below the rim." If you're looking for a simple walk or stroll, try sections of the scenic Rim Trail or wander around the village area. If you decide to enter the realm below the rim, start with one of the South Rim's corridor trails: Bright Angel and South Kaibab. The maintained and patrolled corridor trails are easy to follow and so popular that help usually isn't far away, should you need it.

When hiking below the rim, don't let the ease of traveling downhill lure you into hiking farther than you have water, time, or energy for. As a rule of thumb, it takes twice as long for the return trip.

Planning Your Hike

Hiking in Grand Canyon is an experience like no other. The views, of course, are awe inspiring, but so is the sense of walking into the past as you descend through rock layers and vegetation zones. Even a short day hike below the rim can shift your perspective as you enter a kingdom of stone castles and sublime views.

Yet, even though Bright Angel Trail is only steps away from park lodges, hiking in Grand Canyon isn't for the spontaneous. Careful planning is important, even for an autumn or spring day hike on a corridor trail.

SUMMER

Hiking in summer requires an entire set of strategies encompassing timing, water, and sun protection. Extreme summer heat can turn any canyon hike into a dangerous, even life-threatening, ordeal. The South Kaibab Trail, in particular, is shadeless and dry. From July to mid-September, afternoon thunderstorms are possible, adding the danger of lightning strikes and flash floods.

WINTER

Icy winter conditions can also create many trail dangers. While South Rim trails are open year-round, upper sections may be snow packed and slick for days or even weeks after a winter storm. Crampons, which you can rent or buy at the General Store, are a must to help prevent a serious fall. A steel-tipped trekking pole can help with traction and balance.

SPRING AND FALL

Spring and fall are ideal times to hike, although the weather can be unpredictable. At any time of year, trail closures are possible. Check online (www.nps.gov/grca) or at the visitor centers for the latest conditions and water availability.

Rim Trail

Distance: 13 miles one-way
Duration: 6.5-7 hours
Elevation change: 480 feet
Effort: Easy-moderate
Trailhead: This mostly paved trail can be accessed at several points from the South Kaibab Trailhead west to Hermits Rest.

South Rim Hikes

Trail	Effort	Distance	Duration
Rim Trail	easy to moderate	13 miles one-way	6.5-7 hours
Kolb Studio to Mather Point	easy	2.6 miles one-way	1-1.5 hours
Mather Point to South Kaibab Trailhead	easy	2.4 miles one-way	1-1.5 hours
Powell Point to Mohave Point	easy	1.1 miles one-way	30-40 minutes
Mohave Point to Monument Creek Vista	easy	2 miles one-way	1 hour
Monument Creek Vista to Hermits Rest	easy	2.8 miles one-way	1.5 hours
Bright Angel Trail	moderate to very strenuous	9.5 miles one-way	2 days
Mile-and-a-Half Resthouse	moderate	3 miles round-trip	2-4 hours
Three-Mile Resthouse	strenuous	6 miles round-trip	4-6 hours
Indian Garden	very strenuous	9 miles round-trip	6-9 hours
South Kaibab Trail	moderate to very strenuous	7 miles one-way	2 days
Ooh Aah Point	moderate	1.8 miles round-trip	1-2 hours
Cedar Ridge	strenuous	3 miles round-trip	2-4 hours
Skeleton Point	very strenuous	6 miles round-trip	4-6 hours
Hermit Trail	very strenuous	20 miles round-trip	2-3 days
Hermit Basin	strenuous	2.8 miles round-trip	2-4 hours
Santa Maria Spring	strenuous	5 miles round-trip	4-6 hours
Dripping Springs Trail	strenuous	7 miles round-trip	5-7 hours
Grandview Trail	strenuous	6 miles round-trip	6-8 hours
New Hance Trail	very strenuous	14 miles round-trip	3 days
South Bass Trail	very strenuous	16 miles round-trip	2-3 days
Tanner Trail	very strenuous	20 miles round-trip	2-3 days
Boucher Trail	very strenuous	21.5 miles round-trip	3 days

Directions: From March through November you can ride the Hermit Road shuttle to one overlook and hike the Rim Trail to another, catching the next shuttle. Keep in mind that shuttle stops are limited on the return (eastward) route.

Over its 13-mile length, the character of the Rim Trail changes from wide, paved, and populated to a narrow dirt path winding in and out of piñon-juniper woodland. Even on the busiest sections of the Rim Trail, however, wildlife sightings are common. Fence lizards—oblivious to midsummer heat—dart over rocky outcrops. Mule deer wander through the forest most mornings. Ravens chortle to each other from juniper trees, while ponderosa pines near the village are home to tassel-eared Abert's squirrels. (Their ruder relatives, rock squirrels, will try to bully you for food; don't give in.) And from late spring through early fall, the heady scent of cliffrose may drift across your path. Most people will choose to hike this trail in shorter sections, described below.

KOLB STUDIO TO MATHER POINT

Distance: 2.6 miles one-way
Duration: 1-1.5 hours
Effort: Easy
Shuttle Stop: Bright Angel Lodge, Village Route (Blue)
Trailhead: Kolb Studio in Grand Canyon Village (see map p. 48-49)

The paved section from Kolb Studio to Mather Point is often crowded where it passes through Grand Canyon Village yet is still pleasant, particularly if you're a history or architecture buff.

It's just 0.6 miles from Kolb Studio to **Verkamp's,** passing the **Lookout Studio, El Tovar,** and **Hopi House.** The 1.3-mile stretch between Verkamp's and **Yavapai Point** is the **Trail of Time,** with hands-on geology exhibits, a bonus for those who want to learn more about the canyon's rock layers. The Rim Trail continues 0.7 miles from Yavapai Point to Mather Point.

You can also make short forays through the ponderosa pine forest to see a ranger program at **McKee Amphitheater** or **Shrine of the Ages,** explore the **Pioneer Cemetery,** or spend some time in the geology museum.

MATHER POINT TO SOUTH KAIBAB TRAILHEAD

Distance: 2.4 miles one-way
Duration: 1-1.5 hours
Effort: Easy
Shuttle Stop: Mather Point, Kaibab/Rim Route (Orange)
Trailhead: Mather Point, near Grand Canyon Visitor Center (see map p. 38-39)

You'll leave the crowds behind shortly after leaving Mather Point (but keep an eye out for bicycles; the Greenway joins this section of the Rim Trail 0.5 miles east of the overlook). The paved trail follows the rim for fine views into Pipe Creek Canyon. Continue one mile past **Pipe Creek Vista** to **Yaki Point,** where the South Kaibab Trail begins. You'll see a water bottle filling station here; thirsty elk occasionally hang out nearby. The Rim Trail officially ends here, but photographers should add a side trip to the **overlook,** another 0.5 miles via footpath (or a little farther via the shuttle bus road), to capture a colorful panorama of Cedar Ridge and O'Neill Butte.

POWELL POINT TO MOHAVE POINT

Distance: 1.1 miles one-way
Duration: 30-40 minutes
Effort: Easy
Shuttle Stop: Powell Point, Hermits Rest Route (Red)
Trailhead: Powell Point on the West Rim (see map p. 37)

If views are your objective, the unpaved section from Powell Point to Mohave Point offers one of the South Rim's widest vistas. This section includes popular **Hopi Point,** so you probably won't have the trail to yourself, but the views are big enough to share.

MOHAVE POINT TO MONUMENT CREEK VISTA

Distance: 2 miles one-way
Duration: 1 hour
Effort: Easy
Shuttle Stop: Mohave Point, Hermits Rest Route (Red)
Trailhead: Mohave Point on the West Rim (see map p. 37)

If it's solitude you're seeking, strike out from one of the overlooks along the West Rim. The unpaved two-mile section of the Rim Trail that leads from Mohave Point to Monument Creek Vista hugs the edge of the canyon, passing by the plunging **Abyss.**

MONUMENT CREEK VISTA TO HERMITS REST

Distance: 2.8 miles one-way
Duration: 1.5 hours
Effort: Easy
Shuttle Stop: Monument Creek Vista, Hermits Rest Route (Red)
Trailhead: Monument Creek Vista on the West Rim (see map p. 37)

The Rim Trail is paved for 2.8 miles from Monument Creek Vista to its end at Hermits Rest. This section is part of the Greenway, so you'll likely be sharing the view with bicyclists. The trail meanders from rim to woodland and back, reaching **Pima Point** at 1.7 miles. Linger here for a while to see if you can hear the sound of **Granite Rapid** churning on the Colorado River far below before continuing to Hermits Rest.

★ Bright Angel Trail

Distance: 9 miles round-trip to Indian Garden
Elevation change: 3,040 feet
Effort: Moderate to very strenuous
Shuttle Stop: Bright Angel Lodge, Village Route (Blue)
Trailhead: near Kolb Studio in Grand Canyon Village (see map p. 62)

Both scenic and historic, Bright Angel Trail is a good choice for novice hikers, even if you have time for only a short walk below the rim. And if you go the distance, you'll experience the element that makes a desert hike magical—water, in this case the clear streams of **Garden** and **Pipe Creeks.**

Bright Angel Trail begins just west of Bright Angel Lodge. On this well maintained and well-traveled trail, mules have the right of way. Step to the inside of the trail and stand quietly while they pass. Wait until the last mule is 50 feet away before continuing your hike.

MILE-AND-A-HALF RESTHOUSE

Distance: 3 miles round-trip
Duration: 2-4 hours
Elevation change: 1,120 feet
Effort: Moderate

One of the first highlights on Bright Angel Trail greets hikers about 0.5 miles down. After passing the first tunnel, pause to look toward the rim. Below a Kaibab limestone overhang are reddish **pictographs,** evidence of the trail's long history. A second tunnel leads to the canyon's Coconino sandstone layer. After a steep descent through reddish Hermit shale, you'll arrive at **Mile-and-a-Half Resthouse**

at—you guessed it!—1.5 miles. Here, you'll find seasonal **water** (early May-mid-Oct.), **toilets,** and an emergency phone.

THREE-MILE RESTHOUSE

Distance: 6 miles round-trip
Duration: 4-6 hours
Elevation change: 2,120 feet
Effort: Strenuous

From Mile-and-a-Half Resthouse, Bright Angel Trail serves up more switchbacks and more red rocks—this time the Supai layer—leading to Three-Mile Resthouse. Here you'll find seasonally available **water** (May-Oct.), **toilets,** a telephone, and great views, especially from the nearby overlook perched atop the Redwall formation.

Mile-and-a-Half Resthouse is a highlight on the Bright Angel Trail.

Bright Angel and South Kaibab Trails

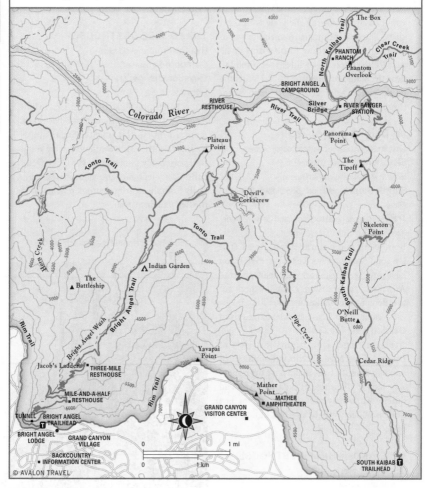

INDIAN GARDEN

Distance: 9 miles round-trip

Duration: 6-9 hours

Elevation change: 3,040 feet

Effort: Very strenuous

After a long series of switchbacks known as **Jacob's Ladder,** Bright Angel Trail descends from Three-Mile Resthouse through the Redwall to Indian Garden, a popular turnaround for strong day hikers. Indian Garden, watered by springs and Garden Creek, has a rest area of benches shaded by cottonwoods, with piped **drinking water** and nearby **toilets.** The Havasupai people grew crops here, on the gentle slope of the **Tonto Platform.** In the early 1900s, Ralph Cameron established a tourist camp here, charging mule riders a toll to use the trail. As mule parties started down the trail, Emery and Ellsworth Kolb took photos. One of them, usually Emery, would run down the trail to develop the photographs here, where there was clear running water, then dash back up ahead of the mule riders to sell them their portraits, a round-trip he sometimes made twice a day. (Think about that when you're heading up Jacob's Ladder gasping for breath.)

Short spur trails lead to a **ranger station** and **campground**. The main trail intersects the westbound Tonto Trail at 4.6 miles and the eastbound **Tonto Trail** at 4.9 miles. Though you may be tempted, keep in mind that the National Park Service *strongly discourages day hikers* from crossing the Tonto Platform to Plateau Point, a 12-mile round-trip hike from the rim (about 9-12 hours).

South Kaibab Trail

Distance: 1.8-6 miles round-trip to Skeleton Point
Elevation change: 2,040 feet
Effort: Moderate to very strenuous
Shuttle Stop: Yaki Point, Kaibab/Rim Shuttle (Orange)
Trailhead: Yaki Point along East Rim Drive (see map p. 62)
Directions: Yaki Point is closed to private vehicles year-round. Take the shuttle from Grand Canyon Visitor Center or the morning Hikers' Express shuttle from Grand Canyon Village.

The South Kaibab Trail follows ridgelines from the South Rim to the river, offering wide-open panoramas of the canyon's monuments and, as you get closer, overlooks of the **Colorado River.** Built by the park service in 1924, the South Kaibab Trail is steeper and shorter than Bright Angel Trail, making it a relatively fast way to get to the inner canyon (unless you have tricky knees). Like Bright Angel, the South Kaibab is well maintained and well trafficked; but because of its openness, *do not hike it midday (10am-4pm) in summer.* Water is available year-round at the trailhead, but there's nary a drop along the trail, so pack plenty, even for a day hike. (As you hike, remember that mule trains have the right of way; step to the inside of the trail and let them pass.)

OOH AAH POINT

Distance: 1.8 miles round-trip

Duration: 1-2 hours
Elevation change: 760 feet
Effort: Moderate

The South Kaibab Trail immediately starts its steep descent into the canyon, switching back and forth through the Kaibab Formation. In less than a mile, views open up dramatically at Ooh Aah Point.

CEDAR RIDGE

Distance: 3 miles round-trip
Duration: 2-4 hours
Elevation change: 1,120 feet
Effort: Strenuous

From Ooh Aah Point, the trail descends 1.5 miles through a series of more switchbacks to Cedar Ridge, the park's most popular day-hike destination. This section of the trail is wide-open to views (and the sun) and only becomes more colorful as it descends through Coconino sandstone into reddish Hermit Shale. You'll find **toilets** at Cedar Ridge, but no water.

SKELETON POINT

Distance: 6 miles round-trip
Duration: 4-6 hours
Elevation change: 2,040 feet
Effort: Very strenuous

The South Kaibab Trail continues along the east side of Cedar Ridge toward prominent **O'Neill Butte.** At three miles is Skeleton Point—a good spot to soak up some views before you turn around. From here, switchbacks make a steep descent to the **Tonto Platform** and **Tipoff.**

Hermit Trail

Distance: 2.8-7 miles round-trip
Elevation change: 1,600 feet from rim to Dripping Spring
Effort: Strenuous
Shuttle Stop: Hermits Rest, Hermits Rest Route (Red)
Trailhead: Hermits Rest on the West Rim (see map p. 64)
Directions: Hermit Trail begins at the end of the service road west of Hermits Rest. December-February,

Hermit Trail

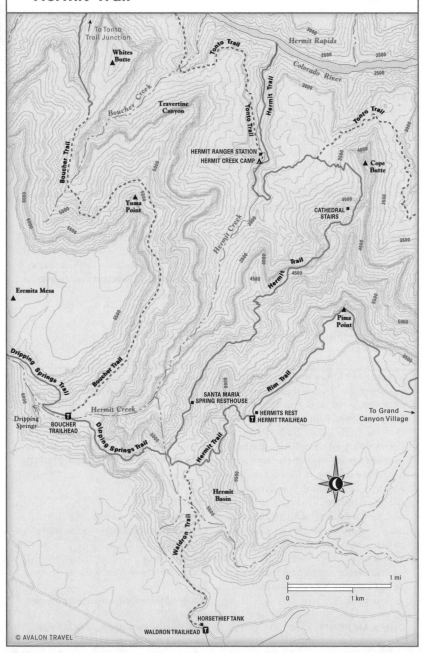

To Tonto
Trail Junction

Whites
Butte

Tonto Trail

Hermit Rapids

Colorado River

Boucher Creek

Travertine
Canyon

Tonto Trail

Hermit Trail

HERMIT RANGER STATION
HERMIT CREEK CAMP

Tonto Trail

Cope
Butte

Boucher Trail

Yuma
Point

CATHEDRAL
STAIRS

Hermit Creek

Eremita Mesa

Hermit Trail

Pima
Point

Dripping Springs Trail

Boucher Trail

Rim Trail

Dripping
Springs

BOUCHER
TRAILHEAD

Hermit Creek

SANTA MARIA
SPRING RESTHOUSE

HERMITS REST
HERMIT TRAILHEAD

To Grand
Canyon Village

Dripping Springs Trail

Hermit Trail

Hermit
Basin

Waldron Trail

0   1 mi

0   1 km

HORSETHIEF TANK
WALDRON TRAILHEAD

© AVALON TRAVEL

Santa Maria Spring on the Hermit Trail

Waldron Trail at 1.5 miles, make a good turnaround point for a two- to four-hour day hike.

SANTA MARIA SPRING

Distance: 5 miles round-trip
Duration: 4-6 hours
Elevation change: 1,680 feet
Effort: Strenuous

Stronger day hikers can continue another mile along Hermit Trail from Hermit Basin down to Santa Maria Spring. En route, at 1.75 miles, the trail intersects the **Dripping Springs Trail.** Take the right fork to continue on the Hermit Trail to the **Santa Maria Spring Resthouse** (2.5 miles). The undependable trickle of water here must be treated before drinking.

DRIPPING SPRINGS TRAIL

Distance: 7 miles round-trip (via Hermit Trail)
Duration: 5-7 hours round-trip
Elevation change: 1,600 feet
Effort: Strenuous
Trailhead: Hermits Rest

Most hikers reach Dripping Springs from the east via the Hermit Trail. This route is a good day hike, and spring hikers may see blossoming barberry, cliffrose, mock orange, and redbud on the way to the spring-fed "garden" of ferns and scarlet monkey flowers.

From the trailhead, the Hermit Trail descends 1,440 feet over 1.75 miles to its junction with Dripping Springs Trail. Take the left fork and continue another 1.5 miles along Dripping Springs Trail across the Hermit Shale Formation to the spring. The intersecting **Boucher Trail** leads deep into the canyon, where "hermit" Louis Boucher had a cabin, orchard, and copper mine around the turn of the 20th century. Keep left to reach Dripping Springs, where Boucher had another camp.

Approximately three miles from the trailhead, the alcove that shelters the **spring** is a good day-hike destination. The historic Dripping Springs Trail continues west to another (more remote) trailhead, but most hikers choose to return the way they came. Spring

private vehicles can drive Hermit Road to Hermits Rest and park at the signed parking area at the end of the road. March-November, access is via the Hermits Rest Route shuttle.

Completed by the Santa Fe Railway in 1912, Hermit Trail is steep but relatively easy to follow—a good option for those who've had some experience on the corridor trails. It offers beautiful views of **Hermit Creek Canyon,** access to other trails, and fine day hikes or an overnight not far from the lush riparian environment of year-round Hermit Creek.

HERMIT BASIN

Distance: 2.8 miles round-trip
Duration: 2-4 hours
Elevation change: 1,240 feet
Effort: Strenuous

The Hermit Trail descends toward Hermit Creek Canyon, passing through piñon-juniper woodland and chaparral of the Kaibab, Toroweap, and Coconino Formations. The reddish slopes of Hermit shale that mark Hermit Basin, near the intersection with the water must be treated before drinking; begin the hike with enough water for the return trip.

BACKPACKING

Overnight hikes require a **backcountry permit** or **reservations** at Phantom Ranch. Rim-to-river trails (even corridor trails like South Kaibab and Bright Angel) are steep and exposed to the sun, with sheer drop-offs and other potential hazards. Non-corridor trails often require route-finding skills—the ability to read both a map and the landscape to locate an obscure trail. In Grand Canyon, reading the landscape also means being able to identify rock layers by their name and characteristics.

Several trailheads in the park have designated overnight parking, but you may prefer to park at the Backcountry Information Center and take a shuttle or taxi to the trailhead. (And never leave food or snacks in your car overnight. Rodents are small but relentless.)

Devil's Corkscrew on the Bright Angel Trail

Backcountry Permits

Backcountry permits are required for all overnight camping outside of developed campgrounds, whether you are backpacking, trail riding, river camping, or cross-country skiing. Permit applications can be made four months in advance and can be submitted in person or by mail or fax to **Grand Canyon Permits Office** (National Park Service, 1824 S. Thompson St., Suite 201, Flagstaff, AZ 86001, fax 928/638-2125, www.nps.gov/grca). Fees are $10 per permit plus $8 pp per night if you are camping below the rim, or $8 per group if you are camping above the rim. The lengthy and detailed process is explained further in the *Essentials* chapter (page 281) and on the park website.

Corridor Trails
BRIGHT ANGEL TRAIL

Do not attempt to hike from rim to river unless you're prepared to spend a night in the canyon.
Distance: 9.5 miles one-way to Bright Angel Campground

Duration: 2 days or more
Elevation change: 4,380 feet from rim to river
Effort: Moderate to very strenuous
Shuttle Stop: Bright Angel Lodge, Village Route (Blue)
Trailhead: near Kolb Studio in Grand Canyon Village (see map p. 62)

Bright Angel Trail descends 3,060 feet along 4.9 miles to **Indian Garden.** Below the shady oasis of Indian Garden, the trail twists and turns and flirts with lovely **Garden Creek,** tempting you to continue. About six miles from the trailhead you'll reach the **Devil's Corkscrew,** a section of steep, sunbaked switchbacks. Past the confluence of Pipe Creek and Garden Creek, you'll come to **River Resthouse** at 7.8 miles. There's no potable water here, but you'll enjoy the shady riparian surroundings of cottonwoods and willows. Just past the resthouse the trail joins the **River Trail,** which parallels the river for 1.1 miles to the **Silver Bridge.** The short but scenic River Trail was the canyon's most difficult to construct, built by the Civilian Conservation

Corps in the 1930s using ropes, jackhammers, and 40,000 pounds of gunpowder. Hikers can cross the Silver Bridge to continue through **Bright Angel Campground.**

An option for exceptionally fit hikers (or for backpackers spending a night at Indian Garden Campground) is to take the three-mile (round-trip) trail across the Tonto Platform to **Plateau Point.** Here you'll have stunning overlooks of the Colorado River, more than 1,000 feet below, and the Inner Gorge, where the canyon's oldest geological layers are revealed.

SOUTH KAIBAB TRAIL

Distance: 7 miles one-way to Bright Angel Campground
Duration: 2 days or more
Elevation change: 4,780 feet from rim to river
Effort: Strenuous
Shuttle Stop: Yaki Point, Kaibab/Rim Shuttle (Orange)
Trailhead: Yaki Point along East Rim Drive (see map p. 62)
Directions: Access to Yaki Point is closed to private vehicles year-round. Take the shuttle from Grand Canyon Visitor Center or the morning Hikers' Express shuttle from Grand Canyon Village.

South Kaibab Trail descends steeply for three miles to **Skeleton Point.** From Skeleton Point, switchbacks make a steep descent to the Tonto Platform. The South Kaibab Trail intersects the **Tonto Trail** 4.4-miles below the rim. From this intersection, it's 1.4 miles to the **Tipoff,** where the walls of the Inner Gorge descend sharply toward the river.

About five miles from the rim, you'll reach **Panorama Point,** with views of the **Colorado River** and the Black (South Kaibab) and Silver (Bright Angel) Bridges. The trail continues its steep descent to the junction with the **River Trail.** In another mile the trail passes through a 50-yard tunnel leading to the **Black Bridge,** which spans more than 400 feet across the river.

After crossing the bridge, the trail heads west, passing alongside **Bright Angel Ruin**

and the boat beach before turning north. You'll encounter two small footbridges; the second crosses Bright Angel Creek and enters **Bright Angel Campground.** Stay on the main trail to reach the Ranger Station. **Phantom Ranch** is 0.5 miles farther.

South Kaibab Trail is open and shadeless; *do not hike it midday (10am-4pm) in summer.* Water is available year-round at the trailhead and at Bright Angel Campground, but there is no water along the trail.

Wilderness Trails
HERMIT TRAIL

Distance: 20 miles round-trip to the Colorado River
Duration: 2-3 days
Elevation change: 4,240 feet from rim to river
Effort: Strenuous
Shuttle Stop: Hermits Rest, Hermits Rest Route (Red)
Trailhead: Hermits Rest on the West Rim (see map p. 64)
Directions: Hermit Trail begins at the end of the service road west of Hermits Rest. December-February, private vehicles can drive Hermit Road to Hermits Rest and park at the signed parking area at the end of the road. March-November backpackers can take the shuttle or go to the Backcountry Information Center and request the gate combination to Hermit Road in order to park a private vehicle at the trailhead.

Hermit Trail descends 2.5 miles to **Santa Maria Spring,** then continues through the red rocks of the Supai to the top of the Redwall Formation. From here, the unmaintained trail steps sharply down switchbacks known as the **Cathedral Stairs** before angling west and intersecting with the **Tonto Trail** at the seven-mile point. Take the west (left) fork, and follow the Tonto Trail to the Hermit Creek campsites. Once you've set up camp, take time to explore the area, including the remnants of **Hermit Creek Camp,** operated by the Santa Fe Railroad from 1913 to 1930, and the narrow canyon of Tapeats sandstone that leads 1.4 miles to a sandy beach above Hermit Rapids, another area where **backpackers** can set up camp.

BOUCHER TRAIL

Distance: 21.5 miles round-trip; 8 miles to the Colorado River, plus 2.75 miles to the trailhead
Duration: 3 days or more
Elevation change: 2,520 feet from rim to river
Effort: Very strenuous
Trailhead: Dripping Springs junction with Hermit Trail on the West Rim (see map p. 64)

To reach the Boucher Trail, you'll need to start on the **Hermit** and **Dripping Springs Trails,** adding 2.75 miles to your trip. Sections of the trail are hard to follow, and route-finding experience is necessary. The trail isn't recommended for day hikers, but experienced backpackers will have expansive views of the Inner Gorge and Granite Rapids, along with the chance to explore the remnants of an old mining camp. Louis D. Boucher, the French-Canadian "hermit" who inspired so many Grand Canyon place names, built this trail to his copper mine and cabin in the 1890s. One modern-day drawback, though, is the nearly constant drone of tour helicopters during daylight hours.

The Boucher Trail begins on a piñon- and juniper-studded Supai shelf above Hermit Creek Canyon. As the trail edges the canyon, **Hermit Camp** and **Hermit Trail** come into view below. At 2.5 miles, below Yuma Point, the Colorado River and Granite Rapids are visible. There are fine **campsites** along this slickrock shelf.

The trail continues west toward the head of **Travertine Canyon,** where a very steep and dangerous descent leads down through the Supai layers to the floor of the side canyon. From here the trail climbs north toward Whites Butte, leading toward a saddle where you'll begin the final descent through the Redwall to **Boucher Creek,** another 1.5 miles. En route, you'll pass the junction (unsigned) with eastbound **Tonto Trail;** bear left to continue to the creek. The side canyon is narrow but pleasant, with room for a couple of **tent sites** not far from what remains of Louis Boucher's cabin. Creek water must be treated before drinking.

To reach the Colorado River, follow the creek bed another 1.5 miles. As Topaz Canyon joins Boucher Creek, cairns mark the route of the intersecting westbound **Tonto Trail.** Bear right, continuing down Boucher Creek. Dark gray Vishnu schist—the canyon's oldest and deepest rock layer—forms the creek bed as the side canyon approaches the river and Boucher Rapid. The beach has room for a few **campsites.**

SOUTH BASS TRAIL

Distance: 16 miles round-trip to the Colorado River
Duration: 2-3 days
Elevation change: 4,400 feet from rim to river
Effort: Strenuous
Trailhead: 30 miles west of Grand Canyon Village
Directions: To get to the trailhead, head south on Rowe Well Road. Turn west, following signs for Pasture Wash or Forest Road 328, a rough dirt road that may be impassable in wet weather. Even long after a rain, ruts remain, making a high-clearance vehicle a necessity and 4WD recommended. Depending on the conditions, getting to the trailhead may require two hours or more. Take a good map and ask rangers about current conditions before starting out. You'll be crossing the Havasupai Reservation, and you may be asked to pay a fee (usually $25). Close all gates behind you after you pass through.

Backpackers should consider scheduling more than two days to hike to the river and back. The rewards are scenic views that encompass the Shinumo Amphitheater monuments backed by Powell Point, plus a journey along the trail used by the first nonnative man to raise a family at Grand Canyon.

The South Bass Trail descends from the rim to a series of switchbacks leading to the **Esplanade,** a broad terrace of reddish-pink and gray sandstone topped with delicate cryptobiotic crust. Stay on the trail to avoid trampling this miniature universe.

After dropping below the Esplanade, the trail descends southward to a break in the Redwall at the head of **Bass Canyon.** It follows the east side of the canyon, then drops to the dry creek bed leading toward the river. The route crosses from one side of the canyon to the other several times, and you will hike past cairn-marked junctions with the westbound, then eastbound, **Tonto Trail.** At a third junction, a faint shortcut leads uphill back to the westbound Tonto Trail; continue right, and less than a mile later, look for a cairn marking the descending route to the beach. The route passes by the *Ross Wheeler,* a metal boat chained to the rocks above the water, abandoned by a 1915 river expedition.

The beaches here and across the river are popular with boat parties, who stop to explore or camp. They often shuttle back and forth across the river, and you may be able to catch a ride to explore the other side, where the **North Bass Trail** leads to historic **Bass Camp.** Like many pioneer miners, William Bass improved what was once a Native American trail to make it accessible by horseback, then supplemented prospecting with guiding tourists. (One was music teacher Ada Diefendorf, whom he married in 1895.) Bass built a cable crossing to complete this rim-to-rim route, the first in Grand Canyon, by 1900.

If you're limited to exploring the south side of the river, you can climb back up the route you took to the beach and walk another 0.5 miles west to a cairned scramble that leads down to **Shinumo Rapid.**

East Rim Wilderness Trails
GRANDVIEW TRAIL
Distance: 6 miles round-trip
Duration: 6-8 hours round-trip
Elevation change: 2,600 feet
Effort: Strenuous
Trailhead: Grandview Point (see map p. 70)
Though Grandview Trail doesn't lead to the bottom of the canyon, it's an easily accessed scenic and historic route. Views are spectacular, but the trail is steep and unmaintained so, as the old saw goes, "Don't walk and gawk at the same time." This trail is icy and treacherous after a winter snow, and dangerously hot on a summer afternoon. The **Coconino Saddle** (2.2 miles round-trip, 1-2 hours) makes a fine day-hike destination. Strong hikers can make the entire round trip to and from **Horseshoe Mesa** in a day. Backpackers can

camp on the mesa and spend time investigating its mining history or link to other trails for a longer trip.

You'll find the trailhead at Grandview Point, 12 miles east of the village off Highway 64 (East Rim Dr.). Trailhead parking is signed, and the trail begins at the east side of the overlook's stone wall. Hikers will notice log cribbing on historic sections of the trail, used when mules carried loads of ore from the Last Chance copper mine on Horseshoe Mesa.

After dropping steeply from Grandview Point, the trail traverses the **Coconino Saddle** between Hance and Grapevine Canyons. The saddle, just over a mile, is a good turnaround for a short hike. From here the trail descends again toward **Horseshoe Mesa,** heading straight toward the ruin of Pete Berry's **stone cabin,** just beyond the three-mile point. The mine is on the National Register of Historic Places, and all artifacts are protected by law. Most day-hikers will want to turn around here, although the trail continues another two miles across the west arm of the mesa and down to an intersection with the **Tonto Trail.**

From the cabin, a spur trail leads east to a **toilet** and several dry **campsites** (no drinking water). Backpackers can use this as a base camp to explore the remains of the historic mining camp and the edges of the mesa, enjoying great views of the Inner Gorge before returning up Grandview Trail or before continuing onto other trails for a loop trip using the Tonto Trail as a connector. Check with the Backcountry Information Center regarding possible water sources.

NEW HANCE TRAIL
Distance: 14 miles round-trip from rim to river
Duration: 3 days or more
Elevation change: 4,400 feet from rim to river
Effort: Very strenuous
Trailhead: Desert View Drive, between Buggeln picnic area and Moran Point
This trail, the South Rim's most difficult, gives hikers a sense of the effort pioneering miners and their mules expended to bring minerals

Grandview Trail

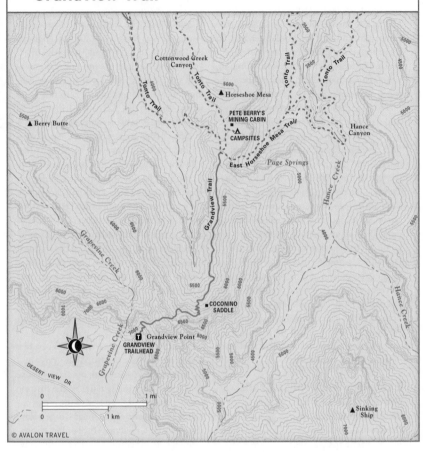

© AVALON TRAVEL

out of the canyon. Though best suited for sea-soned backpackers, the top of the **Redwall** (seven miles round trip) makes a strenuous day-hike destination for strong and experienced desert hikers. Washouts, rock falls, and side trails can make route-finding difficult. Allow plenty of time for the hike out; consider spending a night en route.

Just getting on the trail, 18 miles east of Grand Canyon Village, requires some strategizing. There's no parking at the trailhead, which is one mile southwest of **Moran Point.** You can cache your packs near the trailhead, then park at Moran Point and walk back,

adding two miles to the total distance. The park service also permits parking at the first turnout east of Buggeln picnic area (on the south side of the highway), a 0.25-mile walk to the trailhead.

The trail is referred to as *New* Hance because pioneer John Hance built it when his original trail washed out. It's also known as Red Canyon Trail because it follows the bed of Red Canyon, where bright orange-red Hakatai shale, part of the Grand Canyon Supergroup, makes an appearance.

The trail begins as a deceptively easy walk to the rim on an old road before dropping sharply through switchbacks in the Kaibab limestone. The **Sinking Ship** formation tilts up from behind Coronado Butte as you clamber over and around boulders and slabs. Just over a mile, you'll reach a **saddle** at the base of the Coconino sandstone layer.

From this saddle, the trail descends into the Supai Group, and then follows the east rim of Red Canyon for about a mile, a rough up-and-down traverse across several rocky drainages. The mile-long section along the top of the Redwall formation edges a 500-foot vertical drop—step carefully. **Cairns** mark a break in the Redwall limestone at approximately 3.5 miles. For experienced day hikers, this is a good turnaround point, offering views into fault-formed **Red Canyon** and across the main canyon to the North Rim's **Cape Royal** and **Wotans Throne.**

The trail drops from a fin of Redwall limestone down steep talus slopes, reaching the bottom of seasonally dry **Red Canyon** at about five miles. The winding creek bottom leads a couple of miles farther to the Colorado River, where you'll see—and hear—the "rock garden" of **Hance Rapids,** the most challenging rapids that river runners face in Grand Canyon's upper half. The park service implores hikers not to disturb sand dunes by walking on them or using them for toilet waste. Since the creek bed, camp areas, trail, and beach are all inappropriate for waste disposal, and nearly everything else is solid stone, pack out your toilet paper and consider using a carry-out method for human waste.

TANNER TRAIL
Distance: 20 miles round-trip from rim to river
Duration: 2-3 days
Elevation change: 4,600 feet from rim to river
Effort: Very strenuous
Trailhead: Lipan Point (see map p. 72)

The challenging and unmaintained Tanner Trail offers views of the **Colorado River** and the broad eastern canyon, where the layers of the Grand Canyon Supergroup have been sculpted into colorfully banded hills and folds. An old Native American route later improved by Seth Tanner and other prospectors, this trail was once favored by horse thieves moving stock to and from the Arizona Strip. You'll be able to see the Colorado River for much of the hike—a view you might find taunting, considering that there's no water and virtually no protection from the sun anywhere along the trail. The park service *strongly discourages* hiking Tanner Trail in summer; recent fatalities underline the danger. For experienced desert hikers, day-hike destinations include **Seventyfive Mile Creek** (four miles round trip) or **Cardenas Butte** (seven miles round trip).

The trailhead is 23 miles east of Grand Canyon Village at Lipan Point, east of the overlook's loop-shaped parking area. After its start in the piñon-juniper woodland of the rim, the trail descends steeply toward Tanner Canyon. The trail switches back and forth across talus slopes, reaching a saddle ridge between **Tanner Canyon** and **Seventyfive Mile Creek Canyon** at just under two miles. Considering this section's steep profile (a 1,700-foot elevation loss over two miles), this makes a good turnaround for most day-hikers.

After crossing the saddle, the trail traverses **Escalante** and **Cardenas Buttes** (named for the Spanish explorers). Once past Cardenas Butte, the trail descends the Redwall Formation to a **fork** at about 3.5 miles. The left spur leads to an overlook with excellent views of **Tanner Rapids** and broad Tanner beach, all the way upriver to the point where the canyon narrows at the Palisades of the Desert. For strong hikers, this is another possible day-hike destination.

Tanner Trail continues to the right, descending steeply through the Redwall before traversing open slopes above the edge of Tanner Canyon. The loose gravel is like walking over ball-bearings; take your time. The trail drops sharply again before reaching the **Colorado River** near Tanner Rapids. The large sand dune at the mouth of the Canyon is closed to visitors. **Campsites** can be found near the river on the east side of Tanner Canyon, and you may be sharing them with river runners.

Tanner Trail

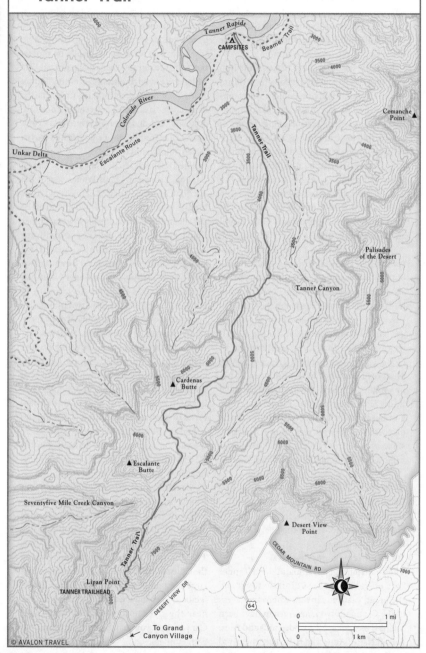

Tanner Rapids

Beamer Trail

CAMPSITES

Colorado River

Comanche Point ▲

Unkar Delta

Escalante Route

Tanner Trail

Palisades of the Desert

Tanner Canyon

Cardenas Butte ▲

▲ Escalante Butte

Seventyfive Mile Creek Canyon

▲ Desert View Point

Tanner Trail

CEDAR MOUNTAIN RD

Lipan Point
TANNER TRAILHEAD

DESERT VIEW DR

64

0   1 mi
0   1 km

To Grand
Canyon Village

© AVALON TRAVEL

BIKING

If you left your bike at home, you can rent one from **Bright Angel Bicycles** (928/638-3055, www.bikegrandcanyon.com, 8am-6pm daily May-mid-Sept., shorter hours Oct.-Apr.), located near the Grand Canyon Visitor Center's P4 (Lizard) parking lot. Rates are $12 per hour to $40 per day for adult bikes, including helmets. Also available are child-size bikes, pull-behind trailers, strollers, adult tricycles, and wheelchairs. The staff will help you choose a route, and they offer guided tours daily, weather permitting. Bright Angel Bicycles also operates an hourly **shuttle** service for their customers, allowing them to bypass the traffic-congested village area.

Traffic throughout the park is heaviest on summer weekends. Play it safe—wear a helmet and bright colors, use hand signals, and ride single-file in the same direction as traffic. In Arizona, bikes are subject to the same traffic rules as automobiles. Biking is allowed on all paved and dirt roads on the South Rim. All South Rim hiking trails, including the Rim Trail, are off-limits to bicycles. The only exception is the multiuse Greenway Trail, which joins the Rim Trail for short sections.

Hermit Road

Scenic Hermit Road is closed to passenger vehicles March-November. Shuttle buses travel Hermit Road during those months, and bicyclists need to use caution, allowing the large vehicles to pass. At the **Monument Creek** overlook, bikers can leave Hermit Road for the Greenway Trail, a paved, nonmotorized, multiuse trail traveling along the rim for 2.8 miles to Hermits Rest. Much of this section of the Greenway follows the 1912 alignment of Hermit Road, when stagecoaches toured the rim. Shuttle buses are equipped with bike racks, making one-way rides possible.

Greenway Trail

The Greenway is a nonmotorized bicycle and pedestrian pathway, a pleasant alternative for getting to the park and exploring the rim. The longest section (6.6-miles) leads from

the **Grand Canyon Visitor Center** outside the park to the town of Tusayan. A 2.3-mile section leads from the Visitor Center east to the South Kaibab Trailhead at Yaki Point. (Cyclists can continue another 0.6 miles on Yaki Road to reach the overlook.) Another 2.3-mile section links the Visitor Center with the historic village area. To reach the 2.8-mile section that begins at Monument Creek Vista and travels west along the rim to Hermits Rest, cyclists can ride 5 miles on Hermit Road.

Forest Roads

The adjoining Kaibab National Forest has miles of dirt roads and trails open to mountain bikers. Most are lightly traveled, so you'll have a good chance of seeing deer and elk while enjoying natural quiet, shady ponderosa forests, historic sights, and glimpses of the canyon. One possible side trip is to take **Forest Road 307** to Hull Cabin. You can start your adventure by climbing the 80-foot-tall **Grandview Lookout Tower,** built in 1936 by the Civilian Conservation Corps. The tower was used by forest rangers to spot smoke plumes or other signs of wildfire. Today, it marks the start of the Arizona Trail. Built in 1888, **Hull Cabin** is the oldest standing cabin in the Grand Canyon area, the home of sheepherders Philip and William Hull, who partnered with John Hance to bring the first tourists to Grand Canyon. The cabin is on the National Register of Historic Places and is available for overnight rental (877/444-6777, www.recreation.gov). Respect the privacy of guests and residents.

Depending on winter snow depths, unpaved forest roads can be muddy through April. For current conditions, maps, or additional information about these rides, contact the Tusayan Ranger District of the **Kaibab National Forest** (928/638-2443, www.fs.usda.gov/kaibab) or stop by the ranger station, located one mile north of Tusayan on the west side of Highway 64.

Arizona Trail

The Arizona Trail offers several options for

mountain bikers. This scenic nonmotorized trail, when complete, will cross the state from the Utah border to the Mexican border, 800 miles in all. To get to the Arizona Trail from inside the park, take Desert View Drive (Hwy. 64) east about nine miles, passing the Grandview Point overlook and continuing two more miles, turning right (south) at the Arizona Trail sign. The trail begins at the **Grandview Lookout Tower,** built in 1936 by the Civilian Conservation Corps. If you're starting from Highway 64 in Tusayan, turn east on Forest Road 302 and follow the signs to Grandview Lookout (16 miles). You'll be traveling over old logging roads that meander through ponderosa pine forest. With the aid of a good map, you can loop back on different roads for the return trip. Maps are available at the **forest ranger station** (176 Lincoln Log Loop, 928/638-2443, www.fs.usda.gov/kaibab), one mile north of Tusayan.

The 12-mile **Coconino Rim** segment of the Arizona Trail, which is open to mountain bikers, hikers, and equestrians, begins south of Grandview Point. The trail follows the edge of a 500-foot-high escarpment that curves to the southeast, offering unusual perspectives on Grand Canyon and distant views of the **Painted Desert.** At eight miles, a bypass route for bikes avoids a steep series of switchbacks. Just past 10 miles, the trail crosses Forest Road 310. If you like, you can loop back to the park on Forest Road 310, another seven miles.

For a longer ride, you can continue onto the **Russell Wash** segment of the trail, which begins just south of Russell Tank and parallels a historic stagecoach route. In about three miles, the trail crosses Forest Road 313 and nears the historic **Moqui Stage Station,** a remnant of the route from Flagstaff to Grand Canyon, in operation from 1892 to 1901. This station was a stop on the 20-hour, $20 ride to the Grandview Point area, the center of tourist accommodations at the time. The Arizona Trail continues all the way to Flagstaff, but you'll probably want to head back to the Grandview area and the national park boundary.

For an especially picturesque side trip, add the **Vishnu Trail,** a 1.1-mile scenic loop that starts just north of the fire tower. The trail leads to an overlook on the Coconino Rim offering distant Grand Canyon views and then loops back to the Grandview area via the Arizona Trail.

TRAIL RIDING

Equines (horses, mules, and burros) are allowed on primitive roads and specific trails: the South Kaibab, Bright Angel, River, and Plateau Point Trails, and the Tonto Trail between Indian Garden and the South Kaibab Trail. Contact the **livery stables** (928/638-2526, ext. 6095) when planning a trip. In addition, all riders must check in at the **Backcountry Information Center** (928/638-7875, 1pm-5pm Mon.-Fri.) before setting out, even on a day trip.

A backcountry permit is required to stay at inner canyon campgrounds, and there are restrictions on the number of animals per group. Permit fees and additional stock fees apply. If riders plan to stay at Phantom Ranch, at least one member of the group must stay in Bright Angel Campground with the animals. On the South Rim, Mather Campground has two stock sites available.

Riders must stay on specified trails and travel according to the park's uphill/downhill "traffic" schedules; mule parties have right of way. No grazing is allowed, and feed must be packed in. Hay must be weed-certified, and riders must carry a current health certificate for each animal. Tree-savers must be used for tying up animals. Pack animals must be tied together and led single file. Riders accept all responsibility for their own and their animals' safety.

Trails and roads in neighboring Kaibab National Forest are open to equine use (horses, mules, or burros) unless otherwise posted, or unless the animals pose a danger to free-ranging livestock. Contact the Tusayan

A rider leads a packhorse down Bright Angel Trail.

Ranger District of the **Kaibab National Forest** (928/638-2443, www.fs.usda.gov/kaibab) for more information about trail riding and camping.

WINTER ACTIVITIES

The South Rim is open year-round, and winter hikes into the canyon might start in ice and snow, making trails treacherous, before leading into pleasant low-desert temperatures along the Colorado River. Due to lengthy shaded or north-facing sections, Bright Angel, Grandview, New Hance, and Tanner Trails are usually the iciest. Trails may be snow-covered down to the Redwall Formation (roughly one-third to halfway from rim to river)—but with crampons or snow cleats to negotiate icy sections, winter hiking offers solitude and quiet; clear air; beautiful sunrises and sunsets, due to the lower angle of the sun; and plenty of wildlife-watching.

The park website (www.nps.gov/grca) has current weather information as well as valuable trail-specific information about typical winter conditions. Backcountry updates are posted online, and notices about current trail conditions and closures are also available as an RSS feed. For the latest information, contact the **Backcountry Information Center** (928/638-7875, 1pm-5pm Mon.-Fri.).

Cross-country skiing and **snowshoeing** opportunities are relatively limited on the South Rim. Snowfall varies from year to year—the most likely place to find adequate snow cover is the Grandview Point area on the East Rim, and the best time is mid-December to early March. The ponderosa forest shelters a winter population of juncos, chickadees, nuthatches, and Steller's jays. Below the pines, deer and elk tracks trail through the snow.

Two miles east of Grandview Point, the **Arizona Trail** parking area offers access to the **Kaibab National Forest** (928/638-2443, www.fs.usda.gov/kaibab). If snow cover is adequate, and if you don't mind breaking trail, you can head off into the forest in any direction, including historic Hull Cabin or the scenic Coconino Rim.

Entertainment and Shopping

If your alarm isn't set for dark-thirty to get an early start on a hike or to watch the sunrise, you'll find a few things to while away the evening in Grand Canyon Village. The Village Route shuttle runs until 10:30pm daily June-August (be at your stop by 10pm), and many venues are within walking distance of rim lodges. It's a good idea to carry a small flashlight for getting around the village area after dark.

Inside Maswik Lodge, the **Pizza Pub** (11am-11pm daily) has wine, beer, and TVs tuned to current games. The **Bright Angel Bar** (11am-11pm daily) has occasional live entertainment, generally folk or acoustic country music. **El Tovar Lounge** (11am-11pm daily) is a comfortable place to gather for conversation or a light meal, and the wine list is impressive. **Yavapai Tavern** (11am-11pm daily summer, 3pm-10pm daily fall-spring) serves cocktails, beer, wine, and bar snacks in stylish surroundings, though if the weather's fine, you can gather around the outdoor fire pit.

RANGER PROGRAMS

From **June to September** more than a dozen ranger programs are offered each day, including guided walks and nature talks, at various locations around Grand Canyon Village, Grand Canyon Visitor Center, Tusayan Museum, and Desert View. These free programs, lasting from 20 minutes to four hours, are a great way to gain a more in-depth understanding of Grand Canyon, whether your interest is condors or constellations, birds or brachiopods. Many programs are geared toward families and children, such as storytelling, easy nature hikes, or activities leading to a Junior Ranger certificate and badge.

Seasonal programs include **campfire talks** at McKee Amphitheater. Offerings are fewer during the winter but still include a variety of lectures, hikes, and other activities. Check at visitor centers and lodges for current schedules. Sometimes additional programs are added at the last minute.

EVENTS

Park events might include free digital camera workshops offered by vendors, art openings at Kolb Studio, or nature festivals. Annual events are posted on the park's website (www.nps.gov/grca) and include the following:

Archaeology Day has plenty of family-oriented activities, such as making split-twig figurines like those on display in Tusayan Museum. It's the highlight of several events held at the park each March, Arizona's Archaeology and Heritage Month.

The wildly popular **Star Party** takes place over a week each June—book room reservations early to enjoy guided explorations of the canyon's dark, star-studded skies. Rangers lead nightly constellation tours, and amateur astronomers present slide shows at the main visitor center and set up telescopes for nighttime viewing.

Grand Canyon Music Festival (928/638-9215 or 800/997-8285, www.grandcanyonmusicfest.org) has grown since its inaugural 1984 season to more than half a dozen concerts over a two-week period beginning in late August. The festival embraces a wide repertoire of classical to contemporary music, and some events are free. Past performers have included Robert Bonfiglio (a festival cofounder), R. Carlos Nakai, the Amadeus Trio, and the Catalyst Quartet. Most of the concerts are held at the Shrine of the Ages auditorium.

During the weeklong **Celebration of Art** in September, landscape painters from around the United States travel to the South Rim to work *en plein air,* painting outdoors on location. A highlight is the "quick draw,"

Astronomers offer free programs during the annual Star Party.

architecture. If you make your other shopping stop at one of the stores operated by the nonprofit **Grand Canyon Association,** you'll have seen the cream of the canyon's retail crop.

Hopi House

Mary Colter designed her first Grand Canyon building, **Hopi House** (generally 8am-5pm daily, hours vary seasonally), to showcase indigenous cultures and their traditions. Downstairs you'll find the usual T-shirts, books, and gifts, but the upstairs gallery boasts a selection of Native American arts and crafts that is unmatched anywhere else in the park. Climb the narrow staircase to see museum-quality work by some of the leading artisans from Hopi, Navajo, and other regional cultures.

Grand Canyon Association Stores

If you're looking for learning games for kids, books on local history, or trail guides and maps, the selection at stores operated by Grand Canyon Association (GCA, www.grandcanyon.org) is superb. A nonprofit organization founded in 1932, Grand Canyon Association uses money from sales to support national park programs and publications. Staffed by canyon-savvy employees, GCA stores are located at **Kolb Studio, Verkamp's, Yavapai Geology Museum, Tusayan Museum,** and inside **Desert View Watchtower.** The largest is the **Park Store** (928/638-7145, 8am-8pm daily summer, 8am-5pm daily winter) across from Grand Canyon Visitor Center. GCA members receive a 15 percent discount online or in GCA shops.

Gift Shops

Grand Canyon's rich history of traders includes the Fred Harvey Company and the pioneering Verkamp and Babbitt families. The **Fred Harvey Company** (acquired by Xanterra Parks & Resorts in 1968) opened Hopi House in 1905 and continues to operate

when artists create paintings in two hours to be auctioned later in the day. The Celebration of Art culminates in a juried exhibit with an opening reception at Kolb Studio.

From late August to early November, **HawkWatch International** (www.hawkwatch.org) volunteers record the annual raptor migration over Yaki Point. Public participation is welcome. The park often hosts lectures or informal talks on Grand Canyon's raptors to coincide with this event.

SHOPPING

You'll find roughly three shopping categories at the canyon (or four, if you count necessities like groceries and gear): inexpensive souvenirs, education-themed items, and art. Many of the canyon's shops carry some of each, so unless you're a retail maven, you can get all your shopping done in a couple of stops.

If you have time to browse only two stores, make one **Hopi House,** notable not only for its selection but also for its landmark

Combine history and shopping at Hopi House.

it and half a dozen other gift shops at the South Rim and in Tusayan.

The gift shops inside **Bright Angel and Maswik lodges** (generally 7am-10pm daily, hours vary seasonally) carry similar inventories, a broad selection that ranges from inexpensive souvenirs to well-made Native American jewelry, sand paintings, and tapestries. American-made merchandise is clearly labeled, but if you're unsure, ask. Newer selections include eco-friendly products and refillable water bottles.

Head to **El Tovar gift shop** (7am-10pm daily) for quality Southwestern-style clothing, lavishly illustrated gift books, and fine Navajo and Hopi jewelry.

Mary Colter's imaginative architectural creations are attractions themselves. Built in 1914, **Lookout Studio** (generally 9am-5pm daily, hours vary seasonally) offers a wide selection of rocks and fossils to please the kiddos but continues its historic focus on photography with posters and photographic prints.

Another 1914 Colter building, the West Rim's **Hermits Rest** (generally 9am-5pm daily, hours vary seasonally), has just enough room for a little bit of everything, though brightly painted Navajo folk art is a specialty.

Delaware North Companies recently updated the **Yavapai Lodge gift shop** (7am-9pm daily summer, 8am-8pm daily winter), which carries videos, apparel, jewelry, and canyon-themed items.

The East Rim's **Desert View Trading Post** (8am-sunset daily summer, 9am-5pm daily winter) has a selection of locally made handicrafts, including kachina carvings, jewelry, and rugs.

Outdoor Gear and Supplies

The **Canyon Village Market general store** (928/638-2262, 7am-9pm daily summer, 9am-5pm daily winter) is a crossroads of campers, day-trippers, residents, and rangers. If you need some serious outdoor gear, such as crampons or a camp stove, you'll find it, along with groceries, sundries, and souvenirs. You can also rent tents, packs, poles, sleeping bags, stoves, and other equipment here, a brilliant alternative to airline baggage restrictions and fees.

The smaller **Desert View general store** (928/638-2393, 8am-8pm daily summer, 8am-5pm daily winter) near the park's East Entrance has gear, groceries, souvenirs, and snacks.

Food

South Rim meal options range from hot dogs to fine dining. Leave your white tie at home, though—"canyon casual" is the style here. As long as you stow the backpack, a clean shirt and jeans will do fine, even in elegant El Tovar. All the lodges in the park except Thunderbird and Kachina have their own restaurants or cafeterias, and Tusayan boasts fast-food chains, steak houses, and several options in between. You won't need reservations for in-park restaurants, with the exception of the El Tovar dining room, but queues are likely during peak hours. It's also a good idea to make reservations for dining rooms in Tusayan hotels.

INSIDE THE PARK
Grand Canyon Visitor Center

Bright Angel Bicycles Café (6am-8pm daily Apr.-Nov., 7am-7pm daily Dec.-Mar., under $15) serves coffee from Flagstaff's popular Firecreek Coffee. Grab-and-go items include a selection of pastries, sandwiches, wraps, and energy drinks.

Grand Canyon Village
EL TOVAR

The warm and gracious ★ **El Tovar Dining Room** (dinner reservations 928/638-2631, ext. 6432, eltovar-dinner-res-gcsr@xanterra.com, breakfast 6:30am-10:30am, lunch 11am-2pm, dinner 5pm-10pm daily) offers the only white-tablecloth dining inside the park. Dinner reservations fill quickly and can be made up to six months in advance by guests who have a hotel reservation or 30 days in advance without room reservations.

Breakfast can be as simple as a pastry ($5) or as hearty as one of the chef's Southwestern egg specialties ($11-13). Lunch selections ($7-18) encompass soups, salads, sandwiches, and entrées like the popular Navajo Taco ($12) made with fry bread. Dinner entrées ($11-36) highlight organic and sustainable ingredients

and include steaks, pasta, and vegetarian selections. A perennial favorite is the Salmon Tostada ($26). Half-portions are offered for children at discounted prices. The impressive wine list includes many organic or sustainable options.

The adjoining **El Tovar Lounge** (11am-11pm daily, under $20) offers light fare indoors or on the veranda. No reservations are necessary, but you might have to wait for a table. It's one of the best spots in the village to sit back and people-watch with the canyon as backdrop.

BRIGHT ANGEL LODGE

The menu at the **Bright Angel Restaurant** (928/638-2631, breakfast 6am-11am, lunch 11:30am-4:30pm, dinner 5pm-10pm daily, $3-15) focuses on traditional American comfort food like pancakes, chili, stew, and burgers. For ambience, try to get a table in the mullion-windowed ell that overlooks the rim. Next door, but with its own outdoor entrance, **Bright Angel Fountain** (11am-5pm daily spring-fall, under $5) tempts people off the Rim Trail for ice cream cones, hot dogs, and other light fare.

The **Bright Angel Bar** (11am-11pm daily, hours vary seasonally, under $10) serves up refreshing beverages and light fare. Canyon murals cover the walls, and on summer evenings you might catch some live western or folk music. If you overindulge and fall asleep at your table, you're in luck: The bar transforms into the **Canyon Coffee House** (6am-10am daily, under $5) in the morning, serving coffee, pastries, and cereal.

The **Arizona Room** (928/638-2631, lunch 11:30am-3pm daily Mar.-Oct., dinner 4:30pm-10pm daily Mar.-Dec.) is a classic Western-style steak house. Lunch offerings ($6-20) range from soup and salad options to burgers and barbecue. Dinner highlights grilled meats ($18-33), but vegetarians can opt for the roasted vegetable-and-black-bean enchiladas ($14). Beer, wine, and cocktails are available; margaritas are a specialty. Reservations aren't accepted, and sometimes the wait list is lengthy, but you can spend the time browsing the lodge's history room or gift shop.

MASWIK LODGE

Maswik Cafeteria (928/638-2631, 6am-10pm daily, under $10) has five food stations to help lines move quickly, and a good selection of grab-and-go items for hikers anxious to hit the trail. Choices include hot and cold breakfasts, burgers and sandwiches, pasta, and Mexican cuisine.

The adjoining **pizzeria** (11am-11pm daily) sells pies ($15-20) and slices ($3) to eat in or take out. A pub atmosphere takes over in the evening, with beer, wine, and TVs tuned to sports events.

Market Plaza

The **Yavapai Lodge Restaurant** (928/638-2631, 6am-10pm daily late May-Sept., hours vary seasonally, $5-20) serves up family favorites like pizza, chili, burgers, rotisserie chicken, and steak. Beer and wine are available. Diners can customize their selections with an assortment of toppings. Food is semi-cafeteria style, using interactive kiosks for ordering. Skip the lines and grab a beverage, pastry, fruit, or trail-ready sandwich at the **Coffee shop** (5am-5pm daily late May-Sept., hours vary seasonally, under $10), adjacent to the Yavapai Lodge Restaurant.

Unwind later at the ★ **Yavapai Tavern** (11am-11pm daily late May-Sept., hours vary seasonally, under $10), also inside the lodge. The full bar includes some local brews, along with light fare like sliders, flatbread, or guacamole and chips. The tavern's modern lodge atmosphere is pleasant, with plenty of forested views through the big windows for those not tuned in to the big game on TV.

In Market Plaza at Grand Canyon Village, the General Store's **Canyon Village Deli** (928/638-2262, 7am-8pm daily summer, shorter hours Sept.-Apr., under $15) serves up

salads, sandwiches, fried chicken, and more from a counter at the front of the store. You'll note a lot of locals eating here, including park rangers. There's plenty of bright and pleasant seating inside and out. The deli is located at the front of the **General Store** (928/638-2262, 7am-9pm daily summer, shorter hours Sept.-Apr.); check the store aisles for grab-and-go fare and smoothies. Here you'll also find groceries (including plenty of fresh produce), picnic supplies, and everything you need to cook at your campsite, from stoves and firewood to fully loaded s'mores kits.

West Rim

The **Hermits Rest Snack Bar** (West Rim Dr., 8am-6pm daily summer, 9am-5pm daily fall-spring), located at the end of Hermit Road, is convenient when the overlooks and Rim Trail have tempted you into lingering longer than you planned. For a couple of bucks, you can get a cold or hot drink and a snack to sustain you until you get back to the village.

East Rim

Inside the trading post near the Watchtower, the **Desert View Deli** (928/638-2360, 8am-7pm daily late May-Sept., shorter hours Oct.-Apr.) has sandwiches, chili, and hot breakfasts for a few dollars—a welcome convenience for nearby campers. **Desert View Market** (928/638-2393, 8am-8pm daily Apr.-Sept., shorter hours Oct.-Mar.) may be on the small side, but if you've forgotten something for your cooler or campsite, you'll probably find it here.

OUTSIDE THE PARK
Tusayan

Tusayan caters to Grand Canyon travelers, and you'll find lots of middle-of-the-road dining here, including a few fast-food chains. Among the local options are **We Cook Pizza and Pasta** (605 Hwy. 64, 928/638-2278, 11am-9pm daily, $10-30); the name says it all. **RP's Stage Stop** (Red Feather Lodge, 114A Hwy. 64, 928/638-3115, www.rpsstagestop. com, 7am-5pm daily, under $10) has all-day breakfasts, fresh sandwiches, and free Wi-Fi. Colorful **Sophie's Mexican Kitchen** (Hwy. 64, across from IMAX Theatre, 928/638-4679, 11am-9pm daily, $10-17) serves tacos, burritos, quesadillas, and the like, with vegetarian and gluten-free versions.

Three local hotels have seasonal buffets and off-the-menu meals, including **JJK's** (406 Canyon Plaza Lane, 928/638-2673, 7am-9pm daily, $10-30) inside the Canyon Plaza, and the Western-themed **Canyon Star** (149 Hwy. 64, 928/638-3333, dinner daily 4:30pm-10pm summer, 5pm-9pm winter, $10-30) at the Grand Hotel, where you're likely to catch some live country music or perhaps a Navajo singer or storyteller. The Best Western Squire Inn's ★ **Coronado Room** (100 Hwy. 64, 928/638-2681, dinner daily 5pm-10pm spring-fall, 4pm-9pm winter, $20-35) is a frequent choice for locals marking a special occasion. Make dinner reservations for hotel restaurants, especially during peak season.

You'll find a few Tusayan destinations with Old West ambience, including **Big E Steakhouse and Saloon** (395 Hwy. 64, 928/638-0333, http://bigesteakhouse.com, 2pm-9pm daily, $15-40, reservations recommended). The menu includes rib eye, strip, filet, and T-bone, as well as some fish, chicken, and pasta selections.

Tusayan's midsize grocery, the **General Store** (928/638-2854), also sells souvenirs, RV supplies, camping gear, and firewood. Look for it on the east side of Highway 64.

Valle

Valle lies 20 miles south of the South Rim, at the junction of U.S. 180 and Highway 64. Here, the **Grand Canyon Inn** (928/635-9203, www.grand-canyon-inn.com, 7:30am-1:30pm and 6pm-9pm daily summer, 6pm-8pm winter, $7-23) has a reasonably priced full-service restaurant serving American-style food, and a lounge that stays open late. The adjacent gas station and convenience store has snacks and sandwiches to go.

It's a café, it's a campground, it's a roadside curiosity: Enter Bedrock City, a *Flintstones*-themed camper village (a bit time-worn but fondly remembered by many boomers) for a bronto burger at **Fred's Diner** (928/635-2600, 6am-8:30pm daily summer, shorter hours fall-spring, $5-15).

Accommodations

INSIDE THE PARK

Staying inside the park might mean sacrificing amenities like swimming pools and free breakfasts, but you can roll out of bed for a sunrise, stay up late to stargaze, and never have to squander precious minutes queuing up at the entrance station or looking for parking. Lodges are all within walking distance of the canyon's edge and linked by the free shuttle system. Most have basic amenities, including TVs, in-room coffeemakers, and mini-refrigerators.

Make reservations early; lodges are often completely booked from late spring to early autumn. In winter, some lodges may close for a few weeks—even though visitors number fewer, so do available rooms. Plan to spend $100-250 per night for a room. Winter rates and promotions are often available November-February, the canyon's off-season. Most lodges have some accessible guest rooms. Note that all lodges are nonsmoking, and pets aren't allowed, with the exception of Yavapai Lodge.

Grand Canyon Historic Village

Xanterra Parks & Resorts (928/638-2631 for same-day reservations, 888/297-2757, www.grandcanyonlodges.com), operates five hotels in the South Rim's Grand Canyon Village, including historic **El Tovar Hotel** and **Bright Angel Lodge.**

EL TOVAR

★ **El Tovar** (from $217) was built in 1905 by the Santa Fe Railway to lure well-heeled tourists to Grand Canyon. ET is still the most elegantly appointed lodging at Grand Canyon and further refurbishment is scheduled for early 2018. With room service, a concierge desk, a stately dining room, and morning coffee on the mezzanine, guests here might feel like they're in a major city . . . until they look out the windows to see mule deer or bighorn sheep wandering along the rim. Standard guest rooms have one double or queen ($217-263), and deluxe rooms have two queens or a king ($354). Twelve of the hotel's 78 rooms are uniquely decorated suites ($442-538), some with a porch or balcony.

BRIGHT ANGEL LODGE

Mary Colter designed **Bright Angel Lodge** (from $97) in 1935 to look like a pioneer settlement of log, clapboard, and pueblo-style cabins. The lodge is central to rim activities, and the Bright Angel Trail begins nearby. The lodge has a family restaurant, a steak house, a coffeehouse and bar, and a soda fountain. Accommodations range from simple "hiker rooms" (no TV, shared bath, $97) to private cabins ($140-217) or suites ($213-469). The cabins perched along the rim—some with their own fireplaces—book quickly.

KACHINA AND THUNDERBIRD LODGES

The midcentury **Kachina** and **Thunderbird Lodges** ($225-243) are steps away from the Rim Trail in the center of Grand Canyon Village. Guest rooms have two queens or one king, with the higher price for canyon-view rooms. If you're staying at the Kachina, you'll check in at El Tovar. Thunderbird guests check in at Bright Angel Lodge.

MASWIK LODGE

Maswik Lodge (from $112) has 250 guest rooms tucked into the ponderosa pine forest about 0.25 miles from the canyon's edge. The lodge's north section is a few years newer than the south section, and Maswik North guest rooms ($215) are a little larger, with air-conditioning and a choice of two queens or one king. Maswik South rooms ($112) have two queens. The main lodge building includes a food court, pizza pub, and gift shop.

a cabin at Bright Angel Lodge

Market Plaza

YAVAPAI LODGE

With 358 guest rooms in its two wings, Delaware North's **Yavapai Lodge** (928/638-4001 or 877/404-4611, www.visitgrandcanyon.com) is the South Rim's largest in-park motel. It's also the farthest from the rim and the historic village (about a mile), although it is conveniently close to Market Plaza, the general store, and the campgrounds. Most guest rooms (from $150) have two queens. Family rooms with bunk beds, accessible rooms, and pet-friendly rooms are also available. Note that Yavapai West doesn't have air-conditioning, although ceiling fans are usually adequate for South Rim summers. The main lodge building has a casual restaurant, a coffee shop, a tavern, and a gift shop.

Campgrounds

Three South Rim campgrounds are located inside the park: two near the South Entrance Station and Market Plaza, and the other at Desert View, near the park's East Entrance. **Backcountry permits** ($10 per permit, plus $8 pp per night) are required for overnight hiking and backpacking, river camping, or any camping outside developed campgrounds.

MARKET PLAZA

Mather Campground (877/444-6777, www.recreation.gov, year-round, $18) has more than 300 sites. Shaded by ponderosa pines, the campground is located a mile from the rim on the east side of Grand Canyon Village, a short walk from Market Plaza and the general store. Sites can be reserved up to six months in advance. Campers sometimes depart ahead of schedule, making spaces available—check early and in person for last-minute spots. During high season, the campground is usually full by noon. December-February, reservations aren't accepted and availability is first-come, first-served. Fees are discounted for Golden Age and Golden Access pass holders.

Tent sites can accommodate up to two vehicles, three tents, and six people, with grills, picnic tables, and paved parking. There's enough room for RVs up to 30 feet but no hookups. Group sites ($50) are available for groups of up to 50 people with a maximum of three vehicles.

The adjacent **Trailer Village** (928/638-1006, 877/404-4611, www.visitgrandcanyon.com, year-round, $44 for 2 people) has 84 paved pull-through RV sites with full hookups for vehicles up to 50 feet long. Sites can be reserved up to 13 months in advance, and high season books quickly. Sites have picnic tables, grills, and cable TV hookup. A dump station (closed in winter) is located next to Mather Campground.

Serving both campgrounds, the **Camper Services** building has coin-operated showers ($2 for eight minutes) and laundry. It's located at the entrance to Mather Campground, about 0.5 miles from Trailer Village. Internet access is available here and at Yavapai Lodge or the general store.

DESERT VIEW

★ **Desert View Campground** (May-mid-Oct., $12), 26 miles east of Grand Canyon Village near the park's East Entrance Station, has 50 first-come, first-served campsites tucked into a juniper woodland along the East Rim. This seasonal campground usually fills by early afternoon. Sites can accommodate two tents, six people, and two vehicles or one small RV (up to 30 feet). Each site has a grill and picnic table but no water. Two faucets are available in the campground, and there are restroom buildings nearby with cold-water sinks and flush toilets but no showers. The Desert View general store and trading post-deli are nearby.

OUTSIDE THE PARK

For those who prefer resort-style accommodations, the town of Tusayan (two miles south of the Main Entrance Station) offers several options, along with a handful of moderately priced motels and two campgrounds. For additional campgrounds and motels, travel south on Highway 64 toward Williams.

Tusayan

Tusayan owes its existence entirely to the park, so the town is heavy on motels and restaurants but not on charm. Tourism businesses line both sides of Highway 64 just 1-2 miles south of the South Entrance Station. Several Tusayan hotels offer the amenities of resort or business travel, and many are pet friendly. During summer months the park's free shuttle route extends here. Although the town was recently incorporated, addresses continue to read "Grand Canyon, Arizona." But don't let the address confuse you: There are no canyon views here, even though you're only a few miles away from the Rim. Expect deep discounts—up to half-off—on winter rates.

The expansive **Best Western Grand Canyon Squire Inn** (100 Hwy. 64, 928/638-2681 or 800/622-6966, www.grandcanyonsquire.com, $205-270) has an outdoor swimming pool, fitness room, spa, beauty salon, and a family activity room featuring everything from billiards to video games. The Squire Inn has two full-service restaurants, and the downstairs lounge serves drinks and snacks. Standard guest rooms, deluxe rooms, and suites are available. The 318-room hotel offers vacation packages with plane, helicopter, or raft tours. Meetings and banquets can be accommodated.

The 121-room **Grand Hotel** (149 Hwy. 64, 928/638-3333 or 888/634-7263, www.grandcanyongrandhotel.com, $300-330) was built in 1998 in a nostalgic mountain-lodge style, with a piano lobby, a fireplace, exposed timbers, and modern amenities that include an indoor pool and a hot tub, a fitness center, a lounge, a sports bar, meeting rooms, and event-planning services. Some guest rooms and suites have patios or balconies, and pets are allowed in some guest rooms. Lodging packages can be customized to include tours.

Canyon Plaza Resort (406 Canyon Plaza Lane, 928/638-2673 or 800/995-2521, www.grandcanyonplaza.com, $260-280) has standard or deluxe rooms and suites. Amenities include a dining room, a lounge, a spa, an outdoor swimming pool, and a hot tub. Meeting and banquet facilities are available, and pets can be accommodated. Packages can include air, horse, and raft tours. The hotel shares a driveway with the IMAX Theatre on Highway 64.

Grand Canyon Holiday Inn Express (226 Hwy. 64, 928/638-3000 or 888/465-4329, www.hiexpress.com, $270-280) has standard guest rooms and suites. Special kids' suites have bunk beds, TVs, stereos, and video games. Rates include breakfast. To make the kiddos even happier, there's an indoor pool and a spa.

The **Red Feather Lodge** (106 Hwy. 64, 928/638-2414 or 866/561-2425, www.redfeatherlodge.com, $150-200) still welcomes guests with a neon sign that dates back to the 1960s. Guest rooms in the original motor lodge can accommodate pets and smokers. The adjacent hotel, built in 1995, has larger guest rooms and interior hallways. Together, the buildings house a total of 231 rooms. The lodge has an outdoor pool and spa.

Seven Mile Lodge (56 Powell Ave., 928/638-2291, $110-150) is seven miles from Mather Point, the first canyon overlook past the park's entrance. The unpretentious motel's 20 guest rooms each have two queens, a TV, and air-conditioning, but no phones. The motel doesn't take advance reservations, and it fills up early during high season. Savvy budget travelers stop and reserve a room on the way to the park. It's located on the west side of Highway 64.

CAMPGROUNDS AND CABIN

Grand Canyon Camper Village (milepost 236, Hwy. 64, 928/638-2887, www.grandcanyoncampervillage.com), one mile south of the park's South Entrance, has 50 tent sites ($30) and 250 RV sites with electric ($35), water and electric ($46), or full hookups ($50-56). Off-season and group rates are available. Campground amenities include coin-operated showers and laundry, free Wi-Fi, a camp store, a playground, restrooms, and a dump site. Tusayan's grocery store, shops, and restaurants are within walking distance.

★ **Ten X Campground** (Hwy. 64, 877/444-6777, www.recreation.gov, May-Sept., $10), four miles south of the park's South Entrance, is operated by the U.S. Forest Service. Some of the campground's 70 sites can be reserved, but most are first-come, first-served, and the campground often fills in summer months. Each site accommodates up to eight people, with a picnic table and a fire pit or grill. Most sites are pull-through, and RVs up to 30 feet long can be accommodated, although there are no hookups. The campground has vault toilets but no showers. There's a nearby nature trail and an amphitheater with occasional evening ranger programs during the summer. Two group sites ($75-125) accommodating up to 50 and 75 people can be combined. The group sites have covered picnic areas and tent pads.

Kaibab National Forest (928/638-2443, www.fs.usda.gov/kaibab) rents historic **Hull Cabin** (877/444-6777, www.recreation.gov, Apr.-Sept. $140), built by sheepherders who hosted the canyon's very first tourists in 1884. Amenities are limited: There's a vault toilet in the bathhouse, where guests can attach their own solar shower bladders. The one-bedroom cabin accommodates groups up to six, with twin beds and a queen-size futon. Guests need to bring bedding and other supplies, but those willing to handle their own housekeeping and forgo cell phone service will be rewarded with wildlife-viewing opportunities and great access to forest roads and trails, which are open to mountain bikers and equestrians as well as to hikers. The cabin is located 16 miles east of the town of Tusayan and about five miles southeast of Grandview Point.

DISPERSED CAMPING

Primitive-style camping is available in the Tusayan Ranger District of the **Kaibab National Forest** (928/638-2443, www.fs.usda.gov/kaibab), which borders the national park. Stays are limited to 14 days, and no camping is allowed within 0.25 miles of water, on open meadows, within one mile of a developed campground, within 200 feet of main roadways, or within 20 feet of forest roads. Bury human and pet waste at least six inches deep and pack out all trash. Many forest roads are rugged, and depending on rainfall and winter snow cover, they can be quite muddy as well. During the summer, fire restrictions may be active. Check with the forest service for current conditions and maps.

Valle

If guest rooms and campgrounds near the park's South Entrance are full, you can travel 20 miles south to Valle, a small community with an airport and a few businesses at the junction of U.S. 180 and Highway 64. For a budget-friendly campground and hostel, drive 43 miles south on Highway 64 to Red Lake.

On the northeast corner of the U.S. 180-Highway 64 junction, the **Grand Canyon Inn and Motel** (928/635-9203, 800/635-9203, www.grand-canyon-inn.com, $110-170, rates vary by season) offers a range of guest rooms in two buildings. The inn has simple double queen rooms and an outdoor swimming pool, a restaurant-lounge, a gift shop, and a gas station. Guests at the motel across the highway can use the inn's facilities. Pets are not allowed. Advance reservations are recommended. The adjacent convenience store has a park pay station: You can purchase a park pass here and use the express lane when you get to the South Entrance Station.

CAMPGROUNDS AND HOSTEL

Bedrock City (U.S. 180 at Hwy. 64, 928/635-2600, www.bedrockaz.com, year-round), 20 miles south of the park, has tent ($12) and RV ($16) sites and a *Flintstones*-themed camper village with a grocery store, a diner, a gift shop, a game room, laundry, and showers. This campground has amenities you won't find anywhere else near the canyon: a theater showing *Flintstones* cartoons, plus tram rides in the Fredmobile. Community grills are available if you're too late for a bronto burger at the diner.

Red Lake Campground and Hostel (928/635-4753 or 800/581-4753, year-round) is located 43 miles south of the park between Williams and Valle. Some campsites ($25) have full hookups. Rooms in the hostel ($20 pp) are dorm style, although private rooms are often available. Baths and coin-operated showers are down the hall, and there's a common area with satellite TV, free Wi-Fi, and a refrigerator and microwave. You'll find snacks and souvenirs in the adjacent gas station and market.

Transportation and Services

The **South Entrance** lies 60 miles north of Williams (via Hwy. 64) and 78 miles north of Flagstaff (via U.S. 180). The park has made a number of infrastructure changes, so don't rely on your GPS to navigate. The park's pocket map (available at the entrance station and other locations) is up to date and accurate.

Road closures due to construction are possible any time of year, and winter storms occasionally result in the closure of **Highway 64** between the South Rim's main entrance and Desert View. The windswept section of Highway 64 around Valle, 20 miles south of the park entrance, can also be troublesome after a winter snow. The National Park Service website (www.nps.gov/grca) provides construction updates and current weather reports.

Traffic on the South Rim can be beastly during **peak season,** with street-parked cars hiding driveways, "deer jams" bringing vehicles to a standstill, pedestrians wandering everywhere, and tempers growing as heated as an Arizona summer afternoon. The best solution is to liberate yourself from your car as quickly as possible and use the free shuttle to get around.

Parking

During crowded summer months, village-area parking is at a premium. You'll find it a relief to park your car and rely on the **shuttle,** which stops near all major parking areas. The largest parking area is one mile past the entrance station at **Grand Canyon Visitor Center.** Day-trippers can leave their vehicles here to avoid entering the traffic swarming around Grand Canyon Village lodges. There are hundreds of spaces; Lot 1 is closest to canyon overlooks and has spaces large enough for RVs and trailers. Lots 2 and 4 are closest to the Visitor Center.

If you continue to the village in your vehicle, you'll find several smaller parking lots—though you may not find a parking space. **Lot A** is near Shrine of the Ages and Park Headquarters; this lot often has open spots. **Lot B** is in Market Plaza, where the bank and general store are located. **Lot C** is a small lot near the intersection of Center and Village Loop Roads. **Lot D,** a large paved lot near the **Backcountry Information Center,** has spaces large enough to park a trailer or RV (though you can't camp here). Lots A-D have nearby shuttle stops.

Village Loop Road is mostly one-way and runs counterclockwise, which means staying right is the correct choice when you reach the stop sign at the start of the loop. For El Tovar guests, there's a small lot east of the hotel, but even if you circle like one of the canyon's turkey vultures, you may not find a parking place here. If you're driving an RV or pulling a trailer, don't even try. Thankfully, El Tovar has a baggage-handling service. The other lodges have larger guest parking areas, short-term loading zones, and bell services.

Gas and Garage Services

Your last chance to fill up is in Tusayan, seven miles south of Grand Canyon Village, or at Desert View, just inside the park's East Entrance, about 30 miles from the village. The pumps at the park's **Desert View Gas Station** (9am-5pm daily) have 24-7 credit-card service, though the cashier and convenience store closes from late October to early April.

Garage services (926/638-2631, 8am-noon and 1pm-5pm daily, emergency service after hours) are available in Grand Canyon Village east of the train depot. The garage can provide basic repairs, including tires, belts, batteries, and hoses. If more serious repairs are needed, tow service is available to Williams or Flagstaff.

Park Shuttle Buses

The South Rim's **free shuttle system** offers three main routes, encompassing Hermit Road (the West Rim), Grand Canyon Village, and the Kaibab Trailhead (Yaki Point). Buses arrive at each shuttle stop every 10-30 minutes. Have faith—the wait is shorter than the time it would take to drive around in search of a parking place. During peak months (June-Aug.), shuttle buses operate from an hour before sunrise until an hour after sunset.

Pets are not allowed on shuttle buses, with the exception of trained service animals. All park shuttle buses are equipped with bicycle racks and are wheelchair accessible. (Most motorized scooters are too large to fit on buses.)

Route maps are available online and are included on the park's pocket map. Routes are color coded and buses display the route name on front and indicate if the bus is westbound or eastbound. Transfer locations (for changing from one route to another) are near the Bright Angel Trailhead and at Grand Canyon Visitor Center.

- The Village Route (Blue) stops at lodges, campgrounds, Market Plaza, Shrine of the Ages, the train depot, and also travels to Grand Canyon Visitor Center. The round-trip takes about 50 minutes, and riders can get on or off at any stop to dine, shop, or stroll in the historic district. The Backcountry Information Center is on the Village Route.

- The Hermits Rest Route (Red) travels back and forth between the village and Hermits Rest, eight miles away. You can ride the loop, which takes 80 minutes and stops at a dozen overlooks, or leave the shuttle to spend some time photographing or hiking the Rim Trail, and then board another bus. After leaving Hermits Rest, the return (eastbound) route stops only at Pima, Mohave, and Powell Points. The Hermits Rest route is not in service December-February. During these three months only, passenger cars can travel Hermit Road, weather permitting.

- The Kaibab-Rim Route (Orange) travels between the Grand Canyon Visitor Center, Mather Point, Yavapai Geology Museum, and Yaki Point. The bus stops en route at the South Kaibab Trailhead and Pipe Creek Vista. This scenic round-trip takes 50 minutes.

- The Hikers' Express is an early-morning shuttle that stops at Bright Angel Lodge, the Backcountry Information Center, and Grand Canyon Visitor Center before traveling directly to the South Kaibab Trailhead. In May and September, the Hikers' Express stops at Bright Angel Lodge at 5am, 6am, and 7am daily. June-August it stops at 4am, 5am, and 6am. In April and October, express shuttles stop at the lodge at 6am, 7am, and 8am, and in November at 7am, 8am, and 9am. December-February, the Hikers' Express stops at Bright Angel Lodge at 8am and 9am.

- Tusayan (Purple): Early May-early October, free shuttle buses travel from the town of Tusayan to Grand Canyon Visitor Center, a trip of about 20 minutes (one-way). The shuttles make four stops in Tusayan, including the IMAX Theatre and the Grand Canyon Airport. Passengers must present valid park passes to enter the park. This park-and-ride shuttle operates at 20-minute intervals 8am-9:45pm daily.

Taxis and Bike Rentals

Taxi services (928/638-2631) are available 24 hours daily year-round. Destinations include

Where Can I Find...?

- **Banks and ATMs:** Chase Bank (928/638-2437, 9am-5pm Mon.-Thurs., 9am-6pm Fri.) has an office near Market Plaza and an ATM outside. ATMs are also located in the Maswik Lodge lobby and at the IMAX Theatre in Tusayan.

- **Day Care:** The Kaibab Learning Center (928/638-6333, grandcanyonchildcare.org) offers day care services for infants and children up to 12 years old, when space is available. Immunization records must be provided.

- **Laundry:** The Camper Services building near the entrance of Mather Campground offers laundry services (hours vary by season).

- **Lost and Found:** If you left something in a guest room or lodge, contact Xanterra (928/638-2631) or Delaware North (928/638-4001). For all other lost items, call park administration (928/638-7798). Take found items to the Grand Canyon Visitor Center.

- **Newspapers:** El Tovar and the general store sell national newspapers. The weekly *Grand Canyon News* covers Grand Canyon Village and the towns of Williams and Valle.

- **Post Office:** At Market Plaza (928/638-2512, 9am-3:30pm Mon.-Fri.). Stamps are available in the lobby (5am-10pm daily).

- **Public Restrooms:** Grand Canyon Visitor Center, Market Plaza, Bright Angel Trailhead, Hermits Rest, Desert View

- **Religious Services:** Schedules of services are posted at Grand Canyon Visitor Center, Mather Campground, Park Headquarters, Shrine of the Ages, and at the information kiosk near the post office.

- **Showers:** Coin-operated showers are in the Camper Services building (hours vary seasonally) near the entrance of Mather Campground.

- **Water:** Water is no longer sold in individual bottles inside the park. Bring (or buy) reusable containers and fill them up for free at one the South Rim's "filling stations" at Grand Canyon Visitor Center, Market Plaza, Hermits Rest, Desert View, Bright Angel and South Kaibab trailheads, and other locations.

Grand Canyon Airport. Taxis will even deliver hikers and backpackers to South Rim trailheads.

Bright Angel Bicycles (928/814-8704, www.bikegrandcanyon.com) rents bicycles and operates a shuttle from the visitor center to Hopi Point, giving customers an option for avoiding the congestion around Grand Canyon Village and the first few miles of Hermit Road.

TO THE NORTH RIM

From the South Rim, it's 215 miles (4.5 hours) by car to the North Rim. From Grand Canyon Village, take Highway 64 east to Cameron.

Turn north (left) on U.S. 89 and continue to Bitter Springs. Turn west (left) on U.S. 89A and continue to Jacob Lake. Turn south (left) on Highway 67 and proceed to the park entrance.

Two companies offer daily shuttle service between the North and South Rims. Reservations are required.

The **Trans Canyon Shuttle** (928/638-2820 or 877/638-2820, www.trans-canyon-shuttle.com, May 15-Oct. 31, $90 one-way) leaves the South Rim twice daily at 8am and 1:30pm, arriving at the North Rim at 12:30pm and 6pm. Charter shuttles can be arranged, and bag-only deliveries ($25) are available for weary cross-canyon hikers who want clean clothes waiting on the other rim. **Grand Canyon Shuttle Service** (888/215-3105, www. grandcanyonshuttles. com) has 24-7 customizable on-demand service between the rims, a good option for groups. Call or email (admin@flagshuttle. com) for more information.

TO GRAND CANYON SKYWALK

From the South Rim, it's 250 miles (5.5 hours) to the Hualapai Reservation's Grand Canyon West, home of the Grand Canyon Skywalk. From Grand Canyon Village, take Highway 64 south toward Williams, then take I-40 west to Kingman. In Kingman, turn north on U.S. 93 and continue for about 30 miles to Pearce Ferry Road. At the junction with Pearce Ferry Road, turn right and continue for 28 miles, making a right onto the Diamond Bar Road. It's another 21 miles to Grand Canyon West, all paved.

SERVICES
Groceries and Supplies

Market Plaza is like a village within a village, hosting a general store, post office, bank, and public restrooms. The **General Store** (928/638-2262, 7am-9pm daily summer, shorter hours Sept.-Apr.) sells everything from souvenirs to groceries to fishing licenses. You can buy or rent camping and hiking equipment, including some pretty serious gear like water-filter systems, sleeping bags, and camp stoves. And if camp cooking isn't your idea of a vacation, the store's deli has sandwiches, pizza, fried chicken, and other takeaway items.

Internet Access

Free Wi-Fi is available at Camper Services, **Park Headquarters** (8am-5pm daily), the lobby of Yavapai Lodge, and the General Store. Computers with Internet access are available for public use at the village's community **library** (928/638-2718, 10:30am-5pm Mon.-Sat.) and in the research library at Park Headquarters (8am-4:30pm Mon.-Fri.). Internet service in Tusayan has been notoriously slow, and the town is negotiating with new service providers.

Emergencies

Hikers can find emergency phones at ranger stations and along corridor trails: on Bright Angel Trail at Mile-and-a-Half Resthouse, Three-Mile Resthouse, and River Resthouse, and on the South Kaibab Trail at its junction with the Tonto Trail. Inner canyon ranger stations are located at Cottonwood Campground (summer only), Indian Garden, and Phantom Ranch. Emergency phones are connected to a 24-hour dispatch center and do not require coins. If your situation requires search-and-rescue services, you will be charged expenses.

For urgent medical care or pharmaceutical needs, contact **North Country HealthCare** (928/638-2551, 9am-6pm daily Memorial Day-Labor Day, 8am-5pm daily Labor Day-Memorial Day). The Grand Canyon clinic (1 Clinic Rd.) is located south of the village and can be reached from Center Road or from Highway 64.

The North Rim

Discover the quieter side of Grand Canyon on the North Rim, where shady forests of spruce, fir, and aspen yield to grassy meadows and wildflowers. Though it's only 10 miles from Grand Canyon Village as the raven flies, getting here

from the South Rim takes five hours by car or two to three days on foot. The payoff for making the journey: miles of unpopulated trails, natural quiet, and crisp, pine-fresh air that makes views seem infinite.

Open only from mid-May to mid-October, the North Rim hosts far fewer visitors than the South Rim, about 500,000 annually. The pace is slower, and activities are refreshingly low-tech, from ranger hikes and campfire talks to mule rides and scenic drives. Take advantage of the opportunity to unplug and recharge by connecting with nature.

Park activities center on Bright Angel Point, home to gracious Grand Canyon Lodge and the North Rim Campground. Trails that start near the lodge include the shady rim-side Transept Trail and the 14-mile North Kaibab Trail, which leads to the river. From the North Rim's lofty heights, river views are rare, but strolling to the tip of Bright Angel Point will

take you within earshot of Roaring Springs, the source of the park's fresh water.

Other activities include traveling scenic Cape Royal Drive, which leads across the Walhalla Plateau, connecting overlooks, picnic areas, and trailheads. Mountain bikers can try their legs on the 17-mile route to the aptly named Point Sublime. And for the truly adventurous, there's Toroweap, a primitive campground nearly six hours from Bright Angel Point with jaw-dropping views of Lava Falls.

Most visitors arrive during Arizona's blazing summers, when the North Rim's high elevations offer sweet relief, or in autumn, when aspens shimmer gold among evergreens. Visitor services close for the season on October 15, but hardy travelers can ski or snowshoe into the park during winter months to camp in the park's yurt and enjoy the snowy solitude.

Previous: veranda of Grand Canyon Lodge; view from Transept Trail. **Above:** a Kaibab squirrel.

Highlights

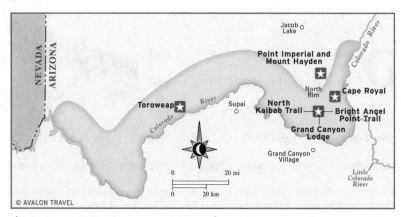

© AVALON TRAVEL

★ **Grand Canyon Lodge:** From the lodge's inviting limestone terrace, you can gaze all the way across the canyon to the South Rim (page 99).

★ **Point Imperial and Mount Hayden:** See Mount Hayden, Saddle Mountain, the Painted Desert, and the eastern end of Grand Canyon from this overlook, the highest point on either rim at 8,800 feet (page 101).

★ **Cape Royal:** Cape Royal, located at the end of a winding 23-mile drive, curves into canyon like a rocky fin (page 103).

★ **Toroweap:** If you have a high-clearance vehicle and a taste for adventure, drive to this lonely spot along the western canyon (page 103).

★ **Bright Angel Point Trail:** This paved 0.5-mile trail leads to the very tip of Bright Angel Point, where the views will take your breath away (page 106).

★ **North Kaibab Trail:** Hike or ride a mule into the canyon's depths to see how the canyon's vegetation and rock layers change with elevation (page 107).

PLANNING YOUR TIME

North Rim lodges and park services are open May 15-October 15, but it's Mother Nature who really calls the shots. You can drive to the North Rim until the first snowfall closes Highway 67 (usually late November), and winter sports enthusiasts can ski or snowshoe into the park even when it's blanketed by snow. Most of us, however, will visit in summer or fall. Lodging on the North Rim is limited, so plan early and make reservations several months in advance.

Even in **summer,** nights are cool—bring some warmer clothes as well as a jacket in case of afternoon showers. The Arizona monsoon rolls north in early July and lingers until mid-September, bringing brief, localized thunderstorms with possible lightning and heavy rain.

In **fall,** aspens and maples put on a colorful show, with bursts of gold and red among the North Rim's mixed boreal forests. From October 15 until December 1, or until snow closes Highway 67, visitors can drive into the park and spend the day—no overnight parking is allowed. The park's administrative services, including the Backcountry Office, continue to operate until October 31. Backcountry hikers with a permit can spend the night in the campground (walk-ins only; no car camping) until December 1.

Once you've found your way to the North Rim—the more remote, less visited side of Grand Canyon—you'll want to spend at least three days exploring its trails, forests, and overlooks.

Day 1

Plan on several hours at **Bright Angel Point** for touring the historic lodge, hiking the **Transept Trail,** and taking in a ranger program or two. Drink plenty of water and get used to the high elevation and low humidity. Set aside at least half a day during your visit to drive the **Cape Royal Road,** with a side excursion to **Point Imperial,** the highest point on both rims. Along this paved, winding road, signs direct hikers to several trails, from the short, easy **Roosevelt Point Trail** to the more ambitious **Ken Patrick Trail.**

Day 2

Descending even a short way into the canyon will reward you with an intimate perspective on the canyon's geological layers and life zones. The **North Kaibab Trail,** the only maintained North Rim trail that leads into the canyon, can be explored either on foot or by mule. Shadier rim hikes, such as the **Widforss Trail,** make better options for summer afternoons.

Day 3

Spend a day exploring beyond Bright Angel Point, traveling to **Toroweap** or **Point Sublime,** or into neighboring **Kaibab National Forest.** Many dirt forest roads are suitable for passenger cars, while some are best explored in a high-clearance 4WD vehicle. Before venturing off main thoroughfares, stop at a visitor center for maps and information about road conditions and backcountry permits.

on the Widforss Trail

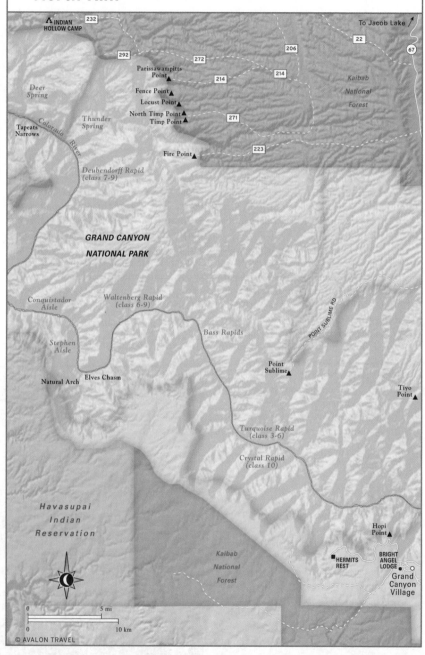

North Rim

INDIAN HOLLOW CAMP

232

292

272

206

22

67

To Jacob Lake

Parissawampitts Point

214

214

Fence Point

Locust Point

North Timp Point

Timp Point

271

Kaibab National Forest

Deer Spring

Thunder Spring

Tapeats Narrows

Colorado River

Fire Point

223

Deubendorff Rapid (class 7-9)

GRAND CANYON NATIONAL PARK

Conquistador Aisle

Waltenberg Rapid (class 6-9)

Bass Rapids

POINT SUBLIME RD

Stephen Aisle

Natural Arch

Elves Chasm

Point Sublime

Tiyo Point

Turquoise Rapid (class 3-6)

Crystal Rapid (class 10)

Havasupai Indian Reservation

Kaibab National Forest

Hopi Point

HERMITS REST

BRIGHT ANGEL LODGE

Grand Canyon Village

0   5 mi
0   10 km

© AVALON TRAVEL

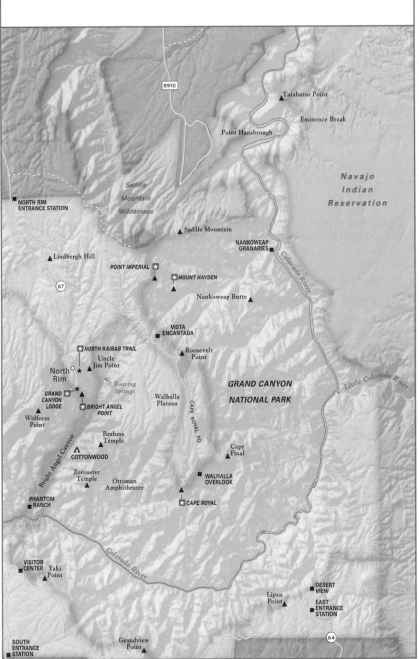

Exploring the North Rim

At the canyon's North Rim, you'll find fewer tour options and no shuttle buses to whisk you between overlooks and sites. Shopping, dining, and entertainment choices are more limited here too, allowing Mother Nature to take center stage. This side of Grand Canyon is most easily explored by car, and the focus of your explorations will be the exquisite natural setting. Many North Rim sights lie along the Cape Royal Road, which travels more than 20 miles across the Walhalla Plateau. Hiking, trail riding, and scenic drives take you through lush forests and meadows sprinkled with wildflowers to overlooks with sweeping canyon vistas. Pack a picnic, wear comfortable shoes, and plan to enjoy the fresh, pine-scented air and natural quiet.

VISITOR CENTERS
North Rim Visitor Center

The **North Rim Visitor Center** (928/638-2481, 8am-6pm daily) is at the end of Highway 67 at Bright Angel Point, just south of the main parking area. Get your bearings by looking at the visitor center's large, three-dimensional

map of the canyon. It shows major viewpoints, landforms, and trailheads as well as park, forest, and reservation boundaries. Weather forecasts for the North Rim, South Rim, and Phantom Ranch are posted daily.

The visitor center hosts a Grand Canyon Association (www.grandcanyon.org) **bookstore,** with an excellent selection of books, maps, videos, and other items. Proceeds benefit the GCA, which partners with the park to create interpretive materials. Restrooms are located around the back of the building, where there's also a shady ramada with vending machines, a water refill station, and public phones. (Cell phone reception can be spotty on the North Rim, so pay phones aren't merely quaint artifacts here.)

Kaibab Plateau Visitor Center

You can preview your visit to the rim with a stop at the **Kaibab Plateau Visitor Center** (928/643-7298, 8am-4pm daily mid-May-mid-Oct., some weekends through Nov.), operated by the U.S. Forest Service in Jacob Lake, 45 miles north of Bright Angel Point. Displays

North Rim Visitor Center

emphasize the Kaibab Plateau and Kaibab National Forest, although information on Grand Canyon National Park is also plentiful. Purchase forest maps here if you plan to make any back-road excursions.

ENTRANCE STATION

The North Rim entrance station is 12 miles from Bright Angel Point on scenic **Highway 67,** at the boundary between Kaibab National Forest and Grand Canyon National Park. The highway is usually open to travel **mid-May to November,** a few weeks after most visitor services close for the season. When the entrance station is staffed, you can pick up a copy of the *North Rim Pocket Map,* which lists services and activities, including ranger programs and hikes.

TOURS

Cape Royal Driving Tour
23 MILES

Cape Royal Drive, a 23-mile (one-way) paved road with spectacular overlooks, trailhead parking, and fascinating sights, may be the highlight of your visit to the North Rim. You can drive this winding, paved road in less than an hour, but you'll regret it if you don't set aside two or three hours to explore—longer

if you plan to hike or picnic, or if you enjoy a slower pace. The canyon's colors are resplendent in early morning or late afternoon, and shadows add texture and depth to panoramas of the Marble Platform, Saddle Mountain Wilderness, and Unkar Delta. The road begins three miles north of **Grand Canyon Lodge,** forking right at about five miles.

- At the **Vista Encantada** overlook, six miles south of the fork, tables shaded by ponderosa pines make a fine spot for a picnic. The woodsy picnic area is carpeted with pinecones and lupine, and it's often visited by Kaibab squirrels and mule deer. Long, colorful views stretch across the Painted Desert to Navajo and Hopi lands.

- Stop at **Roosevelt Point,** eight miles from the fork, to stretch your legs on the short, easy **Roosevelt Point Trail.** Below, you'll see the confluence of the **Colorado** and **Little Colorado Rivers.** The curtain of cliffs forming the South Rim is known as the **Palisades of the Desert.**

- About 12 miles south of the fork, a dirt parking area on the left marks the trailhead for the four-mile **Cape Final Trail.** One of the North Rim's most satisfying day hikes, leads across the **Walhalla Plateau** to views

Smokey Bear greets visitors at the Kaibab Plateau Visitor Center.

of **Unkar Delta,** a large sandy bend along the Colorado River.

- At **Walhalla Overlook,** a viewpoint 13 miles from the fork, you can learn more about the plateau's ancient residents, the Ancestral Puebloans. Below is **Chuar Canyon,** marking the route the ancients traveled to reach their inner canyon home at Unkar Delta.

- At 16 miles the drive ends at **Cape Royal,** a rocky peninsula that curves into the canyon. Follow the easy 0.5-mile paved trail to the rim and take in magnificent views of **Wotans Throne.** There's plenty of room to picnic, and restrooms are located at the north end of the parking lot.

Point Sublime Driving Tour
17 MILES

If you have a sturdy, high-clearance 4WD vehicle—and steady nerves—consider traveling the rugged 17-mile route to Point Sublime. (Calling this a road would be overly generous.) You'll pass through deep ponderosa forest splashed with purple lupine and yellow butterweed, mostly over a rocky two-track. About halfway, an overlook offers up-close views of the **Dragon,** a limestone formation extending from the rim. The end of the road, Point Sublime, is a stark and isolated peninsula utterly surrounded by the canyon and monuments.

Before you head out, check with the **North Rim Backcountry Office** (8am-noon and 1pm-5pm daily) to find out the latest road conditions. Be sure to travel with a good spare tire and plenty of water—this infrequently traveled route presents plenty of hazards, including deep sand, high crowns, and tire-eating rocks. Allow at least five hours of daylight to drive to the point and return, longer if you plan to picnic along the way.

The route begins 2.5 miles north of Grand Canyon Lodge on Highway 67. Turn left onto the gravel road that leads to the **Widforss Trail.** Just past the trailhead parking area, the road begins to change to a rocky two-track, and it will change character several more times as it heads west to Point Sublime.

As you near Point Sublime, you'll pass over a narrow causeway of dirt and stone lined with a half-dozen picnic tables, cliffrose, and beavertail cactus. The rocky causeway leads to what feels like the very ends of the earth. A short footpath leads still farther, until you are standing on a narrow spit of limestone, the canyon dropping away on all sides. It's like being on a diving board high over the ocean, but instead of water you are surrounded by stone. With a **backcountry permit,** you can spend the night at this primitive overlook, which has fewer than a dozen campsites.

Guided Walks and Tours

Daily ranger-guided activities include nature walks, usually a relaxed morning stroll through the forest lasting about an hour. Rangers introduce participants to the North Rim's forest ecosystem and answer questions about the canyon. Check the *Pocket Map* for departure times, or stop by the North Rim Visitor Center to see if additional tours have been scheduled.

Mule Trips

Wranglers from **Grand Canyon Trail Rides** (P.O. Box 128, Tropic, UT 84776, 435/679-8665, www.canyonrides.com) guide hour-long mule trips and half-day mule trips along the rim or partway into the canyon. (Note that on the North Rim, mule trips don't descend all the way to the river.) No previous riding experience is necessary, but riders must understand English and be suitably dressed in long pants and shoes or boots (no sandals). Each rider can take a camera or binoculars, and guides will stop at points of interest.

The **one-hour rim tour** (8:30am or 1:30pm daily, $45 pp) is suitable for children as young as seven years old. The **half-day rim tour** (7:30am or 12:30pm daily, $80 pp) travels to Uncle Jim Point, with views of the North Kaibab Trail and Roaring Springs Canyon. **Half-day canyon trips** (7:30am or 12:30pm daily, $90 pp) descend via the North Kaibab Trail and travel to the Supai Tunnel before riding back the same route, a four-mile roundtrip. Children must be 10 or older for half-day trips. Weight limits are 220 pounds for the rim tours and 200 pounds for the canyon tour. Prices include shuttle transportation from the lodge to the trailhead; the shuttle leaves 30 minutes before tour departures. If you haven't made an advance reservation, check at the lodge's **transportation desk** (7am-5pm daily) to see if same-day spots are available.

Audio Tours

If you have a cell phone, you can listen to two-minute audio tours describing four locations on the North Rim. Look for the numbered **Park Ranger Audio Tour** signs, dial 928/225-2907, enter the stop number, and listen to park rangers talk about Grand Canyon Lodge, Bright Angel Point geology, the night sky, or Roaring Springs. The prerecorded mini-tours are free, but be aware that cell coverage is sketchy at the North Rim, and not all service providers cover park locations.

Learning Adventures

Guided activities are a great way to make the most of a visit. **Grand Canyon Field Institute** (P.O. Box 399, Grand Canyon, AZ 86023, 928/638-2485 or 866/471-4435, http://grandcanyon.org/fieldinstitute) offers a wide variety of expert-led classes and service trips. Difficulty ranges from single-day, rim-side classes to multiday backpacking trips. A few focus on the North Rim, including a family day-hike ($49 pp), or four-day photography workshop ($515 pp) highlighting fall color.

Sights

Scenic Highway 67 crosses the Kaibab Plateau on its way from Jacob Lake to the park's Bright Angel Point, almost 50 miles. The serene drive passes through grassy meadows edged by forests of pine and aspen. Travel in the early morning or evening and you may see deer, elk, coyotes, or even bison. Paved turnouts are a good place to stop and watch the action with a pair of binoculars.

BRIGHT ANGEL POINT

The heart of the North Rim is **Bright Angel Point,** a peninsula extending between the Transept and Roaring Springs Canyon. Nearly all visitor services, including the lodge and campground, are situated on this forested peninsula. Past the lodge, the peninsula narrows and descends to jut into the canyon like the prow of a ship. You can walk to the very tip on the short-but-sweet **Bright Angel Point Trail,** which hugs the edge of a narrow ridge with stunning views on both sides. Kaibab limestone along the trail bears fossilized remains of marine life, and gnarled pines make interesting foreground elements for photo buffs. As you near the end of the trail, you may be able to hear **Roaring Springs,** 3,100 feet below, the source of the canyon's drinking water.

★ Grand Canyon Lodge

"Parkitect" Gilbert Stanley Underwood designed Grand Canyon Lodge in 1928. He sited it at the rim, with its foundations rising up out of the limestone cliffs, setting the stage for a grand entrance: Guests' first glimpses of the canyon are framed by the large windows across the lobby.

Now a National Historic Landmark, Grand Canyon Lodge is the center of visitor activities on the North Rim, with an air of Western hospitality that extends not just to the lodge's guests but also to the canyon's guests. Even if you're not staying in one of the cabins, you can enjoy a meal in the dining room, attend a program in the auditorium, or find a sunny spot on the veranda to sip your morning coffee.

Bright Angel Point and Walhalla Plateau

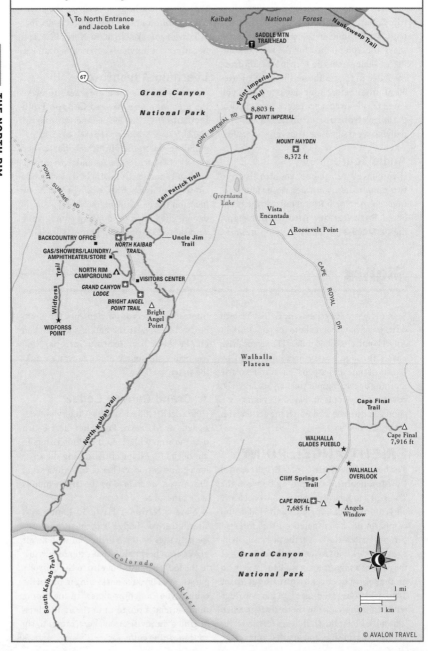

To North Entrance and Jacob Lake

Kaibab   National   Forest   Nankoweap Trail

SADDLE MTN
TRAILHEAD

67

Grand Canyon
National Park

POINT IMPERIAL RD

Point Imperial Trail

8,803 ft
POINT IMPERIAL

MOUNT HAYDEN
8,372 ft

POINT SUBLIME RD

Ken Patrick Trail

Greenland
Lake

Vista
Encantada

Roosevelt Point

BACKCOUNTRY OFFICE
NORTH KAIBAB
TRAIL
Uncle Jim
Trail
GAS/SHOWERS/LAUNDRY/
AMPHITHEATER/STORE

NORTH RIM
CAMPGROUND

VISITORS CENTER

GRAND CANYON
LODGE

BRIGHT ANGEL
POINT TRAIL

Bright
Angel
Point

Widforss Trail

WIDFORSS
POINT

CAPE ROYAL DR

Walhalla
Plateau

Cape Final
Trail

Cape Final
7,916 ft

WALHALLA
GLADES PUEBLO

WALHALLA
OVERLOOK

North Kaibab Trail

Cliff Springs
Trail

CAPE ROYAL
7,685 ft

Angels
Window

Grand Canyon
National Park

South Kaibab Trail

Colorado   River

0   1 mi
0   1 km

© AVALON TRAVEL

Designing Grand Canyon Lodge

To complete its Grand Circle Tour of Zion National Park, Bryce National Monument, Cedar Breaks National Monument, and the North Rim, the Union Pacific Railroad hired architect Gilbert Stanley Underwood, designer of the stunning Ahwahnee Hotel in Yosemite. Considered the father of "parkitecture," **Gilbert Stanley Underwood** excelled at creating a deeper experience of nature from within his designs.

Limestone for the lodge's foundation was quarried two miles away. Timber came from the Kaibab Forest, about 10 miles north. Because the mill required water and power, a hydroelectric plant was built on the Colorado River, more than 3,000 feet below the construction site.

Underwood banked the stonework foundation into the rim, with multiple levels of open terraces overlooking the canyon. He sited 120 guest cabins according to the forested, hilly topography.

UP officials altered the design in one key respect: Underwood's original plan called for a structural core of concrete and steel, but they made the fateful decision to use a timber frame instead.

On June 1, 1928, the lodge opened its doors. Only four years later, early in the morning of September 1, 1932, sparks from a fireplace started the largest structural fire in the history of Grand Canyon National Park. The fire destroyed the lodge and two cabins, leaving only the stone foundations and chimneys.

Rebuilt and reopened in 1936, the lodge retains Underwood's flair for dramatic scale, with a steeper roof pitch helpful for shedding North Rim snows. The east terrace boasts a huge fireplace—a popular location to gather for ranger talks. Inside, beams painted and carved with Native American symbols contribute to the building's sense of place. Soaring above the lodge's public areas are exposed roof trusses—logs with a hidden core of steel.

★ POINT IMPERIAL AND MOUNT HAYDEN

Arrive at Point Imperial—the highest point on both rims at 8,800 feet—by taking Highway 67 to the Cape Royal Road (also known as the Fuller Canyon Road). Take the left fork toward Point Imperial and drive another three miles. The road ends at a large parking area.

For the best views, descend the short path to the overlook. The spire of **Mount Hayden** (8,372 feet) rises above **Nankoweap Canyon.** Late-afternoon or early-morning sunlight turns this Coconino sandstone peak from buff to rosy gold. The 40,000-acre **Saddle Mountain Wilderness,** part of the Kaibab National Forest, sprawls to the north, and to the east is the colorful **Marble Platform,** edged by reddish cliffs.

Picnic tables are scattered beneath the shade of a ponderosa pine forest with restrooms nearby. Two trails lead from the parking lot: the **Point Imperial Trail** and the **Ken Patrick Trail.**

WALHALLA PLATEAU

Across the road from the Walhalla Overlook parking area, a short path leads to the North Rim's most extensive prehistoric site, **Walhalla Glades.** This village was occupied by the Ancestral Puebloans approximately 1050-1150. Archaeologists have studied their 10-room dwelling, now a rocky ruin, learning about Ancestral Puebloan daily life from pottery shards, chipped stone, and architecture.

Scattered over the Walhalla Plateau are more than 100 farming sites where the Ancestral Puebloans grew corn, beans, and squash during summer months. Because the plateau is lower than surrounding elevations, warm updrafts melted winter snow and made earlier planting possible. During winters, many residents migrated into the canyon, where they could farm in the desert climes of **Unkar Delta,** visible from the overlook. At Unkar Delta, a two-day journey from the rim,

Mount Hayden from Point Imperial

they built a pueblo of more than 50 rooms, the inner canyon's largest archaeological site.

When staffing allows, rangers lead **guided tours** from Walhalla Overlook to the Walhalla Glades ruin, discussing how people

Wotans Throne from Cape Royal

subsisted here on the North Rim 1,000 years ago. Check at the visitor center for times.

An ancient granary can be seen along the **Cliff Springs Trail.** To access the trail, drive one mile farther up the road and park at the paved overlook for **Angels Window** (about 14 miles south of the fork to Cape Royal). The trail begins across the road.

★ Cape Royal

Cape Royal Road continues almost all the way to the southern edge of the Walhalla Plateau, ending at a large parking area, where an easy, 0.5-mile paved trail leads to the rim through a natural bower of cliffrose and other high-desert vegetation. Be sure to stop along the way for a closer look the natural limestone arch called **Angels Window,** which frames a slice of the Colorado River and Unkar Delta. A spur trail leads 150 yards to the top of the arch itself, where you can stand and enjoy precipitous views of the canyon below.

Continue on the main trail to Cape Royal, which extends into the canyon toward **Wotans Throne,** the centerpiece of a spectacular panorama. Pause for a heady inhalation of cliffrose before taking in equally intoxicating views of **Vishnu Temple** and **Freya Castle.** All three peaks rise past 7,200

feet, taller than any mountain in the eastern United States, and yet all three are below you, tucked into the rocky folds of Grand Canyon. See if you can make out Desert View Watchtower, sticking up like a thimble far across the canyon on the South Rim. Explore nearby to find the outdoor "wedding chapel" where couples can tie the knot in front of a stunning canyon backdrop.

★ TOROWEAP

At 4,550 feet, **Toroweap** (a Paiute word meaning "dry or barren valley") is the lowest rim overlook in the park, but one of the most precipitous: Sheer cliffs fall away 3,000 feet below to the Colorado River. You can see—and hear—**Lava Falls** by walking to the rim, a few hundred feet beyond the overlook parking area. There are no guardrails or fences or even pavement at this primitive overlook, and peering over the edge to look at tiny rafts floating past on the Colorado River far below can stir up a strong sensation of acrophobia. Views up- and downriver are stunning, especially at sunrise and sunset. You may decide not to visit this lonely spot the first or second time you travel to Grand Canyon, but it belongs on your Grand Canyon bucket list.

To get to Toroweap (also known as Tuweep)

Toroweap overlooks the western canyon.

Toroweap

To Fredonia

TUWEEP
RANGER
STATION

GRAND CANYON
NATIONAL PARK

Toroweap
Point

TUCKUP TRAIL
JUNCTION

TUWEEP
CAMPGROUND

Vulcan's
Throne
5,102 ft

TOROWEAP
OVERLOOK

Colorado River

Vulcan's
Anvil

Lava
Falls

0   2 mi

0   2 km

© AVALON TRAVEL

you'll have to travel nearly 150 miles from Bright Angel Point before you're back inside park boundaries. The journey spans some 60 miles of dirt roads through Bureau of Land Management (BLM) holdings on the Arizona Strip, including a small stretch of the **Grand Canyon-Parashant National Monument.** The reward for this trip through the Strip is a perspective of Grand Canyon that few people see outside book covers, a vertiginous drop to the river with no crowds or barricades, and a clear view of the ancient lava flows that captured John Wesley Powell's imagination in 1869, when he wrote: "What a conflict of water and fire there must have been here!"

Volcanic activity along the Toroweap fault began about seven million years ago. Lava flowed into the canyon several times, damming the Colorado River. About 1.2 million

years ago, lava flows created dams more than 1,000 feet high, forming a lake that extended for hundreds of miles. Basalt remnants of the lava dams are visible today.

Day hiking possibilities include meandering along the rim near the **campground** and overlook, hiking nearby **Tuckup Trail** for a mile or so, or bushwhacking up **Vulcan's Throne,** a 700-foot-high cinder cone west of the overlook.

Camping

With fair weather, dry roads, and good fortune, it's possible to travel to Toroweap and back to Fredonia in a day, about six hours round-trip. However, because of the time and effort needed to get to this remote corner of the canyon, most people will want to spend at least one night at **Tuweep Campground,** a cluster of 10 sites one mile from the rim overlook. The National Park Service requires **permits** for the Tuweep Campground (www.nps.gov/plan-yourvisit/tuweep.htm). Be aware that there's no water, gas, food, lodging, or phones—and no cell phone coverage. The chief amenities, after amazing views, are picnic tables and composting toilets. If the campground is full, stop at the Tuweep Ranger Station, about six miles north of the rim, for information about camping on nearby BLM land.

Getting There

Plan ahead and be prepared. You'll need a high-clearance vehicle and at least one good spare tire. Because 25 percent of visitors experience one or more flats, the park service recommends bringing a second spare, a tire repair kit, and everything you need for an extra night in the backcountry. Don't count on your GPS unit; bring a map. From Jacob Lake, take U.S. 89A to Fredonia, turning left on Highway 387. About seven miles west of Fredonia, look for a dirt road with a sign reading "Mt. Trumbull." At 46 miles, the road forks. Continue straight to Toroweap, following the signs. Once you cross the park boundary, the road becomes rougher. Check in at the Tuweep Ranger Station on your way to the overlook, another six miles.

Recreation

DAY HIKES

The North Rim's unspoiled beauty and natural quiet is best enjoyed on foot. Because of its remoteness, your chances for solitude are much greater here. The flip side is that if you get into trouble, help can be farther away and slower in coming. Novice canyon hikers should stick to rim trails or hike on **North Kaibab Trail** before attempting other descents.

Though no permit is needed for a day hike, planning is important. Be prepared, pace yourself, and be sure to allow enough time for the return trip. It takes twice as long to hike the same distance coming out of the canyon as it does going in, and the North Rim's 8,000-foot elevation can make even the best-conditioned hikers gasp for breath.

On summer afternoons, shady rim hikes like the **Widforss Point Trail** are the best options. Temperatures rise quickly, and the sun is intense at this elevation. Drink plenty of water and take some time to get used to the high elevation and low humidity before setting out on a challenging trail.

North Rim Hikes

Trail	Effort	Distance	Duration
Bright Angel Point Trail	easy	0.5 miles round-trip	30 minutes
Bridle Path	easy	3 miles round-trip	1 hour or less
Transept Trail	easy to moderate	3 miles round-trip	1.5 hours
Uncle Jim Trail	easy to moderate	5 miles round-trip	3 hours
North Kaibab Trail	moderate to very strenuous	14 miles one-way to the river	3 days or more
Coconino Overlook	moderate	1.5 miles round-trip	1-2 hours
Supai Tunnel	strenuous	4 miles round-trip	3-4 hours
Redwall Bridge	strenuous	5.2 miles round-trip	4-6 hours
Eye of the Needle	very strenuous	7 miles round-trip	6-8 hours
Roosevelt Point Trail	easy	0.2 miles round-trip	20 minutes
Cliff Springs Trail	easy	2 miles round-trip	1 hour
Cape Final Trail	easy	4 miles round-trip	2 hours
Point Imperial Trail	easy	4.4 miles round-trip	2 hours
Widforss Trail	easy to moderate	10 miles round-trip	5 hours
Self-guided tour	easy	4.2 miles round-trip	2-3 hours
Tuckup Trail	easy to strenuous	70 miles one-way	multiple days
Ken Patrick Trail	moderate	10 miles one-way	6 hours
Thunder River Trail	very strenuous	15 miles to the river	3 days or more
North Bass Trail	very strenuous	13.5 miles rim to river	4 days or more
Lava Falls Route	very strenuous	3 miles round-trip	8 hours
Nankoweap Trail	very strenuous	28-29 miles round-trip	4-6 days

Bridle Path

Distance: 3 miles round-trip
Duration: 1 hour or less
Elevation change: Negligible
Effort: Easy
Trailheads: Grand Canyon Lodge or the North Kaibab Trail parking lot (see map p. 100)

More of a stroll than a hike, this easy trail allows visitors to leave their cars behind in order to get from one place to another on Bright Angel Point. The path connects the lodge and campground and leads through a forest of ponderosa pines to the **North Kaibab Trailhead.** It's the only trail on the North Rim where you can **bicycle** or **walk your pet** (on a leash). Like a small-town sidewalk, this path has a friendly, social feel. You might see mule deer wandering nearby or catch a glimpse of a Kaibab squirrel leaping from branch to branch in the tall ponderosas. If no one's watching, stop and sniff a tree—the ponderosa's bark smells like butterscotch or vanilla.

★ Bright Angel Point Trail

Distance: 0.5 miles round-trip
Duration: 30 minutes
Elevation change: 200 feet
Effort: Easy

Trailheads: Log shelter near the easternmost cabins, or at the corner of the lodge's veranda (see map p. 100)

This paved trail leads to spectacular canyon views along a narrow ridge. At either trailhead, look for a box containing brochures for a self-guided nature tour highlighting canyon geology. Though the Bright Angel Point Trail is short, the elevation (8,148 feet) and narrowness of the trail—not to mention the views—can take your breath away. This is a popular trail, and you may need to make way for other hikers, especially the vertigo sufferers hugging the inside of the trail.

En route, you can see fossils embedded in the Kaibab limestone that forms the canyon's rim. Peer over the edges into **Transept** or **Roaring Springs Canyons** or across the horizon to the **South Rim,** 10 miles away as the raven flies. On a clear day, the **San Francisco Peaks** near Flagstaff stand out on the southern horizon. Landmarks nearer the point include **Brahma, Deva,** and **Zoroaster Temples.** Any of these stone monuments would be major attractions if they were located elsewhere—but here at the canyon, they are among hundreds of stony sentinels, many named by geologist Clarence Dutton in the

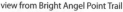
view from Bright Angel Point Trail

Roaring Springs can be reached from the North Kaibab Trail.

late 1800s to reflect their lofty and inspiring forms.

Transept Trail

Distance: 3 miles round-trip
Duration: 1.5 hours
Elevation change: 100 feet
Effort: Easy to moderate
Trailhead: Grand Canyon Lodge or the North Rim Campground

The Transept Trail is an up-and-down meander through a ponderosa pine forest that gives way to Gambel oaks along the rim of Transept Canyon. Even though it leads along busy Bright Angel Point, the trail offers many spots to enjoy the forest solitude and rim views. If you hike in the early morning, you have a good chance of seeing mule deer, Kaibab squirrels, and several bird species. Stop midway, where a rustic bench offers views of **Zoroaster, Brahma,** and **Deva Temples**—fabulous at sunset. Nearby, a small **prehistoric ruin,** approximately 1,000 years old, stands next to the trail. The ancients spent summers here on the rim, hunting and gathering wild plants in the nearby forest. Return the same way, or make a three-mile loop by taking the **Bridle Path** that parallels Highway 67 between the lodge and the campground.

Uncle Jim Trail

Distance: 5 miles round-trip
Duration: 3 hours
Elevation change: 200 feet
Effort: Easy to moderate
Trailhead: Ken Patrick Trailhead on the east side of the North Kaibab Trail parking lot (see map p. 100)

This lollipop trail travels through the forest between Roaring Springs Canyon and Bright Angel Canyon. Because it's shaded, it's a good choice on hot summer days. You'll be sharing the trail with mule parties, who have the right-of-way. For the first 0.5 miles, the **Uncle Jim** and **Ken Patrick Trails** are a single path, skirting the rim before heading into a dense fir forest. At the signed junction, the Uncle Jim Trail veers to the right, descending toward the head of **Roaring Springs Canyon.**

After about one mile, you'll come to another junction, this one unsigned, marking the beginning of the loop to **Uncle Jim Point.** Whether you go right or left, it's another mile to the point. The left fork continues east toward the rim of Bright Angel Canyon before looping back toward Uncle Jim Point, named for the Grand Canyon's first game warden.

From the rim, you can look down into **Roaring Springs Canyon.** Three thousand feet below, Roaring Springs is the source of Grand Canyon's drinking water, piped to both rims. Looking at the opposite side of the canyon, you can see the North Kaibab Trail switchbacks. On the southern horizon, 12 miles away, is the **South Rim,** and beyond that the **San Francisco Peaks.** Return the same way, or take the other half of the loop on your way back to the parking lot.

★ North Kaibab Trail

Distance: 1.5-7 miles round-trip
Elevation change: 5,770 feet
Effort: Moderate to very strenuous

North Kaibab Trail

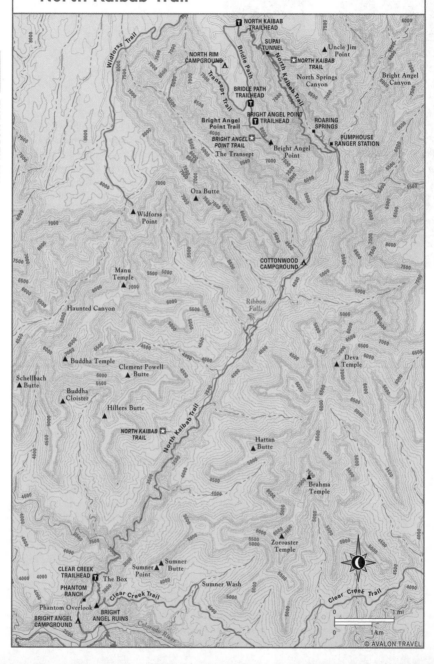

North Rim Names

ROOSEVELT TRAIL

President Theodore Roosevelt, an avid sportsman and canyon booster, proclaimed Grand Canyon Game Preserve in 1906 and Grand Canyon National Monument in 1908. He called Grand Canyon the "one great sight that every American should see." The canyon gained National Park status in 1919.

UNCLE JIM POINT AND TRAIL

James T. Owens began working as a cowboy at age 11. In his 40s, Owens led two bison drives from Utah to House Rock Valley. His scheme to breed buffalo with cattle and sell them proved unprofitable, but his other gigs—as guard, game warden, and guide—put his name on the map. His clients included novelist Zane Grey, Arizona historian Sharlot Hall, and Teddy Roosevelt, who accompanied Owens on a cougar hunt in 1913. All three recounted their adventures, and Uncle Jim's skill as a lion hunter became legendary.

BRIGHTY OF GRAND CANYON

Another member of Roosevelt's 1913 hunting party was Brighty, a burro named for Bright Angel Creek. Brighty's job was to haul spring water to a tourist camp, where young campers would ride him for hours. Years later, author Marguerite Henry read about Brighty in an old *Sunset* magazine, and his real-life adventures became the basis for her award-winning children's book and later a movie, both titled *Brighty of Grand Canyon*. Brighty's likeness—nose shiny from petting—rests in a corner of the sunroom at Grand Canyon Lodge.

WIDFORSS POINT AND TRAIL

Born in Sweden, artist Gunnar Widforss lived and painted at Grand Canyon, defying a doctor's warning to move to a lower elevation. He died of a heart attack at age 55 and was buried in the South Rim cemetery. His love for the canyon is evident in his exquisite watercolors, which can be viewed at the Museum of Northern Arizona and other locations.

Trailhead: 1.5 miles north of Grand Canyon Lodge at a large parking lot (see map p. 108)

The North Kaibab is a popular corridor trail—patrolled, wide, and well maintained—and also congested with backpackers, day hikers, mule riders, and the occasional ranger patrol. It's the only North Rim trail within park boundaries that descends into the canyon, and it offers many day-hike options; trailhead parking often fills up by late morning. Arrange for a shuttle from the lodge or walk to the trailhead via the Bridle Path.

Don't underestimate this trail: The upper sections are steep, and at this elevation, even a short day hike can be a workout. Time summer hikes so that you're off the trail between 10am to 4pm.

COCONINO OVERLOOK

Distance: 1.5 miles round-trip
Duration: 1-2 hours
Elevation change: 800 feet
Effort: Moderate

The North Kaibab Trail leaves the piney rim and drops quickly into **Bright Angel Canyon,** whose rugged walls frame the view as you step down 800 feet of elevation in 0.75 miles. The lush vegetation may lend the impression that you're entering a high-desert oasis, but you'll quickly realize the upper sections of this trail are hot and exposed. The **overlook**—a natural platform of Coconino sandstone—is a good place to catch your breath and befriend your water bottle before climbing back up to the rim.

SUPAI TUNNEL

Distance: 4 miles round-trip
Duration: 3-4 hours
Elevation change: 1,450 feet
Effort: Strenuous

Even a short hike below the rim will give you a different perspective of the canyon as you pass through different geological layers and life zones. From the trailhead to the Supai Tunnel is a 1,450-foot elevation change, and ponderosa pine, firs, and aspen give way to Gambel oak, New Mexican locust, and wild rose. Past the tunnel, vegetation shifts to piñon pine, juniper, manzanita, and cliffrose.

REDWALL BRIDGE

Distance: 5.2 miles round-trip
Duration: 4-6 hours
Elevation change: 2,150 feet
Effort: Strenuous

As the North Kaibab Trail descends to the Redwall limestone layer, the trail crosses a bridge over **Roaring Springs Canyon.** This bridge is a good turnaround for strong day hikers. But be warned: The Redwall section of the trail is so seductively gorgeous that you may find it hard to turn back.

EYE OF THE NEEDLE

Distance: 7 miles round-trip
Duration: 6-8 hours
Elevation change: 2,400 feet
Effort: Very strenuous

Another possible turnaround for strong hikers on the North Kaibab Trail is the **Needle** at 3.5 miles. As you hike, start listening for the sound of **Roaring Springs**—you'll hear flowing water about a mile before you reach it. At 4.7 miles from the rim, the springs mark the point of last return if you are day hiking, and only the most experienced canyon hikers should attempt it.

Roosevelt Point Trail

Distance: 0.2 miles round-trip
Duration: 20 minutes
Elevation change: Negligible
Effort: Easy

Trailhead: Roosevelt Point overlook, 12 miles up Cape Royal Road

This short, easy trail passes through forest burned by the Outlook Fire in 2000, offering beautiful views of the eastern canyon as well as an up-close look at how the forest responds to wildfires. Young aspen, grasses, and wildflowers grow among blackened stumps. Snags (dead trees that still stand) shelter birds and chipmunks. A **bench** in this mini-Eden offers a quiet respite from road noise. Before returning to your vehicle, soak in the views, scanning the southern horizon for **Comanche Point,** which rises above the confluence of the Colorado and Little Colorado Rivers.

Cape Final Trail

Distance: 4 miles round-trip
Duration: 2 hours
Elevation change: 150 feet
Effort: Easy
Trailhead: A dirt parking area 17 miles up Cape Royal Road, 2.5 miles from road's end (see map p. 100)

This pleasant trail passes through a forest of ponderosa pine on its way across Cape Final (a thumb-like extension of the Walhalla Plateau) to rim overlooks with views of Unkar Creek, Chuar Valley, and the Painted Desert.

From the dirt parking area on the left (east) of the road, the trail climbs a forested ridge before meandering toward a rim clearing, about 1.25 miles. Here, a dramatic drop reveals views of the **Chuar Valley,** with **Gunther's Castle** rising above its soft folds. The trail narrows as the cape, a peninsula of land, becomes narrower. As the trail turns south and west, the vegetation changes to piñon and cactus. An **intersecting path** heads east through scrubby vegetation to the very tip of Cape Final. Far below, **Unkar Delta,** a wide, sandy curve in the Colorado River, marks the site of a large Ancestral Puebloan village, occupied seasonally until AD 1150.

The main trail continues to the southern edge of Cape Final, where **Freya Castle** rises above Unkar Creek Canyon. With a backcountry permit, it's possible to **camp** overnight on Cape Final, and you'll find yourself

Cliff Springs

down and follow sandal prints left behind by the ancients who walked here. Sheltered by a soaring stony overhang, water seeps from the base of the Kaibab limestone walls, converging into shallow pools at the 0.5-mile point.

You can linger here for a while, enjoying the sound of dripping water and watching quietly as birds visit the spring. This is the end of the maintained section of the trail, but it's possible to explore a bit farther along the cliff to a rugged path that descends toward **Clear Creek Canyon,** ending with views of **Cape Royal** and **Vishnu Temple.**

Point Imperial Trail

Distance: 4.4 miles round-trip
Duration: 2 hours
Elevation change: Negligible
Effort: Easy
Trailhead: North end of the Point Imperial parking area

This trail leads toward **Saddle Mountain,** just across the park boundary. The trail starts out paved but soon turns to dirt. Pine and fir yield to areas scorched by the 2000 Outlet Fire, and soon the trail is surrounded by ghostly white aspen snags and blackened pine stumps. **Saddle Mountain, Marble Canyon,** and—on the horizon—**Navajo Mountain** are visible through the burned areas. The surrounding landscape is a good example of how the natural environment recovers from fire. Wildflowers and young aspens are the first stage in a forest's rebirth. Nature is reclaiming the trail in spots; watch out for thorny New Mexico locust. At 2.2 miles, you'll reach the **gate** that marks the park's northern boundary, a fine day-hike destination.

For bonus views, go beyond the park boundary into **Kaibab Forest.** Shortly after crossing the dirt road (Forest Rd. 610), you'll come to the signed trail for **Saddle Mountain.** A spur to the right heads up a rocky outcrop with a view across Marble Platform to the **Vermilion Cliffs,** worth the extra few minutes of hiking.

envying those who made plans to spend the night in this beautiful area.

Cliff Springs Trail

Distance: 2 miles round-trip
Duration: 1 hour
Elevation change: 150 feet
Effort: Easy
Trailhead: Across the road from Angels Window Overlook, a paved pullout 19 miles up Cape Royal Road

Short it may be, but this trail offers a variety of riches. Starting at the paved pullout 0.3 miles north of Cape Royal, cross the road to find the trail marker. The well-defined dirt trail descends through ponderosa pine forest to an Ancestral Puebloan **granary** tucked beneath a large chunk of Kaibab limestone. The trail curves around this boulder and continues to descend through mixed forest into a rugged wash. You'll leave behind the road noise and enter a magical world where the past feels near, as though you could look

Widforss Trail

Distance: 4.2 miles round-trip
Duration: 2-3 hours
Elevation change: Moderate ups and downs totaling 1,100 feet
Effort: Easy to moderate
Trailhead: About one mile north of the North Kaibab Trail parking lot, turn left onto a dirt road and drive another mile to the trailhead.

This rim trail is an excellent choice for a hot day. At the trailhead, pick up a brochure for the **self-guided tour.** This section of the trail leads from Harvey Meadow to the edges of Transept Canyon, with peekaboo views of Bright Angel Point and Zoroaster Temple. Points of interest are marked with numbered stakes. The day-hike turnaround point is marker 14.

Lava Falls Route

Distance: 3 miles round-trip
Duration: 8 hours
Elevation change: 2,500 feet
Effort: Very strenuous
Trailhead: 3.5 miles south of the Tuweep Ranger Station, a 4WD road leads another 2.5 miles to the trailhead. During or after wet weather, the road may be impassable (see map p. 104).

Although this route is the shortest rim-to-river trail in the park, it is extremely difficult, passing down a steep slope of loose basalt cobbles and boulders to **Lava Falls.** (The Class-10 rapid, formed by debris from Prospect Canyon, drops 13 feet, making it one of the most challenging for river runners.) Temperatures along the Lava Falls route can reach dangerous heights, and there's no shade or water along the way. The route, indiscernible in loose scree, is marked by cairns. Even the most experienced hikers should not attempt to hike this trail during summer months. It's no exaggeration: *People die here.*

BACKPACKING

Rim-to-river trails on the North Rim tend to be longer than the South Rim's because they start at a higher elevation and descend tributary canyons before reaching the Colorado River. Only one maintained trail, North Kaibab, leads to the river, a 14-mile (one-way) journey. The North Rim's other rim-to-river trails are wilderness trails—remote forest trailheads, no water, faint routes, steep descents. Do not attempt to hike from rim to river and back in one day, a trek that's barely feasible (for a few) on the South Rim but suicidal on the North Rim.

Transept Canyon from the Widforss Trail

BACKCOUNTRY PERMITS

If you want to spend the night in the canyon, you'll need to apply for a **backcountry permit** ($10 per permit, plus $8 pp per night). Permits are required for overnight hiking and backpacking, river camping, or any camping outside developed campgrounds. Permit applications can be made up to four months in advance and can be submitted online, in person, and by mail or fax to **Grand Canyon Permits Office** (National Park Service, 1824 S. Thompson St., Suite 201, Flagstaff, AZ 86001, fax 928/638-2125, www.nps.gov/grca). The lengthy and detailed process is explained further in the *Essentials* chapter (page 281) and on the park website.

North Kaibab Trail

Distance: 28 miles round-trip to the river
Duration: 3 days or more
Elevation change: 5,770 feet to the river
Effort: Very strenuous
Trailhead: 1.5 miles north of Grand Canyon Lodge at a large parking lot (see map p. 108)

If you plan to hike the North Kaibab Trail to the river, make **reservations** well in advance for Phantom Ranch, or get **permits** for Bright Angel and Cottonwood Campgrounds. **Piped water** is available seasonally at the trailhead, Supai Tunnel (2 miles), Roaring Springs pump house (5.4 miles), and Cottonwood Camp (6.8 miles). Be prepared for the occasional pipeline break, which can affect water supplies at inner canyon campgrounds. Spring or river water must be treated before drinking. Plan your hike so that you're off the trail during the heat of the day (10am-4pm).

The North Kaibab Trail descends 4.7 miles from the rim to **Roaring Springs.** From the springs, it's 0.7 miles to the **pump house,** where you'll find piped water and a picnic table. At 6.8 miles, **Cottonwood Campground** has water and a ranger station. Often, backpackers spend the night here before continuing to Bright Angel Campground (mile 14). Past Cottonwood Campground, desert vegetation predominates—yucca, cactus, and catclaw. At 8.5 miles, a short spur leads to **Ribbon Falls,** an oasis shrouded in ferns, columbine, and monkey flower. The waterfall drops 100 feet onto a mound of travertine, creating a refreshing spray. In 2017 the footbridge leading to the falls was closed indefinitely for repairs; check with the park service before your hike to see if the trail has reopened.

The main trail continues down Bright Angel Canyon, which narrows at **The Box,** a schist-walled maze that's oven-hot on a summer afternoon. After zigzagging across the creek several times, the canyon opens up again. The **Clear Creek Trail** junction is at 13 miles, signaling your approach to **Phantom Ranch** and, 0.5 miles beyond, **Bright Angel Campground.**

Ken Patrick Trail

Distance: 10 miles one-way
Duration: 6 hours
Elevation change: 300 feet, with 1,090 feet of up-and-down
Effort: Moderate
Trailheads: Point Imperial overlook and the North Kaibab Trail parking lot

Much of this trail's 10-mile length is shaded by mixed forest. Day hikers can walk part of the trail, or leave a car at the North Kaibab parking lot to hike the trail one direction. The section of the trail nearest **Point Imperial** is the most scenic. A good out-and-back day-hike destination is the **Cape Royal Road** (6 miles round-trip, 3-4 hours).

The trail starts at the end of the Point Imperial parking lot, offering striking views of **Mount Hayden** and the eastern canyon to the **Painted Desert.** As the trail continues in a generally southwest direction, you'll go up and down gently rolling terrain with occasional peeks into **Nankoweap Canyon.** Watch your step along weathered areas; steel posts used to support timber cribbing and water bars have begun to protrude from the soil.

The trail edges a recovering burn, where you'll spot splashy wildflowers; you may need to shimmy through a thicket of New Mexico locust. At three miles, the trail ascends a rocky stair to the Cape Royal Road; most day hikers will turn back here, unless they've left a second vehicle at the North Kaibab parking lot, another seven miles through the forest.

Nankoweap Trail

Distance: 28-29 miles round-trip
Duration: 4-6 days
Elevation change: 4,800 feet
Effort: Very strenuous
Trailhead: Saddle Mountain Wilderness
Directions: There are two possible routes to this trailhead: from House Rock Valley and Forest Road 445, or south of Jacob Lake on Forest Road 610. The latter may be snowy or muddy into June. You will start outside park boundaries on the Saddle Mountain Trail for 3 miles (from Forest Rd. 445) or 3.5 miles (from Forest Rd. 610).

Nankoweap Trail is considered one of Grand Canyon's most strenuous hikes, with downclimbs, dangerous drop-offs, and no water along most of its length. Only experienced canyon backpackers should attempt it. Those who do will gain close-up looks at the colorful Grand Canyon Supergroup rocks and Marble Canyon panoramas, as well as the opportunity to explore Nankoweap Delta's prehistoric sites.

From its junction with the **Saddle Mountain Trail,** Nankoweap Trail drops from the rim through the **Esplanade,** then descends gradually eastward, narrowing to an inches-wide ledge at times. A couple of downclimbs require handholds and footholds. From **Tilted Mesa** (6.8 miles), the trail descends steeply to **Nankoweap Creek** (at 10.6 miles), with switchbacks, ledges, and plenty of loose scree. Follow the creek bed to the Colorado River, a little more than three miles. The shrubby Low Sonoran Desert along the river offers good **campsites,** though you may have to share them with river runners.

Widforss Trail

Distance: 10 miles round-trip
Duration: 5 hours
Elevation change: Moderate ups and downs totaling 1,100 feet
Effort: Easy to moderate
Trailhead: About one mile past the North Kaibab Trail parking lot, turn left onto a dirt road and drive another mile to the trailhead.

This rim trail is an excellent choice for a hot day: It's **shaded** much of the way, and you won't have to slog your way out of the canyon in midday sun. A self-guided tour covers the first 2.1 miles of trail. Beyond that, stronger hikers and backpackers can continue through a forest of fir and aspen; the trail climbs to a ridge west of the Transept. As you traverse the ridge, the forest changes to ponderosa pine and gradually opens. Look for the picnic table and **campsite** (a backcountry permit is required to camp here). Just beyond, the trail drops toward the rim for a splendid view of the South Rim's **Coconino Plateau.**

See if you can spot Grand Canyon Village by pinpointing El Tovar Lodge. Below you is **Haunted Canyon,** and before you are several of the canyon's monumental peaks, including **Buddha** and **Isis Temples.** To the southeast, a limestone spire marks **Widforss Point,** named for artist Gunnar Widforss.

North Bass Trail

Distance: 13.5 miles rim to river
Duration: 4 days or more
Elevation change: 3,300 feet
Effort: Very strenuous
Trailhead: Swamp Point

Suitable for veteran canyon backpackers, this historic trail ranks with Nankoweap as the canyon's most difficult. It leads from remote Swamp Point to the mining camp of canyon pioneer William Bass. The easiest route to the trailhead (relatively speaking) is via Swamp Ridge, a couple of hours of driving over forest roads that get rougher as you approach the rim. Roads may be muddy into June; stop at the Kaibab Plateau Visitor Center in Jacob Lake for current conditions and a map. Do not attempt the hike if rain threatens; the trail follows two creek drainages, and flash floods are possible.

The trail starts with a steep, mile-long descent to a junction at **Muav Saddle,** a good day-hike destination (though hikers with time and energy can take the middle fork another mile or so up to **Powell Plateau**). Take the left fork to continue on the **North Bass Trail**. After passing **Queen Anne Spring,** about 0.25 miles, the trail descends to **White Creek,** another mile. The trail follows the boulder-strewn creek bed, bypassing a waterfall, to the edge of the Redwall. Look for cairns marking the descent through the Redwall back into the creek bed.

Keep looking for cairned bypass routes as the trail descends toward **Shinumo Creek,** reaching it a little over 10 miles from the trailhead. The trail follows the creek for 1.5 miles before climbing a saddle, then descending toward the river. The beach is popular with river runners; you'll likely be sharing it.

Thunder River Trail

Distance: 15 miles to the Colorado River
Duration: 3 days or more
Elevation change: 4,400 feet
Effort: Very strenuous
Trailhead: Indian Hollow Campground in Kaibab National Forest (see map p. 116)

In several locations along the North Rim, access to trailheads is on U.S. Forest Service land. Trails (like this one) enter the national park only after they descend from the rim. The Thunder River Trail is a challenging multiday trip to see one of the world's shortest rivers and the impressive waterfall near its start.

The trail descends to the **Esplanade,** turning east to intersect with the **Bill Hall Trail,** which offers an alternate start to this hike (three miles shorter but much steeper). From this intersection, the Thunder River Trail heads south across the Esplanade for about three miles.

At the Redwall formation, the trail drops sharply to **Surprise Valley,** hot and shadeless in summer. In Surprise Valley, the **Deer Creek Trail** intersects the Thunder River Trail from the right. Turn left (east) to continue to Thunder River. You'll hear the river before you see it tumbling 100 feet from the cliffs.

Thunder River ends at the confluence with Tapeats Creek, 0.5 miles from its spring-fed origins. The **Upper Tapeats campsites** are near the confluence. The trail crosses the creek and continues toward the Colorado River, where the **Lower Tapeats campsites** are located.

Tuckup Trail

Distance: 70 miles one-way
Duration: Multiple days
Elevation change: Mostly level
Effort: Easy to strenuous
Trailhead: Five miles south of the Tuweep Ranger Station

The Tuckup Trail leads across the Esplanade shelf to **150-Mile Canyon,** starting as an old road that soon fades to a barely discernible route. The old road is closed to vehicles, so hikers must find room to park along the narrow dirt road, or start from the Tuweep campground, about one mile farther.

For a splendid day hike, walk a couple of miles down the trail, enjoying rim views of the western canyon before returning the same way. The trail follows the old roadway for the first three miles, but past that it's little more than a faint route that winds around finger canyons. The route is relatively level to **Tuckup Canyon,** the halfway point. Experienced backpackers can use the **Tuckup Trail** to access other routes, creating multiday loop trips into remote stretches of Grand Canyon. Popular destinations include **Big Cove Point, Cottonwood Canyon,** and the **Dome.** The Tuckup is very exposed, with few water sources, some of which may be contaminated by livestock. Careful advance planning is a must.

BIKING

In the park, biking is allowed on all paved and dirt roads open to public traffic. Bicycles are subject to the same traffic rules as automobiles. Traffic on Highway 67 can be heavy on summer weekends, and Cape Royal Road is narrow and curving—treacherous on a bike.

Hiking trails are off-limits to bicycles, except for the **Bridle Path** that travels between the lodge and the campground. One option for

Thunder River Trail

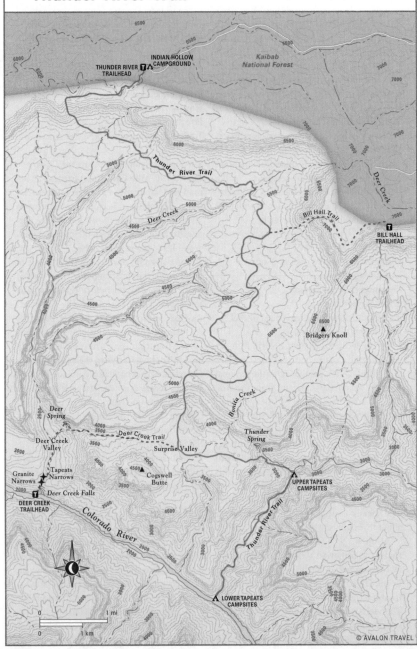

© AVALON TRAVEL

mountain bikers is to take the **Point Sublime road,** a rugged two-track that begins near the Widforss Trail parking area, and travel part or all the way to Point Sublime. At 17 miles (one-way), the point is nearly a day's journey.

You must obtain a **backcountry permit** if you plan to camp overnight at Point Sublime. Applications are available online (www.nps.gov/grca). If you arrived at the North Rim without a permit, you can check in at the North Rim Backcountry Office (8am-noon and 1pm-5pm daily) to see if last-minute permits are available. The office is housed in a small trailer, located off Highway 67 just north of the campground road.

Neighboring **Kaibab National Forest** (928/643-7395, www.fs.usda.gov/kaibab) offers bicyclists miles of trails, dirt tracks, and gravel roads, many bordering the canyon rim. Note that bicycles are not allowed within the forest's Kanab Creek or Saddle Mountain wilderness areas. For maps and information about road conditions on the Kaibab Plateau, visit or contact the **North Kaibab Plateau Visitor Center** (928/643-7298) in Jacob Lake.

TRAIL RIDING

Private stock (horses, mules, burros, or donkeys) are allowed on unpaved public roads as well as North Kaibab Trail, Uncle Jim Trail, and Ken Patrick Trail. The North Rim's **horse camp** is near the North Kaibab Trail; overnights require a backcountry permit. Grazing is not allowed within the park, so riders must bring feed for their stock. Call 928/638-7809 for more information about stock use in the park. Neighboring **Kaibab National Forest** (928/643-7395, www.fs.usda.gov/kaibab) offers additional trail-riding and camping opportunities for equestrians.

Outside the park, **Allen's Trail Rides** (435/644-8150 or 435/689-1660, from $40 pp) offers horseback trips in Kaibab National Forest near the North Rim and Jacob Lake. Short tours are usually available without a reservation; for a multiday pack trip, make arrangements in advance.

WINTER ACTIVITIES

In winter, deep snows may cover the high meadows between Jacob Lake and the entrance station, and the only way into the park's North Rim is on foot, skis, or snowshoes. But for experienced and prepared winter campers, an off-season visit to the North Rim can be peaceful and rewarding.

Before making a winter trip to the North Rim, check with the Arizona Department of Transportation (dial 511 or 888/411-7623, www.az511.gov) for road conditions. Snowmobiles are not allowed on the highway or beyond the park boundaries. It's a 45-mile ski trek from Jacob Lake to the rim, and the highway is the most direct route. Cross-canyon hikers can access the North Rim from Cottonwood Campground, though North Kaibab Trail is often icy and treacherous as it climbs toward the rim.

Winter conditions on the Kaibab Plateau vary. Deep snowpack, extreme cold, and blizzard conditions are possible. Some years, snows may arrive late, but travelers should be prepared and stay aware of changing weather. The meadows and forests north of the park's boundaries often get heavier snowfalls than along the rim, where updrafts from the canyon create warmer microclimates.

During winter months, all overnights at the North Rim require a backcountry permit ($10 per permit, plus $8 pp per night). The North Rim's group campsite and the winter yurt can be reserved between December 1 and April 15. About 10 minutes' ski time from the North Kaibab trailhead, the yurt accommodates up to six people, with a table, chairs, a wood-burning stove, and a nearby portable toilet. Groups reserving the yurt are limited to four nights.

Water is turned off seasonally at the North Kaibab trailhead and below the rim at Supai Tunnel, Roaring Springs, and Cottonwood Campground. Water is available at the North Rim's Backcountry Information Center (near the campground) during winter months. Always bring extra water in case of a pipeline break.

A Shining Beacon

Brighty's statue at Grand Canyon Lodge

Another member of Theodore Roosevelt's 1913 hunting party was Brighty, a burro named for Bright Angel Creek. A working animal, Brighty hauled water from a spring below the rim up to a tourist camp. He lived at the warmer canyon bottom in the winter and in the cooler rim forests in the summer, much beloved by the camp's children, who would ride him for hours on end.

Years later, author Marguerite Henry read about Brighty in an old *Sunset* magazine, and his real-life adventures became the basis for her award-winning children's book and later a movie, both titled *Brighty of Grand Canyon*. The film company commissioned artist Peter Jepson to create a bronze statue commemorating Brighty for the park's visitor center.

Years later, Brighty inspired the children who read about his adventures to help save his wild cousins from doom. Feral burros, descended from pack animals abandoned by Grand Canyon prospectors, numbered in the hundreds by the mid-1900s. Roaming burros damaged canyon trails and over-grazed native plants, impacting desert bighorn sheep and other species. A Park Service plan to shoot the burros from small planes was supported by environmental groups but shot down by a coalition that included schoolchildren, the Humane Society, and author and animal rights activist Cleveland Amory, who proposed airlifting burros from the canyon.

The airlift operation involved two helicopters, several horses, and a group of cowboys working morning and evening to herd, hobble, and secure each burro in a sling. Dangling from cables, the burros were lifted one by one from the canyon's depths as cameras recorded the operation for evening newscasts. By 1981 nearly 600 burros had been saved, thanks in part to children's letters to Congress, who responded by passing the Wild Free-Roaming Horse and Burro Act.

During the height of the controversy, park administrators decided to remove Brighty's statue from the visitor center, an act that only added fuel to the fire. Years later, Brighty was quietly returned to public view at Grand Canyon Lodge, where he sits today, a reminder not to underestimate the enduring power of childhood icons.

Entertainment and Shopping

North Rim night owls are the feathered kind, and star-studded entertainment is just that—gazing at the night sky. After a day in the great outdoors, most people are happy to hit the sack early and rest up for another full day of adventure. But if you're searching for something to do after sunset, the **Roughrider Saloon** (11:30am-10:30pm daily) occasionally hosts live acoustic music in the evenings. Located next to the lodge, the saloon is a relaxed spot to unwind over a hot coffee drink or a beer.

RANGER PROGRAMS

Free ranger programs are scheduled throughout the day and evening at various locations, including the terrace and auditorium of **Grand Canyon Lodge** and the **North Rim Campground** amphitheater. Ranger talks are entertaining and educational, and most are family friendly. For more information, refer to the *North Rim Pocket Map and Guide* or check the schedules posted in the visitor center, lodge, and campground.

EVENTS

Each June, the North Rim hosts a weeklong **Star Party** (the celestial kind, not the Hollywood variety). Miles from city lights, the skies here are velvety black, and the stars are breathtaking. During the annual star party, the lodge auditorium hosts a nightly slide show. Amateur astronomers volunteer their expertise and set up their telescopes outdoors on the lodge's terrace, where park visitors can view planets, constellations, nebulae, and galaxies. The festivities spill beyond park boundaries to Kaibab Lodge, a few miles north of the park entrance, where guests can eye the starry skies from telescopes provided by members of the Saguaro Astronomy Club (www. saguaroastro.org). Visit the website for future event dates.

In July, **Western Arts Day** celebrates pioneer culture with cowboy poetry and music, saddle-making, and other activities. A few weeks later, **Native American Heritage Days** focuses on the region's indigenous cultures. Past events have included cedar flute music and traditional dances. For more information, contact the **North Rim Visitor Center** (928/638-7870).

Also in August, the annual **Symphony of the Canyon** brings together musicians from southern Utah and northern Arizona. They perform a sunset concert on the lodge's terrace, usually for a standing room-only audience. Visit the symphony's website (www. symphonyofthecanyons.org) for more information.

SHOPPING

Shopping choices are limited on the North Rim, but if you run out of toothpaste or want to pick up a few souvenirs to take home, you'll find what you need. The **gift shop** (8am-9pm daily) in the lodge complex has a wide selection of items, including hiking hats, T-shirts, jewelry, Native American art, books, and plenty of souvenirs for the kiddies. Additional camping gear can be found at the campground's **General Store** (928/638-2611, ext. 270, 7am-8pm daily) along with sundries, snacks, and picnic supplies.

The Grand Canyon Association operates a small but superb bookstore at the **North Rim Visitor Center** (8am-6pm daily May 15-Oct. 15, 9am-4pm daily Oct. 16-31), stocking nature guides, posters, videos, and coffee-table books as well as learning-themed items for kids of all ages.

Outside the park, **Kaibab Lodge** (Hwy. 67, five miles north of the park entrance, 928/638-2389) has a selection of gifts and souvenirs, from cutesy, country-themed items to flint knives and arrowheads knapped by a local artisan.

If you're interested in Native American art, be sure to stop at the **Jacob Lake Inn** (928/643-7232), 45 miles north of the rim, near the junction of Highway 67 and U.S. 89A. The Navajo rugs decorating the walls of the dining room are for sale, as are silver and turquoise jewelry, sand paintings, pottery, kachinas, baskets, and other traditional crafts made by Navajo, Hopi, Zuni, and Paiute artists and artisans. The inn also has a wide selection of books, maps, and gifts.

Food

When dining at the North Rim, expect traditional American fare with an occasional Southwestern twist. Because this side of the canyon is more remote, dining options are fewer, and most venues close during the winter. Jacob Lake Inn stays open year-round, serving hearty meals to winter travelers. Casual dress is the norm—you might even spot the occasional cross-canyon hiker limping around in bedroom slippers.

INSIDE THE PARK
Grand Canyon Lodge
The ★ **Grand Canyon Lodge Dining Room** (www.grandcanyonforever.com/dining, 928/638-2611, ext. 760, breakfast 6:30am-10am, lunch 11:30am-2:30pm, dinner 4:30pm-9:30pm daily) is impressive: The high ceiling is supported by exposed log trusses (with hidden steel beams for support), and expansive windows overlook the Transept. The dining room uses all-natural, hormone- and antibiotic-free meats, organic vegetable selections, and fair-trade coffee and tea. Children's menus and gluten-free options are available.

The breakfast buffet ($14 adults, $8 children) includes something for everyone, from granola to hot items. From the menu, you can choose a hearty breakfast of eggs, pancakes, or country-fried steak ($9-13), or order lighter fare. For lunch, try the soup, sandwich, and salad bar ($14 adults, $8 children), or order from menu selections ($6-20) such as burgers, elk chili, and Navajo tacos.

Grand Canyon Lodge Dining Room

Dinner choices ($15-45) include light fare and Western classics like prime rib, grilled salmon, or venison. **Dinner reservations** (928/645-6865 Jan.-Apr., 928/638-2611 May-Oct.) are required and can be made as early as February 1 of the year you arrive. If you arrive without a reservation, check with the dining room host or hostess. You may be able to get a table, especially if you're willing to wait for a seating after 8pm. Another option is the **dinner buffet** (4:30pm-7pm daily), held in the auditorium. Opt for all-you-can-eat or one-time-through and head out to the lodge's **veranda,** for an al fresco meal with stunning views.

West of the lodge's main entrance you'll find the **Deli in the Pines** (10:30am-9pm daily). Selections range from grab-and-go salads and sandwiches to pizza and soft-serve ice cream. Most items are under $10. The deli lacks atmosphere, but you can take your sandwich and find a pleasant spot under the trees.

ROUGHRIDER SALOON

Just east of the lodge entrance, the **coffee shop** (5:30am-10:30am daily) serves the earliest—and best—cup of joe along with an assortment of pastries or breakfast burritos. Later in the day, it magically transforms into the **Roughrider Saloon** (11am-11pm daily), offering appetizers and snacks to accompany soft drinks, beer, wine, and cocktails.

OUTSIDE THE PARK
Kaibab Lodge

Seven miles north of the park entrance, **Kaibab Lodge** (Hwy. 67, 928/638-2389, www.kaibablodge.com, daily mid-May-Oct. 25, $4-25), cooks up hearty breakfasts and casual dinners. From the dining room's large windows, you can watch deer grazing in the meadows morning and evening. Boxed breakfasts or lunches are prepared on request. Children's menus are also available.

Across the highway from the Kaibab Lodge, the **North Rim Country Store** (928/638-2383, 7:30am-7pm daily May 15-Nov. 2) has a limited selection of snacks and camping supplies as well as souvenirs, newspapers, and fuel.

Jacob Lake

Jacob Lake Inn (928/643-7232, www.jacoblake.com, 6:30am-9pm daily summer-fall, 8am-8pm daily winter-spring, $6-25) serves breakfast, lunch, and dinner year-round to grateful guests and travelers. If you arrive at the restaurant at the same time as a bus tour, consider skipping the dining room experience and head for the small deli where you can pick up a loaf of freshly baked bread and a bottle of wine for a picnic. But if you lack willpower, avert your eyes when you pass by the bakery counter's glass cases: The giant, homemade cookies are irresistible.

Accommodations

Although there are fewer visitors to this side of the canyon, summer is the North Rim's busiest season, and lodging availability is limited. Bright Angel Point makes an ideal hub, with accommodations at the lodge or the campground. Most activities and services are centered here, including food, ranger programs, and hiking trailheads.

Plan early and make reservations, or you may find yourself anxiously awaiting cancellations or commuting from far outside the park. Be sure you understand cancellation policies; many lodges on this side of the canyon require advance notice of cancellations to avoid forfeiting a deposit. If you hope to visit during the annual Star Party in June, or in early October, when fall colors splash across plateau forests, make reservations a year in advance. Campgrounds fill up quickly all season long.

If Grand Canyon Lodge and the North Rim Campground are booked, expand your search to Kaibab Lodge (18 miles), Jacob Lake (45 miles), or Kanab (82 miles).

INSIDE THE PARK
Grand Canyon Lodge

★ **Grand Canyon Lodge** (877/386-4383, http://grandcanyonlodgenorth.com, $124-182, May-Oct.) has more than 200 guest rooms, but they book quickly. Reservations are accepted beginning in July for the next season. Last-minute rooms due to cancellations are possible—check at the lobby desk on your arrival. Rooms range from historic cabins to motel-style accommodations. All have private baths, and all are nonsmoking. A few of the cabins meet ADA-accessibility standards. No pets are allowed in the lodge buildings, including the guest cabins. Rates listed below do not include tax. Rollaway cots can be delivered to some guest rooms for an additional charge.

The Craftsman-inspired **Western cabins** ($199-221) east of the lodge are the North Rim's nicest, complete with shady porches and rocking chairs. Each cabin has two queen beds, a full bath, and a mini fridge. Rim-view cabins overlook Bright Angel Canyon.

On the west side of the lodge are the **Frontier** ($141) and **Pioneer cabins** ($181-191). Each Frontier cabin has a shower, a double and a single bed, and can accommodate up to three people. The larger Pioneer cabins can accommodate up to six in two rooms, one with a queen, mini fridge, and coffeepot, the other with a twin bed and a full-size futon, with a shared shower in between. Some of the Pioneer cabins overlook Transept Canyon.

Motel-style guest rooms ($130) may lack the atmosphere of the cabins, but they have all the basics, including a queen bed and a shower, plus a mini fridge. (Television, by the way, is not considered a basic. If having one in your room is a must, your nearest option is Jacob Lake Inn.)

Campgrounds

Because North Rim elevations range 6,300-8,000 feet, campers should be prepared for cool evenings, even in the summer. Inside the park, camping is permitted only in designated campsites; violators may be cited and fined. If you plan on spending the night in the backcountry (including Point Sublime or Cape Final), a **backcountry permit** is required.

Western cabins at Grand Canyon Lodge are built from native stone.

NORTH RIM CAMPGROUND

The **North Rim Campground** (877/444-6777, www.recreation.gov, May 15-Oct. 15, $18-25) has 80-plus sites, available by reservation only. Sites can be reserved two days to six months in advance, up to a year in advance for the three group campsites. Senior and Access pass holders qualify for a 50 percent discount. A maximum of two vehicles, three tents, and six people are allowed per site. Towed trailers, pop-ups, and campers count as a second vehicle. Some sites accommodate RVs up to 40 feet. There are no hookups, but there is a dump station. Generator hours are strictly enforced.

Sites 11, 14-16, and 18 are considered premium sites because they have canyon views. Even more scenic are the tent-only sites perched at the rim of Transept Canyon, a reward for minimalism. (Tent-only sites have a 16-foot square pad and require walking a few steps from a shared parking lot.) A communal area along the canyon's edge has additional space for hikers and bikers.

The campground is shaded by ponderosa pines, with the General Store and coin-operated showers and laundry a short stroll away.

Both the Transept Trail and the Bridle Path connect the campground to the lodge, about a mile away. Pets are allowed in the campground but must be leashed and cannot be left unattended. Charcoal or wood fires are permitted in campsite grills. Wood gathering is not permitted; wood can be purchased at the General Store.

After the lodge, restaurants, and other facilities close on October 15, campsites and limited services may be available on a first-come, first-served basis until snow closes Highway 67. Group campsites are available throughout the winter to hikers, snowshoers, and skiers with a backcountry permit. A permit is also needed to reserve the North Rim **winter yurt,** available December 1 to April 15.

OUTSIDE THE PARK
Kaibab Lodge

The nearest rooms outside the park are in **Kaibab Lodge** (Hwy. 67, 928/638-2389, www.kaibablodge.com, May 15-Oct. 20, $90-185), 18 miles north of Bright Angel Point. The historic main building, a former cattle ranch constructed in the 1920s, sits at the edge

the winter yurt at North Rim Campground

of DeMotte Park, a meadow along Highway 67. Comfortable and homey, it has a pleasant dining room with meadow views, a gift shop, and a lounge anchored by a stone fireplace on one side and a TV on the other.

Guest accommodations vary from rustic "hikers' specials" with a double bed and shower to larger cabins accommodating up to eight people. All guest rooms have private baths and heaters but no TVs or phones. All are nonsmoking. Special rates are available for groups (10 rooms or more). Pet-friendly rooms are available, and the lodge offers pet-sitting services.

Jacob Lake

About 45 miles north of Bright Angel Point, at the intersection of Highway 67 and U.S. 89A, **Jacob Lake Inn** (928/643-7232, www.jacoblake.com, $96-146) has welcomed North Rim visitors for more than 80 years. Accommodations include rustic cabins, a vintage motel, and a modern hotel. All rooms are nonsmoking. Pets are allowed in some guest rooms. Rates are discounted in winter, when the inn becomes a hub for snowmobilers, cross-country skiers, and snowshoers.

Cabins ($90-140) have one or two rooms with doubles, queens, or kings and can accommodate two to four people. Family cabins have two rooms and can accommodate up to six people. All cabins have small decks for enjoying the numerous birds that frequent the woodsy setting—but no air-conditioning, TV, phones, or Internet access. **Motel rooms** ($128) have air-conditioning; they come with doubles or queens and accommodate up to four people. **Hotel rooms** ($146) have two queens or a king for two to four people and include TVs, phones, and air-conditioning. Family units can be arranged with adjoining rooms.

Campgrounds

DeMotte Campground (928/643-7395, www.fs.usda.gov/kaibab, May 14-Oct. 15, $18) is located 18 miles north of the rim and six miles north of the entrance station on the edge of a meadow just off Highway 67. Operated by the U.S. Forest Service, the campground has 38 sites for up to six people with tables and grills, drinking water, and vault toilets. Tents, trailers, and small motor homes are allowed, but there are no hookups. Half the sites are available by **reservation** (877/444-6777, www.recreation.gov); the other half are available on a first-come, first-served basis. The campground does fill up, so arrive early. Campers can dine at nearby Kaibab Lodge and shop for supplies at the North Rim Country Store, both less than a mile away.

The Forest Service also operates ★ **Jacob Lake Campground** (928/643-7395, www.fs.usda.gov/kaibab, May 14-Oct. 15, $18) 45 miles north of the rim at the intersection of U.S. 89A and Highway 67. The campground has two group sites and 51 sites for up to six people. Half are available by **reservation** (877/444-6777, www.recreation.gov) and half on a first-come, first-served basis. Sites can accommodate tents, trailers, or small motor homes, but there are no hookups. Amenities include tables and grills, drinking water, and toilets. Nearby, campers will find horseback and nature trails as well as the amenities of Jacob Lake Inn.

Kaibab Camper Village (Forest Rd. 461, 928/643-7804 or 800/525-0924, off-season 928/526-0924, http://kaibabcampervillage. com, May 15-Oct. 15, $17-85) is located just south of Jacob Lake, less than one mile off Highway 67. The campground offers sites with full hookups for RVs ($36), dry sites and tent sites ($17), and a small cabin with two queens ($85). A small fee ($4-11) is added for additional guests and vehicles. Amenities include fire pits, picnic tables, toilets, outdoor sinks, laundry, and showers. The camp store has groceries and supplies. The forest service offers interpretive programs at the nearby ranger cabin. As a bonus, park hosts can hook you up with guided horseback tours or river-rafting trips.

Dispersed camping is allowed in **Kaibab**

National Forest (928/643-7395, www. fs.usda.gov/kaibab, free). Restrictions include stays no longer than 14 days and no camping within 100 yards of the highway or near the East Rim Day Use Area along Forest Road 611. Campsites are accessible by dirt roads, many of them suitable for passenger cars. For road conditions and maps with camping suggestions, visit the Kaibab Plateau Visitor Center (928/643-7298, 8am-4pm daily mid-May-mid-Oct., some weekends through Nov.) in Jacob Lake.

Transportation and Services

Scenic **Highway 67** is the only paved route to the North Rim. U.S. 89A intersects Highway 67 from the east (Marble Canyon area) and northwest (Fredonia and Kanab). All routes to the North Rim converge at Jacob Lake, 30 miles from the park's north entrance station on Highway 67. From the entrance station, it's another 14 miles south to the lodge and visitor services at Bright Angel Point.

Getting around the park's North Rim in your own vehicle is a breeze. With the exception of the large public parking lot shared by the lodge and visitor center, and the occasional wait at the entrance gate, you've left traffic congestion far behind you on the canyon's South Rim.

For park road conditions, check with the **North Rim Visitor Center** (928/638-2481 or 928/638-7496 for recorded message, 8am-6pm daily). For forest road conditions, contact the **Kaibab Plateau Visitor Center** (928/643-7298, 8am-4pm daily mid-May-mid-Oct.). For information about highway conditions, contact the **Arizona Department of Transportation** (dial 511 or 888/411-7623, www.az511.gov).

Driving and Parking

Keep your gas tank full if you plan on backroad explorations. You can fuel up at the **Chevron station** (8am-5pm daily or pay at the pump 24-7, mid-May-Oct.), along the entrance road to the North Rim Campground. Minor car repairs are also available here. After the park closes to overnight visitors in the fall, gas pumps remain accessible 24 hours a day with a credit card until December 1.

The nearest fuel available outside the park is at the **North Rim Country Store** (928/638-2383, 7:30am-7pm daily mid-May-mid-Oct.), across the highway from Kaibab Lodge, about seven miles from the park entrance station. Basic mechanic services and propane can also be found at the service station next to **Jacob Lake Inn** (928/643-7232). Gas is available here year-round, with 24-7 pay-at-the-pump service.

Shuttles

The **hiker shuttle** travels from Grand Canyon Lodge to the North Kaibab Trail (1.5 miles away) twice each morning (5:45am and 7:10am daily); reservations can be made at the front desk of the lodge and are required 24 hours in advance. The shuttle is complimentary for lodge guests (nonguests $7 pp).

Kaibab Lodge (928/638-2389, www.kaibablodge.com), 18 miles north of the rim, offers ATV tours and shuttle services to Bright Angel Point.

TO THE SOUTH RIM

From the North Rim, it's 215 miles (4.5 hours) by car to the South Rim. From the lodge at Bright Angel Point, drive north on Highway 67 to Jacob Lake. Turn right (east) on U.S. 89A and continue through the Marble Canyon area and across Navajo Bridge. Turn right (south) on U.S. 89. At Cameron, turn right (east) on Highway 64 and proceed to the park's East

Where Can I Find...?

- **ATMs:** ATMs are in the Roughrider Saloon (east of the lodge's main entrance), the General Store (adjacent to the campground), and outside the park at the North Rim Country Store.

- **Laundry:** A public, coin-operated laundry (7am-10pm daily) is located along the entrance road to the North Rim Campground.

- **Lost and Found:** Check at the Visitor Center (928/638-2481) or the front desk of Grand Canyon Lodge (480/998-1981 or 888/386-4383).

- **Pay Phones:** Cell phone service can be iffy on the North Rim; there's a bank of pay phones behind the visitor center.

- **Post Office:** Look for the mail window (8am-noon and 1pm-5pm Mon.-Fri.) next to the gift shop.

- **Public Restrooms:** Located behind the visitor center, in the lodge complex adjacent to the deli, and at the General Store in the North Rim Campground. All are wheelchair accessible.

- **Religious Services:** Check the bulletin board inside the Grand Canyon Lodge for a schedule of religious services.

- **Showers:** The building along the entrance road to the North Rim Campground has coin-operated showers (7am-8pm daily).

- **Water:** Individual water bottles are not available. Bring (or buy) refillable containers, and fill them up for free at any of the North Rim's three "filling stations" (the visitor center, the backcountry office, and North Kaibab Trailhead).

- **Wi-Fi:** If you can't log on at the lodge, head for the porch of the General Store (adjacent to the campground).

Entrance Station at Desert View. From here, it's another 30 miles to Grand Canyon Village.

Two companies offer shuttle service between the North and South Rims, a 4.5-hour trip with stops in the Marble Canyon area. Reservations are required. The **Trans Canyon Shuttle** (877/638-2820 or 928/638-2820, www.trans-canyonshuttle.com, 7am and 2pm daily May 15-Oct. 16, 2pm daily Oct. 16-31, $90 one-way) leaves the North Rim twice daily in high season. Charter shuttles can be arranged, and bag-only deliveries ($25) are available. **Grand Canyon Shuttle Service** (888/215-3105, www.grandcanyon-shuttles.com) has 24-7 customizable on-demand service between the rims, a good option for groups. Call or email (admin@flagshuttle.com) for more information.

SERVICES
Groceries and Supplies

Inside the park at the North Rim Campground, the **General Store** (928/638-2611, 7am-8pm daily) sells camping and picnic supplies, snacks, groceries, and sundries, from insect dope to bars of soap. You can take your sandwich or ice cream bar outside to the shady veranda, where a couple of small tables offer a comfortable spot to watch campground comings and goings, or log onto free Wi-Fi.

Emergencies

For emergencies, dial 911, adding an extra 9 (9-911) if you're calling from a lodge phone. Cell phone reception is spotty, even along the rim. If you're closer to the river, you may be able to flag down a rafting party. River

The North Rim's General Store sells camping and picnic supplies.

guides carry satellite phones for emergencies (928/638-7911). Helicopter evacuations are very expensive, so it's best to avoid hiking emergencies by planning thoroughly.

EMT-certified rangers can respond 24 hours a day to medical emergencies. The nearest clinic is more than 80 miles away in Kanab, Utah. Hospitals are even farther, located in Page, Flagstaff, and St. George, Utah.

If you are hiking the North Kaibab Trail, the only emergency phone is located at the Cottonwood Campground, seven miles below the rim. The Tuweep Ranger Station has an emergency phone.

The Inner Canyon

Only 5 percent of visitors enter Grand Canyon's inner reaches. The rest don't know what they're missing. Below the canyon rims, grand views shift to microcosmic experiences—glimpses of darting lizards or ancient pictographs,

the sound of a creek tumbling over stones, the changing colors and textures of rock as the miles pass. Time seems to slow with every footfall, hoof beat, or sweep of an oar.

Along the chilly waters of the Colorado River, you can touch rocks that are two billion years old. You can hear the power of a churning rapid and watch sunset colors lift from canyon walls as shadows creep higher. If you've made it this far, you'll be spending the night under a narrow ribbon of sky, tucked into your sleeping bag or enjoying the hospitality of Phantom Ranch, a cluster of cottonwood-shaded cabins offering cold beer, hot showers, and mail service by mule train.

The only way to get to this oasis along Bright Angel Creek is on foot, by mule, or by rafting the Colorado River. Outside the central corridor formed by Bright Angel, South Kaibab, and North Kaibab trails, the canyon is desert wilderness contrasted by 160-plus white-water rapids, more than a dozen waterfalls, and countless side canyons with hidden seeps and springs.

To see them, you'll pay for the privilege with time, effort, and sweat. There are no easy trails into or out of the canyon, as the park service warns, and even mule tours and river trips demand a certain level of attention and fitness. Summer temperatures soar into the hundreds, with little or no water on most trails. Unmaintained trails become faint routes that require sharp orienteering skills and backcountry strategies. The Colorado River's peaceful greenish blue hides dangerous currents and bone-chilling cold. Fierce summer thunderstorms spout lightning and send debris-laden water racing down side canyons and slopes.

The dangers are real, but don't let them scare you away. Those who approach the inner canyon with preparation and humility will earn a place in its heart.

Previous: rafting the Inner Canyon; desert bighorn sheep. **Above:** a resting dragonfly.

The Inner Canyon

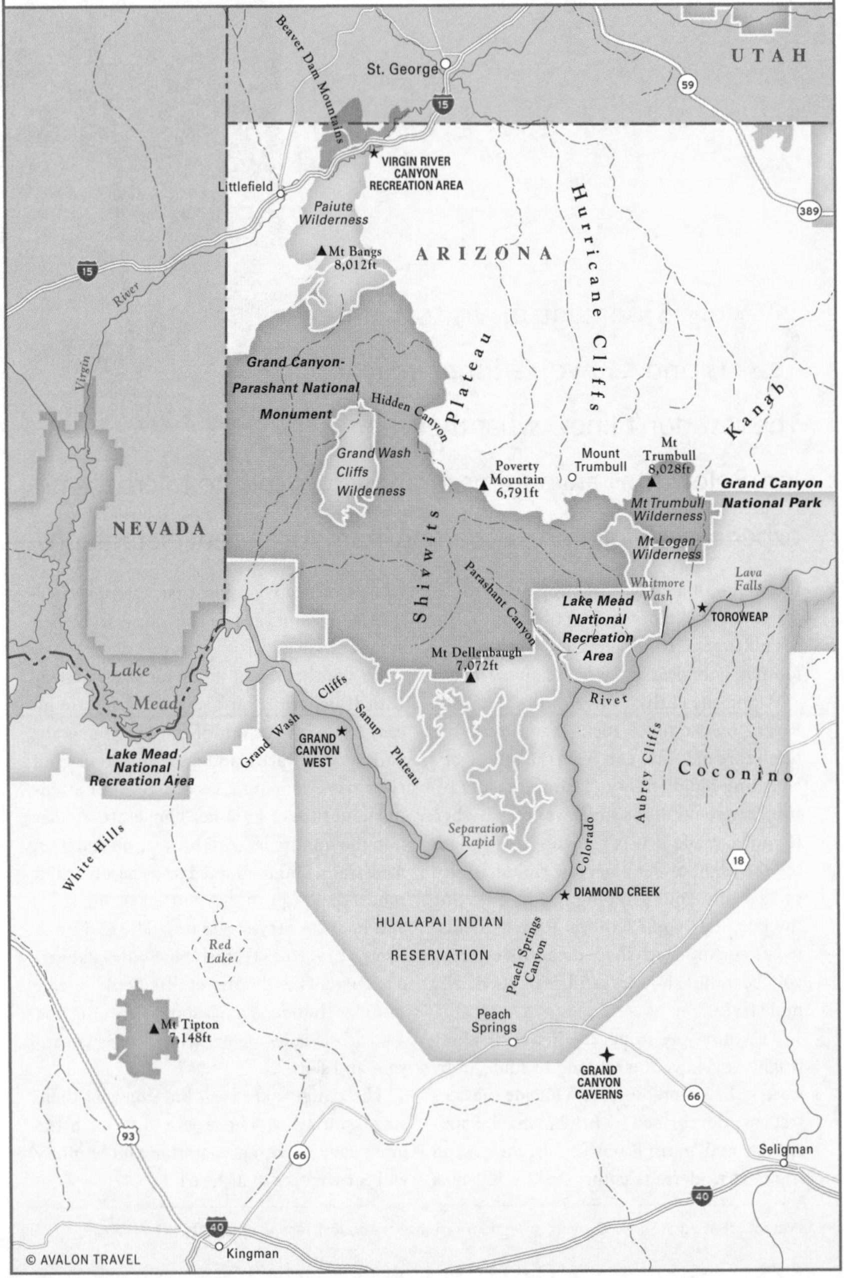

UTAH

St. George

Beaver Dam Mountains

VIRGIN RIVER CANYON RECREATION AREA

Littlefield

Paiute Wilderness

Mt Bangs 8,012ft

ARIZONA

Hurricane Cliffs

Grand Canyon-Parashant National Monument

Hidden Canyon

Shivwits Plateau

Kanab

Grand Wash Cliffs Wilderness

Poverty Mountain 6,791ft

Mount Trumbull

Mt Trumbull 8,028ft

Grand Canyon National Park

NEVADA

Mt Trumbull Wilderness

Mt Logan Wilderness

Parashant Canyon

Whitmore Wash

Lava Falls

Lake Mead National Recreation Area

TOROWEAP

Mt Dellenbaugh 7,072ft

Lake Mead

River

Lake Mead National Recreation Area

Grand Wash Cliffs

Sanup Plateau

GRAND CANYON WEST

Coconino

Aubrey Cliffs

White Hills

Separation Rapid

Colorado

Red Lake

DIAMOND CREEK

18

Mt Tipton 7,148ft

HUALAPAI INDIAN RESERVATION

Peach Springs Canyon

Peach Springs

GRAND CANYON CAVERNS

66

Seligman

93

66

40

Kingman

40

© AVALON TRAVEL

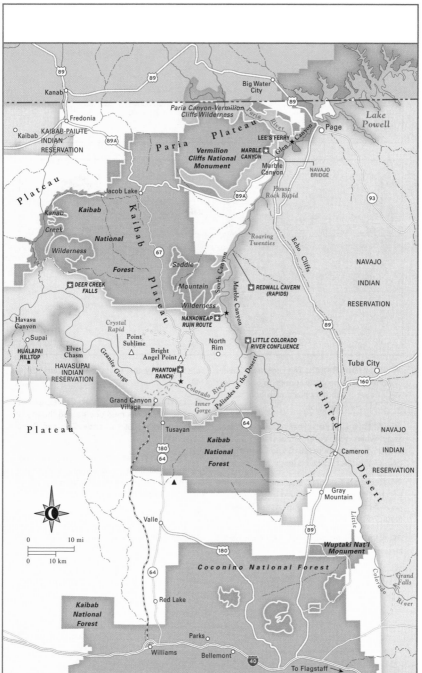

Look for ★ to find recommended
sights, activities, dining, and lodging.

Highlights

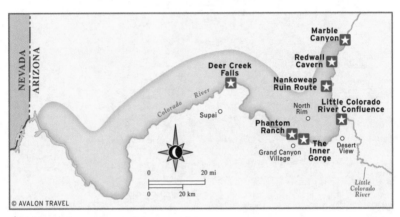

★ **Phantom Ranch:** This creek-side cluster of stone-and-wood cabins designed by architect Mary Colter is the only place with hot showers and cold beer (page 135).

★ **Marble Canyon:** Feel worldly cares melt away when you enter sheer-walled Marble Canyon, the introduction to Grand Canyon's gorgeous Paleozoic rock layers (page 145).

★ **Redwall Cavern:** Stop for lunch on the beach at this large cave, carved by the Colorado River from the Redwall limestone formation (page 147).

★ **Nankoweap Ruin Route:** Scramble up a steep route to these 1,000-year-old granaries,

constructed by the Ancestral Puebloans (page 148).

★ **Little Colorado River Confluence:** Pause to play in the mud pools along the warm turquoise waters of the Little Colorado River (page 148).

★ **The Inner Gorge:** Marvel at schist and granite two billion years old as the Colorado River swings west, entering the darker, harder rocks of the Inner Gorge (page 149).

★ **Deer Creek Falls:** Frolic under the spray of this 100-foot-high waterfall as it tumbles out of Tapeats sandstone on the lower river (page 151).

PLANNING YOUR TIME

If your goal is to reach the Colorado River, take note: The National Park Service strongly discourages anyone from attempting to hike from rim to river and back in a day. This means you'll need to prepare ahead to **spend at least one night in the canyon.**

An overnight canyon trip isn't something to do on impulse: Careful planning and preparation are essential. You may need weeks or months of lead time to apply for backcountry permits or to make tour reservations. You may also need time to improve your personal fitness, even for a one- or two-night mule trip from the South Rim. It's possible to backpack the canyon's central corridor in **one or two nights,** but it's preferable to spend three or more on wilderness trails from rim to river, and **one to three weeks** if you plan to explore the length of the inner canyon by raft.

Because of the myriad challenges (heat, limited water, remoteness, topography), the inner canyon is an area best experienced with companions. If you haven't been to Grand Canyon before, or if you and your companions don't have a lot of hiking experience, consider joining a guided trip that matches your interests and abilities.

Backcountry Permits

Permits are required for overnight hiking and backpacking, river camping, or any camping outside developed campgrounds. Permit applications can be made up to four months in advance and can be submitted online, in person, and by mail or fax to **Grand Canyon Permits Office** (National Park Service, 1824 S. Thompson St., Suite 201, Flagstaff, AZ 86001, fax 928/638-2125, www.nps.gov/grca). Fees are $10 per permit, plus $8 pp per night if you are camping below the rim or $8 per group per night if you are camping above the rim. The lengthy and detailed process is explained further in the *Essentials* chapter (page 281) and on the park website.

Exploring the Inner Canyon

Foot, mule, or boat—those are your choices for exploring the inner canyon. Backpacking and hiking excursions will originate from river or rims. Mule trips begin from the South Rim year-round. Most white-water raft trips put in at Lees Ferry on Grand Canyon's eastern end. If these options seem limited, well, that's what makes a trip inside Grand Canyon rare and special. Even if you ride on a raft or mule, you need to be relatively fit to handle the terrain and temperatures. Mental attitude is even more important: Determination, focus, and a sense of adventure can make the difference between a positive experience and an ordeal. You may be here to learn about the canyon, but in the process you'll learn more about yourself.

TOURS

Guided trips and tours to the inner canyon include mule tours, backpacking trips, and commercial river trips. Mule trips from the South Rim to Phantom Ranch are scheduled year-round. The best times for backpacking are spring and fall, although during winter, when both rims may be covered with snow, inner canyon temperatures average 50-60°F—great hiking weather.

Mule Trips

Mule trips to the inner canyon originate from either rim. The **Phantom Ranch Mule Tour** (303/297-2757 or 888/297-2757, daily year-round, 1 night $552, 2 nights $961, reduced rates for 2 or more people) departs from the South Rim and is the only mule trip with an

Phantom Ranch

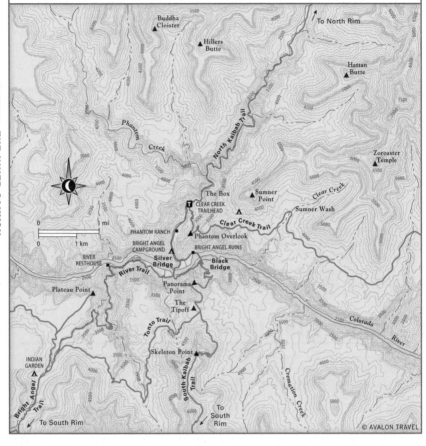

overnight in the canyon. Reservations can be made up to 13 months in advance. Tours fill up quickly, but last-minute cancellations are possible, and you can add your name to the waiting list at one of the transportation desks when you arrive at the canyon. The waiting list is shortest in winter, when cancellations are most likely.

Backpacking Tours

If you've never backpacked before, it's a good idea to make your first overnight hike to the inner canyon with a guide and other travelers. Not only will you be safer, you'll also learn

much more about the canyon's flora, fauna, and geology, enriching your experience as you gain new skills.

Backpacking trips led by the **Grand Canyon Association Field Institute** (GCAFI, 928/638-2485 or 866/471-4435, gcfi@grandcanyon.org, www.grandcanyon.org/fieldinstitute, $650-900) last two or more nights and focus on a variety of topics such as basic wilderness skills, photography, or geology. Some beginner classes are suited to kids 12 and older, accompanied by a parent or adult guardian. Participants must be able to carry a pack weighing 30-50 pounds,

a mule tour approaching Phantom Ranch

although occasional mule-assisted trips are offered. As a nonprofit organization and park partner, GCFI also leads service trips, such as archaeological surveys.

Road Scholar (800/454-5768, www.road-scholar.org) offers several Grand Canyon trips, including an all-inclusive rim-to-rim backpack with a layover at Phantom Ranch. Formerly known as Elderhostel, Road Scholar now includes family tours and grandkid getaways.

More than 20 concessionaires hold permits to lead backpacking trips within the canyon, among them nationally known organizations like **National Outdoor Leadership School** (800/710-6657, www.nols.edu) and regional guide services such as **Discovery Treks** (480/247-9266 or 888/256-8731, www. discoverytreks.com) and **Four Seasons Guides** (928/525-1552 or 877/272-5032, www.fsguides.com). Look for guides who have Grand Canyon experience, wilderness first aid certification, and wilderness first responder (WFR) training, and don't be shy about asking for testimonials from past clients.

A riparian oasis situated between Bright Angel Creek and the Colorado River, **Phantom Ranch** (303/297-2757 or 888/297-2757, www.grandcanyonlodges.com) opened in 1922. Begun as a rustic inner canyon camp operated by canyon pioneer David Rust, it was modernized and expanded by architect Mary Colter. The cluster of guest cabins and a canteen, shaded by cottonwoods and surrounded by native seep willow and coyote willow, are the only accommodations in the inner canyon. In the 1930s the young men of the Civilian Conservation Corps (CCC) stayed here while improving canyon trails and amenities. Though decades have passed, Phantom Ranch retains the warm and welcoming ambience of a family-run guest ranch. Keep your camera handy: Deer, foxes, and other critters enjoy this Eden as much as hikers, mule riders, and river runners do.

Those who spend a night or two will find plenty to explore. The CCC-built **River Trail** overlooks the south side of the river, leading to Pipe Creek. On the opposite side of the river, the CCC also built **Clear Creek Trail,** which climbs the cliffs for hawk's-eye views of Phantom Ranch and the Inner Gorge. But it's almost as entertaining to lounge near the Boat Beach and watch mule wranglers, river guides, and park rangers go about their daily routines.

HIKING AND BACKPACKING

Inner canyon trails range from rigorous multiday backpacking adventures to short explorations from river camps. Backpackers often make the Colorado River their goal, but "halfway hikes" can also be very rewarding, offering beautiful river panoramas from viewpoints on the **Tonto Trail** or along the **Esplanade.** Hiking the inner canyon adds an intimate perspective, revealing details that are hidden from the rim.

Keep in mind that the Navajo, Hualapai, and Havasupai nations hold land surrounding the park. Be sure to apply for permits from their offices if you will be hiking into or across reservation lands. Once your group has set up camp, your backcountry permit must be displayed in plain view (such as on a pack or tent) so that rangers can check it easily. Much of the inner canyon is wilderness—hike with others and be aware that help is a long way away.

Planning Your Hike

A permit is not necessary to day hike in Grand Canyon National Park, but in order to camp anywhere other than the developed rim campgrounds, a **backcountry permit** is required. You'll need to spend at least one night in the canyon, and that means applying for a backcountry permit months ahead.

At river elevations of 1,200-3,200 feet, the inner canyon's Sonoran Desert climate is like being in Tucson or Phoenix. Expect a 20- to 30-degree difference between rims and river, choosing gear—and food—accordingly. **Sun protection** is crucial: appropriate clothing, a hat, sunglasses, and sunblock. Many trails have exposed sections, and at midday even the river is in full sun. The Park Service recommends staying off exposed trails from 10am to 2pm or later in summer months. Some hikers hit the trail well before dawn in order to reach a shady rest area like Indian Garden, and then resume hiking in late afternoon.

A light, long-sleeved shirt can help shield you from the intense desert rays. For **summer** hikes, thin cotton works well. The rest of the year, polyester fleece and quick-drying fabrics

are best. Be prepared for afternoon showers during Arizona's **monsoon season,** July to mid-September. If you are hiking near the rims during **winter** months, you may need crampons, for sale or rent at the General Store.

Bring boots that are broken in, extra socks, and an emergency kit. Pack salty snacks and **adequate water.** Water supply issues due to pipeline breaks and pump failures are becoming increasingly likely as the canyon's infrastructure ages. A critical section of the 16-mile long transcanyon pipeline was replaced in 2015, but the cost of full replacement has been estimated at $100-150 million. (Think that's a lot of money? The park's deferred maintenance backlog is estimated at $330 million, and the entire national park system is underfunded to the tune of nearly $12 billion.) Backpackers and hikers should be prepared to carry all drinking water or to treat creek water.

A good trail map is a must for wilderness backpackers, along with an understanding of desert hiking and route-finding. For example, "Creek" on a map might refer to a dry wash, a year-round stream, or a stream that flows seasonally during spring melt or briefly after a rainstorm. Always research potential water sources. Good resources include the park's website (www.nps.gov/grca), detailed hiking guides, and the Facebook group managed by the **Grand Canyon Hikers and Backpackers Association** (www.gchba.org).

Inner Canyon Hikes

Trail	Effort	Distance	Duration
Plateau Point	easy	3.4 miles round-trip from Indian Garden	2 hours
Clear Creek Trail	moderate to strenuous	18 miles round-trip	2 days or more
Beamer Trail	moderate	19 miles round-trip	2 days or more
Tonto Trail	moderate to strenuous	93 miles from Garnet Canyon to Red Canyon	multiple days

Water: Too Much or Too Little?

Garden Creek as seen from Bright Angel Trail

The National Park Service recommends that hikers drink a quart of water every 30 minutes to one hour while hiking. Because sweat evaporates rapidly in the canyon's high elevation and low humidity, you might not realize how much moisture you're losing. Don't wait until you feel thirsty to drink. The earliest signs of dehydration can be very subtle: crankiness and mild headache.

If you're hiking the Bright Angel or North Kaibab Trails, you can usually refill your water bottles at trailside **resthouses.** If you're planning a long hike in warmer weather, it's important to research water availability before you set out. Water from springs, creeks, and the Colorado River must be filtered or treated before drinking.

Hikers should be prepared with a few iodine pills. Although **iodine pills** aren't recommended for several days' use, they are handy for emergencies, such as a broken pipeline or a failed water filter.

Just as dangerous as dehydration is water intoxication, or **hyponatremia.** This happens when hikers drink water without replacing electrolytes—the minerals that nerves and muscles need to function. Pack salty snacks, eating a little each time you take a water break, or mix an electrolyte-replacement powder or concentrate with your water.

Rangers treat up to 20 cases of heat exhaustion (serious dehydration) each summer day, but water intoxication is also common. Some symptoms of hyponatremia are very similar to heat stroke: altered judgment, nausea, and arrhythmia.

Plateau Point

Distance: 3.4 miles round-trip from Indian Garden
Duration: 2 hours
Elevation change: 30 feet
Effort: Easy
Trailhead: Indian Garden (see map p. 134)

This side trail leaves from the **Bright Angel Trail**'s Indian Garden rest area, following the Tonto Trail for about 0.75 miles before forking northwest. It's another 0.75 miles to the point itself, where hikers have a fine view of the Colorado River snaking through the Inner Gorge, 1,300 feet below. It's an easy day hike for campers at Indian Garden, but making it a side-trip on a rim-to-river hike bumps up total mileage and hike time to challenging levels.

Clear Creek Trail

Distance: 18 miles round-trip
Duration: 2 days or more
Elevation gain: 1,520 feet
Effort: Moderate to strenuous
Trailhead: 0.3 miles north of Phantom Ranch (see map p. 134)

The Clear Creek Trail climbs up to the Tonto Platform before descending again to Clear Creek. For backpackers or mule riders staying at Bright Angel Campground or Phantom Ranch, a couple of miles on the Clear Creek Trail make a scenic side trip, though it's dangerously hot and dry in the summer. There are campsites and a pit toilet at **Clear Creek,** the trail's only water source. Spring backpackers may see seasonal **Cheyava Falls,** while day hikers at any time of year can enjoy aerial views of **Phantom Ranch** and the **Silver and Black Bridges.**

From its junction with the **North Kaibab Trail,** the Clear Creek Trail ascends 0.75 miles to **Phantom Overlook,** a good day-hike destination with views of Bright Angel Canyon and the oasis of Phantom Ranch, 550 feet below. When the Civilian Conservation Corps constructed the Clear Creek Trail, they made a bench of Vishnu schist so hikers could rest and enjoy the view. The trail continues up to the rim of Granite Gorge, offering stunning views up and down the river. Another good turnaround point for a day hike is **Sumner Wash,** about 2.5 miles from the trailhead, where the trail turns north, away from the gorge, to reach the Tonto Platform.

The trail rises gradually through the Tonto's scrubby desert terrain, with wide-open eastern views, before reaching the edge of Clear Creek Canyon. From here, it's a steep descent to the creek and its cottonwood-shaded campsites. Depending on the season, adventurous hikers may want to explore farther: It's another five miles north to **Cheyava Falls,** tumbling 800 feet from the Redwall during spring snowmelt. The rough route crosses the streambed several times. For those with rock-climbing skills, it's the same distance south to the Colorado River.

Tonto Trail

Distance: 93 miles from Garnet Canyon to Red Canyon
Duration: Multiple days
Elevation gain: 1,200 feet
Effort: Moderate to strenuous
Trailhead: Accessed from other trails, including Bright Angel Trail

The Tonto Trail crosses the Tonto Platform,

Despite its name, Clear Creek Trail is dry and exposed.

a broad east-west shelf of Tapeats sandstone roughly two-thirds of the way from rim to river. The Tapeats forms the rim of the canyon's Inner Gorge, a steep-walled canyon-within-a-canyon. Backpackers use the Tonto Trail as a connector to make loops with other trails. The most traveled segments are the four-mile section closing the loop between the **Bright Angel** and **South Kaibab Trails,** and the 12-mile link between the **Bright Angel** and **Hermit Trails.**

If you're planning a loop route anywhere in the canyon, be sure to research water sources and cache points in advance. Although the Tonto Platform appears relatively level from rim overlooks, the trail climbs up and down numerous drainages across the shadeless and dry Upper Sonoran Zone. The terrain can make route-finding a challenge, and summer heat is deadly. In *The Man Who Walked Through Time,* Colin Fletcher described his two-month-long journey through the length of the inner canyon, much of it over the Tonto Platform.

Beamer Trail

Distance: 19 miles round-trip
Duration: 2 days or more
Elevation gain: 960 feet

Effort: Moderate
Trailhead: Tanner Beach or Little Colorado River confluence

More route than trail, this path paralleling the Colorado River leads to the remnants of Ben Beamer's cabin. Beamer, a prospector who arrived at the canyon around 1890, remodeled an Ancestral Puebloan dwelling to fashion a cabin at the mouth of the Little Colorado River. His trail followed part of the salt trail, a pilgrimage route used for centuries by the Hopi people and their ancestors. The route is rich in cultural history, but the real reward is at the Little Colorado River (LCR): The turquoise-blue waters are warm enough to soak in and edged with mud pools that are more fun than any spa treatment.

Backpackers can start the Beamer Trail at either end, but because of camping restrictions at the Little Colorado River, most will begin at **Tanner Beach** (accessible by the Tanner Trail from the South Rim), following bright-red Dox sandstone cliffs that line the beach. At mile 4, the trail reaches **Palisades Creek,** the site of an old copper mine worked by Seth Tanner, where there's a small **campsite.** From here, the trail makes a series of steep switchbacks, topping out on a bench of Tapeats sandstone. The cliffs are

Tonto Trail passes through blackbrush and Bright Angel shale as it traverses the canyon above the Inner Gorge.

narrow in places, and the trail crosses several drainages, making it difficult to find routes.

Beamer's cabin is on the west side of the LCR. Depending on the flow, you may be able to ford the LCR to the other side. Camping and fishing are prohibited near the confluence due to the archaeological resources and endangered native fish species found here.

CANYONEERING

Scores of tributary canyons lead to the Colorado River, many of them originating on the Navajo Reservation to the east, Kaibab National Forest to the north, and the Hualapai Reservation to the west. (Permits are required on reservation lands.) To ascend or descend these canyon routes combines rock climbing, boulder hopping, hiking, and wading or swimming, a.k.a. canyoneering.

In wild tributaries like **Rider Canyon, South Canyon,** and **Kanab Canyon,** canyoneers will encounter obstacle courses of pourovers, pools, chockstones, and boulder fields. Some routes are official trails; others demand route-finding skills and creative problem solving, which might involve rope, dry bags, and other gear. The rugged terrain presents many dangers, foremost among them the possibility of catastrophic flash floods. But if you are experienced and prepared, canyoneering can take you to wild and enchanting places seldom seen.

CLIMBING

In 1958 climbers Dave Ganci and Rick Tidrick made the first technical ascent in Grand Canyon, to the top of Zoroaster Temple. During the decades since, climbers have made technical and nontechnical ascents of some 150 of the canyon's peaks, including **Vishnu** and **Shiva Temples.** Famed canyon hiker Harvey Butchart is said to have climbed 83 summits, making 50 first ascents. Even more daring are routes scaling walls, faces, and features like the pinnacle in Monument Creek.

Many of the Grand Canyon's rock layers are limestone and sandstone, notoriously

Shiva Temple

In 1937 the American Museum of Natural History sent a team of scientists to Grand Canyon to climb Shiva Temple. The museum hoped to find isolated species and other marvels, but their most embarrassing discovery (not divulged in any of the expedition's reports) was an empty Kodak box. Canyon insiders correctly guessed that **Emery Kolb,** perhaps miffed that he hadn't been asked to guide the expedition, had beaten the scientists to their goal and left his calling card.

unstable surfaces, and research is essential to a safe climb. The National Park Service discourages sport climbing, and there are no official routes. That's not to say climbers don't try their skills in the canyon. Some hikes prized by canyon backpackers (such as the Royal Arch route) require rappels or technical climbs, and occasionally, experienced climbers put together private raft trips that focus on inner canyon climbs. To learn more, connect with climbing enthusiasts and local experts on social media, particularly via the **Grand Canyon Hikers and Backpackers Association** (www.gchba.org) and the **Grand Canyon Private Boaters Association** (www.gcpba.org), or within **Flagstaff's climbing community** (www.flagstaffclimbing.com).

FISHING

After Glen Canyon Dam impounded the waters of the Colorado River, cooler downstream temperatures changed the river's environment. Today, the chilly waters below the dam provide a good habitat for rainbow trout. Introduced species commonly found in the river include rainbow, brown, and brook trout as well as carp. Channel catfish and striped bass are seen occasionally, although they prefer the warmer downstream waters of Lake Mead. Of the native species, only speckled dace are common, with several others, including bonytail chub, considered extinct in Grand Canyon.

The best time for trout fishing is in the fall or winter. Popular spots include **Bright Angel Creek,** accessible from the Bright Angel, South Kaibab, or North Kaibab Trails; Tapeats Creek; and **Nankoweap Creek.** No fishing is allowed near the confluence of the Little Colorado River and the Colorado. The warmer waters of the LCR are a refuge for several threatened and endangered species of native fish such as the humpback chub. If you should catch a protected fish, it must be immediately released unharmed. If the fish has been tagged, note the tag number and contact

the USGS research station (928/556-7323, wpersons@usgs.gov).

To fish in the canyon, you'll need an Arizona state fishing license (unless you're under age 14) and a trout stamp. Bag limits vary, depending on area. For most of the canyon, from 21-Mile Rapid to Separation Canyon, trout, striped bass, and catfish are unlimited. No live baitfish may be used. Licenses are sold at the General Store on the South Rim, Lees Ferry, or Jacob Lake. You can also purchase a license online. For more information about fishing regulations, contact the **Arizona Game & Fish Department** (602/942-3000, www.azgfd.gov).

Exploring the Colorado River

The Colorado River runs 277 miles through the canyon from Lees Ferry to the Grand Wash Cliffs, dropping 2,220 vertical feet. Many of the inner canyon's special places are readily accessible only from the river, and chances are you'll get a wider range of sightseeing in a two-week river trip than you could in years of hiking from the rim. The commercial rafting season runs April to October, and most white-water raft trips put in at Lees Ferry.

COMMERCIAL RIVER TRIPS

A guided river trip through the canyon is the experience of a lifetime, combining jaw-dropping scenery with camaraderie and relaxation. Typically, you'll spend four to eight hours on the river each day, with the rest of the time for hiking and exploring, or relaxing along the water's edge. All the clichés you've heard are true: It *is* like entering another world, and time *does* lose its meaning. Ten days will feel like 10 hours—you won't believe the trip is over so quickly. Luckily, 10 days will also feel like 10 months because you've packed each one with so many experiences: great hikes, good food, gorgeous

views, lots of white-water thrills, and plenty of peaceful moments. If possible, give yourself a day or more to transition back to civilization.

Choosing a River Trip

One of the most basic decisions in choosing a river trip is—to paraphrase Shakespeare—whether to motor or not to motor. **Nonmotorized** trips on paddle rafts, oar rafts, and wooden dories are slower and quieter—because there are no motors—and more exciting, because you sit closer to the water. On the other hand, **motorized** trips on large rafts allow you cover more canyon miles in a shorter period of time.

You can also choose between general and focused trips. Focused trips might feature more hiking; some showcase experts like professional geologists, photographers, historians, and even musicians, who share their knowledge and skills. And if you can get together a large enough group to charter a trip, you may be able to suggest your own theme.

Reservations are a must for summer trips, which can fill a year in advance. Cancellations do occur, however, and often space is available on short notice.

Commercial White-Water Outfitters

More than a dozen outfitters have concessionaire agreements with the park to lead 3- to 18-day trips through the canyon. Prices start around $300 per day; meals, gear, and guide services are included. Trip length and guest-to-guide ratio influence price. Compare boat types, origin and end points, and whether additional lodging or shuttle services are included. Also consider your comfort level: half-canyon trips require a long hike into or out of the canyon. Some outfitters offer supported kayak trips or specialties like hiking or yoga, while others include a mid-journey layover at Phantom Ranch. For more information:

- **Aramark-Wilderness River Adventures** (P.O. Box 717, Page, AZ 86040, 928/645-3296 or 800/992-8022, www.riveradventures.com)

- **Arizona Raft Adventures** (4050 E. Huntington Dr., Flagstaff, AZ 86004, 928/526-8200 or 800/786-7238, www.azraft.com)

- **Arizona River Runners** (P.O. Box 47788, Phoenix, AZ 85068, 602/867-4866 or 800/477-7238, www.raftarizona.com)

- **Canyon Explorations/Canyon Expeditions** (P.O. Box 310, Flagstaff, AZ 86002, 928/774-4559 or 800/654-0723, www.canyonexplorations.com)

- **Canyoneers** (P.O. Box 2997, Flagstaff, AZ 86003, 928/526-0924 or 800/525-0924, www.canyoneers.com)

- **Colorado River & Trail Expeditions** (P.O. Box 57575, Salt Lake City, UT 84157, 801/261-1789 or 800/253-7328, www.crateinc.com)

- **Grand Canyon Dories** (P.O. Box 216, Altaville, CA 95221, 209/736-0805 or 800/877-3679, www.oars.com)

- **Grand Canyon Expeditions** (P.O. Box 0, Kanab, UT 84741, 435/644-2691 or 800/544-2691, www.gcex.com)

- **Grand Canyon Whitewater** (P.O. Box 2848, Flagstaff, AZ 86003, 928/779-2979 or 800/343-3121, www.grandcanyonwhitewater.com)

- **Hatch River Expeditions** (5348 E. Burris Lane, Flagstaff, AZ 86003, 928/526-4700 or 800/856-8966, www.hatchriverexpeditions.com)

- **O.A.R.S.** (P.O. Box 67, Angles Camp, CA 95222, 209/736-2924 or 800/346-6277, www.oars.com)

- **Outdoors Unlimited** (6900 Townsend Winona Rd., Flagstaff, AZ 86004, 928/526-4546 or 800/637-7238, www.outdoorsunlimited.com)

- **Tour West** (P.O. Box 333, Orem, UT 84059, 801/225-0755 or 800/453-9107, www.twriver.com)

- **Western River Expeditions** (7258 Racquet Club Dr., Salt Lake City, UT 84121, 801/942-6669 or 800/453-7450, www.westernriver.com)

Some outfitters include pre- or post-trip lodging and transportation to and from the canyon from Flagstaff or other cities. Lower rates may be available for groups or youths. Deposits are typically required at the time of reservations, and discounts may be offered for early payment. Trip cancellation insurance—strongly recommended—is available from a few outfitters; more likely, you will shop around for your own.

If time or money are issues, you can sign on for a **half-length trip** starting at $1,300 pp. Upper-canyon trips from Lees Ferry to Phantom Ranch (about 90 miles) feature stunning scenery and milder rapids. Lower-canyon trips (about 130 miles) beginning at

Phantom Ranch navigate the river's biggest rapids. If you leave a river trip at Phantom Ranch, you'll have to hike out of the canyon—more than nine miles and 8,000 feet of elevation. Conversely, if you join a river trip halfway, you'll have to hike down to Phantom Ranch to meet the rest of your group. Either way, you can arrange ahead of time for a mule duffel service to transport your gear.

Preparing for a River Trip

River trips are physically active, and you'll need to consider any health issues or limitations. Being in good physical condition will help make your experience more enjoyable, but most outfitters are willing to work with people whose abilities are limited. Some outfitters have age restrictions, particularly on longer, more challenging trips. Crew members aren't there to act as babysitters or personal valets, but they will do their utmost to make sure you are safe and having a great time.

Commercial trips are scheduled **April to October,** with peak months being **June to August.** Discounts are sometimes available for early-spring or late-fall trips, when storms or cold spells are more likely: Bring fleece and rain gear. During the summer, when temperatures in the canyon soar past 100°F, the Colorado River remains a chilly 45-55°F, and splashing through rapids is welcome refreshment. Another way to beat the heat and relentless sun is to create your own wearable evaporative cooler by soaking a cotton hat, shirt, bandana, or sarong in the Colorado's cool water.

Outfitters provide necessary gear, including dry bags to store your belongings. You may want a smaller dry bag for a camera or other items you want to access quickly while on the boat. If you bring your lucky Cubs cap or wear prescription sunglasses, be sure they're attached with a clip or retainer before you go bouncing through the rapids. And no matter what type or length of trip you choose, bring plenty of sunscreen and moisturizer, especially if you plan to paddle.

NONCOMMERCIAL RIVER RUNNING

Experienced river runners wait eagerly for a chance to challenge the canyon's rapids themselves, choosing their own pace and campsites. If you have your own gear, a private (noncommercial) trip costs a fraction of the price of a guided commercial trip. The hallmark of a private trip is that all participants (maximum 16) contribute, and no one gets paid a fee. But private trips have been hard to score on a river with strict limits on the number of annual visitors. In order to keep a sense of the wild in this wilderness and protect the canyon's fragile environments, the National Park Service doles out a certain number of **private-trip permits** each year. The most coveted are for 12- to 25-day trips, available only by lottery.

Diamond Down Trips

Are you the impatient type? Skip the lottery and get a permit for a two- to five-day noncommercial trip through the Lower Granite Gorge, launching from Diamond Creek on the Hualapai reservation. **Diamond Down** trips navigate about 15 miles of white water on the 52-mile stretch to Lake Mead. The National Park Service issues permits for two trips per day of up to 16 people each. Applications are available online or from the **River Permits Office** (1824 S. Thompson St., Suite 201, Flagstaff, AZ 86001, 800/959-9164, fax 928/638-7844, grca_riv@nps.gov) and can be submitted up to a year in advance. The National Park Service doesn't charge for Diamond Down permits, but arrangements and fees must be handled with the **Hualapai River Running Department** (P.O. Box 246, Peach Springs, AZ 86434, 928/769-2210 or 800/622-4409) prior to the trip's launch date.

The Permit Lottery

The National Park Service uses a weighted lottery system for granting permits to noncommercial 12- to 25-day river trips launching from Lees Ferry. The weighted system increases the odds for those who haven't been on a river trip during the past five years. Lottery applications can be submitted a year in advance.

Unlike commercial trips, which have a limited season, **private river trips launch all year.** Winter months are less popular, and you may increase your lottery chances if you apply for a winter launch date. The main lottery is held in **February,** with smaller lotteries throughout the year to fill cancellations or leftover trips. The **application fee** is $25, and you can be listed on only one application per year. If you win the lottery, a $400 deposit holds your reservation. (Final permit fees are $100 pp, due 90 days before launching.)

Applications are available on the park's permit website (https://npspermits.us). You must complete an online profile to apply for the lottery. Scroll down for a link to Frequently Asked Questions (FAQs) about the permit lottery system. If your question isn't on the FAQ list, call the permits office (928/638-7843 or 800/959-9164, 8am-noon Mon.-Fri.).

Spend some time familiarizing yourself with the regulations and issues surrounding a private trip by browsing the park's website (www.nps.gov/grca). You'll find a booklet called *Noncommercial River Trip Regulations* that addresses everything from permit requirements to waste management. Other helpful goodies include a free podcast of the park's River Orientation Video.

Even if you decide that you aren't ready to apply for a trip permit, you can set up a profile and register online. There's no charge, and you'll receive periodic announcements via email regarding future launch dates and other river news. (Don't try to game the system by entering duplicate profiles—doing so will cost you your trip permit.)

Private Trip Support

Numerous companies supply river runners with à la carte trip support, renting boats or gear or providing shuttle services. For the whole enchilada, including equipment, menu planning, food shopping, and more, contact:

- **Canyon REO** (1619 N. East St., Flagstaff, AZ 86004, 928/774-3377 or 800/637-4604, www.canyonreo.com)

- **Ceiba Adventures** (3051 N. Fanning Dr., Flagstaff, AZ 86004, 928/527-0171 or 800/217-1060, www.ceibaadventures.com)

- **Moenkopi Riverworks** (5355 N. Dodge Ave., Flagstaff, AZ 86004, 928/526-6622 or 877/454-7483, www.moenkopiriverworks.com)

- **Professional River Outfitters** (2800 W. Route 66, Flagstaff, AZ 86001, 928/779-1512 or 800/648-3236, www.proriver.com)

One worthy alternative to putting together a private trip yourself is to fill an opening on an existing reservation. The **Grand Canyon Private Boaters Association,** a group of experienced river runners, shares a wealth of information on its website (www.gcpba.org) and manages a Yahoo! group (www.groups. yahoo.com/neo/groups/gc_river_trip_planning/info) helping people who are seeking or filling spots on trips.

Planning a Private Trip

It takes a lot of river savvy not only to navigate the canyon's rapids but also to keep groceries fresh down to the last ice block. The biggest drawback of planning a private trip is, well, the planning—about 300 hours' worth. If this isn't your forte, seek out professional trip support. Several companies specialize in outfitting private Grand Canyon trips. Most are based in Flagstaff, and they offer everything from equipment rental to meal planning to river shuttles.

On a private trip, everybody works. The reward is being able to tailor your canyon experience to match your interests and abilities, perhaps planning layovers around longer hikes or technical climbs, stopping for photography or sketching, or celebrating a milestone event with your nearest and dearest.

LEES FERRY TO PHANTOM RANCH

All white-water rafting trips through the heart of Grand Canyon put in at Lees Ferry, just outside the park's eastern boundary, 15 river miles below Glen Canyon Dam. Lees Ferry is the last developed area river runners will see until Phantom Ranch, nearly 90 river miles away.

Leaving the Navajo sandstone cliffs of Glen Canyon behind at Lees Ferry, the river quickly begins to cut through the rock layers associated with Grand Canyon. Less than a mile downstream from Lees Ferry, the **Paria River's** entry creates a riffle that's choppy but too mild to call a rapid. When the waters of the Paria carry sediment after a rain or flood, they form swirling patterns as they enter the clear, green-blue waters of the Colorado River.

Navajo Bridge
MILE 4

About four miles from Lees Ferry, 467-foot high **Navajo Bridge** links the Arizona Strip country to the rest of the state. Navajo Bridge is considered by many river runners to be the gateway to Grand Canyon. The historic bridge, completed in 1929, is closed to vehicles, though people can walk across it for great views of rafts passing below. The newer highway bridge was built a few feet to the west.

★ Marble Canyon
MILE 5

The easternmost section of Grand Canyon cuts north-south through the Marble Platform of Paleozoic rocks for more than 60 miles. Early canyon explorer John Wesley Powell thought the smoothly polished, almost vertical walls looked like marble, so he named this section **Marble Canyon.** In 1969, the area became Marble Canyon National Monument to protect the river from proposed dam sites. In 1975, Marble Canyon was added to Grand Canyon National Park. Geologically speaking, it is part of Grand Canyon, though its historic appellation remains.

The rocks of Marble Canyon introduce the highest layers found throughout the rest of the canyon: the Kaibab, Toroweap, and Coconino Formations. Past Navajo Bridge, reddish slope-forming Hermit Shale begins to make an appearance. Formed by an ancient swamp, Hermit Shale bears fossils of insects and plants, including ferns. (Hermit Shale becomes a predominant layer farther west, where it erodes to form sloped shoulders on buttes and canyon rims.)

House Rock Rapid
MILE 17

The first sizable rapid that river runners encounter, House Rock Rapid, lies at the mouth of the tributary **Rider Canyon,** about 17

Marble Canyon's Redwall limestone cliffs

miles downriver from Lees Ferry. Like most rapids, House Rock was formed when flash floods pushed debris through this tributary into the Colorado, creating a spillover. In 1890, when engineer Robert Brewster Stanton made his second attempt to survey a railroad route through the canyon, the expedition's photographer, Franklin Nims, was nearly killed in a fall. Stanton and his crew halted their journey to evacuate Nims via Rider Canyon.

The Roaring Twenties
MILES 20-30

A series of small rapids, known collectively as the Roaring Twenties, give river runners a fast and fun run: **North Canyon, Indian Dick, 23-Mile, 23.5-Mile, 24-Mile, 24.5-Mile,** and so on, are a mild roller-coaster ride and a mere hint of things to come. Harmless as it seems today, this section of canyon plagued Stanton's ill-prepared first attempt at running the canyon in 1889, and 25-Mile Rapid is also

Robert Brewster Stanton

One fateful river journey began with the dream of building a rail route through the inner canyon. The idea may seem ridiculous now, but in 1889, engineer Robert Brewster Stanton and 15 others set out to survey the canyon on behalf of the Denver, Colorado, Canyon and Pacific Railroad. To save weight, they omitted lifejackets, and the trip Stanton originally considered "ordinary" became a harrowing ordeal. He lost three boats and three men by the time they reached South Canyon.

Undeterred, Stanton made a second attempt. After the group's photographer fell from a cliff and broke his leg, Stanton finished photographing the journey himself and reached the Gulf of California in April 1890. It was the third expedition (after two by John Wesley Powell) to run the Colorado through Grand Canyon. That dreamed-of railroad route? Another expedition casualty.

known as **Hansbrough-Richards Rapid** for the second and third men drowned on that fateful expedition.

The Supai Group of rocks, which begin to appear about 11 miles downstream from Lees Ferry, form the bedrock of beautiful North Canyon, entering from the west at mile 20. Shortly after that, cliff-forming Redwall limestone appears. This limestone, left by a shallow sea 320-360 million years ago, is actually off-white but stained reddish by the overlying layers. Redwall cliffs are often streaked with tapestries of **desert varnish**—dark manganese oxide stains.

Marble Canyon tributaries like **Rider Canyon, South Canyon,** and **Buck Farm Canyon** not only make fascinating day-hike opportunities for river runners but also offer canyoneering adventures for people entering from the House Rock Valley area above the rim. Canyoneers sometimes need technical climbing gear to negotiate pour-overs (dry waterfalls) or small inflatable rafts to float packs across long, deep pools.

South Canyon
MILE 31

As you float through the Redwall, repetitive neck strain is a real possibility. Who can resist gazing up to examine the cliffs right and left for tapestries, pockets, caves, arches, and alcoves? These natural features formed over time as water dissolved softer deposits in the limestone. Some alcoves protect **Ancestral Puebloan dwellings** built a millennium ago, such as the ruin at the mouth of South Canyon, which enters Marble Canyon at mile 31. River runners often stop to explore South Canyon's polished limestone narrows. Just downstream is **Stanton's Cave,** where scientists found the bones of a Pleistocene-era giant sloth and split-twig figurines from the Archaic period, as well as gear stashed by Stanton's first expedition when they abandoned their attempt to run the Colorado and returned to the rim via South Canyon. The cave is closed to visitors.

★ Redwall Cavern
MILES 33-50

On river left, Redwall Cavern gapes at mile 33. The Colorado River carved this large cave from the Redwall limestone formation at river level. Explorer John Wesley Powell, impressed at its vast size, wrote that it could hold 50,000 people (unlikely, but it *is* big). River runners often stop here for lunch on the beach or a game of Frisbee inside the cavern's sandy expanse, but no camping is allowed.

Grayish Muav limestone, the oldest of the Paleozoic rocks (formed about 500 million years ago), begins to appear at **mile 34.** Five miles downstream is the **Marble Canyon dam site,** proposed and test-drilled in 1963. (Imagine, for a moment, if all the natural beauty you'd just floated through had been drowned by water impounded behind the proposed dam.)

The river continues to meander gently until mile 41, when it bends sharply east around **Point Hansbrough,** toward President Harding Rapid, before turning west toward Saddle Canyon. This hairpin is an entrenched meander, a river bend deepened by downcutting. Above is **Eminence Break,** a northwest-facing escarpment formed along a fault line. A challenging route leads to the rim from the camp below **President Harding Rapid.**

On his second expedition, Robert Brewster Stanton discovered the body of one of the crewmembers lost on the previous attempt at running the river. Stanton buried Peter Hansbrough here, leaving an inscription on the cliff as an epitaph. The rapid was named by a later expedition, a U.S. Geological Survey mapping trip led by Claude Birdseye, with Emery Kolb as chief boatman. The 1923 expedition carried a radio, and when they heard that President Harding had died, they camped here for a day and named the rapid in remembrance.

At **mile 50,** Bright Angel Shale appears, a late-Paleozoic series of mudstone, sandstone, and limestone in shades of green, tan, and lavender. Easily eroded, it forms fantastic shapes farther downriver. In the central canyon, the colorful shale can be spotted on top of the Tonto Platform, where it has mostly eroded away.

★ Nankoweap Ruin Route
MILE 53

High above the Colorado River near Nankoweap Canyon, at river mile 53, the Ancestral Puebloans constructed masonry granaries to protect their food stores. The steep route up to the **Nankoweap granaries**, which are about 1,000 years old, offers striking views of Marble Canyon, the river a gently undulating silver ribbon below. It is one of the finest river views in the inner canyon. This area is also accessible from the North Rim and Saddle Mountain Wilderness via the **Nankoweap Trail**, a 15-mile route that many consider to be the canyon's most difficult.

★ Little Colorado River Confluence
MILE 61

A couple of miles before the confluence of the Colorado and Little Colorado Rivers, Tapeats sandstone makes its first appearance, forming dark-grayish-brown stratified cliffs and ledges that intermingle in places with Bright Angel shale. On river left at mile 61 the turquoise waters of the **Little Colorado River** (LCR) join the deep green Colorado. No camping is allowed near the confluence except by rangers and others who have special research permits. Fishing is also restricted because the warmer waters of the Little Colorado host endangered fish species, including the humpback chub.

Often, river runners ferry across the Colorado to see **Beamer Cabin**, a small Ancestral Puebloan ruin "remodeled" by an 1880s prospector, and to play in the warmer waters of the LCR. At times, the LCR's flow is just right for a waterslide, and it's fun to hike a mile or so along the Tapeats ledges that form the LCR's banks, stopping to try out mud pools for beauty packs or foot soaks. Enjoy the natural splendor while you can: This serene

river view from the Nankoweap Ruin Route

location is currently under threat from above, a proposed development that includes a large rim-side resort and a tram carrying up to 10,000 visitors daily into the canyon.

Just downriver from the confluence, the **Great Unconformity** appears. Think of an unconformity as pages missing from the geological record. In this case, between Tapeats sandstone and an underlying layer of Vishnu schist, the unconformity is a gap of hundreds of millions of years—a series of rocks known as the Grand Canyon Supergroup. You'll see remnants of these layers a few miles downcanyon, uplifted and tilted to form the colorful folds of Unkar Valley.

Chuar Butte to the Palisades
MILES 65-75

Near mile 65, river runners may spot bits of metal reflecting in the sun on the slopes of **Chuar Butte**, marking one of the nation's most horrific midair collisions. On June 30, 1956, a TWA Super Constellation and a United DC-7 collided at 21,000 feet, killing all 128 people aboard and scattering debris on both sides of the river. The National Park Service had most of the wreckage removed in the 1970s, and a memorial for the crash victims stands in the Pioneer Cemetery on the South Rim. (To prevent similar tragedies, Congress passed the Federal Aviation Act of 1958, creating the Federal Aviation Agency and giving it control of U.S. airspace.)

Below the great curtain of rock known as the **Palisades of the Desert,** the river begins to swing west toward Unkar Valley. At Unkar Delta, the ancestors of today's Hopi people, the Ancestral Puebloans, established a village and raised corn, beans, and squash in nearby plots. The warmer inner canyon temperatures meant a longer growing season, and the villagers moved between rim and river according to the season. In the summer, villagers would return to the Walhalla Plateau on the North Rim. To protect the delta's fragile archeological resources, camping is prohibited here. If you are exploring on foot, stay on the trails.

Below **Comanche Point,** the highest point along an undulating section of the rim called the Palisades, Tanner Rapid marks the mouth of the tributary Tanner Canyon. The **Tanner Trail** leads 10 miles from here to the rim at Lipan Point, one of many prehistoric Native American trails later adapted by miners and pioneers. Before the Colorado River was dammed, it was possible to cross to the other side during seasons of low water, climbing up to the opposite rim via the Nankoweap Trail—a route said to be favored by horse thieves who traveled back and forth between Arizona and Utah In the late 1800s.

★ The Inner Gorge
MILE 76

Hance Rapid is the first challenging white water that river runners encounter—a preview of things to come as the river enters the narrower confines of the Inner Gorge, or, as explorer John Wesley Powell called it, the Granite Gorge.

Just past Hance Rapid, the oldest rocks in the canyon make their appearance—pink and red Zoroaster granite and dark-gray Vishnu schist. These harder rocks form steep cliffs below the Tonto Platform, creating the Inner Gorge, a canyon within a canyon. In the Lower Sonoran Desert climate zone, summer temperatures can push toward 120°F, and even lizards take cover in midday. **Cremation Camp,** a popular overnight for river runners at mile 87, appears stark and rocky at midday, but when late-afternoon sun hits the Zoroaster granite, the rocks seem to smolder with inner fire.

Bright Angel Creek
MILE 88

Bright Angel Creek joins the Colorado River at about 88 miles, creating a welcome oasis. Powell and his crew rested here for several days in 1869, and Powell named the creek Bright Angel for its clear and gentle waters. In contrast, the pre-dam Colorado River was so laden with silt that pioneers joked it was "too thin to plow, too thick to drink."

Powell's men weren't the first to appreciate

The Inner Gorge is called the canyon within the canyon.

this peaceful spot. The Ancestral Puebloans settled near the confluence, building a small L-shaped pueblo. Trail builder David Rust established a camp here in the early 1900s, connecting his North Rim trail to trails from the South Rim via a cableway. He planted cottonwood trees and rented tents to guests, including Theodore Roosevelt. After Grand Canyon became a national park in 1919, visitation increased, and the Santa Fe Railway decided to build a lodge on the site.

Phantom Ranch

The oasis of **Phantom Ranch** (888/297-2757, www.grandcanyonlodges.com) marks the boundary between the upper and lower canyon. For some river runners, the trip ends here or about a mile downriver at lovely Pipe Creek, followed by the long, steep hike up **Bright Angel Trail.** For those who've booked lower-canyon trips, this is where the adventure begins.

PHANTOM RANCH TO LAKE MEAD

For passengers who continue downriver, serious white water lies ahead. On most rivers, rapids are rated on the International Scale of River Difficulty, from Class I to Class VI. In Grand Canyon, rapids are ranked on a scale of 1 to 10, with 1 being a small riffle and 10 the highest difficulty that is still navigable. The severity of rapids can fluctuate with changes in river flows (releases from Glen Canyon Dam, runoff from rainstorms), and many rapids have more than one possible run or route, with differences in difficulty. At **miles 93** and **95** are **Granite** and **Hermit Rapids,** both ranked class 9.

Crystal Rapid and the Gems
MILE 98

At mile 98, notorious **Crystal Rapid** was a mere riffle until the river channel filled with flash-flood debris in 1966. Crystal changed again in 1983 when another flood swept downriver, moving boulders and creating a 10-plus rapid with a notorious hole. Boaters

have their own descriptive lexicon, including "washing machine," "cheese grater," and "haystack." The boat-sucking hydraulic on the downstream side of a large rock is called a "hole," and the hole in Crystal is considered the canyon's biggest, capable of trapping and recirculating even very large rafts. Past Crystal, boaters encounter the rapids known as the Gem Series—**Agate, Sapphire, Turquoise, Jasper, Jade, Ruby,** and **Serpentine Rapids.**

Bass Canyon to Granite Narrows
MILE 107

At mile 107, Bass Canyon enters from the southwest. The area near William Bass's historic camp is a popular layover for river runners and backpackers. Bass built a cable crossing here to connect his two trails, the first rim-to-rim route in Grand Canyon. The Tapeats sandstone bench on river right makes a great campsite, with historic **Bass Camp** a couple of miles up the **North Bass Trail.** On river left, along the **South Bass Trail,** is the abandoned *Ross Wheeler,* a metal boat left behind during a 1915 expedition.

Royal Arch Creek and Elves Chasm
MILE 116

Just past mile 116, Royal Arch Creek enters the main canyon from the south. **Elves Chasm,** a magical grotto of maidenhair ferns and trickling water, is a short walk from the river, near the mouth of Royal Arch Canyon. Two straight river passages—**Stephens Aisle,** which runs north-south from **mile 117** to **mile 119,** and **Conquistador Aisle,** heading east-west from **mile 120** to **mile 123**—lead to **Middle Granite Gorge.**

Ask river runners to identify their favorite rock layer in Grand Canyon and many will answer "Tapeats sandstone." This dark-brown sandstone, formed about 545 million years ago, erodes into interesting platforms and ledges and often bears fossilized brachiopods, trilobites, or worm tracks. **Blacktail**

Deer Creek Falls

Canyon, at **mile 120**, and Tapeats Canyon, at **mile 134**, are both carved from the Tapeats. The **Thunder River Trail** leads up Tapeats Canyon to 0.5-mile-long Thunder River, also accessible from the North Rim. The dark, mile-long section of the canyon from Helicopter Eddy to Deer Creek is known as **Granite Narrows,** where the canyon pinches to a width of 76 feet.

★ Deer Creek Falls
MILE 136

At **Deer Creek,** a 100-foot-high waterfall tumbles out of a sinuous Tapeats sandstone tributary, creating a welcome oasis on the lower river at mile 136. River runners often stop at Deer Creek Falls to frolic in the water and hike around the falls to the high slot canyon of **Deer Creek Narrows.** The route is not for acrophobes, as it requires carefully stepping along a trail barely wider than a boot and suspended high above the rushing creek waters. From the falls, it's possible to hike to Thunder River or all the way to the rim, a strenuous 15-mile journey.

Matkatamiba Canyon
MILE 148

Matkatamiba Canyon, at mile 148, is another sinuously carved side canyon and a favorite with photographers and hikers. Its walls, ledges, and pools are formed from Muav limestone, shaped into linear ridges that make scrambling and climbing relatively easy.

Havasu Canyon
MILE 157

Havasu Creek enters the Colorado River at mile 157. From the mouth of Havasu Canyon (formerly known as Cataract Canyon), it's six miles to **Mooney Falls,** one of several waterfalls in the Havasu Canyon area. **Supai Village** is another three miles, roughly halfway between the rim and river.

The Havasupai (People of the Blue-Green Water) lived at Grand Canyon for centuries, widely roaming the rims and tributaries in

hiking up Havasu Creek in Havasu Canyon

search of game and plants until the government established their small reservation in 1882. Today, Havasupai people support themselves with tourism. Each year, about 20,000 visitors come from all over the world to see Havasu Creek's waterfalls and travertine-lined pools, which reflect the sky in exquisite turquoise hues.

Lava Falls
MILE 179

Just past Tuckup Canyon, at **mile 165,** the south edge of the Colorado River forms the boundary of the Hualapai Reservation. A few miles downstream on the right, 3,000-foot-high cliffs loom above the river. On top is **Toroweap,** a remote overlook on the North Rim's western reaches. Below, at mile 179, is **Lava Falls.** In just a couple of hundred yards, the Colorado River drops 37 feet, forming a class 10 rapid, the fiercest white water in Grand Canyon. In 1869, Powell's men chose to make an arduous, three-hour portage rather than risk their wooden boats and remaining food stores against the churning water.

Powell recognized the signs of past volcanic activity along this section of the river. Upriver from the rapid, a volcanic neck, the black monolith **Vulcans Forge,** juts out of the water. Downriver, cascades of basalt rock mark the canyon walls, the flow of a volcano that erupted 1.2 million years ago. The flows created a dam about 1,400 feet high. An even higher dam formed near Prospect Canyon, creating a lake that extended all the way to present-day Moab. Over time, the sediment-laden Colorado River ground its way through these natural dams.

Whitmore Wash
MILE 188

Lava flows are evident at Whitmore Wash, at mile 188. The canyon walls are lower here, and the trail that leads up to the rim is less than a mile long, the shortest rim-to-river route in Grand Canyon. (The **Lava Falls Route,** at 1.5 miles, is the shortest within the bounds of the park.) Because of its proximity to the rim, some outfitters use the beach at Whitmore Wash as a passenger-exchange point. The family-operated **Bar-10 Ranch** (435/628-4010, 800/582-4139, www.bar10.com) offers lodging and an airstrip on the north side of the canyon, and on the south side, the Hualapai nation operates a helipad.

Diamond Creek
MILE 226

At mile 226, Diamond Creek enters the canyon, marking the takeout point for most commercial white-water trips. The wide beach at the edge of the river is also used as a put-in for rafting trips managed by the Hualapai nation and as well as by private boaters who have reserved a "Diamond Down" trip to raft the canyon's remaining 54 miles through **Lower Granite Gorge.** The **Diamond Creek Road** climbs 20 miles from the river to Peach Springs on the Hualapai Reservation, a rugged scenic route.

Separation Rapid
MILE 239

Powell's party camped above the rapid at mile 239 in late August 1869. Weary and disheartened, the men had opened their last sack of flour two days earlier. Several believed the rapid would be impassible. The next morning, three crew members left the expedition, and Powell named the roiling water **Separation Rapid.** Below it, the canyon widened, and the river became quieter. In two days, the six remaining expedition members reached the mouth of the Virgin River and nearby Mormon settlements. Only later did they learn that the three men who left were murdered. The exact fate of the men is still unknown. Though Shivwits people have long been blamed for their deaths, canyon historians have also made convincing arguments that the murderers were Mormon settlers.

Grand Wash Cliffs
MILE 276

At mile 276, the **Grand Wash Cliffs** mark the geographical end of Grand Canyon and the

The Mystery of Glen and Bessie Hyde

the Hydes' abandoned sweep scow, found near Diamond Creek

The canyon makes a dramatic backdrop for tall tales, heroic feats, and terrible tragedies, and river guides love to recount these legends on a moonlit beach. A particularly haunting tale is that of newlyweds Glen and Bessie Hyde, who set out on an adventurous honeymoon trip on October 20, 1928. The Hydes would have joined the elite group of successful Grand Canyon expeditions, and Bessie Hyde would have become the first woman to accomplish the feat. But the fame and fortune they hoped for was not to be. On November 15, they hiked up to Grand Canyon Village to resupply and confer with Emery Kolb. When they didn't return to Idaho in December as planned, Kolb and others launched a search. The Hydes' sweep scow was found in Lower Granite Gorge, but Glen and Bessie had disappeared without a trace, their fate a mystery to this day.

start of the basin-and-range topography of the **Mojave Desert.** The boundary between Grand Canyon National Park and Lake Mead National Monument lies just beyond.

Lake Mead

The waters of Lake Mead, impounded by Hoover Dam, slow the river's current after Separation Rapid. Long-term drought in the Southwest has severely impacted Lake Mead's water levels, evident by the white "bathtub ring" that rises high above the surface of the lake. Sustained drought left the takeout point at **Pearce Ferry** high and dry until 2010, when the Pearce Ferry Road was extended another two miles to the changed waterline, a $1 million project that once again allowed

river take-outs and de-rigging. The alternative is to continue on another 15 miles to busy South Cove beach, navigating the notorious Pearce Ferry Rapid and adding an extra day or two to your trip.

HIKING AND BACKPACKING
Silver Grotto

Distance: 0.5 miles round-trip
Duration: 1-2 hours
Elevation gain: 1,000 feet
Effort: Strenuous
Trailhead: River left, mile 31

This tributary is also known as **Shinumo Wash** or **29-Mile Canyon,** although river runners usually refer to the lower portion,

Hikes from the Colorado River

Trail	Effort	Distance	Duration	River Mile
Silver Grotto	strenuous	0.5 miles round-trip	1-2 hours	mile 31 (right)
South Canyon	easy	0.5 miles round-trip	30 minutes	mile 31 (right)
Nankoweap Granaries	moderate	1.5 miles round-trip	1.5-2 hours	mile 52 (left)
Shinumo Creek Falls	easy	0.2 miles round-trip	1 hour	mile 108 (right)
Elves Chasm	easy	0.5 miles round-trip	1 hour or less	mile 116 (left)
Deer Creek Trail	strenuous	10 miles round-trip	4-6 hours	mile 136 (right)
Kanab Creek	moderate	8 miles round-trip to Whispering Falls	3-5 hours	mile 143 (right)
Matkatamiba Canyon	easy	0.5 miles round-trip	1 hour	mile 148 (right)
Havasu Creek	strenuous	up to 19 miles	varies	mile 156 (left)
Fern Glen	moderate	1 mile round-trip	1 hour	mile 168 (right)
Whitmore Wash	moderate	2 miles round-trip	1 hour	mile 188 (right)
Travertine Canyon	strenuous	up to 4 miles round-trip	2-3 hours	mile 229 (left)

inaccessible from the upper wash, as Silver Grotto, named for its smooth limestone walls. It's less than one mile before progress from the river is halted by a high pour-over, but this is not an easy hike. In fact, it's not a really a hike at all—it is more of a scrambling, swimming, climbing, canyoneering adventure. A boat ferry might be necessary to get across the first pool, and other obstacles await. This series of slickrock scrambles and swims through a lovely limestone narrows is for those who have some climbing and canyoneering experience. It's also for hot afternoons when no rain threatens: The pools are cold, and the canyon is prone to flash flooding.

South Canyon
Distance: 0.5 miles round-trip

Duration: 30 minutes
Elevation gain: 800 feet
Effort: Easy
Trailhead: River right, mile 31

Even a short hike up South Canyon is awe-inspiring, leading through narrows of Redwall limestone. More determined canyoneers can clamber up through boulders and around pour-overs to the confluence with Bedrock Canyon, where Supai narrows await. Those who don't have climbing skills can explore along the Colorado River, up- or downstream from South Canyon.

Just upstream from the mouth of South Canyon is an Ancestral Puebloan **ruin,** occupied about 900 years ago. From the back of the river camp, a short hike up to the Redwall Formation leads to **Stanton's Cave.** A little

Nankoweap Granaries

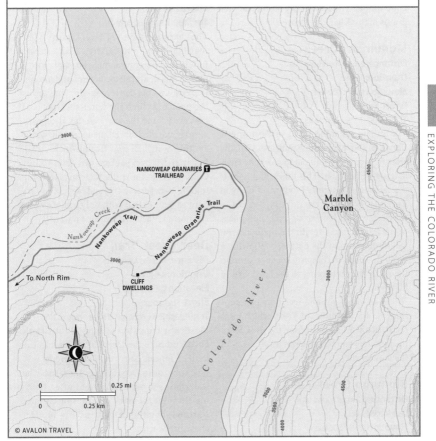

NANKOWEAP GRANARIES
TRAILHEAD

Nankoweap Trail

Nankoweap Creek

Nankoweap Granaries Trail

To North Rim

CLIFF
DWELLINGS

3000

4500

3000

Marble
Canyon

Colorado River

3000

4500

3500

4000

0   0.25 mi

0   0.25 km

© AVALON TRAVEL

farther downstream, reached most safely by boat, is **Vaseys Paradise,** a lush oasis created by a spring erupting from the Redwall. Powell named it in honor of a botanist colleague because it supports a number of species, including redbud, willow, monkey flowers, watercress, and—*beware*—poison ivy. Also be careful of the endangered Kanab ambersnail, which might be crawling underfoot.

Nankoweap Granaries
Distance: 1.5 miles round-trip
Duration: 1.5-2 hours
Elevation gain: 1,500 feet

Effort: Moderate
Trailhead: River left, mile 52 (see map p. 155)

This short-but-steep route starts just downstream (south) of **Nankoweap Creek.** The **camps** in this area are overgrown with tamarisk, and there's a network of unofficial trails. Look for the well-traveled trail paralleling the base of the cliffs, and then locate the spur leading uphill toward the **granaries.** It's a rocky climb through broken Muav limestone, but the view at the top is one of the finest along the river. In late afternoon, the walls of **Marble Canyon** turn shades of peach and rose, reflecting in the waters of the Colorado

River. The delta of Nankoweap Creek must have provided the Ancestral Puebloans with good garden plots, and they stored surplus grains in this high, dry alcove.

Monument Creek

Distance: 2 miles round-trip
Duration: 1 hour
Elevation gain: 500 feet
Effort: Easy
Trailhead: River left, mile 93

The trail begins at the mouth of **Monument Canyon,** above **Granite Rapid,** where many river trips camp or pull out to scout the challenging white water. This hike's highlight is the tall spire that gives Monument Canyon its name. From the river, it's 0.75 miles to the narrows that loop around the monument to the left. You can rejoin the main canyon by climbing out of the narrows, following a small drainage to complete the loop around the spire, then returning to the creek bed to hike out.

Those who want a longer hike can continue on the **Monument Trail,** which joins the **Tonto Trail** 1.5 miles from the river. From the junction, you'll have a raven's-eye view of the monument.

Shinumo Creek Falls

Distance: 0.2 miles round-trip
Duration: 1 hour
Elevation gain: 300 feet
Effort: Easy
Trailhead: River right, mile 108

There's a lot to explore around **Bass Camp,** at the foot of the **North Bass** and **South Bass Trails,** including historic artifacts and a refreshing 15-foot waterfall on Shinumo Creek. For river runners, it's an easy walk about 200 feet up the creek bed to reach the falls. Depending on the season, the pool at the base of the falls may be a couple of feet deep, a comfortable swimming hole, or so flooded that the waterfall is inaccessible.

Elves Chasm

Distance: 0.5 miles round-trip
Duration: 1 hour or less
Elevation gain: 200 feet
Effort: Easy
Trailhead: River left, mile 116

The charming grotto of Elves Chasm is less than 0.25 miles from the river. A delicate waterfall trickles around huge boulders into a pool in this shady canyon of ferns and mosses. It's possible—but dangerous—to swim across the pool and climb the water-slick rocks to the cave behind the waterfall. It's also possible to make the risky climb upcanyon, where another waterfall and **Royal Arch** await. Experienced backpackers can access Elves Chasm from rim trails that involve route finding, rock scrambling, and rappelling—it's hard to believe that with only a short walk, river runners achieve the same reward.

Deer Creek Trail

Distance: 10 miles round-trip
Duration: 4-6 hours
Elevation gain: 1,700
Effort: Strenuous
Trailhead: River right, mile 136 (see map p. 116)

Most river trips stop to enjoy **Deer Creek Falls** and hike the Deer Creek Trail to the head of Tapeats Narrows, a challenging 0.5-mile hike, or to Deer Spring, 1.5 miles. The waterfall is a refreshing sight after floating through the dark confines of Granite Narrows, bursting from the cliffs 100 feet above the beach.

Starting from the river, the trail climbs around Deer Creek Falls and enters a labyrinthine narrows of Tapeats sandstone. With the creek flowing below, the trail hugs the cliff inside the narrows, a serious challenge for any hiker with acrophobia or claustrophobia. The trail exits the narrows at Deer Creek Valley, where cottonwoods shade a few **campsites.**

From here, the trail climbs toward a spur trail that leads to a smaller waterfall created by **Deer Spring.** The main trail ascends through Muav limestone to shadeless Surprise Valley, where it joins the **Thunder River Trail** at five miles. Most hikers starting from the river will turn around long before this point.

Kanab Creek

Distance: 8 miles round-trip to Whispering Falls
Duration: 3-5 hours
Elevation gain: 400 feet
Effort: Moderate
Trailhead: River right, mile 143

Whether you have time for a couple of miles or double that, Kanab Creek and its side canyons are fun to explore. Kanab is Paiute for "willow," and desert willows grow in the lower canyon along with cottonwood, Apache plume, Mormon tea, agave, and cactus. There's no trail, and following the creek bed means going around or over cobbles and boulders, with easier going across ledges of Muav limestone on the east side of the creek.

A good destination for a long day hike is **Whispering Falls Canyon,** which enters from the east at about four miles. A short way up this canyon is the waterfall that gives the canyon its name, sliding down bedrock into a plunge pool surrounded by a grotto of stone.

The mouth of the canyon isn't very interesting, but the farther you travel from the river, the more intriguing the canyon becomes. It's negotiable all the way to Kanab, Utah, 50 miles away. On his second expedition through Grand Canyon in 1872, John Wesley Powell and his crew left the river at Kanab Creek, deciding their boats were too worn to continue down the main canyon. It took them four days to hike to Kanab.

A little more than halfway between the Colorado River and the mouth of Jumpup Canyon, springs emerge from the Redwall Formation, giving lower Kanab Creek its perennial flow. To explore that far, you'll need about two days; sometimes backpackers spend a week or more in this network of canyons, Grand Canyon's largest tributary system on the north side.

Matkatamiba Canyon

Distance: 0.5 miles round-trip
Duration: 1 hour
Elevation gain: 400 feet
Effort: Easy
Trailhead: River left, mile 148

"Matkat," as it's affectionately known to river runners, is a popular stop on river trips. If you like rock scrambling and wading, it's a pleasant 0.25 miles to the **patio,** where the narrows open up into an amphitheater of ledges and platforms decorated with ferns and mosses. The distance is short, but most hikers will linger to practice their Spidey moves in the narrows or to play in the small waterfalls. Stronger hikers have the option of continuing up Matkatamiba Canyon to where it forks. The left fork continues another mile or so before reaching impassable cliffs. The right fork leads to **Mount Akaba,** a difficult canyoneering adventure.

Havasu Creek

Distance: Up to 19 miles
Duration: Varies, depending on length hiked
Elevation gain: 4,400 feet
Effort: Strenuous
Trailhead: River left, mile 156

A **permit** is required to enter Havasupai Reservation land. From the river, Supai Village is nine miles. Most river runners only go as far as **Beaver Falls,** but even a short hike up Havasu Creek leads to shady pools, perfect on a hot summer day.

From the river, the trail up Havasu Canyon crosses the creek several times and can be difficult to follow as it washes out frequently. At about three miles you'll reach **Beaver Falls,** a pretty series of travertine cascades. The trail climbs around Beaver Falls to a ledge before dropping back down to the creek. At about six miles, **Mooney Falls** plummets nearly 200 feet into the turquoise-colored pool below. The trail to the village, another three miles, tunnels through the travertine at Mooney Falls, a slippery route with ladders and chains for handholds. En route to the village the trail passes **Havasu Falls** and **Navajo Falls.**

Although river runners will be wading and swimming a lot during a day hike up Havasu Canyon, they should pack plenty of water. The water in Havasu Creek isn't drinkable, and most day hikers from the river won't have the time or legs to reach the campground or village, where water is available.

Fern Glen

Distance: 1 mile round-trip
Duration: 1 hour
Elevation gain: 300 feet
Effort: Moderate
Trailhead: River right, mile 168

Allow time to linger on this short hike leading to a fern-draped grotto and pool. Redwall and Muav limestone walls have been carved into shelves and chutes. The canyon walls narrow a short way from the beach, creating welcome shade. There's no trail, but scrambling up natural **limestone staircases** is only moderately challenging. Springs, like the one in Fern Glen Canyon, are formed when rain and snowmelt percolate down through the relatively porous layers above until reaching the more resistant Bright Angel shale. Water pools on top of the shale, forming an aquifer in the Redwall formation that is easily dissolved into caves and chambers. Where Redwall is exposed in canyon walls, water issues forth as springs, relatively common in the tributaries along this section of Grand Canyon. **Cliff walls** block further progress up Fern Glen Canyon, but it's pleasant to pause by one of the pools and listen to the trickling water before returning to the river.

Whitmore Wash

Distance: 2 miles round-trip
Duration: 1 hour
Elevation gain: 800 feet
Effort: Moderate
Trailhead: River right, mile 188

A short walk across the beach leads to a masonry **ruin,** protected by cliffs and a retaining wall built by the National Park Service. To the left of the ruin are some **pictographs.** To the right a trail leads up to the rim, where local ranchers built a line shack. At this point, the walls of the canyon rise less than 1,000 feet from the river, and a Bureau of Land Management (BLM) road leading from St. George, Utah, crosses through ranch land to the edge of the canyon.

Travertine Canyon

Distance: Up to 4 miles round-trip
Duration: 2-3 hours
Elevation gain: 900 feet
Effort: Strenuous
Trailhead: River left, mile 229

Depending on how much time you have and how hot it is, you can make the short, mildly challenging scramble to **Travertine Falls,** a lovely 35-foot plunge, or attempt the difficult scramble to the source of the canyon's water, a spring surrounded by dense vegetation. To get to Travertine Falls, follow the creek bed up a steep and slippery slope of Vishnu schist. The waterfall is at the back of a narrows of travertine-covered cliffs. Hiking to the falls and back takes less than an hour.

If you want a longer, more challenging hike, and your climbing skills are sharp, return to the river and walk past the creek (upriver), heading up the ridge to go up and around the falls. Look for **cairns** to guide you back into the creek bed. You'll encounter three smaller waterfalls on your way up the creek, requiring some hand-and-foot climbing to get around. The **springs** are marked by thick vegetation, and you can turn back or go a bit farther to the top of the Tonto Platform for good views.

Food and Accommodations

The only lodging and dining establishment in the inner canyon is Phantom Ranch. But don't worry: Whether you're preparing a package of instant noodles on your backpacking stove or enjoying sunset while a boat crew cooks up steak and strawberry shortcake, everything tastes better with a view. If you're backpacking, be sure not to attract unwanted dinner guests: Use an ammo can or a high-tech food sack to keep ringtails and rodents out of your food supply.

Competition for river camps can be fierce during the high season, and if you're on a commercial trip, you'll notice that guides often pause to confer with each other about where their group plans to spend the night. Some beaches are large enough to offer space for two or three large groups. Other camps have space for only a few boaters and backpackers, so it's important to plan ahead, have a backup, and be courteous to everyone you encounter, since you just might be sharing camp with them downriver.

Commercial rafting companies usually provide tents, sleeping bags, and pads. During the summer rainy season, most thundershowers pass before sunset. Unless the weather is threatening, you'll probably find yourself forgoing a tent and sleeping under the stars.

PHANTOM RANCH

★ **Phantom Ranch** (888/297-2757, www. grandcanyonlodges.com) is the inner canyon's only stopover with sheets and showers, tucked into an oasis-like setting along Bright Angel Creek, 0.5 miles north of its confluence with the Colorado River. Designed by architect Mary Colter, the cluster of historic wood-and-stone buildings include dormitory-style rooms for men and women, 11 rustic cabins, and a canteen serving breakfast, lunch, and dinner. When meals aren't being served, the canteen acts as post office and store.

Phantom Ranch accommodations for mule riders are included in tour fees. Hikers and river runners can make room reservations (888/297-2757 or 303/297-2757) up to 13 months in advance, and available rooms sell out quickly. Men's and women's **dorms** ($49 pp) have shared showers and restrooms. Most

Phantom Ranch cabins

of the **cabins** ($142-246) sleep four. Cabins and dorms have heat and evaporative cooling (a.k.a. "swamp coolers"). **Reservation requests** can be made online, but due to high demand, phoning is recommended, especially on the first of the month.

The ★ **Phantom Ranch Canteen** sells snacks and serves up a simple but hearty breakfast ($20), sack lunch ($14), and dinner ($26-45). Dinner options include steak, stew, or veggie chili, accompanied by salad, bread, and a thick slab of chocolate cake. Meals are part of the package for mule-tour guests, but hikers, campers, and river runners need to make meal reservations well in advance of their trips.

CAMPGROUNDS

Backcountry permits ($10 per permit, plus $8 pp per night) are required for overnight hiking and backpacking, river camping, or any camping outside developed campgrounds. And "developed" is a relative term. Don't expect showers—let alone cable hookups—if you're spending the night in the canyon. Stays are limited to two nights per hike (four nights Nov. 15-Feb. 28), and your site is reserved when you apply for a backcountry use permit. To cut pack weight, some backpackers forgo

tents during summer, but be aware that afternoon thunderstorms are likely July-August.

Bright Angel Campground

★ **Bright Angel Campground,** along Bright Angel Creek near its confluence with the Colorado River, has 31 partly shaded campsites (including two group sites), year-round drinking water, food storage boxes, pack hangers, picnic tables, an emergency phone, and toilets. The campground is accessible from the **Bright Angel, South Kaibab,** and **North Kaibab Trails.** You'll need a backcountry permit to stay here, and sites do fill up quickly in spring and summer. The ranger station is nearby, and during summer months, rangers host evening programs. Phantom Ranch is 0.5 miles north, giving backpackers the option to rough it easy with a cold beer or hot meal from the canteen.

Cottonwood Campground

Cottonwood Campground, 6.8 miles from the North Rim via the **North Kaibab Trail,** has 11 campsites with picnic tables and food storage boxes. The campground also offers toilets, an emergency phone, and a ranger station (staffed May-Oct.) but very little shade, although its name might suggest otherwise.

Bright Angel Campground

Water is available seasonally (May-mid-Oct.). Always check the park website (www.nps.gov/grca) for announcements about seasonal water shut-offs, and be prepared to purify or filter water in case of a pipeline break.

Indian Garden Campground

Indian Garden Campground is an oasis of grapevines and cottonwoods midway down the **Bright Angel Trail**, 4.5 miles from the South Rim. A backcountry permit is required to reserve one of the 15 campsites. Amenities include potable water year-round, pack hangers, food storage boxes, and composting toilets. Indian Garden also has a ranger station and an emergency phone.

Backcountry and River Camps

The backcountry is divided into zones and use areas that may be hundreds or thousands of acres in size depending on ecology, terrain, and popularity. Backcountry camping in the Corridor and Threshold zones is limited to developed campgrounds, where amenities might include piped water and flush toilets, or designated campsites that might have only pit toilets. In the Primitive and Wild zones, at-large camping is allowed, with certain restrictions.

The **Corridor zone** includes Bright Angel, Cottonwood, and Indian Garden campgrounds. The **Threshold zone** includes Clear Creek, Horn Creek, Salt Creek, Cedar Spring, Monument Creek, Granite Rapid, Hermit Creek, Hermit Rapid, Horseshoe Mesa, Widforss, Point Sublime, and Eremita Mesa use areas. Stays in campsites in these areas are limited to two nights, except during winter months (Nov. 15-Feb. 28), when stays of up to four nights are possible.

Backcountry **permits** must be displayed in camp, either attached to a pack or tent or elsewhere in plain view. Backcountry campsites must be a minimum of 100 feet from water sources. This protects water quality for other campers and wildlife (and helps protect you and your food supply from thirsty nighttime critters). Don't try to improve on Mother Nature with trenching or other earth moving—the site should look undisturbed when you leave. Pack out all trash, used toilet paper, and food scraps. Even the tiniest crumb attracts ants, mice, and other unwelcome visitors.

If you're hiking to the river, be aware that you may be sharing camps with boating parties. You might enjoy the company (and they may even feed you or let you cadge a beer), but if you prefer privacy, choose a tent site far away from the most likely boat landing.

Transportation and Services

Visitor services are limited inside the canyon, with Phantom Ranch the only purveyor of such creature comforts as lemonade and postcards. Cell phone service is unlikely, and only a few emergency phones are available at ranger stations and resthouses. River guides carry satellite phones. The biggest concern for hikers and backpackers, however, is water. Inner canyon water pipes are shut off seasonally, and pipe breaks are becoming increasingly common as the park's infrastructure ages. Verifying water sources before you hike is essential.

Shuttles

For those planning rim-to-rim hikes, two companies offer daily shuttle service between the North and South Rims. Reservations are required. The **Trans Canyon Shuttle** (928/638-2820 or 877/638-2820, www.transcanyonshuttle.com, May 15-Oct. 31, $90 one-way) has two daily shuttle runs between Grand Canyon Village (South Rim) and Bright Angel Point (North Rim). Charter shuttles can be arranged, and bag-only deliveries ($25) are available for weary cross-canyon hikers who want clean clothes waiting on the other rim. **Grand Canyon Shuttle Service** (888/215-3105, www.grandcanyon-shuttles.com) has 24/7 customizable on-demand service between the rims, a good option for groups. Call or email (admin@flagshuttle.com) for more information.

Transportation to and from the river is usually included on commercial white-water trips. If you need help getting people, gear, or vehicles to Lees Ferry, Diamond Creek, or Lake Mead, several private trip outfitters in Flagstaff and Meadview offer shuttle services, among them, **Canyon REO** (1619 N. East St., Flagstaff, AZ 86004, 928/774-3377 or 800/637-4604, www.canyonreo.com) and **River Runner's Shuttle Service** (P.O. Box 61, Meadview, AZ 86444, 928/564-2194, www.rrshuttleservice.com).

SERVICES

Lees Ferry, 15 river miles below Glen Canyon Dam, has a campground, parking (with a 14-day limit), pay phones, a picnic ramada, boat ramp, ranger station, toilets, and water.

Navajo Bridge Interpretive Center (928/355-2319, 9am-5pm daily Apr.-Oct.) is located just south of the intersection of Lees Ferry Road and U.S. 89A, six miles from the campground. There's a fine selection of books

and maps here, as well as some last-minute items that can make a river trip more enjoyable, from sketchpads to sunscreen.

At the confluence of the Colorado River and Bright Angel Creek, **Phantom Ranch** and **Bright Angel Campground** offer the widest range of services inside the canyon, including pay phones, an emergency phone, a ranger station, toilets, water, showers, and mail service. Phantom Ranch Canteen closes during meal service but otherwise sells snacks, refreshments, and a few sundries.

Cottonwood Campground has an emergency phone and toilets. The ranger station is staffed seasonally, and drinking water is available May-mid-October. **Indian Garden** has a campground, emergency phone, ranger station, toilets, and water.

Resthouses

Many of the wood or stone resthouses along the canyon's corridor trails were built by the CCC in the 1930s. The CCC was a Depression-era program that provided jobs for young men at parks and forests throughout the United States.

On the **Bright Angel Trail,** Mile-and-a-Half Resthouse has toilets, an emergency phone, and seasonal drinking water

the Tonto Trail Junction Resthouse on South Kaibab Trail

(May-Sept.). Three-Mile Resthouse has an emergency phone and seasonal drinking water (May-Sept.). River Resthouse, at mile 7.7, where Pipe Creek joins the Colorado River, has an emergency phone.

On the **South Kaibab Trail,** Cedar Ridge Resthouse, 1.5 miles below the rim, has toilet facilities. At 4.4 miles, the Tonto Trail Junction Resthouse has toilets. The Tipoff, a few steps farther along, has an emergency phone. No water is available along the South Kaibab Trail.

On the **North Kaibab Trail,** there are toilet facilities and occasional seasonal water at Supai Tunnel, two miles from the rim. Roaring Springs, at 4.7 miles, has toilet facilities and seasonal drinking water (May-Sept.).

Mule Duffel Service

Pack-mule services are available through **Xanterra** (303/297-3175 or 800/297-2757, www.grandcanyonlodges.com, daily Mar.-Dec., Mon.-Fri. Jan.-Mar., $70 one-way) for backpackers and river runners who need assistance shuttling their gear between Phantom Ranch and Grand Canyon Village. Advance reservations are necessary. There's a weight limit of 30 pounds, and items must be properly packed and delivered to the drop-off points by a specified time. If you don't provide your own duffel bag, you'll need to stuff your things into a repurposed grain sack.

Emergencies

It's highly unlikely that your cell phone will pick up a signal inside the canyon. Consider leaving the phone at home or at the rim; electronic devices can be downright irritating to backpackers and river runners who cherish natural quiet.

The **emergency phones** available at some resthouses and campgrounds are connected to a 24-hour dispatch center and do not require coins. Rangers patrol the trails and river, and ranger stations are located at Indian Garden, Bright Angel Campground, and Cottonwood Campground (unstaffed in the off-season). River guides carry satellite phones, and they are trained to assist with emergencies.

Stay on established trails: On numerous occasions, hikers have been rescued only yards away from a trail. The National Park Service rescues about 400 visitors each year, and most are first-time canyon hikers. If you require rescue, you will be responsible for the cost. Exhaustion doesn't constitute an emergency.

You can leave the **park administration telephone number** (928/638-2477) with someone who is aware of your itinerary. If you've told your contact you will call after hiking out of the canyon, be sure to do so to avoid unnecessary search-and-rescue efforts on your behalf.

Beyond the Boundaries

Covering more than 1.2 million acres, Grand Canyon National Park is big, but the canyon's influence extends even farther. The greater Grand Canyon area encompasses large swaths of federal land and the Navajo, Hualapai, and Havasupai Nations. From wild and lonesome plateaus to communities rich with cultural traditions, these places beyond the park offer unique perspectives on the canyon.

Visit reservation lands bracketing the park on the east and west, and you may come to see the canyon in a new light—not simply as an awesome sight but also as a touchstone, a centerpiece of Native American histories, and a place of healing or pilgrimage. Rock formations, animals, trails, and springs figure into stories retold for generations. Hike to the bottom of Havasu Canyon to swim in turquoise-colored pools or tour a series of waterfalls on horseback. Venture onto the glass-bottomed Skywalk or shop at a trading post for pottery, rugs, and other crafts. And, to any question about frybread, the answer is "yes."

North of the canyon, forested plateaus and a geological staircase of colorful cliffs are home to Kaibab National Forest, Kanab Creek Wilderness, Vermilion Cliffs National Monument, and other federal lands. Exploring them can be tame as driving to Lees Ferry for a picnic along the Colorado River, or as wild as canyoneering in a remote tributary. Choose an adventure that suits your abilities and interests—fly-fishing, mountain biking, backpacking, or walking through autumn leaves with your dog.

With the exception of Grand Canyon West, where the Hualapai Nation welcomes commercial tours, you'll be finding your own way in these parts beyond the park. Small towns and even smaller outposts are scattered across wide-open spaces linked by two-lane roads or dirt tracks: Bring everything you need and refuel your vehicle whenever you can. Cell phone service is spotty, and you may drive for miles before seeing another car. But for independent-minded travelers willing to trade modern conveniences for new horizons, the landscape around Grand Canyon is rich with possibilities.

Previous: petroglyphs in Kanab Creek Wilderness Area; the Vermilion Cliffs and Navajo Bridge. **Above:** paintbrush blooming in Paria Canyon.

Look for ★ to find recommended
sights, activities, dining, and lodging.

Highlights

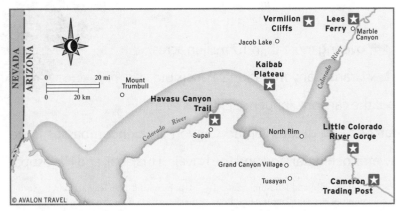

© AVALON TRAVEL

★ **Havasu Canyon Trail:** Journey to the inner-canyon home of the Havasupai people, an oasis of breathtaking waterfalls and turquoise pools (page 171).

★ **Little Colorado River Gorge:** Stop to visit with roadside vendors and peer into the steep-walled canyon carved by one of the Colorado River's major tributaries (page 180).

★ **Cameron Trading Post:** Step into Arizona's past at this historic post, which has welcomed locals and travelers to the Navajo Nation for nearly a century (page 181).

★ **Lees Ferry:** Drive to the edge of the Colorado River, where Glen Canyon ends and Grand Canyon begins (page 185).

★ **Vermilion Cliffs:** Look above these colorful rock walls, part of the Southwest's Grand Staircase, for California condors (page 193).

★ **Kaibab Plateau:** Hike, bike, or drive the plateau's forest roads and trails, which meander through aspen, pines, and wildflowers on the way to remote North Rim overlooks (page 195).

Beyond the Boundaries

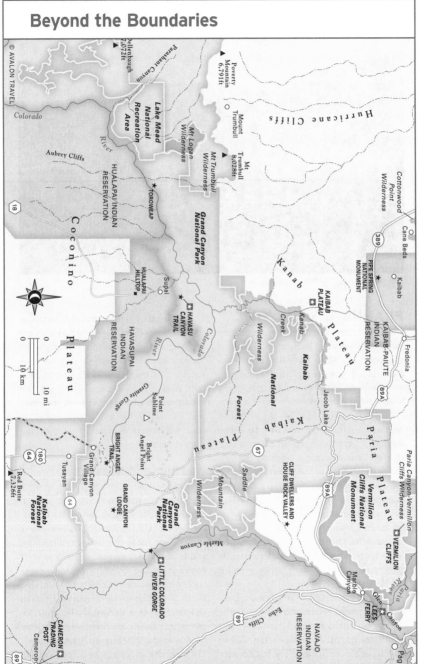

© AVALON TRAVEL

Late-summer clouds gather over Saddle Mountain.

PLANNING YOUR TIME

Grand Canyon is surrounded by fascinating history and stunning landscapes. No matter what roads you take to travel here, spending a couple of days or more exploring beyond park boundaries will literally and metaphorically broaden your horizons.

Travelers interested in history or Native American culture can add **one to three days** to a Grand Canyon itinerary to visit Hualapai and Havasupai lands on the west end of the canyon or the Navajo Nation on the east. Native American governments require permits to hike or camp on reservation land, and reservations for Havasu Canyon fill far in advance, especially during summer months. On Hualapai lands, however, tour choices abound, and you can usually get a reservation on a day's notice, even for the Skywalk.

Outdoor enthusiasts and adventure travelers won't need reservations or permits to explore national forest and Bureau of Land Management (BLM) lands on the Kaibab Plateau or House Rock Valley, but advance planning and backcountry skills are essential.

The driving time to these remote areas is substantial. Set aside at least **two days,** longer for backpacking trips. If you're hiking in the Saddle Mountain or Kanab Creek Wilderness Areas, a good map is a must. Plan routes carefully, researching water availability and trail conditions in advance. Let someone know your itinerary before you set out, and share your wilderness experience with hiking companions.

Weather and Seasons

Spring and **fall** are the best times to explore the greater Grand Canyon region, though Havasu Canyon delights swimmers in hotter months. On the Kaibab Plateau, heavy snows close roads November to mid-May, and muddy roads can persist into June. If you're exploring tributary canyons, especially on the Marble Platform or Vermilion Cliffs, avoid the summer monsoon season (July-mid-Sept.). A storm cell miles away can create flash-flood conditions. No matter what the season, check the forecast before you leave. Elevation changes can mean sudden shifts in the weather, so be prepared.

Havasupai Reservation

On Grand Canyon's western reaches, the Pai peoples occupy land south of the Colorado River. The Havasupai people live eight miles below the rim in Havasu Canyon, a hidden jewel where Havasu Creek flows over ledges to form breathtaking waterfalls. The creek's turquoise waters empty into the Colorado River 35 miles west of Grand Canyon Village as the raven flies. Supai Village, 5,000 feet below the rim, is reached only by foot, horseback, or helicopter. Some 20,000 people visit Havasu Canyon each year.

SIGHTS
Supai Village

The village of **Supai**, population 450, is the center of the historic Havasupai reservation at the bottom of Havasu Canyon. Centuries ago, Havasupai hunters and gatherers roamed vast distances in the canyon and along its rims. Congress restored some of those traditional lands to the Havasupai in 1975. Today, community members rely on tourism, farming, or wage jobs outside the canyon. All supplies and mail are brought into the canyon by pack animals, by helicopter, or on foot. The village has a clinic, a school, a church, a police station, and a post office as well as the lodge, a general store, and a café. The **tourist office** (928/448-2121, 928/448-2141, or 928/448-2180) houses a small museum.

Havasu Canyon

Havasu Canyon is a delight for swimmers and photographers. Spring-fed Havasu Creek contains high amounts of minerals that precipitate, forming travertine basins or pools that reflect the sky. Gorgeous waterfalls tumble over the reddish cliffs into turquoise pools, where the water remains about 70°F year-round. The series of waterfalls begins at the campground and continues four miles along Havasu Creek: **Havasu Falls, Mooney Falls,** and **Beaver Falls.** (A 2008 flood reshaped Navajo Falls into two smaller falls.) The creek joins the Colorado River about eight miles beyond the campground.

Havasu Canyon is inaccessible to vehicles, so visitors must leave cars at the rim. If you plan to hike the eight miles in, make

Havasu Falls

Havasupai and Hualapai Reservations

BUCK AND DOE RD

GRAND CANYON WEST AIRPORT

Guano Point

Huapapai Indian Reservation

SKYWALK

Quartermaster Point

BAT CAVE

GRAND CANYON NATIONAL PARK

Lake Mead National Recreation Area

Mount Dellenbaugh

Gneiss Canyon Rapid (class 3–6)

Bridge Canyon Rapid (class 3–6)

Travertine Falls

Colorado River

POWELL MONUMENT

Diamond Creek Rapid (4)

Price Point

Mollies Nipple

Grassy Mountain

DIAMOND CREEK RD

Thumb

GRANITE PARK

DIAMOND CREEK RIVER ACCESS

Tower of Babylon

205 Mile Rapid (class 7–8)

217 Mile Rapid (class 6–7)

Andrus Point

Lone Mountain

WHITMORE WASH TRAILHEAD

WHITMORE WASH HELIPAD

Hualapai Indian Reservation

Prospect Point

Logan Wilderness

BAR TEN RANCH

1045

Vulcans Throne

Vulcan's Anvil

Mount

TUWEEP RANGER STATION

TOROWEAP OVERLOOK

The Dome

GRAND CANYON NATIONAL PARK

18

Flatiron Butte

Havasupai Indian Reservation

Dead Horse Mesa

Hualapai Canyon

Havasu Canyon

Supai

Hualapai Hilltop 5,200 ft.

0

0

10 km

10 mi

© AVALON TRAVEL

reservations for at least two nights at the lodge or campground so you have time to enjoy the idyllic setting. The canyon's lodge and campgrounds fill up far in advance, especially during the busy summer season. Other options include riding in on horseback or taking a helicopter to the bottom of the canyon. Always check before your departure for current conditions; in recent years, late-summer storms have caused severe flooding. Some areas of the canyon remain off-limits to visitors due to continuing repair work, and additional canyon closures may occur at any time.

All visitors must make **reservations** with the tourist office (928/448-2121, 928/448-2141, or 928/448-2180, httourism0@havasupai-nsn.gov, www.havasupai-nsn.gov) before entering the canyon. Reservations for the season can be made starting in January, and they sell out quickly. Be aware that a reservation is no guarantee that you'll be able to complete your trip; flooding closed Havasu Canyon to visitors several times in recent years. Entrance fees are $35-40 pp; taxes, camping, lodging, and tours are additional. Fees may change and aren't considered final until arrival. The Havasupai Nation asks guests not to bring pets to Havasu Canyon.

RECREATION
Hiking

Contact the reservation office (928/448-2121, 928/448-2141, or 928/448-2180) for permits if you plan to hike or camp on Havasupai lands.

★ HAVASU CANYON TRAIL

Distance: 16 miles round-trip to Supai Village
Duration: 2 days
Elevation loss: 2,500 feet
Effort: Strenuous
Trailhead: Hualapai Hilltop
Directions: The trailhead is about four hours' drive from Grand Canyon Village or an hour from Peach Springs. Take I-40 west from Williams to Seligman, turning north on Route 66 for 28 miles. Turn right on Indian Road 18, a paved road leading northeast for 61 miles to the parking area at Hualapai Hilltop. There are portable toilets here but no water, nor is water

available along the trail. It may be remote, but this is a busy staging area, with helicopters and mule trains leaving daily.

The trail descends steep switchbacks through Toroweap Formation and Coconino sandstone before becoming a more gradual descent through brick-red Hermit Shale. At 1.5 miles, the trail enters **Hualapai Wash,** prone to flash floods after rains. At six miles, the wash joins Havasu Canyon and the perennial waters of Havasu Creek. You'll shortly come to a fork. Go left for **Supai Village.** (The right fork leads to Havasu Spring, off-limits to visitors without a Havasupai guide.)

Not long after the fork, you'll be able to see the creek. The trail crosses a bridge and enters the village. Proceed to the **tourist center** (or lodge, if you have room reservations) to pay the remainder of your fees. The **campground** is another two miles past the village. En route, you'll pass **Supai Falls,** which is hidden by lush vegetation, though you can hear it. From the campground, it's a short distance to the beautiful **Havasu** and **Mooney waterfalls.**

Experienced hikers who've planned an extra night in the canyon can hire a guide to hike the challenging route around Mooney Falls to **Beaver Falls** (4 miles from the campground) or the **Colorado River** (another 8 miles).

Horseback Riding

For a $20 trail fee, you can take your own horse or mule down Hualapai Hilltop Trail to Havasu Canyon, a ride lasting about three hours. You'll need to bring your own feed. Contact the **tourism office** (928/448-2121, 928/448-2141, or 928/448-2180) for more information.

EVENTS

Supai Village hosts the annual **Peach Festival** in mid-August, when peaches ripen in Havasu Canyon orchards. Peaches were introduced by the Spanish and adopted by many Southwestern Native American communities, who still tend historic orchards. If you hope to visit Havasu Canyon during the Peach Festival, make your plans at least a year in advance. This event is a homecoming for community members who live outside Havasu Canyon and also draws many visitors from other Pai nations.

FOOD

Supai Village, at the bottom of Havasu Canyon, has a small **café** ($5-12) that serves breakfast, lunch, and dinner daily to visitors and locals. Cash, debit cards, and credit cards are accepted. Groceries, including frozen entrées that can be microwaved on-site, are available at the general store.

ACCOMMODATIONS

Havasupai Lodge (928/448-2111 or 928/448-2101, htlodge0@havasupai-nsn.gov $145) is in Supai Village at the bottom of Havasu Canyon and is accessible only by helicopter or on foot or horseback via the eight-mile Havasu Canyon Trail. The lodge is at the south end of the village past the church and there are only 24 guest rooms, so make reservations early. All guest rooms are nonsmoking and can accommodate up to four people with two double beds. There are no phones or TVs, but the lodge has air-conditioning.

CAMPING

Havasu Campground (928/448-2121, 928/448-2141, or 928/448-2180, $17 pp plus tax) stretching along Havasu Creek, can accommodate up to 250. There are composting toilets but no showers; bring biodegradable soap for washing in the creek. Piped spring water may need to be treated before drinking. Most sites have picnic tables, but campfires aren't allowed. Bring a pack stove or ready-to-eat meals. All trash must be packed out. Don't leave food or trash in your tent; it will attract critters. A ranger station is staffed during the day, with security service at night.

Sites are selected on a first-come, first-served basis. You must make a reservation in advance and pay a deposit of 50 percent, refundable up to two weeks before your trip

(less a 25 percent surcharge). Exceptions are made if the campground closes (due to flooding, for example) during your travel dates, in which case a full refund is made. If you hike into the canyon without a reservation, all fees are doubled.

TRANSPORTATION AND SERVICES

Peach Springs, the Hualapai Nation's headquarters, also serves as a gateway to the Havasupai Reservation. If you are traveling from the west on I-40, turn north on Route 66 at Kingman and drive 50 miles to Peach Springs. If you are arriving from the east, turn north at Seligman and take Route 66 for 38 miles to Peach Springs.

Trips into Havasu Canyon begin at Hualapai Hilltop, a 66-mile drive from Peach Springs. From Grand Canyon Village, it's about four hours to the trailhead, so most people stay in Peach Springs or spend a restless night in their cars at Hualapai Hilltop in order to get an early start on the hike.

Tours

If the eight-mile hike from Hualapai Hilltop to Supai Village sounds intimidating, you can arrange for a pack mule, or travel on horseback or by helicopter (which lands about two miles from the village). Havasupai packers offer pack mules and horse trips through the **tourist office** (928/448-2121, 928/448-2141, or 928/448-2180, $120-190 pp round trip). Reservations must be made in advance for one-way or round-trip (overnight) rides. Community members also lead horseback tours ($60 pp) of the waterfalls, departing from the lodge.

Riders must have some experience, be able to mount and dismount, know how to guide their horses, and be dressed appropriately (jeans, a long-sleeved shirt, and a brimmed hat or cap). Small fanny packs (less than 25 pounds) can be carried, along with a canteen and camera. Arrangements must be made for a pack mule or horse to carry backpacks or larger packs. Riders must weigh 250 pounds or less and be at least four feet, seven inches tall. Children younger than age five can ride with an adult if their combined weight doesn't exceed 250 pounds. Packhorse loads are limited to 130 pounds.

Airwest Helicopters (623/516-2790, www.airwesthelicopters.com, 10am-1pm Thurs.-Fri. and Sun.-Mon. summer, 10am-1pm Fri. and Sun. winter, from $85 one-way) provides transportation from Hualapai Hilltop to Supai Village. Reservations for the helicopter ride aren't necessary, but community members have first priority, and wait times can be long during busy periods. Schedules are subject to change depending on the weather and federal or community holidays, so it's a good idea to call ahead. (Because of daily use limitations, you'll still need to make a reservation to enter the canyon.)

If you'd rather turn over the work of obtaining the various permits and reservations involved in visiting Havasu Canyon to someone else, the **Wildland Trekking Company** (928/379-6383 or 800/715-4453, www.wildlandtrekking.com, Feb.-mid-Nov., $860-1,400 pp) leads three- or four-day mule-assisted trips to Havasu Canyon. Guides are well-versed in natural and cultural history. Some tour packages include a train ride and hike at Grand Canyon National Park's South Rim. Guide-owned **CenterFocus** (928/567-8580, http://thecenterfocus.com, $695-1,650 pp) leads three- or four-day hiking or fly-in trips emphasizing Havasu Canyon's waterfalls and swimming holes. Prices include transportation from Sedona, Flagstaff, Williams, or Seligman. (Helicopter flights in and out of the canyon cost extra.) **Arizona Outback Adventures** (866/455-1601) leads three- to five-day packhorse-assisted trips and a photography workshop in Havasu Canyon.

Services

The **Havasupai Lodge** (928/448-2111 or 928/448-2101, 8am-5pm daily) and **tourist office** (928/448-2121, 928/448-2141, or 928/448-2180) act as visitor centers at Supai Village, eight miles by foot trail below Hualapai Hilltop. All visitors must check in at one or the other on arrival. Reservations must be made well in advance of a Havasu Canyon trip, and you'll also need to make a down payment for your entry fees and camping or lodging costs in order to hold your reservation. (If you make the mistake of hiking in without reservations, all fees double.) The tourist office takes cash and credit cards, but not traveler's checks. Because of Havasu Canyon's size, the annual number of visitors is limited to 12,000, so plan ahead. The village has a café, a general store, and a post office, one of the few in the United States that sends and receives mail via mule, as well as an Indian Health Service clinic and a resident physician.

At the **Havasupai Trading Post and General Store** (928/448-2951, hours vary) in Supai Village, you'll find a few souvenirs, including postcards, which you can take next door to the post office for the most coveted souvenir in Havasu Canyon: a cancellation stamp that reads "Mule Train Mail, Havasupai Reservation."

Visiting Native American Reservations

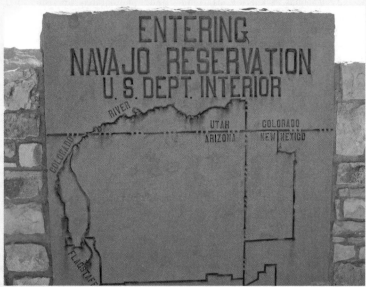

The Navajo Nation occupies the Four Corners region.

Permits are required to hike, camp, or film on the Havasupai, Hualapai, or Navajo Nation lands bordering Grand Canyon. Each nation has its own sovereign government and establishes its own rules for visiting reservation land.

Rules vary among reservations, but photographing, recording, and sketching are usually restricted. You may be asked to purchase a **photography permit** to take photos for personal noncommercial use. Do not take photos of individuals without their permission. (Offering a small tip is an expected courtesy.)

Native American communities may have formal cultural centers. Trading posts or stores sometimes act as unofficial cultural centers, offering directions, sightseeing suggestions, and information about schedules or permits. Most reservations require **permits** for hiking, camping, hunting, fishing, and other backcountry uses, as well as for commercial purposes like professional filming.

Note that there is a distinct difference between performances and ceremonies. **Ceremonies** are held for the benefit of local communities. It is a privilege to be invited to a ceremony, and your good behavior is important to its purpose and outcome. Behave as if you were in a church or temple—dress modestly and neatly and maintain a quiet, respectful attitude. Do not address the dancers during a ceremony, and don't applaud following a ceremony. **Performances,** such as those held at Hopi House or the Museum of Northern Arizona, are reenactments arranged for public enjoyment, and the atmosphere may be more relaxed.

Respect private property. Peoples' homes are not museums or sets. Unless you are invited to enter a private home, perhaps to see baskets or pottery, you should remain in public places like shops and restaurants. Cemeteries, shrines, and other sacred areas are generally off-limits to visitors. **Alcohol and drugs** are prohibited on reservations.

Hualapai Reservation

The Hualapai Reservation borders more than 100 miles of Grand Canyon, covering parts of three counties and encompassing grasslands, ponderosa pine forest, and the rugged canyon rim. The nation hosts thousands of river runners annually, with many trips putting in or taking out on Hualapai land at Diamond Creek. Most tourism activities, including the glass-bottomed Skywalk, are centered at Grand Canyon West.

SIGHTS
Peach Springs

Once a bustling Route 66 tourist hub, **Peach Springs** is the Hualapai Nation capital and home to about 600 people. Though tiny, it's a convenient staging area for a trip to Grand Canyon West or Havasu Canyon. The nation owns and operates Hualapai Lodge, where you can find out more about tour options or purchase the permits required for driving on reservation roads, camping, or hiking.

On your way to Peach Springs, don't pass up the chance to get your kicks on **Route 66,** the American West's most celebrated highway. If you're arriving from Flagstaff or Williams, take I-40 west to Seligman, turning north on Route 66 for 38 miles to Peach Springs. From the west, you can exit I-40 in Kingman and take Route 66 for 50 miles to Peach Springs.

Diamond Creek Road

It's an adventure driving to the inner canyon on Indian Road 6, also known as **Diamond Creek Road** or Peach Springs Canyon Road. The only rim-to-river drive between Lees Ferry and Pearce Ferry, Diamond Creek Road starts at 4,950 feet and travels 20 miles to river level at 1,550 feet, a rugged two-hour round-trip when conditions are dry. Stop at the tourism office at Hualapai Lodge in Peach Springs to get a **permit** ($60 per vehicle plus $60 pp) and inquire about current conditions. The road is prone to washouts and closures,

especially during the late-summer monsoon. A high-clearance 4WD vehicle is recommended, especially for the last few miles, where the creek crisscrosses the road several times. This section is impassable if the creek has flooded recently.

Grand Canyon West

The lands of the Hualapai (People of the Tall Pines) border the rim of western Grand Canyon for 108 miles. If you yearn for wide-open spaces, note that the reservation's 2,300 residents live on more than one million acres, encompassing grassland, desert, piñon-juniper woodland, tall-pine forest, and rugged tributary canyons of the Colorado River. Historically known for their trading skills, the Hualapai today focus on cattle ranching, timber sales, and tourism. The nation has developed **Grand Canyon West** (7am-7pm daily Apr.-Sept., 8am-5pm daily Oct.-Mar.), a tourist area near the Grand Wash Cliffs, which marks the end of Grand Canyon and the beginning of Lake Mead. Tickets for Grand Canyon West start at $50 pp, with additional fees for the Skywalk or activities like river rafting and flight tours.

Although this section of the canyon doesn't have the brilliant colors or temples and monuments of central Grand Canyon, the sheer walls and steep drops to the river are awe-inspiring. No protective barriers separate you from the views, and you won't have to share them with as many people. Grand Canyon West hosts about 3,000 visitors a month, while the South Rim's Grand Canyon Village handles about 10,000 a day.

Grand Canyon West is lightly developed, with three main overlooks accessible by a hop-on, hop-off shuttle. During the 1950s, **Guano Point** was part of a fertilizer mining operation. A short hike leads to the end of the point, where dung from the "bat cave" across the canyon was delivered via a long tramway. The point juts into the canyon for stunning Colorado River views. Another overlook, **Eagle Point,** is home to the Grand Canyon Skywalk. From here you can see the cliff walls that suggested the point's name: a ridge that resembles a large bird with its wings spread wide. It's another short shuttle ride to Quartermaster Point and **Hualapai Ranch,** where you can sign up for a trail ride, watch a gunfight reenactment, or stay overnight in a Western-style cabin.

Visitors tend to have a love-it-or-hate-it reaction to Grand Canyon West, depending mostly on how realistic their expectations are. Remember: This is not a national park. If your plans include the **Skywalk,** expect to spend around $100 pp. Get an early start; it's a long drive here, and the last tour tickets are printed two hours before Grand Canyon West closes.

If traveling to Grand Canyon West from Las Vegas (about 2.5 hours) or from I-40, turn north on U.S. 93 at Kingman and drive 30 miles to Pearce Ferry Road (sometimes spelled "Pierce") and turn right. Paved **Pearce Ferry Road** is a scenic trip through the Mojave Desert, home to jackrabbits and Joshua trees. Drive 28 miles and turn left at **Diamond Bar Road,** now paved, which continues another 20 miles to Grand Canyon West. If you're driving from Peach Springs, the partially paved Buck and Doe Road (Indian Rd. 1) leads 50 miles to Grand Canyon West. Traveling unpaved Hualapai Reservation roads requires a **permit** ($16 per day). Pets are not allowed on any tours and cannot be left in cars; for a fee, you can make arrangements to board pets at Hualapai Ranch.

Grand Canyon Skywalk

From Eagle Point, the 70-foot-long **Grand Canyon Skywalk** juts 25 feet beyond the rim, more than 3,000 feet above the canyon floor. Construction of this ambitious—and controversial—project was completed in 2007 at a cost of $30 million. A Las Vegas architectural firm designed the cantilevered Skywalk. It looks graceful, even delicate, from the side, but it's built to withstand the weight of 71 loaded Boeing 747 jets, or the force of a magnitude 8.0 earthquake within 50 miles. Even so, many visitors feel compelled to hold onto the Skywalk's railings as they make the dizzying walk over the chasm below. The floor's crystal-clear surface is made from five layers of glass that provide support; the topmost layer can be replaced if it becomes clouded from scuffmarks or scratches.

Tours that include a walk on the Skywalk

Grand Canyon Skywalk

The Bat Cave

Dreams of riches lured many prospectors to Grand Canyon in the late 1800s. But miners like **Louis Boucher** (The Hermit) and **John Hance,** a legendary teller of tall tales, quickly learned there were more precious metals to be plucked from tourists' pockets than from canyon walls. That didn't stop the U.S. Guano Company from investing in an elaborate tramway and a giant guano-sucking vacuum to mine the riches of the Bat Cave, estimated to hold 100,000 tons of fertilizer. Construction problems and accidents plagued the company, and by the time it was discovered that profit estimates were off by two decimal places, the enterprise was a losing venture. The mine closed in 1960, but workings are still visible from Guano Point on the Hualapai Reservation's Grand Canyon West.

start at $83. To protect the glass surface, you'll be asked to use shoe covers and check all personal items, including cameras and cell phones, before you proceed. (You can get a good vantage point for a profile shot of the Skywalk before entering and, for about $30, a photographer will snap your photo with the Skywalk in the background.)

Not far from the Skywalk, an Indian Village attraction replicates traditional dwellings of various Native American communities. The amphitheater here hosts demonstrations and performances. Plans for a future visitor center at Eagle Point are on hold until a contract dispute between the Hualapai Nation and the Skywalk developer is resolved.

Grand Canyon Caverns

Just outside the Hualapai Reservation is the oldest and largest dry cave complex in the United States. **Grand Canyon Caverns** (928/422-4565, www.gccaverns.com, 10am-4pm daily fall-spring, longer hours in summer), located nine miles east of Peach Springs on Route 66, is more than just catnip for tourists. Sure, there's plenty of Route 66 kitsch, but the campground, motel, airstrip, and gas station make a handy base of operations for those with reservations for visiting Havasu Canyon, and a stay here wouldn't be complete without a trip underground. More than 20 stories below, selenite, helecite, and calcium formed unusual shapes in the Redwall limestone (the same rock layer that dominates Grand Canyon's cliffs). Tours ($16-90 pp, discounts

for children and seniors) last from 25 minutes to more than two hours.

RECREATION
Hiking

Contact the reservation office (928/769-2636 or 888/868-9378) for permits if you plan to hike or camp on Hualapai lands.

HIGHPOINT TRAIL
Distance: 0.5 miles round-trip
Duration: 30 minutes
Elevation gain: 150 feet
Effort: Easy
Trailhead: Guano Point, Grand Canyon West

This scenic walk starts at **Guano Point**, a three-mile shuttle ride from the Grand Canyon West welcome center. The unpaved trail leads to a small peak on the edge of the canyon, where you'll gain panoramic vistas and a closer look at the historic tram-car infrastructure below the rim. During the mid-20th century, the tram extended across the river to a cave, where bat droppings were mined for use in fertilizer. Don't let the unromantic name discourage you from walking to the top of Guano Point—the views of the western canyon and Colorado River are superb. Wear shoes with lugged soles: The trail may be short, but it travels close to the cliff edge.

River Rafting
Hualapai River Runners (928/769-2636 or 888/868-9378, www.hualapaitourism.com, Mar.-Oct.) guides white-water raft tours that

launch from Diamond Creek, the only one-day white-water trip in Grand Canyon. The trip includes a moderate hike to Travertine Falls, snacks, lunch, and a waterproof storage container to hold minimal gear, although if you want to bring a video camera, you should supply your own dry bag. Children must be at least eight years old to participate. The heli-float adds $187 pp to the Grand Canyon West admission price.

Hunting

The **Hualapai Wildlife Conservation Department** (P.O. Box 249, Peach Springs, AZ 86434, 928/769-2227) sells permits for guided big-game hunts: desert bighorn sheep, elk, pronghorn antelope, and mountain lions.

EVENTS

The Historic Mother Road inspires a number of festivals and events across northern Arizona, including the annual **Route 66 Fun Run** (www.azrt66.com) held the first weekend in May. Open to all street-legal vehicles from bikes to buses, the run covers 140 miles between Seligman and Topock, passing through Peach Springs, Kingman, Oatman, and other towns. Each community en route welcomes visitors with its own spin on the celebration, such as traditional Native American dances, car shows, barbecues, and live music.

FOOD

The **Diamond Creek Restaurant** at Hualapai Lodge (900 Rte. 66, Peach Springs, 928/769-2800, www.hualapaitourism.com, 6:30am-9pm daily summer, shorter hours in winter, $5-20) offers American-style meals and Native American cuisine in a casual setting. The restaurant will pack a picnic lunch for travelers heading down the Diamond Creek Road. Meals at the Hualapai Reservation's **Grand Canyon West** are usually reserved with tour bookings, but you can find snacks at the welcome center and at each of the three overlooks.

Just outside the reservation, the **Caverns Restaurant** (mile marker 115, Rte. 66, Peach Springs, 928/422-3223, www.grandcanyoncaverns.com, noon-8pm daily summer, 12:30pm-7pm daily winter, hours may vary, $5-20) serves breakfast, lunch, and dinner daily, although hours are limited during winter months. The restaurant will also prepare box lunches for hikers heading into Havasu Canyon. A full bar and patio dining are offered in the summer.

If you're packing a picnic for a day of exploring, Peach Springs has a general store, and there's a convenience store nine miles east of town at Grand Canyon Caverns.

ACCOMMODATIONS

Hualapai Lodge (900 Rte. 66, Peach Springs, 928/769-2230 or 888/868-9378, www.grandcanyonwest.com, $150-170) has refurbished 60 guest rooms with coffeemakers, free Wi-Fi, a seasonal saltwater pool and spa, and a fitness center, along with basic amenities. Hualapai Lodge is a popular staging area for trips to Havasu Canyon and Grand Canyon West, the Hualapai Nation's tourist center. Try to get a room on the side of the hotel opposite the railroad tracks. Rates drop sharply during winter months.

The Caverns Inn (mile marker 115, Rte. 66, Peach Springs, 928/422-3223, www.gccaverns.com, $90-100) is a Route 66 throwback, a 48-room motel with a technological plus—Wi-Fi access. If you're feeling brave, you can spend a night 220 feet underground in the inn's cavern suite ($800). Nine miles east of Peach Springs, the inn is only a few miles from the turnoff to Indian Road 18, the road to the Havasu Canyon trailhead. The inn's staff can help arrange tours of Grand Canyon West, and they have plenty of helpful advice for visiting Havasu Canyon. An outdoor pool and coin-operated laundry are on the premises, with a restaurant and bar nearby. Pets are allowed with a deposit.

If you're hankering for Wild West atmosphere, you have a few options. At Grand Canyon West's **Hualapai Ranch** (928/769-2636 or 888/868-9378), cabins have rim-facing front porches. Overnights start around $150 and include cowboy-style entertainment, wagon rides, dinner, and breakfast.

A few miles outside the Hualapai reservation in Meadview is **Grand Canyon Ranch** (3750 E. Diamond Bar Ranch Rd., 800/359-8727, www.grandcanyonranch.com, from $149). Guests can fly here on a package tour from Las Vegas or drive via the scenic Pearce Ferry Road. The 116,000-acre dude ranch has accommodations in log cabins and tepees, and rates include meals and entertainment.

Nine miles east of Peach Springs, you can saddle up and join a guided ride to a wilderness camp near **Grand Canyon Caverns** (928/422-4565, www.gccaverns.com). Overnight trips start at $300, and the old-time experience is complete with campfire tales, stargazing, and a Dutch-oven breakfast.

CAMPING

Grand Canyon Caverns RV Park (mile marker 115, Rte. 66, Peach Springs, 928/422-3223, www.gccaverns.com, $30-40) has 48 sites with full hookups and additional sites with water but no hookups. The campground has restrooms and showers. As a bonus, you can access the pool, Wi-Fi, and other amenities at the nearby Caverns Inn.

For information about backcountry camping on the Hualapai Reservation, contact the tourism desk at **Hualapai Lodge** (928/769-2636 or 888/868-9378) in Peach Springs. Permits are required for driving on unpaved reservation roads ($16 per day) and for camping ($25 per night).

TRANSPORTATION AND SERVICES

The Hualapai and Havasupai Reservations are both north of I-40. Peach Springs is the Hualapai Nation's headquarters. If you're driving, gas up first in Kingman, Seligman, or Williams. From the west on I-40, turn north on Route 66 at Kingman and drive 50 miles to Peach Springs. If arriving from the east, turn north at Seligman and take Route 66 for 38 miles to Peach Springs. Noncommercial pilots can use the small airstrip near Grand Canyon Caverns.

Tours

A range of tour packages is available for exploring the Hualapai Reservation's rim-side attractions at **Grand Canyon West** (928/769-2636 or 888/868-9378, www.grandcanyonwest.com, $47-360 pp). You can book tours directly with the Hualapai Nation, and several companies in Las Vegas include a visit to Grand Canyon West as part of their packages. Get an early start: The last tour tickets are printed two hours before closing time, and you'll want to spend at least three hours exploring the overlooks.

Tours include viewpoint shuttles and Western-style entertainment, with lodging, meals, rim-side horseback rides, wagon rides, or private guides as options. A popular option is the **Skywalk** ($71 pp), the glass-bottomed bridge that extends 70 feet from Eagle Point and overhangs the canyon. Advance reservations aren't required, but it's a good idea to call ahead and have tickets waiting to save time waiting in line.

Helicopter and airplane tours (928/769-2636 or 888/868-9378) are also available, from a simple 15-minute overflight to descents inside the canyon.

Services

The **Hualapai Office of Tourism** (928/769-2636 or 888/868-9378, www.grandcanyonwest.com) is inside Hualapai Lodge in Peach Springs, about three hours west of Grand Canyon Village. The lodge's front desk, staffed 24 hours daily, has information about tours, and you can obtain permits for driving, hiking, or camping on reservation land.

The Hualapai Nation operates a gift shop in Peach Springs and the **Hualapai Market** at Grand Canyon West. Traditionally, the Pai people are known for basketry, although very few basket makers still practice the craft. Havasupai artisans are also known for beadwork.

Peach Springs Health Center, part of the Indian Health Service, provides urgent care and has after-hours transport services to Kingman.

Navajo Nation

On the eastern end of Grand Canyon, the Navajo Nation borders a 60-mile stretch that explorer John Wesley Powell described in 1869 as "beautifully colored marble." The sheer cliff walls are actually Redwall limestone, but this section of Grand Canyon still bears the name Marble Canyon. Herds of horses, cattle, and sheep graze on Navajo land on the canyon's east rim. As you explore this side of the canyon, keep in mind that the Navajo Nation observes **daylight saving time;** the rest of Arizona does not.

HIGHWAY 64
★ Little Colorado River Gorge

Steep walls of Kaibab limestone and Coconino sandstone confine the **Little Colorado River,** dubbed the LCR or "Little C," to a narrow gorge on its final run to the Grand Canyon. The LCR starts in Arizona's White Mountains and travels 315 miles before joining the Colorado River 61 miles downstream from Lees Ferry. During the LCR's last 30 miles to Grand Canyon, it drops 2,000 feet.

About 10 miles west of the Cameron junction, Highway 64 passes two **overlooks** into the gorge. The Little Colorado River Gorge is a Navajo Nation Tribal Park, and the nation charges a small entry fee to stop at the overlooks. Ramadas provide shade during summer, and there are picnic tables and toilets. A couple of rugged trails explore this area, prone to flash flooding and recommended for experienced canyon hikers only. For more information about current conditions and a permit (necessary for hiking on Navajo land), stop at the **Cameron Visitor Center** (928/679-2303, 8am-5pm Mon.-Fri., shorter summer hours), located at the junction of U.S. 89 and Highway 64 in Cameron.

Shopping

Navajo artisans and their families sell jewelry and other crafts at roadside stands along several reservation routes, including Highway 64, which leads from Cameron to Grand Canyon's East Entrance at Desert View; and on U.S. 89A, across the river from Navajo Bridge Interpretive Center. The specialty at these open-air markets is jewelry, but you may

Little Colorado River Gorge

also find Navajo rugs, pottery, sand paintings, baskets, and souvenirs.

CAMERON

Between Flagstaff and Page, the Navajo Reservation town of Cameron acts as a gateway to the East Rim of Grand Canyon, 30 miles away. The historic trading post is a convenient stop for travelers heading for the canyon, Lake Powell, the Painted Desert, or the Hopi Reservation. If you have only a day or a few hours to add to your canyon visit, and you want to learn more about Native American culture, plan to enter the canyon via the East Entrance and spend some time in the Cameron area.

★ Cameron Trading Post

Hubert and C. D. Richardson established a trading post near this crossing along the Little Colorado River in 1916. In the 1930s, the Grand Canyon Hotel welcomed visitors. A new motel was built near the **Cameron Trading Post** (1 mile north of the junction of U.S. 89 and Hwy. 64, 928/679-2231 or 800/338-7385, www.camerontradingpost.com), which has one of the widest selections of Native American art in northern Arizona. Don't miss the nearby gallery, where you'll find museum-quality artifacts and items crafted by artisans from various Native American communities. The on-site dining room is beautifully adorned with Navajo weavings.

Cameron Suspension Bridge

Next to the Cameron Trading Post, a historic suspension bridge crosses the Little Colorado River at the Navajo Nation town of Cameron. The bridge was named for Ralph Cameron, Arizona's territorial senator, the same man who became a thorn in the side of the Santa Fe Railway at Grand Canyon. Navajo government is organized around "chapters," or settlements, and the name for the Cameron chapter is Na ni' ah' hasani, which translates as "old structure across," in reference to the bridge. Built in 1911, the **Cameron Suspension Bridge** is now listed on the National Register

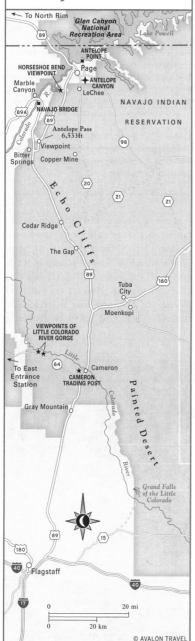

Trading Posts

North of Flagstaff, U.S. 89 passes several historic trading posts, including **Sacred Mountain, Gray Mountain,** and **The Gap.** Once, more than 150 posts dotted the Navajo Reservation, a source of news as well as groceries, tools, and craft supplies. Some traders helped develop markets for indigenous crafts and also acted as interpreters and bankers.

Locals depended on trading posts until highways improved, automobiles replaced horse travel, and regional shopping centers offered a greater variety of goods at lower prices. Most trading posts have closed or transformed into convenience stores, but one of the liveliest examples of a modernized trading post welcomes visitors at Cameron, about 0.5 miles north of the U.S. 89-Highway 64 junction.

Established in 1916 by Hubert and C. D. Richardson, **Cameron Trading Post** is now employee-owned. It's home to a vast selection of crafts made by Navajo, Hopi, Paiute, Tohono O'odham, Apache, and Pueblo artisans. Navajo weavers occasionally work at the large loom in the back, and there's still a small area where locals shop for supplies.

of Historic Places. Once shared by automobiles and flocks of sheep, the 660-foot bridge closed to all traffic in 1958.

Food

The ★ **Cameron Trading Post Restaurant** (U.S. 89, 928/679-2231 or 800/338-7385, www.camerontradingpost.com, 6am-9:30pm daily summer, 7am-9pm daily winter) serves breakfast, lunch, and dinner in a large dining room decorated with Navajo tapestries that offer an introduction to different weaving styles and designs. If you want to fill up before a long afternoon of sightseeing, try the enormous Navajo taco ($13) made from fry bread, a favorite of regional-food junkies. Hearty dinner

Navajo taco at Cameron Trading Post Restaurant

entrées ($12-27) include chops, steak, trout, and Southwestern classics. What you won't find on the menu is alcohol: The trading post is on the Navajo Reservation.

Located on the east side of U.S. 89 near its junction with Highway 64, **Simpson's Market** (Conoco Station, 928/679-2340, 6am-9pm daily summer, 7am-8pm daily winter) has a deli counter, snacks, and a good selection of groceries as well as a few craft items by local artists.

Accommodations

Rates at the **Cameron Trading Post Lodge** (U.S. 89, 928/679-2231 or 800/338-7385, www.camerontradingpost.com, $70-190) vary seasonally, with the lowest rates in January-February and highest in May-October. Some guest rooms are wheelchair accessible, and pets can be accommodated for an additional fee. The lodge complex includes a convenience store, historic and modern trading posts, and a restaurant. Gardens and walkways connect the motel units, situated on a bluff above the Little Colorado River.

Campground

Cameron Trading Post RV Park (U.S. 89, 928/679-2231 or 800/338-7385, www.camerontradingpost.com, $25, monthly $350), 30 miles east of the park's East Entrance Station, has RV sites with full hookups; there are no restrooms or showers. The RV park is within a short stroll of the cliffs overlooking the Little Colorado River and adjacent to historic and modern trading posts, a convenience store, and a restaurant.

Transportation and Services

The Navajo Nation is vast, and most tour companies center on a specific area, such as Monument Valley. You can personalize a journey (starting at $250) that combines sightseeing and cultural events across the reservation by contacting **Navajo Trails** (928/200-5856, http://gonavajotrails.com, suncrane47@gmail.

com) for itinerary planning, logistical support, and guide services.

Cameron Visitor Center (P.O. Box 459, Cameron, AZ 86020, 928/679-2303, lcr@navajonationparks.org, 8am-5pm Mon.-Fri., shorter summer hours), located at the junction of U.S. 89 and Highway 64, serves the western Navajo Nation, including the Little Colorado River Tribal Park. Request camping or hiking permits at least three weeks in advance or stop by the office to see if last-minute permits are available.

The **Cameron Trading Post** (U.S. 89, 800/338-7385, www.camerontradingpost.com, 6am-9:30pm daily spring-fall, 7am-9pm daily winter) complex encompasses a hotel, RV park, restaurant, and convenience market, with a gas station and a post office nearby.

The **Navajo Arts & Crafts Enterprise** (928/679-2244, www.gonavajo.com, 9am-7pm Mon.-Sat., 12pm-6pm Sun.) operates a branch in Cameron. You'll find quality jewelry and crafts here, and NACE can also arrange for repairs and restorations.

U.S. 89 NORTH
The Painted Desert

Those who head for Grand Canyon National Park's East Entrance or the North Rim will get a peek of **The Painted Desert**'s southwestern edge along U.S. 89 near Cameron. Erosion gently rounds the colorful Chinle Formation into soft hills of purples and browns and turns the dark-red Moenkopi sandstone into strange shapes. For a short-but-scenic side trip, continue north to the junction with U.S. 160, about 15 miles from the Cameron Trading Post. Turn right and follow the highway northeast. As the highway climbs toward Tuba City, you'll gain a fine overlook of the Painted Desert, which stretches eastward more than 90,000 acres from Grand Canyon to Petrified Forest National Monument. Warning: Once you head down this road, it will be hard to turn back. If you're not in a hurry to get to Grand Canyon, you might decide to continue to Tuba City's historic trading post and the villages atop the Hopi Mesas.

Echo Cliffs

As you travel U.S. 89 north of Cameron toward Page, Lees Ferry, or the North Rim, you'll be driving alongside the colorful **Echo Cliffs,** a monocline of Triassic and Jurassic rock layers. During the late 1800s, the Honeymoon Trail passed along the base of the cliffs, a wagon route for settlers from St. George, Utah, to Mormon colonies in northeastern Arizona.

A trading post was established below a break in the cliffs at The Gap around 1880, and the area became known for pictorial rugs showing scenes from reservation life. The present red-stone building was erected in 1937 after a fire destroyed an earlier post. Now a **convenience store** (928/283-8932, 9am-5pm daily), it's an interesting place to stop and stretch your legs.

Navajo Bridge

Travelers cross **Navajo Bridge** on their way Grand Canyon's North Rim, or float below it on river trips. Four miles upstream, a ferry once took cars across the river, but it sank in 1928, resulting in a 800-mile detour around canyons and cliffs. No wonder 7,000 people came to this remote corner of the state to celebrate the opening of the bridge in June 1929. Because Prohibition was in effect, Navajo Bridge was christened with a bottle of ginger ale. At the time, it was the highest steel arch bridge in the world.

In 1995, a new span was built alongside the narrow historic bridge. Though it looks like a twin, it's more than twice as wide and designed to carry heavier loads. The 1929 bridge continues its service as a pedestrian crossing, and from its center you can peer 467 feet to the waters of the Colorado River, watching river runners float past. Navajo Bridge is their last view of civilization until they reach Phantom Ranch, 84 miles downriver.

Take a good look at the steel supports underneath to see if you can spot the **California condor** that likes to hang out here. On the Navajo Reservation side of the bridge, vendors sell jewelry and other crafts.

Services

Navajo Bridge Interpretive Center (928/355-2319, 9am-5pm daily Apr.-Oct.) is the southernmost visitor center for the 1.2-million-acre Glen Canyon National Recreation Area. Besides offering travel information, the visitor center has an excellent selection of hard-to-find regional books as well as posters, videos, and restrooms. A stone-and-wood ramada shades plaques and interpretive signs highlighting early river expeditions.

Navajo Bridge Interpretive Center

Marble Canyon and Lees Ferry

Lees Ferry, 14 miles below Glen Canyon Dam, marks the boundary between Glen Canyon and Marble Canyon, and between the Navajo Reservation and public lands managed by Kaibab National Forest, the BLM, and Glen Canyon National Recreation Area. White-water river trips launch from Lees Ferry, which also draws campers, hikers, and anglers. West of Lees Ferry, the Vermilion Cliffs rise above desolate House Rock Valley, where California condors were reintroduced to the Grand Canyon region in 1996.

SIGHTS

★ Lees Ferry

All white-water rafting trips through Grand Canyon put in at Lees Ferry, the former outpost of John D. Lee, a Mormon pioneer who was involved in the Mountain Meadow Massacre of 1857. Brigham Young ordered Lee to this isolated spot, called Lonely Dell, to avoid prosecution for his part in the incident. (It worked, but only for a while—Lee was arrested in 1874 and executed in 1877, though many believe he was merely a scapegoat.) Lee

established a ranch on the Paria River, 0.5 miles above its confluence with the Colorado. The 17th of Lee's 19 wives, Emma, operated the ferry after his death. Short hikes lead to historic ranch buildings, ferry workings, and traces of a placer gold-mining operation.

Today, **Lees Ferry** is a boat launch and popular fly-fishing area, with an adjacent campground and ranger station. The nearest "town" is **Marble Canyon** (pop. 250), a small scattering of motels and restaurants a few miles west along U.S. 89A where you can find gas, limited groceries, and plenty of fishing gear.

Glen Canyon

Lees Ferry marks the southern end of 1.2-million-acre **Glen Canyon National Recreation Area** (www.nps.gov/glca). Most of Glen Canyon, which John Wesley Powell named in 1869, lies under the waters of Lake Powell. If you have your own boat, you can motor up from Lees Ferry to explore the remaining 15-mile stretch of Glen Canyon below the dam. Among the highlights is a

Lees Ferry

Marble Canyon and Lees Ferry

220

HOUSE ROCK VALLEY/
VERMILION CLIFFS
VIEWPOINT

To Jacob Lake

1065

700

Coyote Buttes

89A

CONDOR
RELEASE
VIEWING SITE

Paria Canyon-

Vermilion Cliffs

Vermilion

House Rock Valley

Paria Canyon-

Vermilion Cliffs

Vermilion Cliffs
National
Monument

Paria

Plateau

SAN BARTOLOME
HISTORIC SITE

Wilderness

Cliffs

Vermilion Cliffs

Wilderness

House Rock Rapid
(class 7-9)

Soap Creek

Rider Canyon

CLIFF DWELLERS
LODGE

Paria

River

LEES FERRY LODGE
(VERMILION CLIFFS)

Colorado River

Soap Creek Rapid
(class 5/6)

OVERLOOK

Marble Canyon

Paria Canyon

LEES FERRY

UTAH
ARIZONA

House Rock Wash

89A

Badger Creek Rapid
(class 5-8)

MARBLE CANYON
AIRPORT

NAVAJO
BRIDGE

89

0   0

5 km

5 mi

621

89

Glen Canyon

HORSESHOE
BEND OVERLOOK

GLEN
CANYON DAM

WAHWEAP

Lake Powell

Antelope
Island

98

ANTELOPE
CANYON

Page

PAGE
MUNICIPAL
AIRPORT

ANTELOPE
POINT MARINA

20

20

LeChee

cliff face with archaic and Ancestral Puebloan petroglyphs depicting bighorn sheep and rectangular humanlike figures. This is a great trip for bird-watchers in late fall and winter, when there are fewer boaters and migrant waterfowl take shelter between the beautiful Navajo sandstone cliffs.

Marble Platform

The Colorado River cuts sharply through the rock layers of the **Marble Platform** to create Marble Canyon, bounded by the Navajo Reservation on the east and BLM and U.S. Forest Service land on the west. Marble Canyon, with its colorful Permian-era cliffs, is one of the loveliest sections of Grand Canyon. Dirt roads stretch across the Marble Platform and **House Rock Valley** to remote canyon overlooks, including Triple Arches and Buck Farm.

Tributary canyons zigzag to the Colorado River, and several, including Soap Creek, Rider, and South Canyons, entice canyoneers. **Canyoneering** combines climbing, boulder-hopping, hiking, and wading or swimming in order to explore a canyon's path. Research these routes before attempting them and do not travel alone. Some routes require technical climbs or rappels, most do not have water sources, and all are subject to dangerous flash floods.

Dispersed camping is allowed in most areas managed by the Forest Service or BLM; however, if you hike below the canyon rim, you'll be crossing into Grand Canyon National Park, where permits are required for overnight stays.

RECREATION

Hiking

The Marble Platform is prone to flash floods. If you're hiking and exploring tributary canyons near the Vermilion Cliffs or Marble Canyon, avoid the summer monsoon season (July–mid-Sept.). A storm cell miles away can create flash-flood conditions. No matter what the season, check the forecast before you leave. Always be aware of current conditions: Floods can erase campsites and dump obstacles like trees and boulders in established canyon routes, altering them drastically.

RIVER TRAIL

Distance: 1.2 miles round-trip
Duration: 45 minutes
Elevation gain: Minimal
Effort: Easy
Trailhead: Lees Ferry at launch ramp parking area
This gentle stroll leads upriver through historic ferry and mining operations, beginning a short distance from the parking area at

Lees Ferry and Marble Canyon Hikes

Trail	Effort	Distance	Duration
Lonely Dell Trail	easy	1 mile round-trip	under 1 hour
Triple Alcoves Trail	easy	1 mile round-trip	30 minutes
River Trail	easy	1.2 miles round-trip	45 minutes
Saddle Mountain Trail (Forest Trail 31)	moderate	12 miles round-trip	4-6 hours
Cathedral Wash	moderate	2.5 miles round-trip	1-2 hours
Spencer Trail	strenuous	4.4 miles round-trip	2-3 hours
Nankoweap Trail (Forest Trail 57)	strenuous	8 miles round-trip	3-6 hours
Paria Canyon	strenuous	up to 47 miles one-way	multiple days

Lees Fort. The fort was built in 1874, serving over the years as a trading post, a residence, a school, and a miners' mess hall. Less than 0.5 miles up the trail, the submerged wreck of the *Charles H. Spencer* lies along the river's north bank, brought here in pieces from San Francisco in 1911 to carry coal from Warm Creek, 28 miles upriver, to a short-lived placer gold mining operation at Lees Ferry. Unfortunately, the paddlewheel steamer needed as much coal to get to Warm Creek as she could carry back to Lees Ferry, so she was abandoned after only a few runs. Not far from the wreck, the **Spencer Trail** leads up the rocky cliffs. **The River Trail** continues to the **ruins** of a way station once used by ferry travelers. Look across the river to see cables, the ferry landing, and the old road, built by Robert Brewster Stanton in 1899 after his expedition through Grand Canyon.

SPENCER TRAIL

Distance: 4.4 miles round-trip
Duration: 2-3 hours
Elevation gain: 1,700 feet
Effort: Strenuous
Trailhead: Lees Ferry at River Trail

Cooler spring and fall months are the best times to hike this trail, which leads up an exposed talus slope to the **Vermilion Cliffs,** for outstanding views of the Colorado River and surrounding desert. The trail is named for Charles Spencer, the head of the short-lived placer mining operation that attempted to extract gold from the soft gray hills of Chinle shale at Lees Ferry. Spencer built the trail to transport coal from Warm Creek to the mining site, a feat later undertaken by the steamer submerged about 0.7 miles upriver from the parking lot. The final climb to the top of the cliffs is steep but well worth the effort. From the top, you can see north to **Page** and **Lake Powell.** Marble Canyon is a shadowy gash across the Marble Platform. If you make the hike in late spring or early fall (it's too hot in summer), you'll have a hawk's-eye view of river runners scrambling to load up before departing from Lees Ferry.

CATHEDRAL WASH

Distance: 2.5 miles round-trip
Duration: 1-2 hours
Elevation gain: 300 feet
Effort: Moderate
Trailhead: Along Lees Ferry access road

To reach the trailhead, drive 1.3 miles from the junction of U.S. 89A and the access road leading to Lees Ferry, where there's a large

Follow the Colorado River on the River Trail.

pullout. Park here and descend into the wash, located on the right side of the road. Head for the river, though you may want to explore farther up the wash on your return. Do not attempt this trail if regional rain is a possibility, as the wash is susceptible to flash flooding. The Kaibab limestone walls hold fossils, and water has carved interesting shapes and formations. The hike offers a mild introduction to canyoneering, with some scrambling around and over chockstones or down pourovers. There's even a section of limestone narrows, where wading might be required. The wash opens up at **Cathedral Wash Rapids,** about three miles below Lees Ferry.

LONELY DELL TRAIL

Distance: 1 mile round-trip
Duration: Less than 1 hour
Elevation gain: Minimal
Effort: Easy
Trailhead: Parking lot at Lees Ferry

This easy walk explores the historic buildings, now in ruins, constructed by John D. Lee and others who worked the ferry, which was used until shortly before Navajo Bridge was completed in 1929. The trail follows an old road that leads to **Lonely Dell Ranch,** where Lee brought two of his families to live in 1871. Emma (one of Lee's 19 wives) is said to have exclaimed, "Oh, what a lonely dell," when she saw her new home at the mouth of Paria Canyon. A booklet describing the area's historic buildings is available for $1 at the kiosk. **Historic remains** include a log cabin, a stone house, an orchard, and a cemetery. There are picnic tables and shade but no water, so be sure to bring some with you.

PARIA CANYON

Distance: up to 47 miles one-way
Duration: Multiday backpacking trip
Elevation gain: 1,300 feet
Effort: Strenuous
Trailhead: Multiple

No permit is required for a day hike from Lees Ferry, exploring a mile or two up Paria Canyon. To get here, take the trail past **Lonely**

Dell Ranch. Once you reach the mouth of the Paria, there is no actual trail; you'll be following the bed of the canyon. Depending on how far you hike, you may see the **ruins** of other ranches, petroglyphs, or even a bighorn sheep.

To hike the length of Paria Canyon, which many consider the finest narrow-canyon hike on the Colorado Plateau, you'll need to plan ahead and get a **permit** from the BLM. The best times to hike the Paria are spring and fall, before or after the summer monsoon. Most backpackers start upcanyon and hike down to Lees Ferry. Trailhead options include **Buckskin Gulch, Wire Pass,** and **White House** (all in Utah). Trailheads are relatively remote, so it's wise to leave your car at Lees Ferry and arrange for a shuttle to reach the trailhead or sign up for a guided tour. Make shuttle arrangements in advance; don't expect to get a cell phone signal in this area. For more information and a list of approved shuttle providers, contact the **BLM** (www.blm. gov). **Paria Outpost & Outfitters** (928/691-1047, www.paria.com, outpost@paria.com) can suggest several itineraries, from guided half-day and overnight tours ($125-250 pp) to custom trips to shuttle-only options (starting at $75).

SADDLE MOUNTAIN TRAIL (FOREST TRAIL 31)

Distance: 12 miles round-trip
Duration: 4-6 hours
Elevation gain: 640 feet
Effort: Moderate
Trailhead: Intersects with the Nankoweap Trail in House Rock Valley
Directions: To reach the trailhead, take U.S. 89A (from Jacob Lake or Marble Canyon) to Buffalo Ranch Road (Forest Rd. 445). Follow the road south 25 miles to Forest Road 445G. Take Forest Road 445G west (right) to the end of the road, about five miles. Take the Nankoweap Trail (Forest Trail 57) for one mile to the intersection with the Saddle Mountain Trail (Forest Trail 31).

The Saddle Mountain Trail traverses a bench overlooking Marble Canyon, with the gorgeous **Vermilion Cliffs** and **Kaibab Plateau** as backdrops. The trail fades before it reaches the rim, but it's easy to walk through the open piñon-juniper woodland, approaching the canyon rim for dramatic views of the Colorado River cutting through steep-walled Marble Canyon. In summer months, day hikers can begin from the **Kaibab Plateau trailhead,** reached via unpaved Forest Roads 611 and 610, about 14 miles off Highway 67.

NANKOWEAP TRAIL (FOREST TRAIL 57)

Distance: 8 miles round-trip
Duration: 3-6 hours
Elevation gain: 2,320 feet
Effort: Strenuous
Trailhead: Forest Road 445 in House Rock Valley or Forest Road 610 on the Kaibab Plateau

Forest Service Trail 57 is usually used as a connector route for backpackers attempting the Nankoweap Trail in Grand Canyon National Park. The higher Kaibab Plateau trailhead, snow-covered and inaccessible November to May, is reached from Highway 67 south of Jacob Lake. The lower elevation trailhead begins at the end of the House Rock Valley's Buffalo Ranch Road. Either trailhead takes about 1.5 to 2 hours to reach from Jacob Lake. If the roads are dry, they are suitable for passenger cars.

About a mile up from the **House Rock Valley trailhead,** the trail intersects with the **Saddle Mountain Trail** (Forest Trail 31). Continue on the Nankoweap Trail (Forest Trail 57), cutting through the Saddle Mountain Wilderness. Sections of the steep and narrow trail are difficult to follow, especially as you near the Kaibab Plateau, where postfire growth includes shrubby locust and aspen. At about 2.5 miles, you'll come to **Nankoweap Saddle,** where you can view the network of washes and smaller canyons that drain into Marble Canyon. At the saddle, the Forest Service's Nankoweap Trail intersects with the National Park's Nankoweap Trail, one of Grand Canyon's most difficult routes. If you stay on Trail 57, it's another 1.5 miles to the **Kaibab Plateau trailhead.**

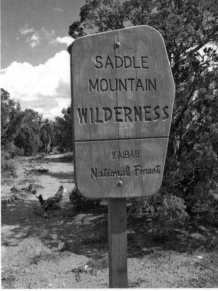

Saddle Mountain Wilderness trails climb from House Rock Valley to the Kaibab Plateau.

TRIPLE ALCOVES TRAIL

Distance: 1 mile round-trip
Duration: 30 minutes
Elevation gain: 250 feet
Effort: Easy
Trailhead: Forest Road 8910 in House Rock Valley
Directions: Take Forest Road 8910 south 23.5 miles to a fork, turning right and driving another seven miles to the trailhead.

More of an overlook than a trail, this easy walk is accessed by a 30-mile drive on unpaved Forest Road 8910, which heads south from U.S. 89A in House Rock Valley, between the Marble Canyon motels and Jacob Lake. If the road is dry, passenger cars can manage it. The road may be washboardy in places, so allow plenty of time for the drive and to enjoy views of the Vermilion Cliffs en route—especially stunning on a fall day when clouds scud across a deep blue sky.

The Triple Alcoves Trail leads 0.5 miles through piñon-juniper woodland to the rim of Marble Canyon. Be sure to bring binoculars to spot **Harding Rapids** below and the **Triple Alcoves** near the mouth of Saddle Canyon. Navajo lands rim the canyon's other side. The river loops around **Point Hansbrough,** an entrenched meander named for the crew-member who drowned here during Stanton's ill-fated 1889 expedition.

Boating

Colorado River Discovery (130 6th Ave., Page, 888/522-6644, www.raftthecanyon. com, from $92 adults, $82 children) leads smooth-water rafting tours through the 15-mile section of Glen Canyon that hasn't been inundated by the lake. Half-day or full-day motorized rafting tours (Mar.-Nov.) start at Glen Canyon Dam and end at Lees Ferry, a pleasant trip suitable for children as young as age four. Oar raft tours ($161 adults, $151 children), available in spring and fall, spend the day floating between the Glen's beautiful Navajo sandstone cliffs.

If you have your own boat (or rent one in nearby Page), you can motor upriver from Lees Ferry to the dam. The trip is only 15 miles, and sandbars and beaches offer several good camp-sites. This is the only remaining section of Glen Canyon, described so lyrically by explorer John Wesley Powell and known to a handful of river runners in the 1950s and 1960s.

These days, it's especially popular with an-glers because the cold, clear waters below the dam are ideal for trout. Along the route, signs distinguish areas set aside for picnicking and day use from Glen Canyon's six official camp-sites, which are available on a first-come, first-served basis. For more information, contact the **Glen Canyon National Recreation Area** (P.O. Box 1507, Page, AZ 86040, 928/608-6200, www.nps.gov/glca). You can also charter a trip with local river guides, or take a guided float tour downstream from the dam.

Fishing

Fishing is available 365 days a year at Lees Ferry. The waters below the dam are a con-stant 47°F, making the area a trophy trout fishery managed by the Arizona Game and Fish Department (www.azgfd.gov). Rainbow trout are common, though brown and cut-throat trout catches have been reported. Fall

and winter are less busy, with more open water for casting. Spawning season begins in mid-November and continues through March. Midges may hatch from March through June (the fish like the midges, but the midges *love* you—wear protective clothing or repellent). Waters are shallower in the fall, good for walk-and-wade fly-fishing.

Only barbless artificial lures and flies may be used at Lees Ferry; no live bait is allowed. The daily bag limit is four trout per person, and it's illegal to possess live fish. You'll find fishing licenses ($55 for out-of-staters) and gear at nearby lodges, where you can also con-nect with a guide. The people who choose to live and work in this sparsely populated area have a genuine passion for their surround-ings. Most local fishing guides have extensive knowledge of the region in addition to angling expertise.

Ambassador Guide Services (928/606-5829, www.ambassadorguides.com) charters trips on the Colorado River and Lake Powell. You can fish the Colorado River elbow-to-elbow with the experienced guides of **Lees Ferry Anglers** (928/355-2261 or 800/962-9755, www.leesferry.com). Their website has detailed fishing reports that can help you de-cide between zebra midges or pink Glo Bugs. The owner of **Marble Canyon Outfitters** (928/645-2781 or 800/533-7339, www.leesfer-ryflyfishing.com) has been fishing the river since childhood.

FOOD

The restaurant and bar at **Marble Canyon Lodge** (U.S. 89A, Marble Canyon, 928/355-2225 or 800/726-1789, www.marblecan-yoncompany.com, 6am-9pm daily summer, 7am-10am and 9pm-8pm daily winter, hours may vary, $5-30) caters to guests, travelers, and river runners who pop in for one last full-service meal before heading downcan-yon. The nearby convenience market has a **deli counter** where you can grab a snack. Better yet, ask the restaurant staff to make you a sandwich for your pack or picnic cooler.

Adjoining Lees Ferry Lodge, the

Vermilion Cliffs Bar & Grille (U.S. 89A, Marble Canyon, 928/355-2231, www.vermilioncliffs.com, 6:30am-8pm mid-Feb.-mid-Nov., hours may vary, $6-25) is famous for its extensive international beer menu. They serve steaks, chops, ribs, chicken, burgers, and even vegetarian fare.

★ **Cliff Dwellers Lodge** (U.S. 89A, Marble Canyon, 928/355-2237 or 800/962-9755, www.cliffdwellerslodge.com, 6am-9pm daily, $5-32) serves hearty breakfasts as well as burgers, wraps, ribs, trout, and steaks. The stone patio is a delightful place to dine, but it can get busy on summer evenings—call ahead for a reservation.

ACCOMMODATIONS

Marble Canyon Lodge (U.S. 89A, Marble Canyon, 928/355-2225 or 800/726-1789, www.marblecanyoncompany.com, $75-150), a former trading post, has basic guest rooms (some with kitchenettes), two-bedroom apartments, and a three-bedroom house handy for groups using the lodge's guide services. Also on the premises: a restaurant, a gift shop, a fly shop, a convenience mart, a coin-operated laundry, a gas station, and a post office. The Marble Canyon Airport is across the highway.

The charming, stone-masonry **Lees Ferry Lodge** (milepost 541.5, U.S. 89A, Marble Canyon, 928/355-2231, www.vermilioncliffs.com, from $80) has 10 guest rooms without phones or TVs, although some have a Franklin stove for chilly nights. Larger guest rooms can accommodate up to five people.

Cliff Dwellers Lodge (U.S. 89, Marble Canyon, 928/355-2261 or 800/962-9755, www.cliffdwellerslodge.com, $80-100) was built in 1949 by a Glen Canyon boatman. Rooms have satellite or cable TV and cell phone service (usually). A three-bedroom guesthouse ($250) has accommodations for groups or families up to six. There's a fly shop and gas pumps as well as a restaurant. Nearby, tucked underneath huge Shinarump boulders, are the "cliff dweller" ruins—actually the remains of a 1920s trading post.

From the Marble Platform, it's about 40 miles to Jacob Lake and another 45 miles to the North Rim. When North Rim services close for the winter, room rates drop sharply in the Marble Canyon area.

CAMPING

★ **Lees Ferry Campground** (no hookups, $18) has 55 designated sites, available on a first-come, first-served basis. Sites have grills, and there are toilets and drinking water nearby. The campground is perched above the river and boat launch, with lovely views of Glen Canyon and the Vermilion Cliffs. To get here, turn right just past Navajo Bridge and drive approximately five miles down Lees Ferry Road, following the signs. For more information, call Glen Canyon National Recreation Area (928/608-6200).

TRANSPORTATION AND SERVICES

From the North Rim, turn right (east) on U.S. 89A at Jacob Lake and drive about 40 miles to reach Marble Canyon and the Lees Ferry Road.

To get to Lees Ferry from the park's East Entrance, take Highway 64 east toward Cameron. Turn north on U.S. 89 and drive 59 miles to Bitter Springs. Turn left (northwest) on U.S. 89A and drive approximately 15 miles to Navajo Bridge. Stay on U.S. 89A to continue to Marble Canyon. To get to Lees Ferry, turn right at the signed turnoff (less than one mile past the bridge). Lees Ferry Road travels seven miles to the edge of the Colorado River, where a large parking area offers access to the boat ramp, picnic ramada, and trails.

From inside the park, you can get to the Marble Canyon area via one of the rim-to-rim shuttle services (mid-May-Nov.): the **Trans Canyon Shuttle** (928/638-2820 or 877/638-2820, www.trans-canyonshuttle.com, $80 pp one-way) or **Grand Canyon Shuttle Service** (888/215-3105, www. grandcanyonshuttles.com), with 24-7 customizable on-demand service. Across the road from Marble Canyon Lodge, a small privately owned airstrip is suitable for single-engine planes—pilots should familiarize themselves with flight restrictions in the Grand Canyon area.

Services

At **Lees Ferry,** six miles from Navajo Bridge, there's a ranger station, where you'll find information about hikes in Glen Canyon National Recreation Area and the eastern end of Grand Canyon. It's possible to score a last-minute backcountry permit at the ranger station for Marble Canyon overnights.

If you're en route to the North Rim, **Marble Canyon Lodge** (U.S. 89A, Marble Canyon, 928/355-2225 or 800/726-1789, www. marblecanyoncompany.com, 7am-8pm daily, hours vary), established as a trading post in Marble Canyon during the 1920s, still carries work by Navajo artists, along with a good selection of books and souvenirs.

En route to the North Rim, you can get gas and ice at Marble Canyon Lodge and Cliff Dwellers Lodge, your last chance to fuel up before Jacob Lake. The nearest hospitals are in Page or Flagstaff. National park rangers and river guides have first-aid training.

★ VERMILION CLIFFS

Two of the Southwest's premier canyoneering adventures lie within the 112,500-acre **Paria Canyon-Vermilion Cliffs Wilderness Area,** administered by the BLM (www.blm.gov/az). Those who wish to explore the slot canyons of the Paria River or Buckskin Gulch usually start north of the Vermilion Cliffs, and permits are necessary for these multiday adventures. For more information, contact the Dixie-Arizona Strip Interpretive Association (435/688-3200, www.d-asia.org) or the BLM's Kanab field office (435/644-1200, www.blm.gov).

Permits aren't necessary to spend a couple of hours exploring the base of the Vermilion Cliffs, where springs and seeps nurture small oases like **Rachel's Pools.** To get here, turn north off U.S. 89A between mileposts 557 and 558; a dirt road leads to an abandoned house and corral at about two miles, where there's room to park. The cliffs, gorgeously layered Triassic and Jurassic rocks, rise 1,000

feet above House Rock Valley, forming part of the geological Grand Staircase that descends from Zion National Park to Grand Canyon. Here and there, large blocks of Shinarump conglomerate have fallen to the valley floor, sometimes supported by small pedestals of mudstone.

As you explore, remember to scan the skies. Six **California condors** were released from the top of the Vermilion Cliffs in 1996, the first time in 72 years that the large birds had flown freely over northern Arizona. Additional releases since have led to a current population of around 60 birds, and several continue to soar over the Marble Canyon area.

Camping

Dispersed camping is allowed in much of the backcountry around the Paria Canyon-Vermilion Cliffs Wilderness Area and in the forest and wilderness areas west of Marble Canyon. The BLM says, "Good campsites are found, not made," and your campsite should look undisturbed when you leave. Restrictions include stays no longer than 14 days, with no camping near archaeological sites or within 200 feet of a water source. Campfires are prohibited in many areas: Check with the appropriate land manager. Contact the BLM's **Arizona Strip Field Office** (435/688-3200, www.blm.gov/az) or **Kaibab National Forest** (928/643-7395, www.fs.usda.gov/kaibab) for more information.

DOMÍNGUEZ-ESCALANTE HISTORICAL MARKER

Along U.S. 89A near milepost 557, a historical marker commemorates the **Domínguez-Escalante expedition of 1776.** The two priests crossed the Colorado River near Lees Ferry before returning to Santa Fe, New Mexico. They failed in their attempt to establish a trail between Santa Fe and missions in California, but their journals include some of the earliest descriptions of the Southwest's canyon country.

Condors at the Canyon

Condors once ranged across North America from Mexico to Canada, but hunting, habitat loss, and lead poisoning decimated their population. By 1985 only nine birds remained in the wild, and biologists made a daring decision, to capture the condors and breed them in captivity. This was no quick fix: Condors don't reach breeding age until they're six years old, and a pair may produce only one egg every year or two. In 1996 six juveniles were outfitted with radio transmitters and identification tags and transported to an acclimation pen on top of the Vermilion Cliffs near Lees Ferry. When released, they became the first condors to fly over Arizona in 70 years.

Grand Canyon's condors have adjusted to life in the wild, despite its hazards. Eagles and other predators (including humans) have killed more than a dozen. Twice that many have died after ingesting lead shot (though the Arizona Game and Fish Department offers hunters free non-lead ammunition). Recently, a breeding female died from **zinc poisoning** after swallowing coins, possibly because she was seeking calcium to produce an egg.

The world's condor population has climbed to 430 captive and wild birds, with over 70 now plying the skies over northern Arizona and southern Utah. A condor can fly more than 100 miles in a single day in search of food. Though they are one of the rarest bird species in the world, condors are curious, and visitors have spotted them investigating campsites and gazing into the windows of Lookout Studio. Sometimes they soar near overlooks, and one likes to hang out on the metal span of **Navajo Bridge.**

To see a condor—the largest land bird in North America—is a thrill. If you spot one during your canyon visit, make note of its tag number and report the sighting to a ranger.

a condor along the Tonto Trail

HOUSE ROCK RANCH

You can watch **free-range buffalo** at the 60,000-acre **House Rock Ranch,** about 20 miles south of U.S. 89A via dirt roads. Charles Jesse "Buffalo" Jones and "Uncle" Jim Owens brought a herd of buffalo to the Kaibab Plateau after the Grand Canyon Game Preserve was established in 1906. Jones convinced backers to invest in his "cattalo" venture, breeding bison with cattle, an experiment that failed (though you may see cattalo wandering the Kaibab Plateau even today). Jones sold his bison to the State of Arizona in the 1920s, and the herd was relocated to the ranch, where 75 to 100 offspring graze on shrubby grassland under permit from the Kaibab National Forest. To get to the ranch, go south on Forest Road 8910 for 19 miles. Turn east at Forest Road 632 and drive two miles to ranch headquarters.

Kaibab National Forest

Administered by the Kaibab National Forest, the Kaibab Plateau doesn't have the amenities of the national park—nor the restrictions. You can hike with your dog, camp at large, and bike almost any trail outside of the designated wilderness areas, terrain permitting.

SIGHTS
★ Kaibab Plateau

John Wesley Powell gave the **Kaibab Plateau** its name from a Paiute word meaning "mountain lying down." The plateau is 8,000 to 9,000 feet in elevation, and its rolling meadows and forests end at the faulted, eroded cliffs of the North Rim. High peninsulas of land extend like fingers toward Grand Canyon, and forest roads and trails lead to the tips, where undeveloped overlooks offer a sense of discovery along with the views. The plateau has the largest stand of old-growth ponderosas in the Southwest and the highest density of the endangered northern goshawk. It's also home to the Kaibab squirrel, an endemic species found nowhere else.

From House Rock Valley, U.S. 89A climbs more than 3,000 feet to the Kaibab Plateau, where the national forest provides more than 1,000 square miles of backcountry hiking and driving for travelers interested in getting away from it all. This lonely stretch between Arizona and Utah is one step in the series of rocky plateaus known as the Grand Staircase.

Scenic Highway 67 heads to the national park's developed Bright Angel Point across the heart of the Kaibab Plateau. Though remote, the rest of the plateau is easily accessed by a network of forest roads that range from good gravel surfaces suitable for passenger cars to rocky two-tracks that can pose challenges even for a high-clearance 4WD vehicle.

The 40,610-acre **Saddle Mountain Wilderness Area** bridges the east side of the plateau and the lower elevations of House Rock Valley. Though winter snows usually close Highway 67, determined hikers can reach the plateau on foot trails, such as the **Nankoweap** or **North Canyon Trails,** which start in the lower elevations and climb toward the plateau's east rim. From the **East Rim Viewpoint** off Forest Road 611, you can access trails and peer into the roadless wilderness.

At the Kaibab Plateau's western reaches is the 68,596-acre **Kanab Creek Wilderness Area,** sharing a boundary with Grand Canyon National Park. The **Jumpup-Nail Trail** leads from the Kaibab Plateau into this wilderness, which protects one of the Southwest's most complex canyon systems. **Crazy Jug Viewpoint** has one of the best views of the canyon's vast **Tapeats Amphitheater,** with **Steamboat Mountain,** the **Powell Plateau,** and other landforms as backdrops. The point, about 55 miles south of Fredonia, can be accessed by passenger cars when roads are dry, via Forest Roads 22, 425, and 292.

Just east, five scenic viewpoints— Parissawampitts, Fence, Locust, North Timp, and Timp—are linked by the 18-mile-long **Rainbow Rim Trail.** Each offers a different perspective, and they are best accessed in a high-clearance vehicle. Before you set out, inquire about forest road conditions at the **Fredonia ranger station** (928/643-7395) or **Kaibab Plateau Visitor Center** (928/643-7298), and be sure to take a current map, as road access can change.

RECREATION
Hiking

On the Kaibab Plateau, heavy **snows close roads November to mid-May,** and muddy roads can persist into June. Elevation changes can mean sudden shifts in the weather, so be prepared. If you're hiking in the Saddle Mountain or Kanab Creek Wilderness Areas, a good topographical map is a must. The Arizona Strip is known as America's Outback

Kaibab Plateau Hikes

Trail	Effort	Distance	Duration
South Canyon Trail (Forest Trail 6)	moderate	5 miles round-trip	2-3 hours
East Rim Trail (Forest Trail 7)	strenuous	3 miles round-trip	2-3 hours
North Canyon Trail (Forest Trail 4)	strenuous	14 miles round-trip	10 hours
Jumpup-Nail Trail (Forest Trail 8)	strenuous	12 miles round-trip	7-8 hours
Rainbow Rim Trail	moderate	18 miles one-way	multiple days

for good reason; this is remote country. Plan backpacking trips carefully, researching water availability and trail conditions in advance. Let someone know your itinerary before you set out, and share your wilderness experience with hiking companions. Always be alert for flash floods when hiking canyon areas, especially during the summer monsoon.

EAST RIM TRAIL (FOREST TRAIL 7)
Distance: 3 miles round-trip
Duration: 2-3 hours
Elevation gain: 1,000 feet
Effort: Strenuous
Trailhead: East Rim Viewpoint off Forest Road 611
Directions: The trailhead is about an hour's drive south of Jacob Lake, suitable for passenger cars in dry weather. Take Highway 67 south 26.5 miles to Forest Road 611, turning left (east). Continue on Forest Road 611 for 2.6 miles to the East Rim Viewpoint. There's parking and a restroom here, but no overnight camping is allowed.

This Saddle Mountain Wilderness Trail is used most often to link to the upper section of the **North Canyon Trail** (Forest Trail 4). The trail is accessible only late spring-early fall, when Highway 67 is open. From the East Rim Viewpoint, the trail descends sharply from the rim, passing through thickets of oak and conifer forests, before ending at the **North Canyon Trail.** Views of **House Rock Valley** and **Marble Canyon** disappear

behind a forest of aspen, bigtooth maple, and ponderosa pine.

NORTH CANYON TRAIL (FOREST TRAIL 4)
Distance: 14 miles round-trip
Duration: 10 hours
Elevation gain: 2,670 feet
Effort: Strenuous
Trailhead: Forest Road 611 (Kaibab Plateau) or Forest Road 631 (House Rock Valley)
Directions: From the Kaibab Plateau, take Highway 67 south of Jacob Lake to Forest Road 611, an hour's drive suitable for passenger cars in dry weather. The trailhead is near the wilderness boundary. From U.S. 89A, take the House Rock Valley Road (Forest Rd. 8910) south to Forest Road 631, turning right. The trailhead is located where Forest Road 631 begins to climb out of North Canyon Wash.

The North Canyon Trail cuts across the Saddle Mountain Wilderness from House Rock Valley to the Kaibab Plateau, connecting with the **East Rim Trail** (Forest Trail 7). The trail can be accessed at either end, but you'll need a high-clearance vehicle to reach the lower trailhead, which is about two hours from Jacob Lake.

The trail loops south a short distance before entering the wash and climbing toward the Kaibab Plateau. In the upper canyon, a perennial stream waters conifer and oak as well as flowers and plants seen nowhere else on the plateau. Here and there, the stream has created pools—some large enough to shelter native Apache trout, a protected species in Arizona.

SOUTH CANYON TRAIL (FOREST TRAIL 6)

Distance: 5 miles round-trip
Duration: 2-3 hours
Elevation gain: 2,200 feet
Effort: Moderate
Trailhead: Forest Road 610 (Kaibab Plateau) or Forest Road 211 (House Rock Valley)
Directions: When roads are dry, access from the Kaibab Plateau is relatively easy, about 1.5 hours from Jacob Lake on Highway 67 south to Forest Roads 611 and 610. From the House Rock Valley Road (Forest Rd. 8910), drive south to Forest Road 211. The trailhead is at the end of the road.

This Saddle Mountain Wilderness trail can be accessed from the Kaibab Plateau or House Rock Valley. Because of the elevations, this shady trail is accessible only late spring-early fall. The trail starts out on an old pipeline access and then climbs sharply to the head of **South Canyon,** a major canyon tributary, passing along rocky outcroppings offering glimpses of Marble Canyon. The narrow, rocky trail tops out on the Kaibab Plateau at 8,800 feet, passing through a forest of ferns, aspen, and mixed conifers.

RAINBOW RIM TRAIL

Distance: 18 miles one-way
Duration: Multiple days
Elevation gain: 800 feet
Effort: Moderate
Trailhead: Parissawampitts Point
Directions: To get to Parissawampitts Point, take Highway 67 south from Jacob Lake for 26.5 miles. Turn right on Forest Road 22 and drive 10.5 miles to Forest Road 206, turning left. Continue on Forest Road 206 for 3.5 miles. Turn right on Forest Road 214 and drive eight miles to Parissawampitts Point. The first 14 miles are good gravel roads. After that, the roads get progressively narrower and rockier, and a high-clearance vehicle is recommended.

The Rainbow Rim Trail traverses the North Rim, linking five points: **Parissawampitts, Fence, Locust, North Timp,** and **Timp.** After leaving the parking area at Parissawampitts, the trail turns south, moving in and out of ponderosa pine forest, playing peekaboo with canyon views that change with each point: the basin of the Tapeats Amphitheater with Powell Plateau, Steamboat Mountain, and Great Thumb Mesa rising above. The lightly used trail has a primeval feel, alternating between mixed forests of conifers and aspen, grassy meadows, and rocky draws overgrown with Gambel oak, New Mexico locust, and ferns. The trail rolls up and down drainages, but grades don't exceed 10 percent.

Most people will hike this trail in sections, starting at one of the trailheads and hiking out and back, but you can arrange to have a second vehicle waiting for you at another of the trailheads. Because the trail lies entirely within the national forest, you can camp at the trailhead or en route, tackle the trail with a **mountain bike** or bring your dog, but be aware that equestrians also use the trail and have the right of way. Mountain bikers can plan loops incorporating forest roads with the trail for long day trips or overnights.

JUMPUP-NAIL TRAIL (FOREST TRAIL 8)

Distance: 12 miles round-trip
Duration: 7-8 hours
Elevation gain: 1,970 feet
Effort: Strenuous
Trailhead: Sowats Point
Directions: To get to the trailhead from Jacob Lake, head south on Highway 67 about 0.25 miles, turning right on Forest Road 461. Forest Road 461 joins Forest Road 462. Continue on Forest Road 462, turning left (south) on Forest Road 22, driving 11 miles to Forest Road 425. Turn right on Forest Road 425, drive eight miles, then take another right on Forest Road 233. Continue nine miles to the trailhead at Sowats Point.

This trail into the Kanab Creek Wilderness Area is difficult to access, requiring a high-clearance vehicle to negotiate nearly 40 miles of dirt road, but the rewards are solitude, scenery, and beautifully sculpted rocks. The trail descends from Sowats Point, providing views of Sowats and Jumpup Canyons. Below the point, the trail follows a bench to the edge of **Sowats Canyon,** crossing the canyon and winding around the point before descending into **Jumpup Canyon.** The piñon-juniper woodland yields to sculpted sandstone formations and steep canyons for a rugged-but-scenic hike. The trail intersects tributary canyons and trails leading to **Kanab Creek,** and experienced wilderness hikers can plan multiday backpacking trips. The Kanab Creek Wilderness Area borders Grand Canyon National Park, and overnight stays across the boundary require a permit.

Biking

The Kaibab Plateau has miles of single-track, double-track, and forest roads for overnight trips or out-and-backs. However, some of the hiking trails leading down the edge of the plateau are steep and rocky, with dangerous drop-offs, and bikes aren't allowed in wilderness areas or on trails that enter the boundaries of Grand Canyon National Park. A couple of good single-tracks for mountain bikes are the 18-mile **Rainbow Rim Trail,** which skirts the southwest edge of the plateau, and the 70-mile **Arizona Trail** on the plateau's east side. The **Kaibab Plateau Visitor Center** (Jacob Lake, 928/643-7298, 8am-4pm daily mid-May-mid-Oct., some weekends through Nov.) has trail maps and suggestions.

Horseback Riding

Allen's Guided Tours (Jacob Lake, 435/644-8150 or 435/689-1660, from $40) offers horseback trips in Kaibab National Forest. The one- to two-hour trip over gentle forest terrain to a rim overlook is suitable for children. Short tours are usually available without a reservation, but if you'd like a longer group tour, make arrangements in advance.

Many of the Kaibab Plateau's forest roads and trails are suitable for equestrians, though some are too steep, rocky, and narrow to be negotiated safely, and lack of water may limit your choices. A good option is the **Arizona Trail,** which travels 70 miles near the plateau's east rim.

Hunting

Contact the Flagstaff district office of the **Arizona Game and Fish Department** (928/774-5045, www.azgfd.gov) for details about hunting on National Forest lands on the Kaibab Plateau.

Grand Canyon views from the Rainbow Rim Trail

FOOD

Jacob Lake Inn (U.S. 89A and Hwy. 67, 928/643-7232, www.jacoblake.com, 6:30am-9:30pm daily summer-fall, 8am-8pm daily winter-spring, $6-25) serves breakfast, lunch, and dinner year-round. The inn also has a small deli where you can pick up picnic items, including gigantic home-baked cookies.

Kaibab Lodge (928/638-2389, www.kaibablodge.com, mid-May-mid-Oct., $4-25), seven miles north of the park entrance, serves breakfast and dinner when the lodge is open. If you're planning an early hike or an afternoon picnic, you can order something to go.

ACCOMMODATIONS

About 45 miles north of the park's Bright Angel Point, at the intersection of Highway 67 and U.S. 89A, the historic **Jacob Lake Inn** (928/643-7232, www.jacoblake.com) has 61 beds in seasonal cabins, a vintage motel, and modern hotel (928/643-7232, www.jacoblake.com, $96-146). All rooms are nonsmoking and some can accommodate pets. The inn is open year-round, becoming a hub for hunters, snowmobilers, and cross-country skiers during late autumn and winter, when rates drop sharply.

Eighteen miles north of Bright Angel Point and seven miles from the park's Entrance Station, **Kaibab Lodge** (Hwy. 67, 928/638-2389, www.kaibablodge.com, May 15-Oct. 20, $90-185) is a former ranch with a collection of cabins, from rustic duplexes to a two-story home that can accommodate up to eight. All guest rooms have private baths and heaters but no TVs or phones. Seasonal closure dates may vary, depending on road conditions.

CAMPING AND CABINS

Elevations on the Kaibab Plateau and North Rim range 6,300 to 8,000 feet, so campers should be prepared for cool evenings, even in the summer (during winter months, campgrounds are closed). Campgrounds near the North Rim's Bright Angel Point tend to fill up quickly.

DeMotte Campground (928/643-7395, www.fs.usda.gov/kaibab, May 14-Oct. 15, $18) is located on the edge of a meadow just off Highway 67, six miles north of the park's entrance station. Operated by the U.S. Forest Service, the campground has 38 sites, half of them **reservable** (877/444-6777, www.recreation.gov), all with tables and grills, drinking water, and vault toilets. Tents, trailers, and small motor homes are allowed, but there are no hookups.

The Forest Service also operates ★ **Jacob Lake Campground** (928/643-7395, www.fs.usda.gov/kaibab, May 14-Oct. 15, $18) 45 miles north of the park's Bright Angel Point. The campground has 53 sites, half of them available by **reservation** (877/444-6777, www.recreation.gov). Sites can accommodate tents, trailers, or small motor homes, but there are no hookups.

Kaibab Camper Village (928/643-7804 or 800/525-0924, off-season 928/526-0924, http://kaibabcampervillage.com, May 15-Oct. 15, $17-85) is located just south of Jacob Lake, less than one mile off Highway 67 on Forest Road 461. The campground offers sites with full hookups to RVers, dry or tent sites, and a small cabin with two queen beds.

Indian Hollow Campground (50 miles south of Fredonia via Forest Roads 22, 435, and 232, free), a primitive Forest Service campground on the Kaibab Plateau, offers nearby access to remote canyon overlooks, the North Rim's Thunder River Trail, and trails leading into the Kanab Creek Wilderness Area. Officially, there are three primitive campsites with tables, grills, and a nearby vault toilet. Unofficially, this little corner of the forest can get busy on summer weekends. A high-clearance vehicle is necessary to negotiate the last few miles. For more information, contact the North Kaibab Ranger District (928/643-7395) or the Kaibab Plateau Visitor Center (928/643-7298).

No-fee dispersed camping is allowed in **Kaibab National Forest** (928/643-7395, www.fs.usda.gov/kaibab). Restrictions include no stays longer than 14 days, and no camping within 100 yards of the highway or near the East Rim Day Use Area along Forest Road 611. Campsites are accessible by dirt roads, many of them suitable for passenger cars. For road conditions and maps, visit the **Kaibab Plateau Visitor Center** (928/643-7298, 8am-4pm daily mid-May-mid-Oct., some weekends through Nov.) in Jacob Lake, or the district ranger's office in Fredonia.

Bordering the Kaibab Plateau on the west, the one-million-acre **Grand Canyon-Parashant National Monument** is managed jointly by the National Park Service and BLM. No-fee dispersed camping is allowed unless otherwise posted. There is a 14-day stay limit, and all trash must be packed out. For more information, contact the BLM's Arizona Strip field office (435/688-3200, www.blm.gov/az) in St. George, Utah.

If you long to get away from it all, but sleeping on the ground isn't for you, consider renting a rustic U.S. Forest Service cabin. (Take note: Though you can hike with your dog on forest service lands, pets aren't allowed in USFS cabins.) The historic **Big Springs Cabins** (877/444-6777, www.recreation.gov, May-Nov. weather permitting, $65) are located off Forest Road 22 (West Side Rd.), approximately 30 miles south of Fredonia and about an hour from Bright Angel Point, with good access to the Rainbow Rim. Each of the seven cabins has one full-size bed and two twins, accommodating up to four people, but you'll need to bring your own linens. The cabins have electricity, and outside you'll find picnic tables, a shared bathhouse with showers and flush toilets, and a communal kitchen and dining hall.

Even more remote and rustic, **Jumpup Cabin** (877/444-6777, www.recreation.gov, May-Nov. weather permitting, $60) is two hours from Fredonia and Bright Angel Point. Though it's accessible by passenger cars when the roads are dry, a high-clearance vehicle is recommended. The cabin has no electricity or running water. It's splendidly isolated, except for the nearby trailhead for popular Jumpup Trail. Pack no-cook meals or be prepared to cook outdoors on the fire ring. You'll also

a cabin at Big Springs Cabins

need to bring plenty of water, unless you're prepared to hike down the trail to Jumpup Canyon to fetch spring water. Bring your own linens or sleeping bags for the double-over-double bunk bed. There's a composting toilet outside, and the cabin has a small woodstove for heat.

TRANSPORTATION AND SERVICES

The tiny settlement of Jacob Lake serves as the gateway to the Kaibab Plateau. Jacob Lake is accessible from the east and west via U.S. 89A, which is open to travel year-round. From Jacob Lake, paved and scenic Highway 67 (open spring-fall) cuts south for 45 miles across the Kaibab Plateau to the park's North Entrance, intersecting with several forest roads en route.

Another north-south route, Forest Road 22, also known as West Side Road, is handy for explorers with sturdy vehicles and a good map. Forest Road 22 begins as a paved road heading south from Fredonia, changing to a good gravel road as it climbs the west side of the Kaibab Plateau, where it connects to a multitude of dirt forest roads that lead to remote trailheads. Most forest road surfaces degrade as they approach the edge of the plateau (i.e., the rim of Grand Canyon), requiring a high-clearance vehicle in dry weather and becoming impassible in wet conditions.

Services

Trails and roads north of Grand Canyon National Park are particularly remote, and cell phone coverage is spotty. Pay phones and first aid are available in Jacob Lake or inside park boundaries at Bright Angel Point, the park's developed area on the North Rim. The nearest hospital is in Kanab, Utah.

In Jacob Lake, the forest service's **Kaibab Plateau Visitor Center** (928/643-7298, www.fs.usda.gov/Kaibab, 8am-4pm daily mid-May-mid-Oct., some weekends through Nov.) has a bookstore with gifts and maps. The helpful staff can field questions about the national park as well as provide information for current conditions, camping, hiking, biking, and driving in the North Kaibab district of the Kaibab National Forest.

You can find a hot meal, gifts, and travel information at **Jacob Lake Inn** (U.S. 89A and Hwy. 67, 928/643-7232, www.jacoblake.com, 6:30am-9:30pm daily summer-fall, 8am-8pm daily winter-spring). Next to the inn is a year-round gas station.

South of Jacob Lake, fuel, camping supplies, and snacks are available seasonally at the **North Rim Country Store** (928/638-2383, 7:30am-7pm daily mid-May-Oct.), located at milepost 605 on Highway 67, less than a mile north of the Forest Road 22 intersection. Across the road is **Kaibab Lodge** (928/638-2389, www.kaibablodge.com, mid-May-mid-Oct.).

In Fredonia, forest service staff at the **North Kaibab District Headquarters** (430 S. Main St., Fredonia, 928/643-7395, 8am-4pm Mon.-Fri.) know the latest scoop on road conditions and can provide maps and information. The BLM operates the top-notch **Kanab Visitor Center** (745 E. U.S. 89, Kanab, Utah, 435/644-4680, www.blm.gov, 8am-4:30pm daily), where you can learn more about Grand Staircase-Escalante National Monument, Paria Canyon, Buckskin Gulch, or the Vermilion Cliffs.

Forest Road 22 leads across the Kaibab Plateau.

Gateways to the Grand Canyon

Flagstaff, Williams, Page, and Kanab all make convenient gateways for Grand Canyon travel. Each is worthy of a day or two of sightseeing to take in its distinct charms. Though the park is only an hour or two from each, add extra time to enjoy the scenery and points of interest along your chosen route.

Museums, trails, skiing, brewpubs—the mountain town of Flagstaff combines urban pleasures with a host of outdoor activities. The largest of Grand Canyon's gateways, Flagstaff also has a number of transportation options for getting to the canyon or touring the region.

Williams, home to the Grand Canyon Railway and Route 66, will delight train buffs and nostalgia-seekers, while boaters and backpackers could spend days exploring the sandstone canyons edging Page's Lake Powell. Just across the Arizona-Utah border, Kanab makes a convenient base for traveling to the North Rim, Zion, Bryce Canyon, and other national parks and monuments on the Grand Circle of the Southwest.

PLANNING YOUR TIME

Kanab, Page, Williams, and Flagstaff are worthy destinations in themselves, with attractions from hikes to historic sites. Plan your itinerary for the park, and then add a couple of days to explore your Grand Canyon gateway.

For maximum scenery on a limited schedule, make a loop through **Flagstaff, Williams,** and the canyon's South Rim. If your Grand Canyon plans include backpacking or camping, you might want to linger in Flagstaff for a few days to adjust to the altitude and stock up on supplies. It's about three hours from Flagstaff to Lees Ferry, the launching point for white-water trips through Grand Canyon.

If your itinerary includes other Grand Circle national parks, stay in **Kanab** so that you can set aside a day or two for the North Rim. If water sports are your favorite activities, a couple of days in **Page** will offer lots of options.

Previous: Flagstaff's visitor center and historic downtown; Horseshoe Bend near Page. **Above:** Route 66 Motel in Seligman.

Look for ★ to find recommended sights, activities, dining, and lodging.

Highlights

★ **Museum of Northern Arizona:** Gain an understanding of the region's natural and cultural history at this splendid museum, tucked among the ponderosa pines north of Flagstaff (page 208).

★ **Arizona Snowbowl:** Take Snowbowl Road up the San Francisco Peaks for access to hiking trails, a gondola ride to the ski resort, and endless views of surrounding mountains and valleys (page 210).

★ **Inner Basin Trail:** Explore the caldera of the San Francisco Peaks on this four-mile round trip hike, which begins in lovely Lockett Meadow and climbs through aspen-and-pine forests (page 212).

★ **Route 66:** Walk, bike, or drive to get your kicks on Route 66, which changes character from bustling Main Street to peaceful forest roads near Williams (page 220).

★ **Bearizona:** Kids and adults love this 20-acre wildlife park with bears, bobcats, wolves, owls, and other woodsy critters (page 221).

★ **John Wesley Powell Memorial Museum:** Learn about Powell's historic voyage down the Colorado River (page 228).

★ **Pipe Spring National Monument:** This oasis on the Arizona Strip is rich with the history of the Kaibab Paiute people and Mormon pioneers (page 237).

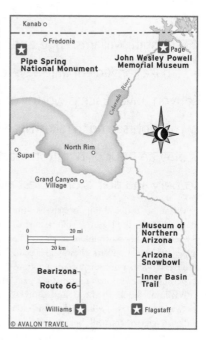

Gateways to the Grand Canyon

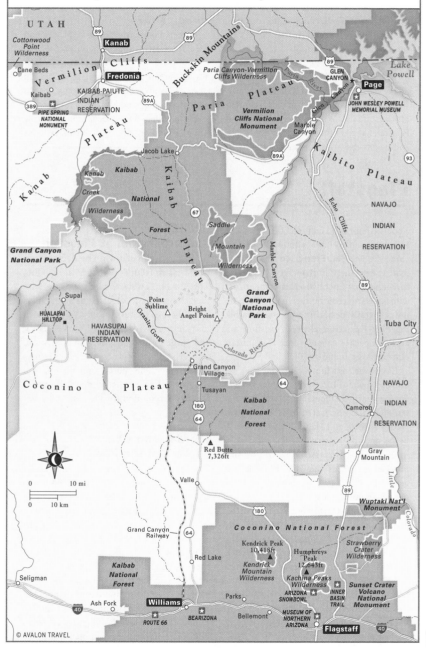

Weather and Seasons

During the busy **summer** season, rooms book quickly, particularly in Page, a destination for desert dwellers hoping to cool off in the sparkling blue waters of Lake Powell. The sun-drenched plateau country around Kanab can be hot in the summer, but it's a short drive up to the cooler temperatures and shady forests of the North Rim and Kaibab Plateau.

Even in summer, the mountain towns of Flagstaff and Williams are cool havens. Flagstaff has plentiful rooms for every budget, and it's possible to find one at the last minute, even during summer. But why wait? Make reservations well in advance so that you can spend your time looking at the scenery instead of looking at vacancy signs.

Winter sports activities make Flagstaff an attractive destination year-round. Even so, you'll find discounts on accommodations during the **winter** off-season, as you will in Grand Canyon's other gateway towns. Keep in mind that in Page and Kanab, some establishments may close for weeks or months during winter, when the park's North Rim facilities are also closed.

Flagstaff

About an hour and a half from the South Rim, Flagstaff (pop. 69,000) is an outdoor lover's paradise. The **San Francisco Peaks** dominate the northern horizon, and the town is surrounded by **Coconino National Forest,** with access to scenic byways, a ski resort, and miles of trails for hiking and mountain-biking. Pine-scented air, plenty of sunshine, and an event-packed calendar lure Flagstaffians outdoors year-round.

Established as a lumbering, ranching, and railroad town in 1876, over the next decades Flagstaff earned a reputation as a science center. Pluto was discovered in 1930 at **Lowell Observatory,** and Flagstaff was the first to be designated an International Dark Sky City in 2001. **Northern Arizona University,** founded in 1899, is known today for its programs in forestry, geology, conservation biology, and climate research.

The university infuses the city with a youthful energy that influences art, music, and an ever-expanding food and brew culture. A number of river guides, landscape photographers, and dedicated canyon worshippers call Flagstaff home. Strike up a conversation with the people sitting next to you at one of the city's numerous coffeehouses, and you're likely to get some valuable inside tips on favorite trails or photo locations.

SIGHTS
The Arboretum at Flagstaff

Four miles south of town, **The Arboretum at Flagstaff** (4001 S. Woody Mountain Rd., 928/774-1442, www.thearb.org, 9am-5pm Wed.-Mon. Apr. 15-Oct., adults $8.50) spotlights the area's natural beauty. Daily guided tours include bird walks, wildflower walks, and garden tours, all free with admission. Concerts and other events are held throughout summer, and there's a picnic area and a nature-themed gift shop. Admission fees are discounted for kids, seniors, and even dogs.

Riordan Mansion State Historic Park

On the edge of the Northern Arizona University campus, **Riordan Mansion State Historic Park** (409 W. Riordan Rd., 928/779-4395, http://azstateparks.com, 9:30am-5pm Thurs.-Mon., adults $10, youths $5) preserves a sprawling, Craftsman-style duplex designed by Charles Whittlesey, the architect of Grand Canyon's El Tovar. Visitors can learn more about Flagstaff's pioneer past on guided tours (included with admission). In winter, expect shorter hours—and vintage holiday decorations. Tour reservations are recommended.

Flagstaff

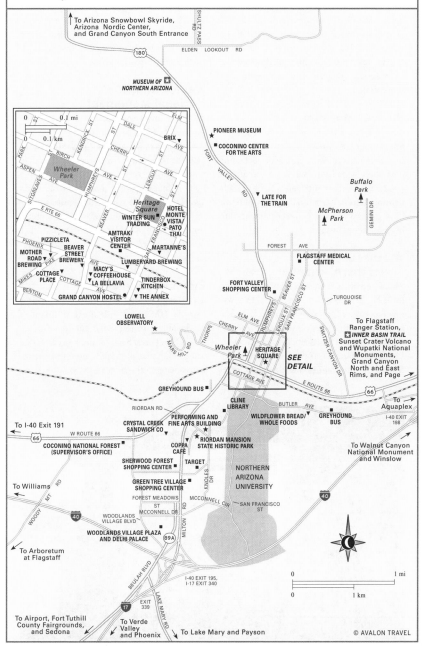

To Arizona Snowbowl Skyride,
Arizona Nordic Center,
and Grand Canyon South Entrance

SHULTZ PASS RD

ELDEN LOOKOUT RD

180

MUSEUM OF NORTHERN ARIZONA

PIONEER MUSEUM

COCONINO CENTER FOR THE ARTS

FORT VALLEY RD

Buffalo Park

GEMINI DR

LATE FOR THE TRAIN

McPherson Park

Detail inset:

0   ST   0.1 mi
0   0.1 km

PARK ST
ASPEN
STIGREAVES
E RTE 66
PHOENIX
PIZZICLETA
MOTHER ROAD BREWING
PIKE
MIKES
BENTON
COTTAGE
COTTAGE PLACE

KENDRICK ST
BIRCH ST
HUMPHREYS ST
BEAVER ST
Wheeler Park
AVE

ELM
DALE AVE
CHERRY AVE
BIRCH AVE
ASPEN AVE
LEROUX ST
SAN FRANCISCO ST

BRIX

Heritage Square
WINTER SUN TRADING
AMTRAK/ VISITOR CENTER
HOTEL MONTE VISTA/ PATO THAI
MARTANNE'S
BEAVER STREET BREWERY
LUMBERYARD BREWING
MACY'S COFFEEHOUSE
LA BELLAVIA
TINDERBOX KITCHEN
GRAND CANYON HOSTEL
THE ANNEX

FOREST AVE

FLAGSTAFF MEDICAL CENTER

TURQUOISE DR

FORT VALLEY SHOPPING CENTER

LOWELL OBSERVATORY

MARS HILL RD

THORPE

ELM AVE
CHERRY AVE
HUMPHREYS
LEROUX ST
SAN FRANCISCO ST
BEAVER ST
SWITZER CANYON DR

To Flagstaff Ranger Station,
INNER BASIN TRAIL
Sunset Crater Volcano and Wupatki National Monuments, Grand Canyon North and East Rims, and Page

Wheeler Park
HERITAGE SQUARE
SEE DETAIL

COTTAGE AVE
E ROUTE 66
66

To Aquaplex

GREYHOUND BUS

RIORDAN RD
CRYSTAL CREEK SANDWICH CO
To I-40 Exit 191
W ROUTE 66
66

CLINE LIBRARY
PERFORMING AND FINE ARTS BUILDING
BUTLER AVE
WILDFLOWER BREAD/ WHOLE FOODS
GREYHOUND BUS
I-40 EXIT 198

COCONINO NATIONAL FOREST (SUPERVISOR'S OFFICE)
COPPA CAFÉ
RIORDAN MANSION STATE HISTORIC PARK

To Walnut Canyon National Monument and Winslow

SHERWOOD FOREST SHOPPING CENTER
TARGET
GREEN TREE VILLAGE SHOPPING CENTER

NORTHERN ARIZONA UNIVERSITY

To Williams

WOODY MT RD
40

FOREST MEADOWS ST
MCCONNELL DR
KNOLES DR
MCCONNELL CIR
SAN FRANCISCO ST

MILTON RD

WOODLANDS VILLAGE BLVD
WOODLANDS VILLAGE PLAZA AND DELHI PALACE
89A

40

To Arboretum at Flagstaff

BEULAH BLVD
LAKE MARY RD

I-40 EXIT 195,
I-17 EXIT 340

EXIT 339
17

To Airport, Fort Tuthill County Fairgrounds, and Sedona

To Verde Valley and Phoenix

To Lake Mary and Payson

0   1 mi
0   1 km

© AVALON TRAVEL

Lowell Observatory

Lowell Observatory (1400 W. Mars Hill Rd., 928/774-3358, www.lowell.edu, 10am-10pm Mon.-Sat., 10am-5pm Sun., adults $12, youths $6, tours and programs included) sits atop Mars Hill, overlooking historic downtown. Daily guided tours are followed by evening telescope viewing and multimedia presentations.

Pioneer Museum

The Arizona Historical Society's **Pioneer Museum** (928/774-6272, www.arizonahistoricalsociety.org, 9am-5pm Mon.-Sat. summer, 10am-4pm Mon.-Sat. winter, adults $6, youths $3) has family-friendly exhibits highlighting Arizona's territorial era. The museum hosts folkway festivals and reenactments during summer months.

★ Museum of Northern Arizona

The superb **Museum of Northern Arizona** (3101 N. Fort Valley Rd., 928/774-5213, www.musnaz.org, 10am-5pm Mon.-Sat., 12pm-5pm Sun., adults $12, youths $8) introduces the cultures and landscapes of the Colorado Plateau and Grand Canyon, exhibiting everything from dinosaur bones to contemporary Southwestern paintings. The museum's heritage celebrations, including the venerable **Hopi Festival** in early July, highlight Native American arts, traditional dances, and demonstrations. In summer, **Thirsty Thursdays** feature later hours—along with live music, libations, and organic cuisine.

Walnut Canyon National Monument

Walnut Canyon National Monument (7.5 miles east of Flagstaff on I-40, 928/526-3367, www.nps.gov/waca, 8am-5pm daily June-Oct., 9am-5pm daily Nov.-June, adults $8, free under age 16) preserves cliff dwellings made by the Sinagua people more than 700 years ago. The shady Rim Trail (0.7 miles round-trip) offers views of the ruins across a pretty limestone canyon. Along the Island Trail (1 mile round-trip), visitors can peer inside masonry rooms.

Elden Pueblo

The Sinagua people also constructed **Elden Pueblo** (U.S. 89, 1 mile north of Flagstaff Mall, sunrise-sunset daily year-round, free), now a U.S. Forest Service site. You can take a self-guided tour of this 65-room village, situated beneath the slopes of a lava dome and

Museum of Northern Arizona

shaded by ponderosa pines, but if you're an Indiana Jones wannabe, time your visit with a workshop or special event. Occasional public dig days are offered spring to fall, and during summer, the **Elden Pueblo Archaeology Project** hosts a field school for avocational archaeologists. For more information, contact the **Coconino National Forest** (928/527-3600, www.fs.usda.gov/coconino).

Sunset Crater Volcano and Wupatki National Monuments

Flagstaff is situated within 200 square miles of cinder cones, lava domes, and other volcanic features. Learn more about the area's volcanic past at **Sunset Crater Volcano National Monument** (U.S. 89, 12 miles north of Flagstaff, 928/526-0502, www.nps.gov/sucr, 8am-5pm daily June-Oct., 9am-5pm daily Nov.-June, $20 per vehicle, includes Wupatki National Monument). The crater—actually a 1,000-foot-tall cinder cone—was named by Grand Canyon explorer John Wesley Powell. Sunset Crater's reddish cinders are colored by oxidized iron particles. Gases from steam and evaporated minerals such as limonite, sulfur, and gypsum tinted the crater's rim yellow, orange, and purple. Park visitors can get a closer look at fumaroles (gas vents) and lava tubes or hike to the top of Lenox Crater.

Sunset Crater is believed to have erupted in AD 1065. Its fiery glow must have been visible for hundreds of miles, a possible factor in the prehistoric population boom that occurred at Wupatki, 33 miles north of Flagstaff. The Sinagua people were among those who constructed pueblos as the cinder cone was erupting. The ruins are now preserved as **Wupatki National Monument** (928/679-2365, www.nps.gov/wupa, 9am-5pm daily, $20 per vehicle, includes Sunset Crater Volcano National Monument). The two monuments are linked by a 36-mile paved loop off U.S. 89, an interesting and scenic side trip for those heading to Grand Canyon National Park's East Entrance.

RECREATION

Flagstaff is surrounded by 1.8-million-acre **Coconino National Forest,** offering a bounty of recreation opportunities that include hiking, cycling, camping, and skiing. Summers are deliciously cool (in Arizona terms), with daytime highs around 80°F and nighttime temperatures dipping into the 40s. The crisp, clean air and 7,000-foot altitude have turned Flagstaff into a high-altitude training destination for Olympic competitors

Wupatki National Monument is a fascinating side trip between Flagstaff and the East Entrance.

and elite runners. Maybe it's from rubbing elbows with world-class athletes, or maybe it's just something in the air, but Flagstaffians are dedicated outdoor enthusiasts.

Buffalo Park

The main draw for outdoor lovers is the cluster of mountains known collectively as the San Francisco Peaks. You can get great views of the peaks while stretching your legs at **Buffalo Park** (2400 N. Gemini Rd., sunrise-sunset daily), the brightest gem among Flagstaff's sparkling city parks. Buffalo Park's wide-open expanse is traversed by an interconnecting network of walking and biking trails. Many link to the city's urban trail system, FUTS (pronounced "foots"), which joins neighborhoods and businesses with more than 50 miles of multiuse trails.

Forest Roads

During summer and fall, unpaved forest roads are gateways to mountainside trails and meadows. While many forest roads in Flagstaff's high country are closed to vehicles during winter months (and may be too muddy to travel in early spring), they can be explored on snowmobile or skis. Check with the **Flagstaff Ranger District** (5075 N. U.S.

89, 928/526-0866, www.fs.usda.gov/coconino, 8am-4:30pm Mon.-Fri.) for current conditions and closures.

Schultz Pass Road (Forest Rd. 420) cuts 26 miles through the mountains and is suitable for passenger cars or bikes. This scenic gravel road can be accessed from the west (2 miles north of Flagstaff off U.S. 180) or the east (11 miles north of Flagstaff off U.S. 89). Take the highway back to town for a drive of about an hour, or continue to Grand Canyon.

Hart Prairie Road (Forest Rd. 151), 10 miles north of Flagstaff on U.S. 180, is spectacular in the fall when aspen groves turn golden. It's a popular picnic destination at this time of year. If you have a high-clearance vehicle, you can continue east onto Forest Road 418 to make the **Around-the-Peaks Loop,** a drive that takes about two hours if you can resist stopping to hike, picnic, or snap photos of deer and wildflowers.

★ Arizona Snowbowl

Seven miles north of Flagstaff on U.S. 180, paved Snowbowl Road winds up the mountainside 6.6 miles, providing access to viewpoints, trailheads, and the ski resort. During summer months, the **Skyride** (928/779-1951, www.arizonasnowbowl.com, 10am-4pm

See golden aspens in the fall on Hart Prairie Road.

San Francisco Peaks

the San Francisco Peaks after a November snowfall

North of Flagstaff, a distinctive cluster of peaks—Humphreys, Agassiz, Fremont, Abineau, Rees, and Doyle—are remnants of a single extinct volcano estimated to have been 16,000 feet high. Known collectively as the San Francisco Peaks, they were created when the stratovolcano—active between two million and 200,000 years ago—erupted and collapsed around an inner basin. Mount Humphreys is Arizona's tallest mountain at 12,633 feet.

Sixteenth-century Spanish explorers drew maps naming the peaks Sierra Sinagua de San Francisco for their patron saint. *Sierra* denotes jagged ridges; *sin agua* (without water) acknowledges that the Spanish found no lakes or streams here.

Long before the Spanish arrived, people throughout the Grand Canyon region revered the peaks, visible for a hundred miles. To the Hopi people, this was the home of the kachinas, benevolent supernatural beings who bestow rain and other blessings. The Hopi called it *Nuva'tuk-iya-ovi*, "Place of High Snows."

The peaks' Navajo name is *Dook'o'oosliid*, "Abalone Shell Mountain." It is the westernmost of the four sacred mountains that mark the boundaries of the nation's homeland, Diné Bikéyah. The Havasupai people once roamed the peaks' northern flanks and called it *Hvehasahpatch*, "Big Rock Mountain." In all, thirteen nations continue to regard the peaks as sacred—a centerpiece of ceremony and stories, and a place for gathering medicinal herbs and other resources.

Anglos entering the area in the mid-1800s valued the peaks for other reasons—as a source of water, minerals, and timber. The peaks were logged intensively, and cattle grazed on lower slopes. For years, railcars transported water from the peaks to Grand Canyon Village. A ski lodge was built in 1930, and in later decades pumice was mined from the mountainside for "stonewashing" denim jeans.

Since 2005 local Native American communities and environmental organizations have fought the ski resort's request to make snow from treated wastewater. After hearings by several courts, the most recent appeal was denied, and snowmaking began in 2012. Yet the controversy continues. In 2015 the Navajo Nation filed a petition with the Inter-American Commission on Human Rights, stating that snowmaking with wastewater violated religious freedom and cultural protections.

Sat.-Thurs., 10am-5pm Fri. Memorial Day-Labor Day, adults $15) carries visitors to 11,500 feet for panoramic views that take in the Grand Canyon. During winter, the **Arizona Snowbowl ski resort** (9am-4pm daily Nov.-mid-Apr., lift tickets $55-80) hosts a ski school and has 40 runs for skiers and snowboarders.

Arizona Nordic Village

Snow sports enthusiasts can spend a few hours or a few days at the **Arizona Nordic Village** (15 miles north of Flagstaff, mile marker 232, U.S. 180, 928/220-0550, www.arizonanordicvillage.com, trail passes $5-18) to enjoy miles of groomed cross-country trails shared with snowshoers, rent fat-tire snow bikes, or camp in a yurt or cabin. In summer months, the trails are open for hiking and horseback riding.

Hiking

Coconino National Forest encompasses the largest contiguous stand of ponderosa pines in world, covering a variety of terrain, including mountains, meadows, and canyons. The forest's **Flagstaff Ranger District** (5075 N. U.S. 89, 928/526-0866, www.fs.usda.gov/coconino, 8am-4:30pm Mon.-Fri.) is home to more than 30 official trails and dozens of unofficial trails, most of them accessed from forest roads.

KACHINA TRAIL

Among Flagstaff's best-known forest hikes is the **Kachina Trail** (10 miles round-trip). Although the trail is not particularly steep, most hikers will find any climb at this elevation somewhat strenuous. The Kachina Trail begins off paved Snowbowl Road (Forest Rd. 516). Take U.S. 180 north of Flagstaff seven miles, then turn on Forest Road 516 and drive another seven miles to the first parking area on the right. The trailhead is at the end of the parking lot. The Kachina Trail meanders through the San Francisco Peaks' aspen-and-pine forests and grassy meadows, offering gorgeous views of the surrounding mountains and valleys.

the Kachina Trail

★ INNER BASIN TRAIL

The **Inner Basin Trail** (4 miles round-trip, moderate) begins in **Lockett Meadow,** a popular hiking and picnicking area during summer and fall. The trail starts out climbing through a mixed forest of ponderosa and aspen, joining with an old jeep road for the last 0.5 miles before reaching the open meadows of the basin. To get to Locket Meadow, take U.S. 89 north of Flagstaff 12.5 miles, turning left on Forest Road 522. After one mile, turn right, following signs to Lockett Meadow and the trailhead. (When fall color peaks in October, the trailhead's 50 parking spots fill quickly, particularly on weekends.)

MOUNT ELDEN

Several trails, including **Fat Man's Loop** (2 miles round-trip, easy), climb the basalt-cobbled slopes of 9,299-foot **Mount Elden,** a petrified lava dome. The loop links to the **Elden Lookout Trail** (6 miles round-trip, strenuous). The trailhead is just north of the Flagstaff Ranger District Office (5075 N.

U.S. 89), where you can get maps and hiking suggestions.

KENDRICK PEAK AND LAVA RIVER CAVE

North of Flagstaff, hikers can choose between three challenging wilderness trails to the top of 10,418-foot **Kendrick Peak**, a lava dome formed by flowing magma. For an easier—and somewhat eerie—adventure, enter **Lava River Cave**, a chilly, mile-long lava tube. Be prepared with flashlights, warm clothes, and sturdy shoes—the uneven lava floor can be slippery and sharp, and the cave temperature hovers around 40°F, even in summer. To reach the trailhead, drive north of Flagstaff on U.S. 180 for nine miles, turning left (west) on Forest Road 245 and continuing three miles to Forest Road 171. Turn left and continue another mile to Forest Road 171B, which leads to the cave.

Fitness

Swim laps, climb a wall, or take a Zumba class at Flag's family-friendly fitness center, the **Aquaplex** (1702 N. 4th St., 928/213-2300, www.flagstaffaquaplex.org, 6am-9pm Mon.-Sat., 10am-6pm Sun.) Day passes ($10 adults) are discounted for kids and seniors. Test your climbing skills at **Beta Bouldering Gym** (495 S. River Run Rd., 928/266-0498, www.betaboulderinggym.com, 10am-10pm Mon.-Sat., 10am-6pm Sun., $14 adults), with 4,500 square feet of wall, a fitness gym, and gear shop.

ENTERTAINMENT AND EVENTS

The best party in town happens on **First Friday** every month, when downtown galleries stay open late for the hugely popular art walk. On summer weekends, **Heritage Square** (E. Aspen Ave., between N. Leroux St. and N. San Francisco St.), hosts live music, family films, yoga classes, and more. Nearby **Wheeler Park** (W. Aspen Ave. and N. Humphrey St.) makes a grassy picnic spot anytime, but on summer weekends, it's often

ground zero for art fairs, wine tasting, and music festivals. For concerts, sporting events, and art exhibits, see what's on at **Northern Arizona University** (www.nau.edu).

Flagstaff residents know how to make the most of winter, but when the high country's sweet and brief summer arrives, the calendar explodes with outdoor festivals and entertainment. For starters: **Flagstaff Rodeo** (June), an **Independence Day** (July) symphony under the stars, the **Flagstaff Yoga Festival** (Aug.), **Route 66 Days** (Sept.), and the **Pickin' in the Pines Bluegrass Festival** (Sept.). Check the online arts calendar (www.flagstaff365.com) for details.

For the scoop on events, as well as restaurant reviews, movie schedules, and entertainment listings, pick up a copy of *Flagstaff Live!* (www.azdailysun.com/flaglive), the free local weekly that hits the streets on Thursday mornings, or *The Noise* (www.thenoise.us), a monthly art-and-news tabloid for northern Arizona.

SHOPPING

For unique gifts, souvenirs, or Native American art, browse through the galleries and trading posts in historic downtown. You can get a window into native culture while shopping at **Winter Sun Trading Company** (107 N. San Francisco St., 928/774-2884, www.wintersun.com, 9am-5pm Mon.-Sat., 11am-4pm Sun.), where you'll find kachina carvings, ethnobotanical remedies, and marvelous natural skin care products, including an herbal salve that river runners swear by for healing chapped hands.

The **Artists' Gallery** (17 N. San Francisco St., 928/773-0958, www.flagstaffartistsgallery.com, 9:30am-6:30pm Mon.-Sat., 9:30am-5:30pm Sun.) is a co-op where you can talk to local artists and photographers about their work.

Flagstaff Mall (4650 N. U.S. 89, 928/526-4827, www.flagstaffmall.com, 10am-9pm Mon.-Sat., 11am-6pm Sun.), anchored by Sears, Dillards, and JC Penney, is located on Flagstaff's northeast side. Not far from the university, off Milton Road, you'll find **Target** (1650 S. Milton Rd., 928/774-3500, 8am-10pm Mon.-Sat., 8am-9pm Sun.), **Walmart** (2750 S. Woodlands Village Blvd., 928/773-1117, 24 hours daily), and other big-box retailers.

Outdoor Gear

Flagstaff is paradise for gearheads, with a host of stores selling sporting goods. (Not surprising for the birthplace of Teva, the sports sandals developed by a Grand Canyon boatman.) You can rent equipment at **Babbitt's Backcountry Outfitters** (12 E. Aspen Ave., 928/774-4775, www.babbittsbackcountry.com, 9am-8pm Mon.-Sat., 10am-6pm Sun.) and **Peace Surplus** (14 W. Route 66, 928/774-4521, www.peacesurplus.com, 8am-9pm Mon.-Fri., 8am-8pm Sat., 8am-6pm Sun.). And if you're putting together a river trip through Grand Canyon, Flag is an ideal starting point—several trip outfitters are based here.

FOOD

Flagstaff has dozens of chain restaurants on its margins, but you'll find the best of a burgeoning local restaurant scene downtown. One exception, close to NAU, is the delightful **Coppa Café** (1300 S. Milton Rd., 928/637-6813, 3pm-9pm Wed.-Fri., 11am-3pm and 5pm-9pm Sat., 10am-3pm Sun., $10-40), open for dinner, happy hour, and weekend brunch. Don't let the strip mall location stop you from stepping inside to enjoy the European atmosphere. Serious foodies should also consider **Tinderbox Kitchen** (34 S. San Francisco St., 982/226-8400, www.tinderboxkitchen.com, 5pm-9pm Sun.-Thurs., 5pm-10pm Fri.-Sat., $20-40) for new twists on comfort food or its **Annex Lounge** (6pm-10pm daily, $5-20) for cocktails, small plates, and burgers. **Brix** (413 N. San Francisco St., 928/213-1021, http://brix-flagstaff.com, dinner Tues.-Sun., $18-40) highlights local producers on its seasonally changing menu.

Focus on three things—coffee, pizza, and craft beer—and you'll get close to the heart of this mountain town. Wake up and follow the scent of freshly roasted beans to longtime local favorite, **Macy's European Coffeehouse and Bakery** (14 S. Beaver St., 928/774-2243, www.macyscoffee.net, 6am-8pm daily, less than $10), then add a pastry or something more substantial like couscous, waffles, or biscuits with vegetarian gravy. Swedish oat pancakes are a standby at nearby **La Bellavia** (18 S. Beaver St., 928/774-8301, 6:30am-2pm daily, $5-10), another popular breakfast spot. Good luck getting a table at **MartAnne's** (112 E. Route 66, 928/773-4701, 7:30am-9pm daily $3-12), where you can fire up your day with *chilaquiles* and enchiladas—or wait for lunch and have carne asada tacos or a bowl of posole.

Befitting a college town, Flagstaff has a host of good pizza joints, but for Neapolitan-style pie approaching the sublime, head south of the tracks to ★ **Pizzicleta** (203 W. Phoenix Ave., 928/774-3242, www.pizzicletta.com, 5pm-9pm Mon., Thurs., and Sun., 5pm-10pm Fri.-Sat., $10-15). Most of the seating at this tiny-but-popular spot is communal, and they don't take reservations. If the waitlist is lengthy, head next door to Mother Road Brewing Company, grab a seat in the taproom or on the patio, and ask for the Pizzicleta menu, available after 5 pm.

While you're at **Mother Road Brewing Company** (7 South Mikes Pike, 928/774-9139, www.motherroadbeer.com, 2pm-9pm Mon.-Thurs., 2pm-10pm Fri., noon-10pm Sat., noon-9pm Sun.), start exploring Flag's burgeoning beer culture with a crisp and light Kolsch. Continue toward the train tracks for **Beaver Street Brewing Company** (11 S. Beaver St., 928/779-0079, http://beaverstreetbrewery.com, 11am-11pm Sun.-Thurs., 11am-midnight Fri.-Sat., $10-20) and a Railhead Red, or follow the Ale Trail to the better-than-dessert Piehole Porter at **Historic Brewing Company** (110 S. San Francisco St., 928/774-0454, 11am-10pm Sun.-Thurs., 11am-11pm Fri.-Sat.). The semi-official trail has ten stops and a passport for collecting stamps and discounts, but it's easy to make your own way along the mile of breweries, pubs, and lounges serving local beers.

ACCOMMODATIONS

Flagstaff has hundreds of guest rooms, from nostalgic motels along Route 66 to national chains with quick access to I-17 and I-40. For nightlife (including a ghost or two), consider staying at **Hotel Weatherford** (23 N. Leroux St., 928/779-1919, www.weatherfordhotel.com, $55-145) or **Hotel Monte Vista** (100 N. San Francisco St., 928/779-6971, www.hotelmontevista.com, $70-175), both downtown landmarks with storied pasts and popular lounges.

Flagstaff's lively Southside neighborhood, between downtown and Northern Arizona University, is home to the highly regarded **Grand Canyon International Hostel** (19 S. San Francisco St., 928/779-9421, www.grandcanyonhostel.com) Choose between dorm-style rooms ($26) or private doubles with a shared bath ($90). Another good choice for budget travelers, boho-chic **Motel Dubeau** (19 W. Phoenix Ave., 928/774-6731, 800/398-7112, http://modubeau.com, $30-90), has four-person dorms or private rooms with baths.

Graciously old school **Little America** (2515 E. Butler Ave., 928/779-7900, 800/352-4386, http://flagstaff.littleamerica.com, $150-200) has large, clean rooms and a woodsy setting that's close to I-40 and U.S. 89, convenient if you're heading for the park's East Entrance or the North Rim.

To live like a local, even for a night, rent one of the ★ **Comfi Cottages** (various locations, 928/774-0731 or 888/774-0731, www.comficottages.com, $150-289), comfortably furnished one- to four-bedroom homes, some historic, several with fireplaces, backyard grills, and other homey touches ideal for long stays or family vacations.

Camping and Cabins

A handful of commercial campgrounds are located on Flagstaff's outskirts, including **KOA** (5803 N. U.S. 89, 928/526-9926 or 800/562-3524, www.koa.com, from $35), with full hookups and loads of amenities. Cabins and tent spaces are also available. Reservations are recommended.

Coconino National Forest operates first-come, first-served ★ **Bonito Campground** (928/526-0866, www.fs.usda.gov/coconino, May-Oct., $18), located just outside Sunset Crater Volcano National Monument, north of Flagstaff near U.S. 89. The campground has no hookups or showers. *Bonito* means "pretty," and it is—a shady haven on the edge of a meadow blooming with sunflowers and paintbrush. In **Lockett Meadow** (May-Oct., no hookups or showers, $14) there are 17 campsites available on a first-come, first-served basis to those ready to tackle bumpy Forest Road 552 on the east side of the Peaks.

Camping at large is permitted in the national forest, but if you'd rather rough it easy, the forest service rents **historic cabins** (800/444-6777, www.recreation.gov, mid-May-mid-Oct., $125). Guests need to bring linens and other supplies, but in exchange for doing your own housekeeping, you'll have privacy and lots of room to roam. **Kendrick Cabin,** accommodating up to 10 people, sits in an open meadow with sweeping views of Arizona's tallest peaks. Grand Canyon's South Rim is a mere 58 miles from its front porch. **Fernow Cabin** is a log A-frame with two bedrooms, accommodating up to eight. It's tucked into the forest about 22 miles south of Flagstaff on Woody Mountain Road (Forest Rd. 231). Both cabins are available April 15 to November 15; rates are lower when water is turned off in spring and fall.

Available year-round, but especially appealing to winter sports enthusiasts, **Arizona Nordic Village** (16848 U.S. 180, 928/220-0550, http://arizonanordicvillage.com) has a campground with tent sites (summer, $20) and year-round cabins or yurts ($45-85). Amenities include coin-operated showers, a camp library, weekly movies, games, and miles of trails for hiking, skiing, or snowshoeing. The campground is 15 miles north of Flagstaff, a mere hour's drive to the South Rim.

TRANSPORTATION AND SERVICES

Driving

Flagstaff is located at the intersection of I-40, which runs from Albuquerque to Kingman, and I-17, which leads north from Phoenix and Tucson. From Phoenix, Flagstaff is a two-hour drive north up I-17. The I-17 freeway ends at its junction with I-40, becoming Milton Road as it travels past the university area, then turning east and becoming Route 66 as it reaches downtown.

South Entrance: It's a fast and easy 90 miles from Flagstaff to the canyon's South Entrance via I-40. Take I-40 west (about 30 miles) to Highway 64 (exit 165). Drive north on Highway 64 to the South Rim (about 60 miles).

For the scenic route via U.S. 180 (78 miles), turn north on Humphreys Street. At Columbus Avenue, turn left. Columbus Avenue becomes U.S. 180. Continue west on U.S. 180 to Highway 64 (about 55 miles). Turn right (north) on Highway 64 and drive to the South Rim, another 23 miles.

East Entrance: The park's less busy East Entrance is 107 miles from Flagstaff via U.S. 89. Follow Route 66 northeast through Flagstaff. Route 66 becomes U.S. 89 as you leave town. Continue on U.S. 89 north for about 65 miles. Turn left (west) onto Highway 64 and drive 30 miles to the East Entrance and Desert View.

DETOUR: SEDONA

You'll regret it if you don't spend a few hours (or longer) in Sedona's scenic red-rock country. U.S. 89A cuts through this small town in the red rocks and climbs 2,000 feet up to Flagstaff via gorgeous **Oak Creek Canyon.**

Although it's only 25 miles from Uptown Sedona to downtown Flagstaff, allow an hour for the winding drive, longer if you plan to stop and picnic, wade, or hike in **Oak Creek Canyon Recreation Area.** You'll rejoin I-17 near the airport, three miles south of Flagstaff.

Air

American Airlines (800/433-7300, www.aa.com) serves Flagstaff's **Pulliam Airport** (FLG, 6200 S. Pulliam Dr., 928/556-1234, www.flagstaff.az.gov), located three miles south of town along I-17. The municipal airport also hosts corporate, charter, and private flights.

Train

The **Amtrak** (928/774-8679 or 800/872-7245, www.amtrak.com) *Southwest Chief* stops at the Flagstaff depot (1 E. Route 66, 3:30am-10:30pm daily), arriving once daily in each direction from Los Angeles or Albuquerque. There's no train service between Flagstaff and Phoenix or Las Vegas.

Bus

Greyhound (880 E. Butler Ave., 928/774-4573 or 800/231-2222, www.greyhound.com) has service in Flagstaff with connections nationwide.

To get around town on the cheap, hop on the **Mountain Line** (928/779-6624, www.mountainline.az.gov). Buses run eight different routes every 15 to 60 minutes (6am-10pm Mon.-Fri., 7am-8pm Sat.-Sun. and holidays), and a day pass is $2.50.

Taxis and Shuttles

Arizona Shuttle (928/225-2290 or 800/563-1980, www.arizonashuttle.com) has daily service between the Phoenix airport, Flagstaff, Sedona, Williams, and Grand Canyon. Shuttles depart Flagstaff three times daily (Mar.-Oct., $30 pp one-way) for Grand Canyon, stopping at Williams and Tusayan before continuing to Maswik Lodge inside the park. November to February, service is once daily. Fares booked online are discounted. **Flagstaff Shuttle and Charter** (888/215-3105, www.grandcanyonshuttles.com) offers on-demand service to Grand Canyon from Flagstaff, Williams, Sedona, and Phoenix for a flat fee or by the hour. Tours or custom itineraries can be arranged.

A Friendly Cab (928/774-4444, 928/214-9000, or 800/853-4445, www.afriendlycab.com) has 24-7 service throughout northern Arizona, including Flagstaff and Grand Canyon. Local rates start at $1.70 per mile, and discounts are available.

Car and RV Rental

Several national car-rental agencies have service counters at Flagstaff's Pulliam Airport or downtown Flagstaff, including **Alamo** (877/222-9075 or 888/826-6893), **Avis** (928/774-8421 or 800/633-3469), **Budget** (928/779-5235 or 800/218-7992), **Enterprise** (928/774-0010 or 800/261-7331), **Hertz** (928/774-4452 or 800/654-3131), and **National** (928/779-1975 or 877/222-9058). **X-Press Rent-A-Car** (928/522-0773, www.xpressrentacar.net) has an office near downtown on Route 66.

Cruise America (4409 N. U.S. 89, 928/774-3339 or 800/671-8042, www.cruiseamerica.com) has a rental office on the north edge of town.

Visitor Centers

The **Flagstaff Visitor Center** (1 E. Route 66, 928/213-2951 or 800/379-0065, www.flagstaffarizona.org, 8am-5pm Mon.-Sat., 9am-4pm Sun.) shares space with Amtrak in downtown's historic train depot. Stop here for information about shuttles, tours, and local attractions. You can even pick up an entrance pass for Grand Canyon, which will get you into the faster prepaid lane at the park's entry station.

Visit the **Flagstaff Ranger District** offices (5075 N. U.S. 89, 928/526-0866, www.fs.usda.gov/coconino, 8am-4pm Mon.-Fri.) for information about recreation on the Coconino National Forest or to buy maps, passes, or permits. You can purchase an interagency pass here, good for admission to national parks and forests.

Walnut Canyon National Monument Visitor Center (7.5 miles east of Flagstaff on I-40, 928/526-3367, www.nps.gov/waca, 8am-5pm daily June-Oct., 9am-5pm daily Nov.-June) has interpretive displays, a small retail area, and a shady picnic area.

Sunset Crater Volcano National Monument Visitor Center (12 miles north of Flagstaff on U.S. 89, 928/526-0502, www.nps.gov/sucr, 8am-5pm daily June-Oct., 9am-5pm daily Nov.-June) has a nearby campground, hiking trails, and fascinating displays about volcanism.

At **Wupatki National Monument Visitor Center** (33 miles north of Flagstaff on U.S. 89, 928/679-2365, www.nps.gov/wupa, 9am-5pm daily), you can learn about the area's ancient cultures, take a nature stroll, or sign up for a guided tour of Wupatki Pueblo.

Medical Services

Flagstaff Medical Center (FMC, 1200 N. Beaver St., 928/779-3366) is a Level 1 trauma center with 24-hour emergency services. **Concentra Clinic** (1110 E. Route 66, Suite 100, 928/773-9695, 8am-6pm Mon.-Fri., 9am-3pm Sat.) provides walk-in urgent care.

Williams

Sixty miles south of Grand Canyon's Main Entrance Station, Williams (pop. 3,100) rests at the foot of forested Bill Williams Mountain, named for the legendary trapper and guide. Mountain men like Williams were the first Anglos to explore the West in the early 1800s, tracing river routes and trading with the indigenous people.

One of these trails became **Route 66,** the celebrated Mother Road that still leads through historic downtown. Motorcycle clubs, vintage auto enthusiasts, and people hoping to recapture the Great American Road Trip make pilgrimages to Williams, the last Route 66 town to be bypassed by a freeway. Despite the town's small size, numerous motels and restaurants welcome visitors, and shops peddle nostalgia along with Grand Canyon souvenirs.

Williams is also home to the **Grand Canyon Railway,** and one of the most popular shows in town is watching as the train pulls out of the depot every morning, its destination the South Rim's Grand Canyon Village.

SIGHTS

Even if you're not planning to travel to Grand Canyon via a vintage railcar, you'll find that the train tracks are a central attraction. On the south side, the former freight depot houses the **Williams Visitor Center** (200 W. Railroad Ave., 928/635-4061 or 800/863-0546, www.experiencewilliams.com, 8am-6:30pm daily summer, 8am-5pm daily fall-spring). While you're here, pick up a tour map for a self-guided stroll along turn-of-the-century **Saloon Row** and **nostalgic Route 66.**

Grand Canyon Railway

On the north side of the tracks, the historic passenger depot now houses the **Grand Canyon Railway** (233 N. Grand Canyon Blvd., 800/843-8724, www.thetrain.com, 7:30am-6:30pm daily, hours vary seasonally).

The train bound for Grand Canyon departs at 9:30am daily and returns at 5:45pm daily, but if you're visiting midday, you can take a look at the locomotives and railcars parked along the tracks or browse through the gift shop housed in the passenger depot. Built

Grand Canyon Boulevard in Williams

Williams

To I-40 and Williams
Ranger District Office

To Buckskinner Park

To Perkinsville

BILL WILLIAMS
STATUE

SAFEWAY ■

CLINIC ■

GRANT AVE

SHERMAN AVE

SHERIDAN AVE

HANCOCK AVE

MEADE AVE

MCPHERSON AVE

COCHISE CT

APACHE BLVD

COCONINO DR N

7TH ST

6TH ST

5TH ST

4TH ST

3RD ST

2ND ST

1ST ST

FABER ST

SLAGEL ST

LEWIS ST

PINE ST

SHERIDAN
HOUSE INN

GRAND CANYON
BREWING COMPANY

CATARACT RD

7TH ST

5TH ST

4TH ST

3RD ST

EDISON AVE

GRAND CANYON
RAILWAY RV PARK

GRAND CANYON
RAILWAY HOTEL

DE BERGE
WESTERN WEAR

CAFÉ 326 ▼

SULTANA ▼

CRUISERS/
GRAND CANYON
BREWING COMPANY

GRAND CANYON
HOTEL/DARA THAI

POST OFFICE ■

LIBRARY ■

VISITOR
INFORMATION CENTER ■

WILLIAMS
TRAIN STATION

PINE COUNTRY
RESTAURANT

RED GARTER BED
AND BAKERY

RED RAVEN ▼

THE
LODGE

ROD'S STEAK
HOUSE

TWISTERS

CANYON
BLVD

FRANKLIN
AVE

GRAND
CANYON
BLVD

FULTON AVE

BURBANK AVE

MORSE AVE

NEWTON ST

HUMBOLT ST

AIRPORT RD

RODEO RD

Rodeo
Grounds

FRANK WAY

STOCKMENS RD

HEREFORD DR

QUARTERHOUSE
RD

HOMESTEAD RD

FARGO DR

RAILSIDE
RV RANCH ▲

CANYON GATEWAY
RV PARK ▲

EXIT 163

40

To Kingman

To Flagstaff

To Canyon Motel
and RV Park

To I-40,
Grand Canyon,
and ✚ BEARIZONA

ROUTE 66 ✚

Route 66

Grand Canyon Railway

RAILROAD AVE

ROUTE 66

0   200 yds
0   200 m

© AVALON TRAVEL

the Grand Canyon Railway

in 1908, the depot is the oldest poured-concrete building in Arizona. The adjacent Fray Marcos Hotel (now offices) was once operated by the Fred Harvey Company, and the railroad district is on the National Register of Historic Places.

★ Route 66

When **Route 66** was born in 1926, a new era of travel began. Though Williams's Main Street was bypassed by I-40 in 1984, the romance of the Mother Road didn't end. Passenger cars can still drive Route 66 for 22 miles east from downtown Williams, with a short segue on the freeway. Two older alignments, dating from the 1920s and 1930s, serve as mountain bike trails, the **Devil Dog** and **Ash Fork Hill** loops.

Enjoy the Route 66 atmosphere by going for a drive or bike ride, or simply by strolling down the Main Street and stopping for a malt shake and some souvenirs.

Route 66 nostalgia in downtown Williams

★ Bearizona

Tucked into the ponderosa pines east of Williams, **Bearizona** (1500 E. Rte. 66, 928/635-2289, www.bearizona.com, 9am-4pm daily, $20 adult, $10 child) is a 160-acre wildlife park that can be explored by car and on foot. Explore the park's natural habitats in your car, then take a self-guided trail for a closer look at bears, bobcats, wolves, raptors, and other critters. Programs throughout the day offer visitors a chance to ask questions or watch animals eat and train. (Be sure to visit the bear cub "kindergarten.")

RECREATION

Williams is surrounded by open prairies and ponderosa pines, offering plenty of back-road drives, hiking and biking trails, fishing lakes, and picnic areas, all under the auspices of **Kaibab National Forest** (www.fs.usda.gov/kaibab). For more information about recreation in the forest's 550,411-acre **Williams Ranger District,** or to pick up maps and learn about current road conditions, contact the **Williams Ranger District Office** (742 S. Clover Rd., 928/635-5600, 8am-4:30pm Mon.-Fri.) or the **Williams Visitor Center** (200 Railroad Ave., 928/635-4061 or 800/863-0546, 8am-6:30pm daily summer, 8am-5pm daily fall-spring).

Forest Roads and Trails

During the 1800s, wagons, stages, and mule trains crossed Garland Prairie, bringing settlers, supplies, and soldiers to and from Prescott via the Overland Trail and other routes. Today, you can retrace the journey via the **Garland Prairie Road** (Forest Rd. 141), which makes a scenic 21-mile loop south of I-40, beginning at exit 167, traveling eastward and rejoining the freeway at exit 178. The gravel road is suitable for passenger cars, and you can complete the loop in 2-3 hours. But give yourself extra time to explore nearby lakes, trails, and historic sites. The prairie comes alive with wildflowers in late spring, and in autumn, aspens turn gold on the slopes of Bill Williams Mountain and Kendrick Peak. Watch carefully as you travel through the open prairie: Here and there, wagon ruts are still visible more than a century later.

Stop at **Laws Spring,** where Lieutenant Edward F. Beale's 1859 expedition left an inscription near petroglyphs made by ancient travelers. From here, it's possible to access the **Beale Road,** now a hiking trail, for an easy stroll. To get to the trailhead, take the Garland Prairie Road (Forest Rd. 171) to Forest Road 100, continuing approximately four miles to its junction with Forest Road 107, where you

entrance to Bearizona

can park. The Beale Road, marked by rock cairns and wooden posts, heads southwest. You can walk as far as you like, but a good turnaround point is at the edge of the prairie, making a five-mile round-trip.

Hikers, mountain bikers, and equestrians can also follow 25 miles of the **Overland Road,** established by the U.S. Army in 1863 to connect to the goldfields near Prescott. There are several trailheads, including one along the Garland Prairie Road, 5.4 miles south of its intersection with I-40 at exit 178.

Mountain Biking

Two older alignments of Route 66, dating from the 1920s and 1930s, serve as mountain bike trails, the **Devil Dog** and **Ash Fork Hill** loops.

The easy five-mile Devil Dog loop begins west of Williams on Forest Road 108 (just south of I-40 exit 157). For the intermediate 12-mile Ash Fork Hill loop, go 12 miles west of Williams on I-40 to exit 151. Drive a short way north on Forest Road 6 and park. A high-clearance vehicle is recommended to reach the trailhead. Begin the loop clockwise so that you can tackle the steepest grade going downhill.

Golf

Golfers who want to aim at a few small holes before traveling to the big one (Grand Canyon) can head northwest of Williams to **Elephant Rocks** (2200 Country Club Dr., 928/635-4935, www.elephant-rocks.com, 8am-dusk spring-fall, $25-40), named for the large dark-gray basalt boulders at its entrance. At 7,000 feet in elevation, this 18-hole course, designed by Gary Panks, is a cool escape for desert dwellers.

ENTERTAINMENT AND EVENTS

Rarely does a summer weekend in Williams pass without some kind of festival or event. If you want to continue the celebration into the wee hours, a fitting place to start is the **Sultana** (301 W. Route 66, 928/635-2021),

which holds the honor of being Arizona's longest-running liquor purveyor. You can shoot pool or shoot the breeze with locals before ambling off to another downtown establishment. Grand Canyon Brewing Company pours beers at **Cruisers** (233 W. Route 66, 928/635-2445, 800/513-2072, 11am-10pm daily) and at its **Grand Canyon Brewing Company Taproom** (301 N. 7th St., 928/635-2168, 11am-11pm daily Mar.-Dec.) west of downtown.

Route 66, train travel, and the Old West are feted in Williams spring-fall. Transportation-themed events include fly-ins, car shows, a motorcycle rally, and the annual **Historic Route 66 Fun Run** (www.azrt66.com), when motor enthusiasts from all over the United States drive the fabled Mother Road from Seligman to Topock during the first weekend in May.

In June, working cowboys gather for the **Cowpunchers Reunion Rodeo** (www.az-cowpunchers.com), one of several annual events that highlight Western traditions. The town's old-fashioned **Fourth of July celebration** features live entertainment all day long and, of course, a parade. On **Steam Saturdays** (1st Sat. of the month, spring-fall), locomotives No. 4960 or No. 29 power the train to Grand Canyon, and even nonpassengers gather at the station to take photos of the historic engines and rub elbows with the crew. (Today, the engines are fueled by waste vegetable oil.)

SHOPPING

Route 66 memorabilia and Grand Canyon souvenirs are a specialty at downtown shops and trading posts. Poke around to uncover such treasures as a Burma Shave sign, hood ornaments and hubcaps, or vintage postcards and the like. Most stores vary their hours with the seasons, with a few opening only on weekends during winter months.

For train-themed items, you need look no farther than the gift shop at the **Grand Canyon Railway** (235 N. Grand Canyon Blvd., 800/843-8724, www.thetrain.com,

7:30am-7pm daily). **De Berge Western Wear** (316 W. Route 66, 928/635-4013, 8am-8pm daily, hours vary seasonally) carries hats and boots, and makes custom saddles for your horse—or Harley. Across from the visitor center, **Quilts on Route 66** (221 W. Railroad Ave., 928/635-5221, 10am-5pm Mon.-Sun. spring-fall, winter hours vary) sells fabric, yarn, supplies, and handmade quilts—you might even find one with a Grand Canyon scene or Route 66 iconography.

More than 20 local artists show their paintings, pottery, jewelry, and other works at **The Gallery** (145 W. U.S. Route 66, 928/635-3006, 9am-9pm daily), a cooperative staffed by the artists themselves. The Gallery becomes the epicenter of the town's **Second Saturday Artwalk** (6pm-9pm 2nd Sat. of the month May-Oct.), with demos, live music, nibbles, and wine.

FOOD

You'll find restaurants on nearly every corner in Williams, from steakhouses to soda fountains with nostalgic ambiance. Expect some seasonal closures and shorter hours during winter months. Local fixtures include **Rod's Steak House** (301 E. Route 66, 928/635-2671, www.rods-steakhouse.com, 11am-9:30pm Mon.-Sat., $15-30), inducted into Arizona's Restaurant Hall of Fame, and **Twisters** (417 E. Route 66, 928/635-0266, 11am-8pm Mon.-Sat., $8-18), an eye-popping, toe-tapping shrine to the 1950s.

The **Pine Country Restaurant** (107 N. Grand Canyon Blvd., 928/635-9718, www.pinecountryrestaurant.com, 6:30am-9pm daily, $5-25) is known for its hearty breakfasts but serves up home-style cooking—including pies—all day long.

Coffee fiends can get their fix at ★ **Café 326** (326 W. Route 66, 928/635-0777, www.cafe326.com, 6:30am-7pm daily, $3-10), along with baked goods fresh from a wood-fired oven, sandwiches, and homemade soups. For spicier fare, a good option is **Dara Thai** (145 W. Route 66, 928/635-2201, 11am-2pm and 5pm-9pm Mon.-Sat., $10-15),

located in the historic Grand Canyon Hotel. For casual, chef-driven cuisine (and a great wine list), try ★ **Red Raven** (135 W. Route 66, 928/635-4980, www.redravenrestaurant.com, lunch and dinner daily, $10-40), or the upscale pub menu at **Barrel & Bottle** (141 Railroad Ave., 928/635-4150, 11am-close daily, $15-30).

ACCOMMODATIONS

Williams has about 30 hotels, motels, and inns with a range of amenities and rates, some discounted steeply during winter. Most are located within a few blocks of I-40 along Route 66 or Grand Canyon Boulevard.

If your trip centers on the train, consider splurging on a room or suite at the stately and comfortable ★ **Grand Canyon Railway Hotel** (235 N. Grand Canyon Blvd., 928/635-4010 or 800/843-8724, www.thetrain.com, $200-290).

Equally elegant but tucked away from the railroad tracks and Route 66 on two woodsy acres, the ★ **Sheridan House Inn** (460 E. Sheridan Ave., 928/635-8991 or 928/814-2809, www.grandcanyonbreadandbreakfast.com, $170-210) is a particularly well-appointed B&B.

The **Red Garter Bed & Bakery** (137 W. Railroad Ave., 928/635-1484 or 800/328-1484, www.redgarter.com, $150-175) is a restored (and some say haunted) bordello in historic downtown, close to the visitor center.

For local color at moderate prices, the **Grand Canyon Hotel** (145 W. Route 66, 928/635-1419, www.thegrandcanyonhotel.com, Mar.-Dec., $70-140), built in 1891, offers boutique accommodations downtown—no cookie-cutter rooms here. The hotel also has dorm-style accommodations ($28-33), suites and a carriage house or cottage ($140-180), ideal for groups or families. Rooms don't have TVs, but Wi-Fi is included in the rates.

The **Lodge** (200 E. Route 66, 928/563-4366 or 877/563-4366, www.thelodgeonroute66.com, $130-270) is a refurbished motor court with rooms and suites.

Camping

For campers and RVers, Williams is a cool summer haven (although in Arizona, "cool" is relative), with a wide variety of campground choices. Two well-equipped, kid-friendly KOAs can be found north and east of town. **Circle Pines KOA** (1000 Circle Pines Rd., 928/635-2626 or 800/562-9379, www.koa.com, Apr.-Oct., from $40) is just off I-40 at exit 167. **Grand Canyon/Williams KOA** (5333 Hwy. 64, 928/635-2307 or 800/562-5771, year-round, www.koa.com, from $40) is located on Highway 64, the route to Grand Canyon. Both have camper cabins, tent lodges, and a gamut of amenities, from bike rentals to movie nights.

If you're planning to ride the excursion train to Grand Canyon, the all-paved **Grand Canyon Railway RV Park** (235 N. Grand Canyon Blvd., 800/843-8724, www.thetrain.com, $43-48) is convenient, offering full hookups, wireless Internet, cable TV, and other amenities, including pet boarding.

Kaibab National Forest (928/635-5600, www.fs.usda.gov/kaibab) operates three lakeside campgrounds near Williams. Sites at **Dogtown Lake, Kaibab Lake,** and **White Horse Lake** have no utility hookups and are suitable for tents and small RVs (877/444-6777, www.recreation.gov, May-Sept., $20-32). **Dispersed camping** is allowed throughout the forest with a few guidelines, including a 14-day stay limit. Many forest roads are rugged and—depending on rainfall and winter snow cover—can be quite muddy as well. During the summer, fire restrictions may be active. Check with the Forest Service for current conditions.

The forest service's historic **Spring Valley Cabin and Bunkhouse** (877/444-6777, www.recreation.gov, $100-150) is ideally situated for an outdoorsy get-together. Located near Parks, midway between Flagstaff (20 miles east) and Williams (20 miles west), the cabin has room for seven people and is surrounded by wide-open vistas of forests, mountains, and prairies. The bunkhouse sleeps an additional seven. The setting is perfect for hiking, mountain-biking, horseback riding, and scenic drives, especially in autumn, when aspens turn the mountainsides into a patchwork of green and gold. Pack binoculars so you can watch for herds of pronghorn or elk grazing the meadow. Winter snowfalls may

wild sunflowers at White Horse Lake campground in the Kaibab National Forest

limit access to those willing to snowshoe, hike, or ski from main roads.

TRANSPORTATION AND SERVICES

Driving

The town of Williams sits along the southern edge of I-40 about 30 minutes' drive west of Flagstaff, four hours east of Las Vegas, and three hours northwest of Phoenix. Three exits lead to Williams from I-40. If you're arriving from the west, use exit 161; a few hotels and motels are located on this side of town. Exit 163 leads to the Grand Canyon Railway depot and the heart of historic downtown. Exit 165 connects with Highway 64, which heads north to Grand Canyon, about an hour's drive.

Air

Although the nearest commercial airport is 35 miles away in Flagstaff, Williams has an airfield for small planes, **Clark Memorial Field** (3501 N. Airport Rd., 928/635-4451).

Train

Amtrak (800/872-7245, www.amtrak.com) has daily service to Williams Junction, about three miles east of downtown Williams. The westbound *Southwest Chief* arrives late at night. The eastbound train (from Los Angeles) arrives in the wee hours of the morning. Make arrangements in advance for the free shuttle that will take you from the junction to the Grand Canyon Railway Hotel downtown. The hotel is adjacent to the historic depot and **Grand Canyon Railway** (235 N. Grand Canyon Blvd., 800/843-8724, www.thetrain. com), which offers four classes of passenger service to Grand Canyon Village, traveling on refurbished vintage rail cars. The train leaves historic Williams Depot in the morning and returns in the afternoon.

Taxis and Shuttles

Williams Taxi and Shuttle (117 W. Route 66, 928/635-1111 or 888/787-4402, www.williamstaxi.com) has local service and shuttles to Flagstaff and Grand Canyon. **Arizona Shuttle** (928/225-2290 or 800/563-1980, www.arizonashuttle.com) has daily shuttle service between the Phoenix airport, Williams, Flagstaff, and Grand Canyon. March to October, shuttles leave Williams for Grand Canyon three times daily (twice daily November-February), stopping at Tusayan and Maswik Lodge ($22 one-way).

Car Rental

Rent a car or van from **I-40 Fleet Services** (3501 N. Airport Rd., Suite 103, 928/635-9199, 7am-4pm Mon.-Fri.), located inside the airport terminal.

Visitor Centers

The historic Santa Fe Railway freight depot houses the **Williams Visitor Center** (200 Railroad Ave., 928/635-4061 or 800/863-0546, www.experiencewilliams.com, 8am-6:30pm daily summer, 8am-5pm daily fall-spring), operated jointly with the U.S. Forest Service. Stop in to browse the museum and find out about tours and recreational opportunities. If you purchase an entrance pass for Grand Canyon here, you can use the faster prepaid lane at the park's entry station.

Kaibab National Forest has additional offices for the **Williams Ranger District** (742 S. Clover Rd., 928/635-5600, www. fs.usda.gov/kaibab, 8am-4:30pm Mon.-Fri.) and the **Forest Supervisor** (800 S. 6th St., 928/635-8200, 8am-4:30pm Mon.-Fri.). Rangers are on hand at both locations with maps and advice about scenic drives, trails, and campgrounds.

Medical Services

The nearest hospital is in Flagstaff. North Country Health Care operates an **urgent care clinic** (301 S. 7th St., 928/635-4441, 8am-8pm daily) in Williams.

Page

Most of Page's two to three million annual visitors come to explore **Lake Powell** and its 2,000-mile, canyon-cut shoreline. "The Big Blue" straddles the border of Arizona and Utah, glittering like a sapphire set among orange sandstone.

Long before there was a town or a lake, John Wesley Powell's Colorado River expedition floated through the canyon he named for its "oak-set glens and fern-decked alcoves." Those who want to experience the charm of the old **Glen Canyon** can float down the Colorado River to Lees Ferry, a 15-mile stretch of vertical sandstone cliffs that shelter ancient petroglyphs and hanging gardens.

The Glen's isolated canyon system made an idyllic but little-known playground for river runners, among them, writer-environmentalist Edward Abbey. When the Bureau of Reclamation decided to turn the lovely canyons into a reservoir, Abbey wreaked fictional revenge on the "Bu-Wreck" with *The Monkey Wrench Gang* (1975), the tale of a motley crew of canyon lovers who plotted to dynamite the dam.

Glen Canyon Dam continues to spark controversy, but Page (pop. 7,500) has grown from a construction camp into a travel destination centered on Lake Powell and the bounty of water sports it provides. Page makes a good gateway for river runners, as well as photographers drawn to the sinuous curves of **Antelope Canyon.**

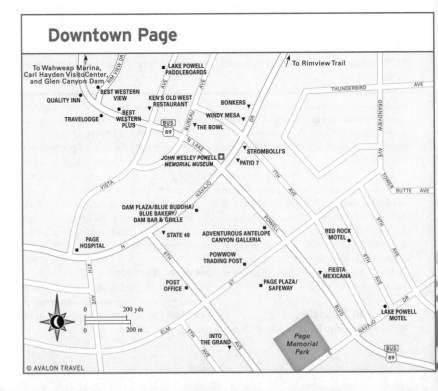

Downtown Page

John Wesley Powell

In May 1869, when a 35-year-old teacher named John Wesley Powell set out to explore the Colorado River through Grand Canyon, the inner canyon was terra incognita—unmapped and virtually unknown to anyone except the region's Native Americans. With the same fascination that later generations felt for the Apollo missions, America waited for news of Powell—a Civil War veteran who'd lost his right arm to a cannonball—and his crew of nine men.

Powell's wooden boat with his chair and life preserver

Fierce rapids battered the expedition's four wooden dories as they journeyed from the Green River to the Grand River and then to the Colorado. Few of the men had river experience. One left a month after they started out. After entering Grand Canyon, the expedition virtually dropped out of sight. Powell wrote in his journal, "We have an unknown distance yet to run, an unknown river to explore. What falls there are, we know not; what rocks beset the channel, we know not; what walls rise over the river, we know not."

The summer sun bore down on them. With food supplies dwindling and their clothing in rags, the men were near starvation. In late August, three more left the expedition rather than face another brutal stretch of white water. Powell named the site Separation Rapid. It proved to be the last difficult rapid they would face.

Two days later, the remaining crew reached the Colorado's confluence with the Virgin River, where they were able to send word of their survival. Their journey had taken 99 days and covered 1,000 miles. Powell learned that the three who'd chosen to leave were murdered on their hike to civilization. He included them in the dedication to his book about the expedition, *The Exploration of the Colorado River and Its Canyons* (1875), which remains one of the finest adventure stories about Grand Canyon.

Powell repeated his canyon journey in 1872 and returned to the Southwest several times to learn about its indigenous cultures. He was named the first director of the Bureau of American Ethnology in 1880 and became the second director of the U.S. Geological Survey in 1881. Remarkably prescient about water issues in the West, Powell warned that communities must plan growth and cooperate to conserve water. He died in 1902, his warnings unheeded. Today the vast reservoir of Lake Powell bears his name, impounded behind the dam that forever changed the river he explored.

SIGHTS
Lake Powell

The canyon country surrounding **Lake Powell** is rugged and isolated, with very few access roads, much of it protected by the National Park Service as Glen Canyon National Recreation Area. The best way to see the lake and its 2,000-mile shoreline is by boat, but if you didn't happen to haul one across the desert, you can hop on a lake tour lasting one to seven hours. From spring through fall, several tours depart daily from **Wahweap Marina** (888/896-3829, www.lakepowell.com, from $45 pp) or **Antelope Point Marina** (928/645-5900, http://antelopepointlakepowell.com, from $28 pp).

Rainbow Bridge

Lake Powell Resorts & Marinas (928/645-1070, www.lakepowell.com, $125 pp) offers a day-long excursion from Wahweap Bay to **Rainbow Bridge National Monument** (928/608-6200, www.nps.gov/rabr). The monument's central attraction is a 275-foot sandstone span carved by water, the largest natural bridge in the world. After docking, visitors can make the short hike (2.5 miles round-trip at current lake levels) to the base of the natural bridge. Sacred to the region's Native Americans for generations, it was "discovered" by nonnatives in 1909. The only way here is by boat or by backpacking from the Navajo Reservation (permit required). Park rangers are on-site May to early October.

★ John Wesley Powell Memorial Museum

The small-but-mighty **John Wesley Powell Memorial Museum** (6 N. Lake Powell Blvd., 928/645-9496, www.powellmuseum. org, 9am-5pm daily Apr.-Oct., shorter hours in winter, $3 adults) is a good place to learn about Powell, the one-armed Civil War major who ran the Colorado River through Grand Canyon in 1869 and 1872. Exhibits include a replica of his boat, prehistoric artifacts, vintage photos, paleontology displays, and more.

The Rainbow Bridge tour, lake excursions, and other adventures can be booked through the museum's visitor services center. If you make your tour reservation here, the museum will receive a percentage of the fee.

Glen Canyon Dam

Whatever you think about **Glen Canyon Dam,** you have to agree that it is impressive, especially when viewed from the **dam overlook** on Scenic View Road west of U.S. 89. The dam contains nearly five million cubic yards of concrete and rises more than 500 feet above the Colorado River. You can get an inside look on a 45-minute tour ($5), departing every half hour from **Carl Hayden Visitor Center** (928/608-6200, 8:30am-4pm daily mid-May-mid-Sept., fewer departures in winter). The visitor center is located on U.S. 89, just west of the dam. Reservations for the tours, which are guided by the **Glen Canyon**

Float the Colorado River below the dam to see cliffs draped in desert varnish.

Natural History Association (928/608-6072, www.glencanyonnha.org), can be made online or by phone up to 24 hours in advance. To make reservations in person, arrive at least 15 minutes prior to tour time.

Glen Canyon

Just below Glen Canyon dam but a world away from the lake, the remaining 15-mile stretch of the Colorado River makes a peaceful downstream passage between Glen Canyon's gorgeous Navajo sandstone cliffs. **Colorado River Discovery** (130 6th Ave., 888/522-6244, 928/645-9175 www.raftthecanyon.com, $90-195) leads full- and half-day motorized trips (Mar.-Nov.), oar-powered trips (spring and fall), and kayak tours (May-Sept.) beginning at the dam and ending at Lees Ferry. If you don't have the time, money, or nerve for a white-water trip through Grand Canyon, this is an enjoyable alternative.

Antelope Canyon

One of the most-photographed sites in the

Southwest, Antelope Canyon is a sinuous and colorful slot canyon carved into a sandstone mesa east of Page. It's exquisitely beautiful—and occasionally deadly. In 1997, a flash flood caused by a storm several miles away killed 11 of the 12 people who were inside. The canyon is a **Navajo Nation Tribal Park** (928/698-2808, http://navajonationparks.org, 8am-5pm daily Apr.-Oct., 9am-3pm daily Nov.-Mar., $8 plus guide), and the only way to enter is in the company of an authorized guide.

Several companies lead tours of the upper canyon, among them **Navajo Tours** (928/698-3384, www.navajotours.com) and **Antelope Canyon Tours** (S. Lake Powell Blvd., 928/645-9102, 22 www.antelopecanyon.com). Prices for hour-long sightseeing tours run $40-60, depending on time of day or season. The number of visitors allowed in the canyon at one time is limited, and advance reservations are recommended. Most guides reserve peak lighting conditions (midday in summer, morning in winter) for serious photographers, the only time that tripods are allowed in the canyon. Photographer-only tours ($90-125) last up to two hours, and guides will often point out highlights and help control traffic for unobstructed photos.

Fewer people visit lower Antelope Canyon, equally beautiful, because doing so requires being able to negotiate a series of steel ladders 3-25 feet high. For more information about guided tours of the lower canyon, contact **Ken's Tours** (928/606-2168, www.lowerantelope.com, $20-45).

The lake end of the canyon can be viewed on an hour-long boat tour departing from **Antelope Point Marina** (537 Marina Pkwy., 928/645-5900, http://antelopepointlakepowell.com, $28), about nine miles east of Page via Highway 98 and Navajo Route 22B.

RECREATION
Hiking
Hike, mountain bike, geocache, or just stretch your legs on the 12-mile **Rimview Trail,** which circles Page along the edges of Manson Mesa. This popular trail can be accessed at several points around town, but the official trailhead on South Navajo Drive, just past the elementary school, provides quick entry to one of the most panoramic sections. Carry water, even for a short out-and-back: There's no shade on this high, dry trail.

Stand-Up Paddleboarding
SUP classes and tours are available from **Antelope Point Marina** (537 Marina Pkwy., 928/645-5900, http://antelopepointlakepowell.com). Classes teach paddling basics plus how to incorporate yoga and Pilates techniques while on the board. The tours feature a meditative, breath-centered journey to a secluded cove.

Experienced paddlers can rent boards and gear from **Lake Powell Paddleboards** (836 Vista Ave., 928/645-4017, http://lakepowellpaddleboards.com); lessons ($75 pp) and tours ($95-225 pp) are also available.

Swimming
Lake Powell's inviting waters can top 80 degrees in summer months, but would-be swimmers need to keep a few precautions in mind. No swimming is allowed at the marinas. Cliff-diving is illegal—the water hides ledges and other hazards. Each year, fatalities result from swimming off houseboats and other watercraft: Dangers include asphyxiation from exhaust as well as injuries from motors or drowning.

While there are no lifeguards or designated beaches at Lake Powell, swimming is a popular activity, especially at **The Chains** (8am-sunset daily). Parking is available east of the bridge, just beyond the Hanging Garden Trailhead. There's no official trail down to the lake—choose a descent along the slickrock ledges. While swimming, wear water shoes or sports sandals: The sandstone ledges are littered with broken glass and sizzling hot after a few hours of summer sun. Be cautious: Depending on current lake levels, water at The Chains can be 500 feet deep, and steep ledges can make it challenging to get back on land. (It's called "slickrock" for good reason.)

Boating

Boat rentals can be arranged at Wahweap Marina through **Lake Powell Resorts** (100 Lakeshore Dr., 888/896-3829, www.lakepowell.com, 8am-5pm daily spring-fall, shorter hours in winter) or at **Antelope Point Marina** (537 Marina Pkwy., 928/645-5900, http://antelopepointlakepowell.com, 8am-5pm daily).

Glen Canyon National Recreation Area

Water, or its absence, is key throughout the tributaries and trails in **Glen Canyon National Recreation Area** (928/608-6200, $25 per vehicle, $25 boating fee). You can take a guided tour of the lake and its canyons, or rent a boat and explore on your own. You'll find most everything that floats, from kayaks to houseboats, at **Wahweap Marina** (100 Lakeshore Dr., 888/896-3829, www.lakepowell.com), operated by Aramark, or Navajo-owned **Antelope Point Marina** (537 Marina Pkwy., 928/645-5900, 800/255-5561, http://antelopepointlakepowell.com). Houseboats start around $750 per day and require a two- or three-day minimum.

Many boaters pull into Lake Powell's canyon tributaries and tie up for a few hours or days to hike or kayak twisting sandstone slots and explore hidden alcoves. **Defiance House,** an Ancestral Puebloan dwelling with associated pictographs and petroglyphs, perches three miles (depending on lake levels) up the middle fork of Forgotten Canyon.

Away from the lake's brilliant blue waters, trails are rocky and sunbaked. Stick to shorter trails until you get a feel for hiking in this high, dry country. **Hanging Garden Trail** (1 mile round-trip), an easy walk to a seep-nurtured oasis, begins across the bridge from the Carl Hayden Visitor Center. **Horseshoe Bend Trail** (1.5 miles round-trip, moderate) offers long views of the **Vermilion Cliffs** as it leads to an iconic Colorado River scene, where the bluish-green waters make a 270-degree turn around a neck of sandstone. For the trailhead, take U.S. 89 five miles south of Page to mile marker 545 and turn west into the parking area.

If you want to dive deeper into the lake and its surrounding canyons, check out the classes and trips offered by **Glen Canyon Field School** (475 S. Lake Powell Blvd., 928/640-3900, www.glencanyonfieldschool.org), the educational arm of the Glen Canyon Natural History Association. From photography workshops to backpacking adventures,

Lake tours to Rainbow Bridge and other sights depart from Wahweap Marina.

trips start at $300 per day, including lodging and meals.

ENTERTAINMENT AND EVENTS

Check at the recreation area's visitor centers for daily ranger programs and special events, such as telescope viewing or beach cleanup parties. Rangers host programs at Wahweap Campground's outdoor amphitheater on Friday and Saturday evenings during the summer months.

Local restaurants and bars host live music on high-season weekends and in March, when the lake is frequented by spring-breakers. Check out the dance scene at **Ken's Old West** (718 Vista Ave., 928/645-5160, 4pm-11pm daily), shoot some pool at **The Dam Bar & Grill** (644 N. Navajo Dr., 928/645-2161, 11am-10pm daily), or rub elbows with the locals at **Windy Mesa** (800 N. Navajo Dr., 928/645-2186, 11am-2am). For craft beers, creative pub grub, and the latest game, head for sports bar **State 48 Tavern** (614 N. Navajo Dr., 928/645-1912, 5pm-10pm Mon.-Sat., 11am-10pm Sun.). Find happy-hour specials at **Blue** (644 N. Navajo Dr., 928/608-0707, hours vary seasonally, under $20) along with tapas and—if your timing is right—live music and fireside seating.

At family-friendly **Into the Grand** (148 6th Ave., 928/660-8593, 7pm-9:30pm daily, $25), you can start with dinner and stay to play horseshoes, browse the river-rafting exhibit, catch some live music, and—the highlight—watch Navajo hoop dancers perform intricate moves. **The Bowl** (24 N. Lake Powell Blvd., 928/645-2682) will take you back to the days when the coolest hangout was the local bowling alley.

If you visit Page during the first weekend in November, you'll be rewarded with low off-season rack rates and the town's premier event, the annual **Balloon Regatta** (http://lakepowellballoonregatta.com). Watch dozens of hot-air balloons float serenely above red sandstone and blue water each morning, then see them glowing along Lake Powell Boulevard during a Saturday-night street fair.

SHOPPING

Hours vary by season in Page's small shops and galleries. The gift shop inside the **John Wesley Powell Museum** (6 N. Lake Powell Blvd., 928/645-9496, 9am-5pm daily summer) has a good selection of local arts and crafts. Seek out traditional Navajo rugs and jewelry (including old pawn) at **Pow Wow Trading Post** (635 Elm St., 928/645-2140, 9am-6pm Mon.-Sat.). The beautiful murals at **Adventurous Antelope Canyon Galleria** (48 S. Lake Powell Blvd., 928/645-6674, 8am-8pm daily) make it a pleasant place to browse Navajo crafts, T-shirts, books, and landscape photography.

FOOD

Page has a wide range of eateries, from fast-food joints to tablecloth-and-a-view seating at the **Rainbow Room** (100 Lakeshore Dr., 928/645-1162, 888/896-3829, www.lakepowell.com, 6am-10am and 5pm-9pm daily spring-fall, dinner reservations recommended, $15-50) overlooking Wahweap Marina. If you want to get even closer to the lake, you can join Aramark's two-hour **dinner cruise** (928/645-1070, 888/896-3829, www.lakepowell.com, 6pm Tues. and Sat. late May-mid-Aug., 5pm Tues. and Sat. mid-Aug-Sept., $80 adults, $35 ages 3-12).

For pasta, pizza, and other classics, follow the scent of garlic and tomato sauce from Page's visitor center to **Strombolli's** (711 N. Navajo Dr., 928/645-2605, www.strombollis.com, 11am-9pm Mon.-Sat., noon-9pm Sun., $8-20) or **Bonkers** (810 N. Navajo Dr., 928/645-2706, www.bonkerspageaz.com, 4pm-close Tues.-Sat. Mar.-Oct., $8-25).

Each local Mexican restaurant has its own loyal fans. Try **Fiesta Mexicana** (125 S. Lake Powell Blvd., 928/645-4082, 11am-9pm Sun.-Thurs., 11am-10pm Fri.-Sat., $10-20) for its superb service, vast menu, and gigantic portions.

The **Dam Plaza** (644 N. Navajo Dr.) hosts three restaurants, including ★ **Blue Buddha** (928/645-0007, 5pm-9pm Tues.-Thurs., 5pm-10pm Fri.-Sat., $10-40), which serves sushi, phat bowls, teriyaki, and steak in a stylish lounge atmosphere.

Spend enough time in the Southwest and you'll learn that there are two kinds of bread: fry bread and "dry bread" (the ho-hum, pre-sliced stuff from the grocery store). Find out why everything tastes better on fry bread at **Patio 7** (707 N. Navajo Dr., 928/645-4900, 11am-9pm Mon.-Sat., $10-15), serving freshly prepared Navajo tacos, lamb stew, burgers, and green chili in a picnic-style setting.

ACCOMMODATIONS

Though many visitors come here to rent houseboats, landlubbers will find several dozen hotels and motels. It's smart to book well in advance for summer months, when water-loving Arizonans escape to Lake Powell. During winter months, hotels slash rates.

At **Lake Powell Resort** (100 Lakeshore Dr., 888/896-3829, www.lakepowell.com, from $255), rooms overlook Wahweap Marina, the closest you can get to the lake without actually being on it. Several

mom-and-pop establishments with moderately priced rooms are located downtown, within a block or two of Lake Powell Boulevard. At **Lake Powell Motel** (750 S. Navajo Dr., 928/645-3919 or 801/831-6905, www.lakepowellmotel.net, $99-160) and **Red Rock Motel** (114 8th Ave., 928/645-0062, www.redrockmotel.com, $95-150) you'll find nicely refurbished rooms with kitchenettes—and owners who enjoy sharing their enthusiasm for the area.

A handful of national chains have staked out territory on the edges of the mesa. **Courtyard by Marriott** (600 Clubhouse Dr., 928/645-5000 or 877/905-4495, www.marriottcourtyardpage.com, $165-325) provides resort-style accommodations near the golf course.

The area's most exclusive resort, ★ **Amangiri** (1 Kayenta Rd., Canyon Point, Utah, 435/675-3999 or 877/695-3999, www.amanresorts.com, from $1,500), is a 30-minute drive from Page. Secluded in a dreamlike high-desert setting, it offers suite accommodations and a 25,000-square-foot spa.

Camping
Aramark's marinas (888/896-3829, www.lakepowell.com) at **Wahweap**

Many visitors come to Lake Powell to rent houseboats.

(928/645-2433), **Bullfrog** (435/684-3000, 70 lake miles from the dam), and **Halls Crossing** (435/684-7000, 95 lake miles from the dam) include large campgrounds with tent sites and RV hookups ($26-46). **Glen Canyon National Recreation Area** (928/608-9200, www.nps.gov/glca, $15 per vehicle) operates the developed campground at Lees Ferry ($18) as well as several primitive campgrounds ($10-14) around the lake.

At-large **backcountry camping** (free) is allowed in the national recreation area, with restrictions that vary between the lakeshore and desert wilderness. All shoreline campsites are required to have a portable toilet, unless toilets are available within 200 yards. Burying waste of any kind on beaches is prohibited, and ground fires (wood only) must be below the high-water line. Choose campsites on dunes or sandstone; avoid vegetation or organic soil. Pack out all trash, including toilet paper. Leave the campsite looking the same as—or better than—it did when you found it.

TRANSPORTATION AND SERVICES

The most practical way to explore the area is by driving your own vehicle or a rental, although you can fly into Page and arrange for air or ground transportation to Grand Canyon. Boat tours and rentals are available at Wahweap and Antelope Point marinas, on either side of town. When making summer tour arrangements, keep in mind that the Navajo Nation observes daylight saving time, while the rest of Arizona does not.

Driving

Page is a little more than two hours' drive north of Flagstaff. To drive from Page to Grand Canyon's North Rim or South Rim takes about two and a half hours.

North Rim: Two routes lead to the North Rim from Page. The Arizona route (123 miles) offers a possible side-trip to Lees Ferry: Head south on U.S. 89, and then right on U.S. 89A at Bitter Springs to continue to Jacob Lake. From Jacob Lake, it's 45 miles to the rim on scenic Highway 67. For the Utah route (153 miles), take U.S. 89 north to Kanab, then U.S. 89A to Jacob Lake.

South Rim: To get to the South Rim (110 miles), head south on U.S. 89, turning west at Highway 64. You'll reach the park's East Entrance Station 30 miles from the junction. It's another 30 miles from the East Entrance to Grand Canyon Village.

Big Water Visitor Center highlights regional paleontology.

Air

A mile east of downtown, **Page Municipal Airport** (PGA, 238 10th St., 928/645-4337) is served by Great Lakes Airlines (928/645-1355 or 800/554-5111, www.greatlakesav.com) with flights to Phoenix and Denver. For charter flights or tours of Grand Canyon or Lake Powell, contact **Westwind Air Tours** (928/645-2494, 888/869-0866, www.westwindairservice.com) or **Grand Canyon Airlines** (702/835-8484, 866/235-9422, www.grandcanyonairlines.com).

Taxis and Car Rentals

Taxi service is available from **Grand Circle Shuttle** (928/645-6806) or **Buggy Taxi** (928/645-6664). **Avis** (928/645-2024 or 800/331-1212) rents cars at the Page airport. At **Canyon Country Jeep Rental** (428 Haul Rd., 928/645-4004, 928/640-0823), you can rent a 4WD vehicle or a boat, or sign onto a guided tour.

Visitor Centers

Sharing space with the John Wesley Powell Museum, the **visitor information center** (6 N. Lake Powell Blvd., 928/645-9496, www.powellmuseum.org, 9am-5pm daily) is well stocked with maps and brochures, and the helpful staff can assist in selecting and booking local tours.

For dam tours and information about Glen Canyon National Recreation Area, stop at **Carl Hayden Visitor Center** (928/608-6200, 8am-5pm daily, hours vary by season), on U.S. 89 near the dam. Boaters will find that the smaller visitor center at **Bullfrog Marina** (435/684-7423) is open intermittently during summer months; the same goes for the ranger stations at Halls Crossing and Dangling Rope.

If there's a budding paleontologist in your family, head 12 miles north of Page for the Bureau of Land Management (BLM) **Big Water Visitor Center** (100 Upper Revolution Way, Big Water, Utah, 435/675-3200, www.blm.gov, 8:30am-4:30pm daily Apr.-Oct., 8:30am-4:30pm Tues.-Sat. Nov.-Mar.). The ammonite-shaped building has displays about recent discoveries in the area, including the remains of a therizinosaur, a feathered dinosaur with wicked sickle-shaped claws.

Medical Services

The 25-bed **Page Hospital** (501 N. Navajo Dr., 928/645-2424) has 24-hour emergency services and helicopter transport. Urgent care is available at **Canyonlands Healthcare** (440 Navajo Dr., 928/645-1700, 7am-8pm Mon.-Sat.).

Fredonia and Kanab

The Arizona and Utah borderlands boasts the largest concentration of national parks and monuments in the United States. Kanab is a convenient gateway not only to the **North Rim,** but also to Zion, Bryce Canyon, Arches, Cedar Breaks, Capitol Reef, and Canyonlands, all less than two hours away.

Kanab is situated between the White Cliffs and Vermilion Cliffs of the **Grand Staircase,** and colorful horizons mark the edges of high, dry plateaus. Big sagebrush *(Artemisia tridentata)* dominates the wide-open landscape, bracingly aromatic after a rainstorm.

At the close of the 19th century, this area was the last blank spot on the map of the continental United States, explored by John Wesley Powell, Jacob Hamblin, Jack Hillers, and other intrepid scientists, surveyors, and photographers. Today, that sense of discovery still lingers, and two-lane roads and red-dirt tracks will tempt you to see what lies beyond the next turn or hill.

Tidy and historic, Kanab has plenty of small-town atmosphere and Western flair. And though its population numbers fewer than 5,000, the town offers numerous lodging

Kanab

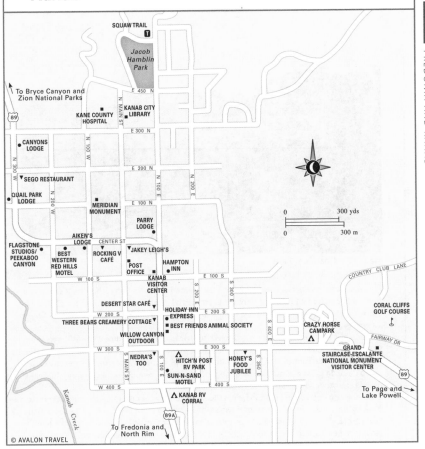

SQUAW TRAIL

Jacob Hamblin Park

To Bryce Canyon and Zion National Parks

89

E 450 N

N MAIN ST

KANE COUNTY HOSPITAL

KANAB CITY LIBRARY

E 300 N

N 100 W

CANYONS LODGE

N 300 W

E 200 N

N 100 E

N 200 E

SEGO RESTAURANT

QUAIL PARK LODGE

N 200 W

E 100 N

MERIDIAN MONUMENT

PARRY LODGE

AIKEN'S LODGE

CENTER ST

FLAGSTONE STUDIOS/ PEEKABOO CANYON

BEST WESTERN RED HILLS MOTEL

ROCKING V CAFÉ

JAKEY LEIGH'S

POST OFFICE

HAMPTON INN

W 100 S

KANAB VISITOR CENTER

S 200 E

E 100 S

S 300 E

COUNTRY CLUB LANE

CORAL CLIFFS GOLF COURSE

DESERT STAR CAFÉ

W 200 S

HOLIDAY INN EXPRESS

E 200 S

THREE BEARS CREAMERY COTTAGE

BEST FRIENDS ANIMAL SOCIETY

S 400 E

CRAZY HORSE CAMPARK

FAIRWAY DR

WILLOW CANYON OUTDOOR

W 300 S

S MAIN ST

E 300 S

GRAND STAIRCASE-ESCALANTE NATIONAL MONUMENT VISITOR CENTER

89

NEDRA'S TOO

S 100 E

HITCH'N POST RV PARK

HONEY'S FOOD JUBILEE

S 360 E

SUN-N-SAND MOTEL

W 400 S

E 400 S

To Page and Lake Powell

Kanab Creek

KANAB RV CORRAL

89A

To Fredonia and North Rim

© AVALON TRAVEL

0 — 300 yds
0 — 300 m

and dining choices about 80 miles from the North Rim.

SIGHTS

See an extensive collection of prehistoric pottery and tools at **Red Pueblo Museum** (900 N. U.S. 89A, Fredonia, 928/643-7777, 9am-5pm Tues.-Sat. spring-fall, $5). For a window into the area's pioneer past, tour **Kanab Heritage House,** an 1894 Victorian standing at the corner of Main and 100 South, or visit the extensive **Kanab Heritage Museum** (13 S. 100 E., 435/644-3966, 10am-5pm Mon.-Fri. May-Sept., free). Everyone is welcome to dig into their family's roots at Kanab's LDS **Family History Center** (20 W. Main St., 435/644-5973, 12pm-9pm Tues.-Thurs., 12pm-6pm Fri.-Sat.).

Even if you aren't looking for backcountry maps or trail info, the BLM's visitor center for the **Grand Staircase-Escalante National Monument** (745 E. U.S. 89, 435/644-1300, 8am-4:30pm daily summer, 8am-4:30pm Mon.-Fri. winter) makes a good stop. Exhibits

Jacob Hamblin, Man with a Mission

the town of Kanab from Squaw Trail

How did Jacob Lake get its name? There is a lake named Jacob, though technically it's an alpine pool—filled seasonally by rain and snowmelt, ringed by meadow grasses, and relied on by wildlife. It's named for Jacob Hamblin—a missionary, scout, peacemaker, and extraordinary Grand Canyon explorer.

Hamblin was born in Ohio in 1816 and converted to Mormonism at a time when followers of the Church of Jesus Christ of Latter-Day Saints (LDS) were being persecuted in the Midwest. After the United States won control of Mexico's territories in 1848, many LDS members migrated to Utah. Jacob Hamblin proved himself adept at negotiating between would-be settlers and the Paiute people and other Native Americans already living in the area.

Hamblin guided young Mormon families to settlements near the Little Colorado River in Arizona Territory, blazing what became known as the Honeymoon Trail. He followed the route of the Spanish friars Domínguez and Escalante, fording the historic Crossing of the Fathers and establishing two more crossings downriver at Lees Ferry and Pearce Ferry. He founded the town of Kanab, Utah, in 1865. In 1870 he assisted Major John Wesley Powell's second canyon voyage by negotiating with local Native Americans for the expedition's safe passage. Of Hamblin, Powell said: "He is a silent, reserved man, and when he speaks it is in a slow, quiet way that inspires great awe."

In his decades of travel, Jacob Hamblin circumnavigated Grand Canyon. He crossed the high Kaibab Plateau and is said to have visited the depths of Havasu Canyon, where he promised Havasupai elders that he would never reveal the location of their idyllic village. (He never did, though others would.)

Hamblin wasn't prone to superlatives, and most of his diaries and letters focus on his mission and his dedication to resolving differences through scripture and friendship. Many people noted that he often didn't carry a gun.

Though Hamblin had homes in St. George and Kanab and a ranch in House Rock Valley below the Vermilion Cliffs, he once wrote: "I have spent more nights under cedar and pine boughs than in a house." After 1882, when the Edmunds-Tucker Act outlawed plural marriages, Hamblin moved his families out of Utah and spent most of his remaining years evading federal authorities. He died of malaria in New Mexico in 1886.

on geology, paleontology, and archaeology provide an excellent primer to the area's natural and cultural riches.

★ Pipe Spring National Monument

Pipe Spring National Monument (406 Pipe Spring Rd., Fredonia, 928/643-7105, www.nps.gov/pisp, 8am-5pm daily May-Aug., 8:30am-4:30pm daily Sept.-Apr., $7), 14 miles west of Fredonia, is operated jointly by the National Park Service and the Kaibab Paiute Nation. Touring the museum and restored buildings are a good way to learn more about those who passed through this high desert oasis or called it home. Mormon leader Brigham Young purchased the stone house (enclosed by a walled courtyard with gun ports) and cattle ranch for the church's herds in 1873. Newly married couples stopped here along the famed Honeymoon Trail, which traveled from the LDS temple in St. George, Utah, to settlements in Arizona.

Best Friends Animal Sanctuary

Love animals? Your heart will melt during a tour of the **Best Friends Animal Sanctuary** (5001 Angel Canyon Rd., 435/644-2001, ext. 4537, www.bestfriends.org, 8am-5pm daily, free), the largest no-kill animal shelter in the United States. The sanctuary, typically home to 1,700 cats, dogs, birds, horses, and other critters, is nestled within the sandstone walls of Angel Canyon, five miles north of Kanab. Best Friends Animal Society also operates a **welcome center** (235 S. 100 E., 435/644-8584, 8am-8pm daily summer, shorter hours in winter) in downtown Kanab, where visitors can stop by to ask questions, cuddle kittens, or reserve tours.

Little Hollywood Museum

Movie buffs will find the series of informative film plaques lining Kanab's main drag to be a bit like eating potato chips—you can't stop at just one. Follow them to the **Little Hollywood Museum** (297 W. Center St., 435/644-5337, www.littlehollywoodmuseum.org, 9am-9pm daily spring-fall, 9am-9pm Fri.-Sat. in winter) in the heart of Kanab, where you can view movie sets and memorabilia, shop for souvenirs, get cast in a Western film, and tuck into a chuckwagon buffet ($16-20).

Movies and TV episodes filmed near Kanab include *The Lone Ranger* (1950), *The Outlaw Josey Wales* (1976), and *Brighty of the Grand Canyon* (1967). If your vehicle is up to

Pipe Spring National Monument preserves Native American and pioneer history.

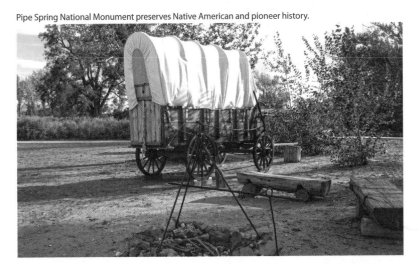

a few bumps, drive 35 miles east on U.S. 89 to the turnoff for the **Pareah Townsite,** where a dirt road leads to a scenic filming location for episodes of *Gunsmoke* (1960) and *Death Valley Days* (1952), among others.

Coral Pink Sand Dunes State Park

If the gorgeously colored landscape of **Coral Pink Sand Dunes State Park** (12 miles southwest of Kanab on U.S. 89A, 435/648-2800, http://stateparks.utah.gov, $6) gives you a sense of déjà vu, you may be remembering scenes from *The Greatest Story Ever Told,* filmed here in 1965. The 3,730-acre park has nature trails, a small campground, and a large area for off-road vehicles.

Maynard Dixon Studio

One of the West's most influential artists, Maynard Dixon (1875-1946) painted striking landscapes as well as Depression-era portraits and scenes, conveying themes that were also captured in photos taken by his second wife, Dorothea Lange. East of Kanab, Dixon's **log cabin home and studio** (mile marker 84, U.S. 89, 435/648-2562 or 800/992-1066, www.thunderbirdfoundation.org) has docent-guided tours (by appointment Mar.-Nov., $20), art workshops, and an annual art festival and campout each June ($150 for four days, through some events are free). Visitors can explore the grounds on a self-guided walking tour (10am-5pm daily, $10).

RECREATION

Besides being the hub for the Grand Circle of national parks, Kanab is also the gateway to the Paria Canyon-Vermilion Cliffs Wilderness, Grand Staircase-Escalante National Monument, and Grand Canyon-Parashant National Monument, all administered by the **BLM** (www.blm.gov), and the Kanab Creek and Saddle Mountain wilderness areas, which lie within **Kaibab National Forest** (www.fs.usda.gov/kaibab). These wild lands offer recreation experiences that range from peaceful back-road drives to challenging

Kanab is known as "Little Hollywood" for its role in the film industry.

canyoneering adventures. Backpackers need to prepare carefully for rugged terrain, poorly marked trails, and infrequent water sources.

Biking

You can bike to the edge of Grand Staircase-Escalante National Monument via the paved **Johnson Canyon Road,** which begins 10 miles east of Kanab on U.S. 89. The route passes ranchland, an old set for the TV series *Gunsmoke,* a sandstone arch, gnarled juniper trees, and beautifully eroded cliffs. The pavement ends at 18 miles, but you can continue a few miles—or more—if you have the legs for it. Be respectful of the surrounding private property.

Hiking

A moderate two-hour hike, the **Squaw Trail** (3 miles round-trip) climbs to great views of Kanab and the series of colorful plateaus making up the Grand Staircase. The trailhead is located just north of **Jacob Hamblin Park** (531 N. 100 E.).

Golf

The nine holes at **Coral Cliffs Golf Course** (755 E. Fairway Dr., 435/644-5005, dawn-dusk Tues.-Sun., weather permitting) are edged on three sides by the foothills of the Vermilion Cliffs.

ENTERTAINMENT AND EVENTS

Western culture, from real cowboys to the celluloid variety, is celebrated in Kanab. Local restaurants host country music and stage shows during the high season, served up with barbeque or chuckwagon-style grub. You can catch a classic Western flick at Parry Lodge's **Old Barn Theater** (89 E. Center St., 435/644-2601, 8pm daily Apr.-Oct.). The **Crescent Moon Theater** (150 S. 100 E., 435/644-2350) stages a variety of entertainment, from cowboy poetry to old Westerns or live music. The annual **Western Legends Roundup** (435/644-3444, www.westernlegendsroundup.com, Aug.) combines food, music, movies, re-enactments, and more, drawing Hollywood celebrities and thousands of fans.

Over three days in late February, the Vermilion Cliffs get even more colorful during the **Balloons & Tunes Roundup** (www.balloonsandtunesroundup.com), when hot air balloons soar over the golf course and bands battle for first place.

Throughout March, prehistoric and historic traditions are highlighted at **Pipe Spring National Monument** (15 miles west of Fredonia on Hwy. 389, 928/643-7105, www.nps.gov/pisp) as part of Arizona Archaeology Month. Events may include beading and rug-making demonstrations or a hike into a canyon to view petroglyphs.

Summer months are filled with classic small-town get-togethers, from concerts at the gazebo to a weekly farmers' market. **Jacob Hamblin Days** (June) honors Kanab's founder with events that include trail rides and a rodeo. **Independence Day** (July) festivities include a parade and fireworks. **Kaibab Paiute Heritage Day** (928/643-7245) is held in September, with most events centering on the band's small reservation near Pipe Spring National Monument.

To learn more about current happenings, check the local paper, *Southern Utah News* (www.sunews.net), pick up a copy of its annual **Vacation Guide** (www.kanabguide.com), or consult **Kane County's tourism website** (www.visitsouthernutah.com).

Parry Lodge screens classic Westerns nightly at its Old Barn Theater.

SHOPPING

Window-shopping in Kanab's historic and walkable downtown is a pleasant way to pass an hour or two. You'll see numerous trading posts and Western-wear shops as well as evidence of the town's shifting demographics in storefronts advertising holistic health services or New Age gifts. You'll also notice a lot of locals walking dogs. Find out why by visiting **Best Friends Sanctuary** (5001 Angel Canyon Rd., 435/644-2001, ext. 4826, www.bestfriends.org). The organization's well-stocked gift shop has toys and necessities for your fur-kids and some pretty cool stuff for humans too.

For hiking guides, outdoor gear, and spot-on advice, head for **Willow Canyon** (263 S. 100 E., 435/644-8884, 7am-8:30pm daily, hours vary seasonally).

FOOD

Fans of home-style cooking will find lots of steakhouses and cafés in Kanab offering simple Western fare. Expect hours to vary during winter months, when some properties limit their service or close for a few weeks.

At **Jakey Leigh's** (4 E. Center St., 435/644-8191, 7am-12:30pm Mon.-Fri., 8am-noon Sat.-Sun., under $10), you can grab a table outside and sip coffee while watching Kanab's dog-loving residents walk past with their pooches. For a hearty Southwestern-style breakfast or lunch, try **Nedra's Too** (310 S. 100 E., 435/644-2030, www.nedrascafe.com, 8am-9pm daily, $6-15), operated by three generations of family cooks. At the **Three Bears Creamery Cottage** (210 S. 100 E., 435/644-3300, www.threebearscreamery.com, 11am-9pm Mon.-Sat., $5-12), sandwiches come on house-baked bread, and the ice cream desserts are legendary.

Foodies will feel at home at the ★ **Rocking V Café** (97 W. Center St., 435/644-8001, www.rockingvcafe.com, 11:30am-10pm daily Mar. 27-Oct. 31, 11:30am-10pm Thurs.-Mon. Nov.-Apr., shorter hours in winter, $12-40). Located in a historic mercantile-turned-art

gallery, this lively spot dishes art and music along with fresh, hip meals. Reservations are recommended during the busy summer season. Another delicious option is **Sego Restaurant** (190 N. 300 W., 435/644-5680, www.segokanab.com, 6pm-10pm Mon.-Sat., $8-26), serving small, sharable plates of farm-to-fork food in a convivial atmosphere. Wood-fired pizza is a specialty at **Peekaboo Canyon Kitchen** (233 W. Center St., 435/689-1959, 8 am-2pm and 5pm-10 pm daily), but you'll also find paninis, salads, and tasty breakfasts on the menu, which focuses on vegetarian dishes.

ACCOMMODATIONS

Kanab's plentiful lodging options include chains, local motels, and home rentals. Many offer discounted rates during winter; a few close for the season. All rooms book early during the peak months from May to October.

Along U.S. 89's bending path through the heart of Kanab, several chains and mid-century motor lodges offer accommodations. Locally owned **Travelers Motel** (544 E. 300 S., 435/644-2228, $75-100) has clean, simple rooms at moderate prices. **Quail Park Lodge** (125 N. 300 W., 435/215-1447 or 844/322-8824, www.quailparklodge.com, $150-180) and sister property ★ **Flagstone Studios** (223 W. Center St., 844/322-8824, $120-130) have stylishly refurbished rooms with a retro flair.

Movie stars from John Wayne to Clint Eastwood have stayed at **Parry Lodge** (89 E. Center St., 435/644-2601 or 888/286-1722, www.parrylodge.com, $120-150). Listed on the National Register of Historic Places, the nostalgic hotel and restaurant highlight Kanab's heyday of Western filmmaking.

For house rentals, contact **Kanab Garden Cottages** (U.S. 89, 844/322-8824, www.kanabcottages.com, $190-230); properties include gracious historic homes that can sleep up to eight people. Guests of **Best Friends Animal Sanctuary** (5001 Angel Canyon Rd., Kanab, 435/644-2001, ext. 4826, www.

bestfriends.org) can stay at the Angel Canyon sanctuary five miles north of Kanab in accommodations that range from RV spaces ($30-50) to cottages ($120-140). You can even invite a shelter cat or dog to bunk with you for some special one-on-one time.

You'll find limited lodging choices in Fredonia, Arizona, seven miles south of Kanab (seven miles closer to the North Rim). A former hunting lodge, the **Grand Canyon Motel** (175 S. Main St., Fredonia, 928/643-7646, http://grand-canyon-motel.com, $20-45) has a dozen rooms and nearby hostel accommodations.

Camping

Kanab has several RV campgrounds, including the **Kanab RV Corral** (483 S. 100 E., 435/644-5330, www.kanabrvcorral.com, $35), located on the east edge of town near the golf course. Public campgrounds include lovely **Coral Pink Sand Dunes State Park** (12 miles southwest of Kanab on U.S. 89A, 800/332-3770, 435/648-2800, http://stateparks.utah.gov, $20), a favorite of off-roaders and photographers.

TRANSPORTATION AND SERVICES

Though only a skip away from several national parks, Fredonia and Kanab are splendidly isolated from major urban areas—about 200 miles east of Las Vegas and 80 miles east of St. George, Utah. The best way to explore the area's colorful, wide-open spaces is in your own vehicle or a rental.

Driving

North Rim: To get to the North Rim from Kanab, take U.S. 89A south. The highway swings east after passing through Fredonia and begins to climb the Kaibab Plateau, turning south again as it nears Jacob Lake, about 30 miles. At Jacob Lake, turn south on Highway 67 and proceed another 43 miles to the North Rim's Bright Angel Point. A backroad alternative to Jacob Lake: Paved Forest

Road 22, beginning a mile east of Fredonia on U.S. 89, is lined with golden-blooming chamiso (rabbitbrush) in early autumn. The road cuts 21 miles through ranch country before joining Forest Road 461, a good dirt road that climbs the Kaibab Plateau for the final nine miles to Jacob Lake.

South Rim: If you're heading for the South Rim, stay on U.S. 89A until it joins U.S. 89. Take U.S. 89 south to Highway 64 and the South Rim's East Entrance Station. Grand Canyon Village is approximately 220 miles from Fredonia.

Toroweap: To get to Grand Canyon National Park's remote Toroweap overlook via the Sunshine Route, take Highway 389 west from Fredonia about seven miles. Turn south on Mount Trumbull Road and travel 60 miles, following signs for Toroweap. Do not attempt this trip unless you have planned carefully, checked current road conditions, and adequately prepared yourself and your vehicle with maps, food, water, and at least one good spare tire (the National Park Service recommends two).

Air

The nearest commercial airport is **St. George Regional Airport** (SGU, 4550 S. Airport Pkwy., St. George, Utah, 435/627-4080, http://flysgu.com) in St. George, Utah, about 80 miles west, served by American Airlines (SkyWest), Delta, and United. The **Kanab Municipal Airport** (2378 S. U.S. 89A, 435/644-2299), accessible to private aircraft, is located two miles south of Kanab.

Car Rental

Xpress RentACar (1530 S. U.S. 89A, 435/644-3408, www.xpressrentalcarofkanab.com) can hook you up with a rental sedan or 4WD vehicle at Kanab's airport or local hotels. You'll find national car-rental companies in St. George, Utah.

Visitor Centers

In Fredonia, the district headquarters for

the **North Kaibab National Forest** (430 S. Main St., 928/643-7395, www.fs.usda.gov/kaibab, 8am-4:30pm Mon.-Fri.) has maps and information about local trails and forest roads to Toroweap and Jacob Lake.

Located 14 miles west of Fredonia via Hwy. 389, **Pipe Spring National Monument** (406 Pipe Spring Rd., 928/643-7105, www.nps.gov/pisp, 8am-5pm daily May-Aug., 8:30am-4:30pm daily Sept.-Apr., $7) has an excellent museum, morning ranger programs, and tours throughout the day.

In Kanab, the **BLM** (www.blm.gov) operates a visitor center for the **Grand Staircase-Escalante National Monument** (745 E. U.S. 89, 435/644-1300, 8am-4:30pm daily summer, 8am-4:30pm Mon.-Fri. winter).

You can't miss the **Kane County Office of Tourism** (78 S. 100 E., Kanab, 435/644-5033 or 800/733-5263, www.visitsouthernutah.com, 8am-5pm Mon.-Fri., 8:30am-4:30pm Sat.), located in a mural-covered building in downtown Kanab.

Medical Services

The **Fredonia Community Health Center** (100 E. Wood Hill Rd., Fredonia, 928/643-6215, 7am-12:30pm and 1:30pm-5pm Mon.-Wed., 7am-11am Thurs.) provides urgent care. **Kane County Hospital** (355 N. Main St., Kanab, 435/644-5811) has emergency services. The attached clinic (435/644-4100, 9am-5pm Mon.-Fri.) provides walk-in urgent care.

Background

The Landscape

GEOGRAPHY

Grand Canyon slices roughly east-west through the southwestern edge of the Colorado Plateau, an uplifted platform with an average elevation of 6,000 feet centering on the Four Corners region. Ninety percent of this vast semiarid plateau is drained by the Colorado River and its tributaries. The plateau's colorful rock layers, broken by faults and carved by streams, are dramatically revealed in Grand Canyon.

Shifts along fault lines have created several distinct smaller plateaus within the 130,000-square-mile **Colorado Plateau.** Grand Canyon's north side is dominated by the Kaibab and Kanab Plateaus. On the south is the Coconino Plateau. The eastern section of Grand Canyon, known as Marble Canyon, runs roughly north-south through the lower elevations of the Marble Platform. Inside the boundaries of Grand Canyon National Park (1.2 million acres), the North Rim's Grand Canyon Lodge sits 1,180 feet higher than Grand Canyon Village on the South Rim, with 10 air miles (220 road miles) between. Grand Canyon ends at the Grand Wash Cliffs, which form the edge of present-day Lake Mead, impounded by Hoover Dam.

Grand Canyon's main artery, the **Colorado River,** flows from north-central Colorado to the Gulf of Mexico. Northeast of Grand Canyon, Glen Canyon Dam impounds the river, restricting flows and changing its muddy, red-brown water to cold, clear green. The distance from rim to river varies but averages 4,000 feet. The river averages about 35 feet deep and varies in width from 76 feet to more than 300 feet.

The 277-mile stretch from Lees Ferry to the Grand Wash Cliffs drops 1,900 feet in elevation and crosses countless tributary canyons. Debris from these side canyons creates the most common type of rapids, constriction rapids, where water tumbles over boulders swept into the main channel by floods. River runners encounter **more than 160 rapids** on the journey through the canyon, and the Colorado River drops in gradient about eight feet per mile. Most of Grand Canyon's tributaries flow only intermittently after rainstorms or during spring melt. About a dozen have year-round water, including the Little Colorado River, Bright Angel Creek, and Havasu Creek.

The Colorado River and Grand Canyon create a barrier between Arizona's northwest corner and the rest of the state. Until the Navajo Bridge was completed in 1929, the **Arizona Strip** was relatively isolated. Even today, the corner of Grand Canyon known as Tuweep or Toroweap requires a long drive through ranch country and Bureau of Land Management (BLM) land.

GEOLOGY

Several forces have combined to create Grand Canyon, and many geological theories about the canyon's formation have been advanced during the hundred-plus years that geologists have studied the region. Most agree that although its rocks are very old, the canyon itself is relatively young. But exactly when and how the canyon was formed is still under debate.

Many geologists believe that sometime between five and six million years ago, the ancestral Colorado River began cutting through rock layers that had been laid down over billions of years. Recent research suggests that canyon formation may have begun as long as 16 million years ago. Although canyon-cutting

---

Grand Canyon by the Numbers

How old?

- Oldest rocks: 1.84 billion years
- Canyon formed: 5-6 million years
- Park established: 1919

How deep?

- 1 mile average; 6,000 feet at its deepest point

How long?

- 277 river miles

How wide?

- 10 miles average; narrowest point, 600 feet; widest point, 15 miles

How big?

- 5.45 trillion cubic yards in volume
- 1,218,375 acres in the park

How high?

- 8,803 feet at the North Rim's Point Imperial overlook
- 2,460 feet at Phantom Ranch

How many?

- 5 life zones
- 1,700-plus plant species
- 373 bird, 91 mammal, 47 reptile, 9 amphibian, and 17 fish species
- 160-plus named rapids
- 900-plus South Rim hotel rooms
- 5 million visitors annually

The pen used by Woodrow Wilson to officially make Grand Canyon a national park is displayed at Verkamps Visitor Center.

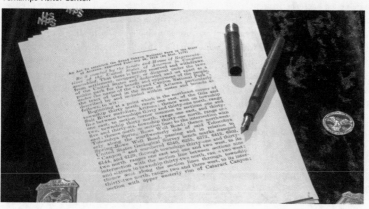

theories conflict in regard to timing, scientists agree that the ancestral Colorado River was a powerful erosional force.

We know that before the completion of Glen Canyon Dam in 1963, the Colorado River carried 380,000 tons of sediment daily through Grand Canyon, giving it a tremendous cutting power that probably pales in comparison to that of the ancestral river. Glen Canyon Dam traps most sediments, but tributaries such as the Little Colorado and Paria Rivers introduce 30,000 to 40,000 tons of sediment daily. Though its colorful cliffs and temples may appear to be frozen in time, the canyon continues to be shaped by wind and water.

Vishnu Schist

Grand Canyon's walls reveal nearly 40 layers of rock that record more than one-third of the earth's history. The oldest, deepest rock found in the canyon's Inner Gorge is Vishnu schist, a hard, fine-grained rock formed by undersea deposits of mud, silt, clay, and sand. Nearly two billion years ago, as the continent collided with a chain of volcanic islands, layers of sediment and ash metamorphosed into schist, and volcanic intrusions solidified to form granite. The gray-to-black Vishnu schist and pinkish **Zoroaster granite** interweave to form the hard cliffs of the Inner Gorge. These rocks are part of the Precambrian Basement Complex on which the North American continent rests.

Grand Canyon Supergroup

Over the next 430 million years, 14,000 feet of marine sediments formed the nine strata collectively known as the Grand Canyon Supergroup. These layers include gray or reddish **Bass limestone,** where the oldest fossils in Grand Canyon formed from clumps of single-celled bacteria. In some areas, Bass limestone has been partly metamorphosed, resulting in asbestos, mined by Grand Canyon pioneers like William Bass and John Hance.

Subsequent layers include bright-orange-red Hakatai shale, 430 to 830 feet thick, and Cardenas lava, forming intrusions and basalt cliffs nearly 1,000 feet thick in places. The volcanic activity was part of a greater collision and uplift that formed mountain ranges along a supercontinent. Widespread geologic unrest began to break the supercontinent apart 820 to 770 million years ago, tilting and uplifting the Supergroup layers along fault lines.

The exposed Supergroup layers eroded as much as 15,000 feet, leaving only colorful wedges and folds near Unkar Delta, Phantom Ranch, Bass Camp, and downriver between miles 130 and 138. In most of the canyon, the Supergroup has completely eroded away, and the contact line between schist and Tapeats sandstone—the edge of the Tonto Platform—represents one billion years of missing geology, the **Great Unconformity.**

Paleozoic Rocks

Over the next 325 million years, the Grand Canyon region lay along a changing coastline. During the Paleozoic era, sediments 3,500 to 6,500 feet deep formed 15 rock layers. These colorful horizontal strata are the canyon's most visible layers, recording a proliferation of life as fossils—the most complete record of the Paleozoic era on the planet. From top to bottom, the Paleozoic layers can be memorized using the mnemonic phrase *Know The Canyon's History, Study Rocks Made By Time:*

gray Vishnu schist and pinkish Zoroaster granite

Kaibab, Toroweap, Coconino, Hermit, Supai, Redwall, Muav, Bright Angel, Tapeats.

- **Tapeats sandstone,** a dark-brown, stratified, 150- to 250-foot-thick cliff lies directly on top of the basement rocks in many areas of the canyon.

- **Bright Angel shale,** a crumbling layer of mud, silt, and sand in shades of green and purple, overlies and intermingles with the Tapeats. Both are riddled with worm burrows and trilobite fossils.

- **Muav limestone** was deposited by deeper waters 535 million years ago. In the Eastern canyon it is overlaid by Redwall limestone, representing another unconformity, in this case a geological gap of about 100 million years.

- **Redwall cliffs** were laid down 360 to 320 million years ago, when ocean covered all of western North America. Nodules of chert (fossilized sponge), along with nautiloids, brachiopods, crinoids, and other fossils indicate a rich marine life. In the central canyon, the Redwall rises 500 to 800 feet above the Tonto Platform, its cliffs pocked with caves and alcoves where softer deposits have been dissolved by seeps. Though Redwall limestone is grayish, it has been stained red by overlying rock layers. In many places, Redwall cliffs are draped with "tapestries" of dark mineralized stains, called desert varnish.

- **Supai Group** layers alternate in cliffs and slopes of shale, limestone, and sandstone, laid down in a coastal environment 310 to 285 million years ago. Reptile tracks can be seen in the upper members of the Supai Group. The topmost member, Esplanade sandstone, forms a hard shelf in western Grand Canyon. In eastern tributaries, such as North and South Canyons, it appears as reddish bedrock carved and fluted by erosion.

- **Hermit shale** was formed 286 to 245 million years ago as steep mountain ranges drained, depositing muddy sediments in a delta-like environment rich with plant life. Fossils of 35 types of ferns and other plants have been identified in the canyon's 250- to 1,000-foot-thick Hermit Shale, which has eroded into dark-red slopes.

- **Coconino sandstone** formed 270 million years ago, in a desert environment of huge sand dunes. This buff-colored sandstone is marked by aeolian (wind-deposited) cross-bedded cliffs 350 feet high in the eastern canyon, pinching out to the west.

- **Toroweap formation,** silty limestone 250 to 450 feet thick, was deposited 265 million years ago when seawater returned, evaporating quickly in the tidal flats of an arid environment. Look for steep slopes of pale yellow, usually vegetated by trees and shrubs.

- **Kaibab formation,** a limestone rich with marine invertebrate fossils, is found at the canyon's rims. This layer, 290 to 500 feet thick, was created as seawater continued to engulf the canyon. By this time, the Grand Canyon area was just north of the equator, part of the supercontinent Pangaea formed as the planet's landmasses collided and slowly coalesced.

Outside the Park

During the Mesozoic era, Pangaea broke up during uplifts, earthquakes, and volcanoes. Mesozoic rocks are visible just outside the park's boundaries: the Chinle Formation of the Painted Desert, the Moenave and Kayenta Formations at the base of the Echo and Vermilion Cliffs, and the Navajo sandstone upstream in Glen Canyon. About 65 million years ago, at the beginning of the Cenozoic era, a mountain-building period raised the Colorado Plateau region, creating the series of monoclines known as the **Grand Staircase.** Mesozoic rocks eroded away from the heights of the Kaibab Plateau, stripping Grand Canyon back to its Permian layers and setting the stage for canyon cutting.

CLIMATE

The Grand Canyon region is semiarid, with great variation in temperature and rainfall due to elevation. Average annual precipitation is less than 10 inches at Phantom Ranch, 15 inches on the South Rim, and more than 20 inches on the North Rim. Most of the moisture arrives during the late summer monsoon season or during the winter. Temperatures vary from below 0°F to higher than 100°F in the inner canyon. Rims are often windy, and the inner canyon "breathes" with upstream winds during daylight and downstream winds at night.

Seasonal descriptions are general and hardly a guarantee. Expect the unexpected: snowstorms in June, 90°F temperatures in October, and dry winters when the North Rim is accessible for stretches of time.

Spring

In late **March** the North Rim may still be tucked under a blanket of snow. On the South Rim it may be cold and windy, but if you find a sunny, sheltered spot, you can already feel the power of the sun's rays. During the next couple of months, spring creeps up from the inner canyon as wildflowers bloom along trails and birds go about the business of establishing territories and nests. Lingering Pacific storm patterns may dump inches of snow on the South Rim into **April,** but the snow melts quickly as the sun gains strength. By May, inner canyon temperatures are already reaching into the 90s, and winter recedes from the North Rim.

May and June are dry and cloudless. While the North Rim begins to experience spring, inner canyon temperatures edge toward the 100°F mark as the dry desert foresummer tightens its grip. Intense sunshine quickly dries the forests surrounding the rims, and by the end of **June, fire danger** may trigger camping and hiking restrictions in the national forest lands surrounding the park. As June comes to a close, prevailing winds shift and humidity rises, leading to the Arizona monsoon.

Temperature and Precipitation

Though much of Arizona is desert, including inner Grand Canyon, the state has two rainy seasons, in winter and late summer. Higher elevations like the North and South Rims receive more precipitation than deserts and valleys.

	South Rim		Inner Gorge		North Rim	
	Low/High	Precip.	Low/High	Precip.	Low/High	Precip.
January	18/41	1.32	36/56	0.68	16/37	3.17
February	21/45	1.55	42/62	0.75	18/39	3.22
March	25/51	1.38	48/71	0.79	21/44	2.63
April	32/60	0.93	56/82	0.47	29/53	1.73
May	39/70	0.66	63/92	0.36	34/62	1.17
June	47/81	0.42	72/101	0.30	40/73	0.86
July	54/84	1.81	78/106	0.84	46/77	1.93
August	53/82	2.25	75/103	1.40	45/75	2.85
September	47/76	1.56	69/97	0.97	39/69	1.99
October	36/65	1.10	58/84	0.65	31/59	1.38
November	27/52	0.94	46/68	0.43	24/46	1.48
December	20/43	1.62	37/57	0.87	20/40	2.83

Summer

As deserts heat up and pull in moisture from the Gulf of Mexico, building clouds herald the arrival of the **annual monsoon.** Hot, dry air may evaporate moisture before it reaches the earth, and dry storms may spawn dangerous lightning. By **mid-July,** the rains arrive—brief, powerful thundershowers that sweep across the canyon, usually in the afternoon. The monsoon pattern lasts through **August,** the month when the inner canyon receives the most rain. A second bloom of wildflowers begins with the rains.

Fall and Winter

By **mid-September** the monsoon retreats and cloudless skies return. Birds begin to migrate south, and aspens turn gold as **October** approaches. In **December,** Pacific storms again march their way eastward, bringing winter moisture to the canyon in the form of rain or snow. The North Rim can receive as much as 120 inches of snow; the South Rim, 65 inches. Ground squirrels hibernate, while deer and elk sink into winter sluggishness, conserving energy by browsing the piñon-juniper woodlands near the village and West Rim. **Mountain snowpack** provides a slow release of moisture as the weather warms, recharging springs and maximizing Colorado River flows. Glimpses of spring begin as early as February in the inner canyon, when brittlebush sends up its golden blooms and the cycle of seasons turns again.

ENVIRONMENTAL ISSUES

Park managers strive to find a healthy balance, not only with regard to nature but also with respect to neighboring communities and various stakeholders—including Native American communities, scientists, park concessionaires, environmental groups, tour guides, boaters, and backpackers—whose interests sometimes overlap and at other times conflict.

Many of these groups weighed in on the **Grand Canyon Enlargement Act (1975),** which doubled the park's size and increased

protection for the Marble Canyon area. And yet the National Park Service has very limited control over Grand Canyon's airspace, underground resources, or impacts outside park boundaries. In 2015 the National Trust for Historic Preservation declared Grand Canyon to be **one of the most endangered sites** in the United States.

Ongoing conservation battles require vigilance from nonprofits and voters as pressure mounts to privatize public lands and profit from them. As Teddy Roosevelt said in a 1903 speech on the South Rim: "We have gotten past the stage, my fellow citizens, when we are to be pardoned if we simply treat any part of our country as something to be skinned for two or three years for the use of the present generation."

Colorado River

During the 1950s and 1960s, momentum was building among environmental groups and canyon lovers to protect the Colorado River within the canyon. Congress approved the construction of **Glen Canyon Dam** in 1956, but President Lyndon B. Johnson created Marble Canyon National Monument in 1969,

Glen Canyon Dam

The Colorado River Lottery

Norman Nevills pioneered commercial river running in the 1930s.

Commercial river running in Grand Canyon launched in 1938 with **Norman Nevills,** who guided a pair of botanists wanting to study the canyon's flora. Nevills designed a broad, flat-bottomed, wooden boat called a cataract boat, and in all his river trips, he never "swam" (river-speak for capsizing).

By mid-century, fewer than 100 people had run the Colorado River through Grand Canyon, but commercial guiding was beginning to catch on. Among the best-known guides was **Georgie White,** who lashed together trios of World War II surplus rafts and added outboard motors to create rubberized people-movers that safely slipped over rapids. She called them G-rigs; others dubbed them baloney boats. Her share-the-expense tours often featured mystery meals—a mishmash of canned food with the labels worn away by the river.

Others followed Georgie White's example, creating rigs that carried large groups, and by the early 1970s river traffic swelled from a few dozen to more than 16,000 people a year. Higher river traffic impacted beaches and water quality, and in 1973 the National Park Service responded by issuing a limited number of river permits in an effort to preserve a sense of wildness within the inner canyon. For some private trip leaders, the wait for a permit stretched to decades.

In 2006, the park shifted to a **weighted lottery** for issuing permits (fewer than 500 each year), hoping to cut long wait times and distribute permits more fairly, improving the odds for those who haven't been on a recent trip.

preventing two other proposed dams that would have flooded Marble Canyon.

The effects of Glen Canyon Dam are still debated. On the one hand, a tamed river with predictable flows and timed releases from the dam makes commercial river running possible. On the other hand, native warm-water fish have become endangered and extirpated, and aggressive nonnative plants, such as tamarisk, have overtaken beaches. And beaches are shrinking—a non-flooding river carries away more sand than it deposits.

After lengthy study and several public hearings, a consensus was reached: Controlled flooding might help replenish beaches and benefit canyon environments. In 1996 dam spillways were opened, the first of many high-flow experiments as scientists and resource managers try to find workable solutions.

Fire

Good intentions can have unintended consequences. Just ask Smokey Bear, who, since the 1940s, has urged generations of Americans to prevent forest fires. Decades of fire suppression are partly to blame for recent high-intensity wildfires. Today, fire ecologists stress the need to reduce fuel loads, and managing fire rather than suppressing it is a good idea that works—most of the time. The Grand Canyon area's largest wildfire to date, the 2006 **Warm Fire,** started with a lightning strike. Foresters decided to manage the fire in order to reduce the fuel burden, but two weeks later, strong winds whipped the smoldering burn into a blaze that jumped across Highway 67, stranding 800 travelers at the North Rim.

The Warm Fire burned nearly 60,000 acres—puny compared to recent catastrophic wildfires that have raged in Western states. A scientific study released in 2016 announced that nearly half of the 23.5 million acres burned in the Western states since 1984 can be attributed to **climate change.** The study also predicted more intense fires are likely in years to come. Smokey's message may be more nuanced today, but we must still be vigilant.

Air Quality

Smoke from Western wildfires, emissions from a nearby coal-fired power plant, even haze blowing in from the Los Angeles basin can impact Grand Canyon's air quality. On a clear day, it's possible to see 200 miles or more. On some days, visibility is less than half that. **Air quality** is perceptible, but many less obvious issues threaten the integrity of the canyon, including stream pollution, noise from air tours, invasive species, archaeological pilfering, wildlife poaching, development, aging infrastructure, and increased groundwater demands.

Development Projects

In 2016 the U.S. Forest Service refused to widen roads and build infrastructure to accommodate a sprawling commercial and residential development that would have increased the population of Tusayan by tenfold, impacting traffic, wildlife habitat, cultural resources, and the canyon's fragile system for delivering drinking water. Even though this proposed megaresort faces strong opposition, backers still haven't abandoned it.

Another massive development project, this one proposed for Navajo Nation lands along the rim near Desert View, would impact one of the most beautiful—and culturally significant—sites within Grand Canyon. Opposed by Navajo families who live nearby, a Scottsdale developer continues to press the nation's council to approve the **Escalade Project,** a megaresort with a **tramway** that would ferry up to 10,000 people a day to the confluence of the Colorado and Little Colorado Rivers.

Mining

On national forest land six miles from Grand Canyon Village, a **uranium mine** has resumed operations despite its potential to contaminate groundwater that feeds into the Colorado River. Overriding objections from environmental groups and the Havasupai Nation, a U.S. district judge ruled in favor of the mining company. The Arizona Department of Environmental Quality (ADEQ) issued permits allowing 24 haul trucks a day to transport ore—covered with a tarp to contain **radioactive dust**—along the same roads that visitors use to reach the canyon. ADEQ granted the company air quality permits for two additional mines, also within the Grand Canyon watershed.

In response, Native American leaders and others have proposed establishing the **Greater Grand Canyon Heritage National Monument** to protect public lands surrounding the park from the effects of toxic mining. Though polls show 80 percent of Arizona residents support the monument, opponents include most of the state's congressional delegation, along with special interest groups funded with dark money from the Koch network.

Plants and Animals

The canyon's natural riches include its flora and fauna. C. H. Merriam, who based his theory of life zones on research he did in the Grand Canyon region in 1889, proposed that plant and animal communities change not only with latitude but also with elevation. From the Colorado River (average elevation 2,200 feet) to the Kaibab Plateau (9,200 feet), the Grand Canyon has a diversity of landscapes, plants, and animals. Hiking from the river to the rim is often likened to traveling from Mexico to Canada.

Although Merriam's system is still used, most scientists today think in terms of biologic communities. Even so, plants and animals aren't aware of the neat scientific boundaries assigned to them. The canyon acts as a barrier to some species and a corridor to others. Orientation to the sun, rainfall amounts, differences in terrain and soils—these factors create a range of microclimates. Desert species extend higher on sunny ridges and slopes, while deep, shady draws allow higher-elevation species to move downward. The intermixture between neighboring biologic communities is referred to as an ecotone, where flora and fauna mingle in amazing variety.

PLANTS

More than **1,700 species** of plants grow in Grand Canyon, nearly half of the flora found in Arizona, which is considered one of the most botanically diverse states in the United States. A dozen plants are endemic, found only in the Grand Canyon area. One is the endangered sentry milk vetch (*Astragalus cremnophylax* var. *cremnophylax).* Its Latin species name means "gorge watchman."

Deserts

The **Lower Sonoran life zone,** found below 3,500 feet, includes plants from the Sonoran and Mojave Deserts. Species vary east to west, with some Great Basin desert plants growing in Marble Canyon, and Mojave Desert species appearing as the canyon approaches Lake Mead. Temperatures rise above 100°F on summer afternoons, and little rain falls. Saltbush

Volunteers helped transplant seedlings to re-establish the endangered sentry milk-vetch.

and creosote are common. On talus slopes, Mormon tea, brittlebush, ocotillo, and crucifixion thorn join prickly pear, hedgehog, fishhook, and barrel cacti.

In sharp contrast, along the river and its tributary creeks or nearby springs, **riparian communities** nourish moisture-loving species. Tributaries may be cooler and more sheltered than the main canyon, nurturing redbuds, cottonwoods, willows, ferns, and monkey flower. Along the river, Apache plume, mesquite, catclaw, and saltbush grow above the old predam high-water line. Above the new high-water line, mesquite, coyote willow, and the common reed compete with thickets of tamarisk, an introduced species that has aggressively overtaken Colorado River beaches.

The **Upper Sonoran life zone,** at 3,500 to 7,000 feet, includes the yucca, agave, and cacti of the Tonto Platform and the piñon-juniper woodland of the South Rim. Within this zone are desert grassland, chaparral, sagebrush, and other plant communities, often intermixed. Blackbrush predominates the Tonto Platform, giving it a gray-green appearance. Cliffrose, New Mexico locust, barberry, and other blooming shrubs grow on and below the South Rim, appearing in sunny pockets below the North Rim. Along trails and roadsides, fleabane, asters, phlox, globe mallow, and Indian paintbrush are part of seasonally changing wildflower displays.

Forests and Woodlands

At 7,000-8,000 feet, the ponderosa forests of the **Transition zone** yield to thickets of Gambel oak near the rims. On the North Rim, lupine and butterweed make purple and yellow carpets below the ponderosas during the summer. Above 8,000 feet the Canadian zone is home to white fir, while the moister and cooler Hudsonian zone is typified by spruce-fir forests. These two zones interweave according to topography, so they are often referred to in combination as the **Boreal life zone.** The Boreal life zone receives 25 to 30 inches of precipitation annually, supporting forests of spruce and fir, with open meadows (often referred to as parks) edged by aspen, shimmering yellow and gold in fall. The first major snowfall can arrive as early as November, and snow can linger into May or even June. High-meadow lakes form from snowmelt in the spring, attracting coyotes, wild turkeys, deer, elk, and other wildlife.

yellow brittlebush in bloom at Tapeats Creek

ANIMALS

Grand Canyon's myriad wildlife habitats are mostly unbroken within the park's 1,217,403 acres. The varied environments support thousands of invertebrates, 17 fish species, 9 amphibian species, 17 reptile species, 355 bird species, and 89 mammal species.

Insects

Along the river, you may encounter moths and butterflies, such as the lovely yellow-and-black swallowtails. The showy **sphinx moth** is an important pollinator, often mistaken for a hummingbird. There are blessedly few mosquitoes, but other biters include fire ants, centipedes, millipedes, and the dreaded cedar gnats that plague piñon-juniper woodlands in late spring. Several scorpion species inhabit the desert areas along the river, including the tiny bark scorpion. Higher up the canyon and along the rims, tarantulas venture across roads and trails around the time of the

Critter Alert

Several poisonous critters inhabit Grand Canyon, including rattlesnakes, Gila monsters, and scorpions. But for the most part, avoiding harm is commonsense: Don't feed or approach wildlife. Look before you step, and never put your hands somewhere you can't see.

- **Scorpions:** The most common bug bite is from scorpions. Always shake out your boots, clothes, and bedding in case a scorpion, spider, millipede, or centipede has decided to make camp along with you. Though scorpion bites can be excruciatingly painful, they are rarely life threatening. If you are bitten, apply a cool compress to the area, and take an antihistamine if the swelling is severe. Monitor any insect bite. If you see signs of infection (redness, swelling, heat, streaking), see a doctor as soon as you can.

- **Tarantulas:** Though they look plenty scary, tarantulas are harmless unless harassed. When provoked, they'll bite or launch hairs from their abdomens, irritating to skin—but seek medical treatment if they end up in your eyes.

- **Rattlesnakes:** The park's six rattlesnake species are most active at snake-friendly temperatures, around 80°F. This means in the shade or at twilight in the summer, so be especially careful hiking after sunset. Most snakebites are a result of provocation, and most victims are young men under the influence (excess testosterone and alcohol are as dangerous as most things Mother Nature can throw our way). Some hikers feel safer packing an **extractor kit.**

- **Squirrels and chipmunks:** The most dangerous canyon critters (not counting humans) frequent trails in search of crumbs and handouts. An estimated 40 rodent bites are reported each day. Unreported bites may be as common as blisters, considering most people would self-treat rather than admit they ignored posted warnings and common sense. Not scary enough? Consider **rabies and bubonic plague**—multiple cases are reported in Arizona each year. Still not scared? **Tick-borne relapsing fever** (TBRF), though rare, was reported by a recent canyon visitor. TBRF is spread by ticks that feed on—you guessed it—small rodents.

- **Deer and elk:** Don't feed these animals and don't approach them for close ups (that's what a zoom lens is for). They have been known to charge and kick.

- **Mountain lions:** Mountain lions have been spotted in areas of the park frequented by humans. It's unlikely you'll encounter one, but it's safest to hike with companions. Rangers monitor the park's mountain lion population—if you see a lion, inform a ranger of the date and location.

- **Condors:** With a wingspan of nine feet, condors are formidable—and curious. They can destroy an unattended campsite, shredding tents and sleeping bags, even making away with shoes or gear. Report sightings to a ranger, noting the bird's tag number if you can.

Park biologists have translocated endangered humpback chub populations.

summer monsoon. Preying on the harmless giant spiders are tarantula hawks, low-flying blue-black wasps.

Fish

The completion of Glen Canyon Dam changed the Colorado River from a sediment-laden river with widely fluctuating flows to a cold, clear river. Since then, several native fish species have become endangered, extirpated, or threatened, including the **humpback chub, razorback sucker,** and **flannelmouth sucker.** Native species are more often spotted near the confluence with the warmer waters of the Little Colorado River. Introduced species include rainbow trout, present in such large numbers that in certain areas they attract bald eagles during spawning season.

Reptiles and Amphibians

Along the river and its tributaries, tree frogs and red-spotted toads serenade campers. Numerous lizard species live in the inner canyon and on the rims, including the chuckwalla, yellow-backed spiny lizard, tree lizard, collared lizard, and short-horned lizard,

a collared lizard

colloquially but incorrectly referred to as a "horny toad." On a hot summer afternoon, when many animals retreat, lizards continue to scramble around rocks and rims.

Snakes do not tolerate extreme heat or cold, spending winter months hibernating underground and reappearing in the spring to sun themselves on rocks. In midsummer, snakes are most active in early morning and at dusk. Six rattlesnake species inhabit the inner canyon and its rims, including a couple not usually seen outside the area, the **Grand Canyon pink rattlesnake** and the speckled rattlesnake. Two rattlesnake predators are also present, with gopher snakes (also known as bull snakes) more common on the rim and king snakes seen more often in the river corridor.

Birds

The canyon is a bird-watcher's paradise, with more than 200 species on the North Rim alone. Willow flycatchers, phoebes, and kingfishers catch insects along the river while mallards, mergansers, teals, goldeneyes, and other waterfowl swim its waters. Great blue herons and spotted sandpipers ply the river's edges. **Canyon wrens** sing from the canyon's rocky walls, a descending, flutelike trill that delights hikers and river runners. Peregrine falcons nest in cliffs, and red-tailed hawks and kestrels are fairly common. In the fall, the canyon becomes a flyway, and members of HawkWatch International (www.hawkwatch.org) station themselves at East Rim overlooks to count migrating **raptors,** usually 10,000 to 12,000 each season. Ponderosa forests are lively with scrub jays, Steller's jays, woodpeckers, chickadees, towhees, wild turkeys, and other species. The most ubiquitous canyon avian is the common **raven,** exceptionally clever and equally at home raiding a river campsite, soaring across the canyon, or entertaining visitors at rim overlooks.

Mammals

Mule deer wander around the North Rim's Bright Angel Point and the South Rim's Grand

Mule deer are a common sight on both rims and near Phantom Ranch.

Canyon Village. **Elk** graze the high-country meadows between Jacob Lake and the North Rim in the mornings and evenings. Though they do occasionally wander the rim, **desert bighorn sheep** are seen more often scrambling inner canyon cliffs. These large prey animals attract the canyon's largest predator, the mountain lion. Coyotes are more likely heard than seen, and black bears, bobcats, and gray foxes are reclusive.

Hike the North Rim's Transept Trail early in the morning to see **Kaibab squirrels** in their native ponderosa pine forest. Found only on the Kaibab Plateau, the squirrels have been designated a National Natural Landmark. Their more common South Rim cousins, **Abert's squirrels,** are often spotted near Grandview Point. Trails along the rim and into the canyon are busy with chipmunks, golden-mantled ground squirrels, and rock squirrels. Accustomed to handouts, small rodents and ringtails raid backpackers' food stores. Even raccoons and skunks can make unwelcome nighttime campsite visits.

History

Grand Canyon's rims and travel corridors are a rich repository of human history, from prehistoric occupation through Euro-American exploration, mining, and early tourism. Scientists have recorded nearly 5,000 archeological sites, and only 3 percent of the park's area has been fully surveyed.

NATIVE AMERICANS

The first humans to see Grand Canyon were Paleo-Indians who traveled large distances in pursuit of megafauna, such as bison and mammoths, around 10,000 years ago. These hunters used large stone points on thrusting spears, moving with game herds and leaving little evidence of their passage.

As the last ice age receded and the megafauna died out, hunters began to rely more on smaller game and plants. During this period, 2,000 to 9,000 years ago, the **Desert Archaic** culture roamed the Grand Canyon Region. Archaic hunter-gatherers traveled in groups, moving with the seasons as plants ripened or game animals migrated. They used atlatls (throwing tools) with darts. Remains from this period include flakes from dart points or other stone tools, grinding stones, hearths, basketry, rock shelters, and perhaps the most intriguing archaeological remains in the canyon, rock art and split-twig figurines.

One canyon rock-art site bears a number of large anthropomorphs (humanlike figures) painted with reddish pigment, perhaps representing shamans. Split-twig figurines may also have a shamanic element. Often in the shape of deer or bighorn sheep, the figurines have been found in caves in the Redwall Formation. The figurines were made 2,000 to 4,000 years ago from a single long piece of wood, usually willow, split down the middle and folded into shape. Some are quite refined, with details that include smaller twigs representing antlers or spears piercing the body of the figurine. Carefully placed in dry caves that

have helped preserve them over the millennia, these are not toys but may be totems used to ensure or reenact a successful hunt.

Around 3,500 years ago, corn agriculture arrived in the Southwest. Archaic people began experimenting with cultivation to supplement hunting and gathering. They seeded flood plains, which hold moisture longer than other areas. Storage cists were used to protect surplus corn or beans, introduced later. Beans require longer cooking, leading to another innovation, pottery, dating to AD 500.

As people began to rely more on agriculture, they became more sedentary, at first building pit-houses, partially underground circular structures. Later, they built aboveground pueblos, structures with multiple rooms, including Tusayan Ruins along the South Rim's Desert View Drive and Walhalla Glades on the North Rim. Both villages were occupied during the summer, linked to the Colorado River via trails leading to the Unkar Delta area, where a broad floodplain and lower elevation offered a longer growing season and comfortable winter temperatures.

By AD 1000, the Puebloans were building kivas and outdoor plazas. Pottery types indicate trade relationships with people living in the Virgin River area north of the Grand Canyon. Archaeologists identify these and other farmers, potters, and pueblo dwellers in the Four Corners area as a single cultural group, known as **Ancestral Puebloan.** Some archaeologists speculate that a combination of internal conflict, drought, and other environmental pressures pushed the Ancestral Puebloans from their homes, beginning around 1200. Others suggest that new cultural developments centered around the Hopi Mesas pulled the Puebloans east. In any case, today's Hopi people are among the descendants of the Ancestral Puebloans.

Sometime around 1300, seminomadic hunter-gatherers moved into the Grand

Canyon area from farther west. **Kaibab Paiute** people foraged along the North Rim. The Pai, or Cerbat, people used the river corridor, supplementing hunting and gathering with agriculture and trade, and living in seasonal camps evidenced by rock shelters and stone rings where they constructed brush shelters known as wickiups. They roasted agave, a staple food, in stone-lined roasting pits. Cactus buds and blooms, piñon pine nuts, and berries added to a varied diet. Their descendants, the **Havasupai** and **Hualapai** people of western Grand Canyon, continued a long trading relationship with the Hopi, while the Paiutes established ties with the Mormon colonists who entered their territories.

The Navajo Reservation bordering Grand Canyon to the east is home to the largest Native American nation in the United States. The ancestors of the Navajo, **Athabascan** hunter-gatherers, entered the area from the north around 1400. Highly adaptable, the Navajo learned agriculture from their pueblo neighbors and stock-raising from Spanish colonists.

THE ENTRADA

In 1540 **Francisco Vázquez de Coronado** led an expedition of 300 soldiers and thousands of horses, cattle, and sheep northward from New Spain. The expedition crossed present-day Arizona, and Coronado sent detachments westward to the Hopi villages. Hopi guides led **García López de Cárdenas** and his men to the edge of Grand Canyon, the first Europeans to gaze into its depths.

Expedition journals describe the soldiers' futile struggle to get to the river, which the Spanish judged to be around six feet wide. This says a great deal about the unprepared mind's ability to grasp the canyon's vast size, as well as the Hopi guides' cleverness at keeping their rim-to-river trails a secret. The Spaniards returned to Mexico City in 1542, their expedition deemed a failure.

Spain established missions in present-day New Mexico and California. In 1776, **Silvestre Vélez de Escalante** and **Francisco Atanasio Domínguez** left the colony of Santa Fe to find a northern route to settlements near Monterey. On their return journey, winter forced them southward, and they crossed the Colorado River in historic Glen Canyon (now flooded by the waters of Lake Powell). A year earlier, the friar **Francisco Garcés,** scouting a southern route, had named the river "Colorado" for its reddish waters. Garcés, Domínguez, and Escalante were the last Spanish explorers to venture near the canyon.

EARLY EXPLORATION

After Mexico gained independence from Spain in 1821, hunters and fur trappers explored the Colorado River and its tributaries at both ends of Grand Canyon. One, James O. Pattie, described his 1827 venture as a "horrid" ordeal. Trappers and traders created new routes west, and after 1848, gold hunters followed. Next came the U.S. Army and government surveyors interested in identifying transportation routes and resources.

At Fort Yuma, steamboats plied the Lower Colorado, transporting settlers, soldiers, and supplies to California. In 1857 the Army sent Lieutenant Joseph Christmas Ives upriver via a stern-wheel steamer; it ran aground downriver from the Grand Wash Cliffs. With help from Havasupai guides, Ives continued his explorations on foot but gave up after a couple of weeks. He summed up the region as "uninhabitable," "impassable," and "altogether valueless."

While exploration and settlement continued north, south, west, and east of Grand Canyon, the canyon itself remained one of the last blank spots on the U.S. map. The man who would change that, **John Wesley Powell,** was a 35-year-old Civil War veteran turned college professor.

After Powell's first and second runs through the canyon in 1869 and 1871-1872, only a handful of expeditions followed over the next half century. One of the most dramatic was led by **Robert Brewster Stanton,** an engineer surveying the inner canyon for a possible rail line, a scheme that sounds

John Hance, former prospector and famed raconteur

and communities sprang up in Flagstaff and Williams, attracting settlers from the East and Midwest. Miners who had scratched out only a meager living saw potential in guiding others to the canyon for sightseeing. One, **William Wallace Bass,** became the first to raise a family at the canyon. He arrived in Williams, established a base camp near Havasupai Point, constructed a wagon road, and improved Native American trails to the river, combining prospecting with guiding tourists.

On the other end of the canyon, the sheepherding Hull brothers and prospector **John Hance** built a wagon road to the Grandview area. Hance guided tourists and erected a tent camp near his cabin on the rim, serving meals and offering accommodations. **James Thurber** bought out Hance's interests and established a regular stage route from Flagstaff, a two-day trip that cost $20. **Pete Berry** began mining copper at Horseshoe Mesa in 1892, building the Grandview Trail to his mines. He and his wife owned and operated the Grand View Hotel until 1901. **Martin Buggeln,** who bought out James Thurber, shifted his attention farther west along the rim, where a Santa Fe Railway spur was nearing completion.

The first to settle at the future Grand Canyon Village was Sanford Rowe, who filed mining claims three miles south of the rim at Rowe Well as early as 1890. He established a small tourist camp and built a road to Hopi Point. Not far away, Pete Berry and **Ralph Cameron** improved a Havasupai trail to Indian Garden in order to prospect their claims in this area. Cameron registered the trail as a toll road with Coconino County. Thurber extended his stage line from Grandview to this part of the rim, building another hotel. He and Rowe guided tourists on Cameron's toll road.

When the **Santa Fe Railway** completed its spur line in 1901, travelers could choose between a $15-20 bumpy, two-day-long stage trip and a comfortable, three-hour train ride from Williams for $3. Most chose the train, and the canyon's pioneer enterprises faded away, with one exception: Over the years, Ralph Cameron acted as sheriff, county supervisor, and U.S.

preposterous today. Stanton aborted his first run in 1889 after three of his crew drowned in Marble Canyon, then successfully navigated the canyon the following year, becoming the second to do so.

PIONEERS

As Utah's Mormon communities expanded, timbermen logged Mount Trumbull and the Kaibab Plateau to supply St. George and Kanab with building materials. Ranchers raised cattle west of the Kaibab Plateau, and colonists settled towns west and east of the canyon.

Prospectors began exploring the inner canyon, mining lead, zinc, silver, copper, and asbestos. **Seth Tanner,** a Mormon scout and guide, settled along the Colorado River in 1876 and established the Little Colorado Mining District in eastern Grand Canyon, mining copper. Dozens of prospectors followed, though few found mineral deposits rich enough to make the effort and expense of mining worthwhile.

The Atlantic and Pacific Railroad completed tracks across northern Arizona in 1882, senator, a man with powerful friends and the resources to take a stand against the railroad. Cameron had moved the Red Horse stage station to the head of his toll trail and remodeled it into the Cameron Hotel. The Santa Fe Railway partnered with Martin Buggeln and his Bright Angel Hotel and camp, a few hundred feet east, until the railroad could complete its own hotel, El Tovar. Bitter competition ensued.

PRESERVATION

In the meantime, interest in conservation was growing on a national level. The Forest Reserve Act passed in 1891. While a senator, Benjamin Harrison had unsuccessfully tried to preserve Grand Canyon as a public park. In 1893, as president, Harrison was able to establish the Grand Canyon Forest Reserve. **Theodore Roosevelt** visited the canyon in 1903, making his famous speech urging its protection for future generations.

After becoming president, Roosevelt signed the 1906 Antiquities Act, which led to the establishment of several national monuments, including Grand Canyon National Monument in 1908. With this act, the canyon was protected from further private development. The Santa Fe Railway partnered with the **Fred Harvey Company** to negotiate government contracts to build and maintain attractions and lodging. They hired **Mary Colter** and other architects to design attractive tourist facilities. In 1913 they built the Hermit Trail and camp to compete with Bright Angel Trail, still a county toll road surrounded by Ralph Cameron's mining claims.

Focused on rail travel, the Santa Fe did little to improve roads. The U.S. Forest Service was ill-equipped to accommodate the growing number of tourists arriving by automobile. In 1916 public sentiment and congressional support led to the establishment of the **National Park Service.** Its first director, Stephen Mather, supported transferring Grand Canyon to the National Park Service, and three years later, on **February 26, 1919,** President Woodrow Wilson signed the bill

proclaiming Grand Canyon the nation's 17th national park.

GOOD TIMES AND BAD

With the National Park Service came improved roads and trails, administrative sites, campgrounds, sanitation, and much-needed utilities. By 1919 the Santa Fe Railway was hauling 60,000 to 100,000 gallons of water daily to the South Rim from Flagstaff via rail car. The septic system installed with the construction of El Tovar, unable to meet increasing demand, had overflowed into an open ditch along the railroad tracks. Employees were housed in a ramshackle collection of boxcars, tents, and shanties literally on the other side of the tracks. The less visited North Rim was virtually ignored.

In order to fund infrastructure, the fledgling National Park Service needed the large capital investment provided by the Santa Fe Railway and Fred Harvey Company on the South Rim, and the Union Pacific Railroad and Utah Parks Company on the North Rim. Only a few family businesses were awarded concession contracts, among them the McKee family on the North Rim, and the Babbitts, Verkamps, and Kolbs on the South Rim. Others, like the Bass family, were bought out. Ralph Cameron's reign ended not long after his unsuccessful reelection bid for the U.S. Senate in 1926. In 1928 Cameron's holdings transferred to the **National Park Service.**

By 1929 the park had housing, utilities, and basic services to meet the needs of employees and visitors, who numbered 184,000 that year. During the Great Depression, the park relied on **Civilian Conservation Corps** labor for needed improvements. World War II brought a loss in funding, drops in visitation, and a scarcity of materials. Nearly half the park's staff left for war-related jobs, and many lodges and attractions closed. During the last year of the war, only 74,000 people visited the park.

Yet it was the post-war boom that threatened the park most. The year after war's end, 334,000 people visited the park, and the National Park Service couldn't keep up with the rising numbers. Vandalism, littering, theft, traffic accidents, and frequent rescues burdened ranger services. Adding to the burden was a bed shortage: 15-30 percent of visitors seeking overnight lodging had to be turned away by 1949.

In 1956 the National Park Service's hopes for government funding materialized with **Mission 66,** a 10-year program intended to add infrastructure to national parks. Efforts focused on the South Rim, and many additions, including the Kachina and Thunderbird Lodges, date to this program.

In 1965 the Union Pacific Railroad donated the North Rim's water system, and the National Park Service launched plans to pipe water from Roaring Springs to the South Rim. Seven footbridges and the cross-river Silver Bridge carried more than 12 miles of pipeline to Indian Garden. Just before its completion, the pipeline was virtually destroyed by a record-breaking flood that swept down Bright Angel Canyon. The transcanyon pipeline was finally completed in 1970. With improvements, the pipeline continues to serve the South Rim today, although there is growing concern about its adequacy and the burden on groundwater in the canyon region.

People and Culture

Many contemporary Native American cultures continue the traditions of their ancestors, farming and herding inside the canyon or along its rims, gathering plants for medicines or basketry, weaving rugs from sheep's wool, or making silver and turquoise jewelry. Some may live far away, but their histories are part of the canyon's history, and for them, the landscape has deep cultural significance.

HOPI

Thirteen villages lie east of Grand Canyon on the Hopi Reservation, 1.5 million acres completely surrounded by the larger Navajo Nation. Most villages sit at the foot or top of three rocky peninsulas known individually as First, Second, and Third Mesa, or collectively as **the Hopi Mesas.** Settlement increased after AD 1100 as people migrated from Homolovi, Chavez Pass, and other ancient sites. The Third Mesa village of **Oraibi,** established in 1150, is considered one of the oldest continuously inhabited settlements in the United States.

According to Hopi stories, their ancestors climbed up to this world, the fourth, on a reed. They were met by Masaaw, who told them to leave their footprints as they journeyed through this world in search of its center. On arriving at the mesas, each group contributed a duty or ceremony to the community, creating cohesiveness among clans. Collectively, the clans became known as *Hopituh Shi-nu-mu,* the peaceful or well-mannered people.

But village life didn't remain peaceful. New Spain sent colonists and priests, who established missions at all the Southwestern pueblos, from the Hopi Mesas to the Rio Grande villages. Priests entered kivas, destroying ceremonial items and forcing villagers to build churches. In 1680, nearly 100 years before Eastern colonists would rebel against British rule, the **pueblos revolted** against Spain. When the Spanish returned in 1692, many people from the Rio Grande pueblos took shelter at the Hopi Mesas, and villages grew. One Hopi village allowed the Spanish to reestablish a mission, sparking strife among the clans. In 1700 the village was destroyed and burned. Nearly 200 years would pass before any missionaries would return to Hopi lands.

In the late 1800s Anglo photographers, artists, and anthropologists "discovered" the Hopi Mesas. Ceremonies grew crowded with curious onlookers, many of them toting bulky box cameras on tripods. The U.S. government started sending agents in 1870, and a boarding school opened in Keams Canyon in 1887 with

Who's First?

Hopi stories say Tiyo was the first person to journey through Grand Canyon.

John Wesley Powell is generally hailed as the first to navigate the Colorado River through Grand Canyon. He made the voyage twice, in 1869 and 1871. But Westerners love a good debate, and a few holdouts still argue the case for **James White,** a Colorado prospector who claimed he rafted the canyon in 1867 in order to escape a band of hostile Native Americans. According to Hopi oral tradition, however, neither man was the first Grand Canyon voyager.

For hundreds of years, Hopi clans have told tales of **Tiyo,** a youth fascinated by the great river flowing through the canyon. Determined to find out where the river led, he enlisted his father, a village chief, to help him make a vessel by hollowing out the trunk of a large cottonwood.

Tiyo traveled many days, until one day his log boat ran aground on a riverbank. Here he met Spider Woman, who guided him to wondrous places, including a village populated by snake people. In order to enter the kiva of the snake people and learn the ceremony for making rain, Tiyo first had to perform feats of courage—including capturing and taming the most frightful of the serpents.

This hideous creature transformed into a beautiful maiden, and Tiyo won the approval of the snake people to marry her and take her back to his own village. Their offspring, however, were young snakes that bit the village children, and Tiyo's clan was cast out.

Tiyo and his family journeyed to Walpi on First Mesa, where the villagers had been suffering from drought. They agreed to accept Tiyo's clan, and in exchange he performed the first Snake Dance. The ceremony was blessed by rain, and ever since, the Snake Clan and Antelope Clan have performed this multiday ceremony at the Hopi Mesas.

On the wall of the South Rim's **Desert View Watchtower,** artist Fred Kabotie painted a striking mural that tells Tiyo's story.

the goal of reeducating Hopi children. Hopi farms were plotted into allotments. Traders arrived with manufactured goods and food staples. The government mandated missionaries to go to the pueblos, parceling them out among different faiths.

Hopi villagers split between those who were hostile or friendly to government interference, with Oraibi village at the center of the storm. Oraibi splintered, and factions moved to Hotevilla, Bacavi, Kykotsmovi, and Moenkopi. Many ceremonies became closed to outsiders. Over time, some ceremonies were lost as the number of clans dwindled. Even so, Hopi remains the most traditional of all the Southwest's pueblos.

The Hopi calendar is divided between social and kachina ceremonials. The basket dances held by women's societies in September and October are often open to the public and highlight one of the oldest art forms on the mesas. Basketry, weaving, and pottery employ forms, symbols, and techniques going back to prehistoric times. Hopi potters still make pottery the way their ancestors did: by coiling and scraping to shape the pot, then firing it over open embers.

Though Hopi ancestors left Grand Canyon centuries ago, clans continued to journey to the canyon to mine salt and trade with the Havasupai. Several Hopi individuals contributed to Grand Canyon Village's growing reputation as an exciting destination, including the celebrated potter Nampeyo, who demonstrated her artistry at Hopi House, and artist **Fred Kabotie,** who assisted architect Mary Colter with Desert View Watchtower and other projects.

ZUNI

By the time the pilgrims stepped off the *Mayflower,* Spain had already explored and colonized the Southwest. The first nonnative to explore the region was a former slave named Esteban. He and three others were survivors of an expedition that landed off the coast of Florida in 1528, following the gulf and wandering west on foot. Eight years later they met a group of Spanish slavers, who delivered them to the viceroy of New Spain.

They had a fabulous story to tell of golden cities they'd heard about in the north. The viceroy assembled an exploring party led by Friar Marcos de Niza, with Esteban as an advance scout, to locate these cities. At the Zuni pueblos, Esteban's luck ran out. Some say he offended the men with his overly familiar behavior toward the village women. Others say it was the women's curiosity and interest in Esteban that offended Zuni's warriors. In any case, Esteban was killed, and Marcos de Niza wisely decided not to approach the hilltop pueblos any closer. He claimed the land for Spain and returned to Mexico City, confirming that the cities of gold did indeed exist. (In the friar's defense, when sunset lights up adobe walls, they can appear gold from a distance.)

Months later, in 1540, the viceroy dispatched an expedition led by conquistador Francisco Vázquez de Coronado. At Zuni, Coronado discovered not seven cities of gold but six villages of mud adobe. Nevertheless, Coronado moved in for the winter, commandeering several rooms, displacing the residents, and appropriating stores of food while sending scouting parties to the Hopi Mesas and other areas.

Coronado and his soldiers eventually returned to New Spain without the riches they'd sought, but in 1598 Juan de Oñate arrived with farmers, priests, livestock, and a soldier escort. Colonists settled along the Rio Grande River, and priests moved into the pueblos to convert the Zuni villagers. During the years of revolt and reconquest, the Zunis left their homes and took refuge on Dowa Yalanne (Corn Mountain) before returning to Halona, where Zuni Pueblo stands today.

The 450,000-acre Zuni Reservation is home to about 10,000 people, most of them residing in **Zuni Pueblo,** the largest of New Mexico's 19 pueblos. The Zuni people, who call themselves A:shiwi, observe an annual ceremonial cycle that includes the winter Shalako activities. The Shalako are 10-foot-tall beings who visit selected Zuni households in December, ensuring continued blessings.

Many Zunis are artisans, creating fetishes, jewelry, basketry, and pottery. Modern Zuni silverwork includes a variety of styles and techniques but is best known for delicate needlepoint and petit point turquoise designs, as well as exquisite inlay depicting birds, Shalako, and other designs.

Fetishes have been carried by Zunis since prehistoric times for use in prayers and ceremonies and also for protection. Modern fetishes (more accurately known as carvings because they haven't been ritually blessed) may depict snakes, foxes, bears, or other animals. It is likely that Zuni individuals carried fetishes during the clans' migrations eastward.

Zunis consider Grand Canyon to be the place where their ancestors emerged into this world. From this place of emergence (which some say is the inner canyon's Ribbon Falls), they traveled for generations. Their migrations roughly trace the path of the Little Colorado River. The people left behind rock art, potsherds, and villages until they reached the middle place, Zuni Pueblo.

HAVASUPAI

The Havasupai people have called the rims and waterways of Grand Canyon home for at least 800 years. Their oral tradition links past events and village life to features in the landscape. One of the many stories Havasupai people associate with their canyon home refers to the twin pillars of reddish stone they call the Wigleeva. According to most versions of the story, if the stone pillars should ever crumble and fall, the walls of the canyon will close in and destroy the community.

Traditionally, the Havasupai hunted in the forests and plains along the rim and farmed within the canyon during summer months, raising corn, beans, squash, sunflowers, and later, peaches. Many of the inner canyon trails used by hikers today were established by the Havasupai. **Indian Garden,** the popular resting point along Bright Angel Trail, was once a Havasupai community.

In the 1880s, the Havasupai were restricted to a 500-acre reservation at the bottom of Havasu Canyon, a mere fraction of their traditional lands. The limited agricultural land, bounded by the canyon's stony cliffs, barely supported the community, and many Havasupai sought work outside Supai Village. Grand Canyon pioneer William Wallace Bass relied on Havasupai guides to establish his mining and tourism activities. Other Havasupai found work with the Santa Fe Railway and Fred Harvey Company at Grand Canyon Village. Many worked for the National Park Service, helping construct the Kaibab Suspension Bridge across the Colorado River.

In 1975, an act of Congress restored 185,000 acres on the plateau to the Havasupai. The present 188,077-acre reservation encompasses **Havasu Canyon** and plateaus along the South Rim west of Grand Canyon Village. The village of **Supai,** reachable only on foot or by horseback or helicopter, lies within the walls of Havasu Canyon (also known as Cataract Canyon). The village is home to 450 people, more than half the total Havasupai population.

For decades the Havasupai have welcomed visitors to their Edenic canyon home, where pools lined with deposits of travertine limestone reflect cerulean-blue skies and gorgeous waterfalls tumble from rocky cliff sides. Tourism has become their main source of income, and the Havasupai have struggled to maintain the delicate balance between tradition, ethnic identity, and economic reality.

In recent years, floods have damaged the village and canyon several times. Tourist facilities have since been rebuilt, though some areas are off-limits due to continuing repair work. The Havasupai government reminds visitors that future closures are possible.

HUALAPAI

Traditionally seminomadic hunter-gatherers, the Hualapai once roamed over five million acres from the canyon south to Bill Williams Mountain, west to the lower Colorado River,

Native American Art

Navajo rug styles vary according to weaver and region.

Whether you're a serious collector or simply want something to remember your visit, you'll discover an impressive variety of Native American arts and crafts—from tiny Zuni fetishes to roomsize Navajo rugs—at Hopi House, Hermits Rest, Cameron Trading Post, and other retail outlets.

Many artists learned their skills from a grandmother, uncle, or other family member, knowledge handed down for generations. Though modern tools and materials have inspired exquisite craftsmanship and experimentation, handwork is still the hallmark of Native American art.

Look for signs of careful craftsmanship, such as fineness of line in designs, pleasing proportions, and symmetry. Keep in mind that some "imperfections" are actually desirable: Hopi potters use dung fires, believing the resulting smoky "fire clouds" make each piece unique. Many kachina carvers use simple tools like Dremels in their work, while others—particularly carvers of old-style dolls—use only a knife and rasp to create a more primitive look. Prices will reflect the skill and reputation of the artist, as well as his or her investment of time and materials.

The high value of Native American art has led to counterfeiting. The Indian Arts and Crafts Act of 1990 makes it illegal to market any non-Native American product as a Native American-made item. Be aware, however, that not everything marked "Indian-made" is handcrafted by an individual artist. Native American-owned factories and co-ops produce lovely jewelry and pottery, for example, but items are created assembly-line style, reflected in lower prices.

Inquiring about the artist and his or her work will not only help you make an informed purchase, but also add to your Grand Canyon memories. And remember, the wisest purchase is one you'll feel good wearing, giving, or displaying in your home. Much more than a good investment, authentic handmade Native American art is a link between you, the artist, and traditions that reach back through time.

and east to the Little Colorado River. Like the neighboring Havasupai, they migrated seasonally, occupying upland plateaus in the winter, returning to inner canyon springs and tributaries in the summer. They participated in a vast trade network with other indigenous nations in the region, trading beads, shells, mineral pigments, and buckskins for salt, wool or cotton blankets, and horses.

When gold was discovered near Prescott, Arizona, in 1863, miners, settlers, and soldiers poured into Hualapai lands. The Hualapai responded fiercely to the incursion. They signed a peace treaty in 1868, and afterward many Hualapai warriors assisted General Crook's Army as scouts. In 1874 the U.S. Army was ordered to relocate the Hualapai to a reservation 150 miles south. The removal sparked a deep sense of betrayal among the Hualapai people. On the reservation, starvation and disease ran rampant, and the Hualapai petitioned the government to return their lands.

In 1883 the Hualapai nation was granted a small reservation along western Grand Canyon. They adopted ranching, lumbering, and wage labor. In 1947, lands that had been given to the railroad were returned to the Hualapai. Today, the Hualapai Reservation includes one million acres along 108 miles of Grand Canyon's rim, south of the Colorado River and west of the national park boundaries. The Hualapai call it Hakataya (the backbone of the river).

The Hualapai people are closely related to the neighboring Havasupai, and also to the Yavapai, Paipai, Maricopa, and Mohave nations, all Yuman-speakers with common ancestors from the lower Colorado River. (The word *pai* means "people.") The Pai nations are linked by the river, reflected in many of their traditions and histories.

According to the Hualapai creation story, the earth was once covered by floodwaters. Only one old man escaped, and a dove brought him instructions from the Creator. Following the instructions, he used the horn from a mountain sheep to dig a hole (some say this became Grand Canyon), and the water drained away. Later, the Creator made two brothers who took the canes growing beside the river and breathed life into them so that they became human. The older brother guided the people to Grand Canyon and taught them what plants to gather and where to find water and game—all that they needed to know to survive in this rugged landscape.

Today, the Hualapai population is approximately 2,100, about half based in **Peach Springs.** The Route 66 town acts as a gateway to neighboring Havasu Canyon as well as to **Grand Canyon West,** the tourist center the Hualapai opened in 1988. The Hualapai have continued to find the means to survive and adapt—enterprises include timber and ranching, hunting permits, river running, helicopter tours, and most famously, the **Skywalk.** The Skywalk's construction was controversial, even among community members. Some find it an affront to nature and say that those who most benefit from it are the Las Vegas businesspeople who developed it. Others see the Skywalk as an investment in the nation's economic future, another way to draw visitors to Grand Canyon West, where they can share Hualapai legends and lifeways with others.

KAIBAB PAIUTE

Many of the names on the canyon's landscape—Kaibab, Kaiparowits, Shivits, Tuweep, and others—are derived from Paiute (Nuwuvi) words. Paiute ancestors migrated east from the Great Basin deserts to the Colorado Plateau about 800 years ago. Seminomadic Southern Paiute bands lived along the North Rim of the Grand Canyon, where a wide range of environments, from desert to forest to meadow, provided diverse resources throughout the year. They cultivated garden plots, hunted game, and gathered wild plants on some of the most isolated land in North America.

Like many of the region's indigenous people, generations of Southern Paiutes saw their territory reduced in size over time. Their traditional lands once extended as far west as California and east to the San Juan River. One Paiute story hints at a migrating population as it describes the creation of Grand Canyon:

A Paiute chief mourned his dead wife until the god Tavwoats told him that she was living in a land far away and that he would take the chief to see her if he would cease to mourn. The chief agreed, and Tavwoats blazed a deep trail westward through the mountains. The chief followed, and he saw his wife living happily in a warm desert. Tavwoats ordered the chief to keep the land a secret, and after they returned, he poured water into the deeply furrowed trail, creating the Colorado River to guard the land to the west.

Many Southern Paiutes were captured by Navajo and Ute raiders and sold as slaves to the Spanish. To avoid capture, Southern Paiute bands moved away from traveled areas along the Old Spanish Trail, a move that furthered their dependence on hunting and gathering. When Mormon pioneers arrived in the Arizona Strip country in the mid-1800s, settlers claimed water sources, including Pipe Spring, that had supported the Paiutes' game and crops.

After his appointment to head up the Bureau of Ethnology, John Wesley Powell returned to the canyon region to document its native peoples. He found the Kaibab Paiute (Kaivavwits) band, the last of the canyon's hunters and gatherers, struggling to continue foraging traditions. On his recommendation, the remaining Paiutes were removed to reservations.

During the latter half of the century, ranching, mining, and timbering continued to impact the Paiutes' resources. Diseases flourished, game vanished, crops withered, and the people starved. By 1913, when the Kaibab Paiute Reservation was at last established, the band's population was decimated.

Today, the Kaibab Paiute's 250 members are spread among five villages on a 121,000-acre reservation about 50 miles north of Grand Canyon. The reservation encompasses **Pipe Spring National Monument,** where the nation operates a visitor center with the National Park Service. Tourism is their major source of revenue.

NAVAJO

From the powerful spires and buttes of Monument Valley to the sweeping sandstone walls of Canyon de Chelly, the landscape of the Navajo people is a rich repository of oral history. Navajo creation stories tell of a great flood. To drain the waters, Humpback God used his cane to draw the Colorado River, forming Grand Canyon. The Holy People, including Salt Woman and Talking God, are said to dwell in Glen Canyon and Grand Canyon.

The Navajo Nation borders Grand Canyon National Park on the east, where sheep pastures extend to the very rim. The reservation is the largest in the United States, sprawling 25,000 square miles across northeastern Arizona, western New Mexico, and into Utah. Even so, the reservation is far smaller than the territory the Navajo once controlled.

BACKGROUND PEOPLE AND CULTURE

log-and-brush shade houses for summer shelter

Navajo ancestors, Athabascan speakers, migrated to the New World and settled in what is now Alaska and Northwestern Canada. About a millennium ago, they ventured south, carrying little with them but the bows they used for hunting. When **The Diné** (the people) arrived to the Four Corners area sometime before 1500, they encountered the pueblo peoples, whose settled lifestyle included corn agriculture. As the Diné adapted to their new homeland, they too incorporated corn into to their repertoire of survival. Life was relatively peaceful, but for all Southwestern peoples, this was the eve of change.

In 1540 Spanish explorer Francisco Vázquez de Coronado led an expedition to the Southwest in search of the fabled seven golden cities of Cibola. Coronado left without the riches he sought, but in 1598 Spanish colonists arrived with priests, servants, and an army escort, trailed by oxcarts and thousands of cattle, sheep, and goats. The Spanish introduced peaches, livestock, metalwork, and horses, but they also took away.

New Spain's mines and ranches spurred an extensive slave trade, especially among the Navajo, who were difficult to convert and difficult to control, since they did not live in large easily targeted villages like their pueblo neighbors. Fierce raiding and shifting alliances ensued. One colonist estimated that 5,000 to 6,000 Navajo slaves lived in New Mexican households, but hundreds of thousands of colonists' cattle, sheep, and horses lived in Navajo herds. The Navajo became such accomplished equestrians they were known as the Lords of the Earth.

Native American lands once claimed by Spain were won by Mexico and later ceded to the United States. Treaties were signed and broken, and raiding continued, followed by harsh punitive expeditions. The Civil War left settlers vulnerable, and frontiersman **Kit Carson** was appointed to defend them. Carson's campaign against the Navajo focused on destroying their herds, fields, and orchards. They sought refuge in places like Canyon de Chelly, Wupatki, and Grand Canyon.

In January 1864 Navajo leaders agreed to go to Fort Sumner, New Mexico, on a treeless plain traditionally claimed by the Comanche. The hardships of the campaign and the grueling 400-mile winter march to Bosque Redondo are known as **The Long Walk.** Those who didn't die or escape suffered four years of poor food, smallpox, Comanche raids, and crop-destroying hail and floods.

Navajo leaders argued eloquently for return to their homeland. In 1868 the Navajo people went home, although tightened boundaries excluded much of their original lands. In exchange for agreeing to stop raiding settlers, the Navajo received rations, and later, sheep and goats. Herding became the foundation of the Navajo economy, and Anglo traders were awarded contracts to supply goods such as coffee and flour.

As tourism to the Southwest increased, **trading posts** offered a ready market for traditional crafts, another economic opportunity for the Navajo and other nations. A few trading posts still dot the reservation. **Cameron Trading Post,** now owned by Navajo people, is the nearest to Grand Canyon.

The political center of the Navajo Nation lies southeast of Grand Canyon in **Window Rock,** Arizona. The population of the "Big Rez" is 250,000, making it the largest Native American nation in the country. Although ranching and herding continue to be important, revenues also stem from mineral resources and tourism. The journey along the edge of the reservation to Grand Canyon involves incredible scenery: the Little Colorado River gorge and Painted Desert near Cameron, the colorful Echo Cliffs en route to The Gap, and long views of the San Francisco Peaks, one of four sacred mountains that mark the traditional boundaries of the Navajo homeland.

Essentials

Getting There

Grand Canyon National Park is in Arizona's northwest corner, close to the Utah and Nevada borders. The nearest major cities are Las Vegas, 278 miles west, and Phoenix, about 230 miles south.

Geography divides Grand Canyon National Park into three areas: the South Rim, the North Rim, and the inner canyon, the river corridor that bisects the park east to west. The South Rim is accessible year-round. Services at the North Rim are available May 15 to October 15, and Highway 67 is closed after the first major snowfall, usually in late November. The inner canyon is accessible on foot from either rim, but the most feasible way to travel its length is by boat. River trips put in at Lees Ferry, east of the park's boundaries.

SUGGESTED ROUTES

The vast majority of Grand Canyon's annual five million visitors head for the South Rim. The South Rim's Main Entrance Station is close to Grand Canyon Village, a developed area with lodging, shops, and visitor centers. The smaller East Entrance is near Desert View, about 25 miles east of the village.

South Entrance
FROM WILLIAMS
This is the simplest route to the canyon, a 60-mile straight shot north from Williams, which lies along I-40 between Las Vegas (260 miles) and Flagstaff (35 miles). To get to the South Entrance Station, take I-40 to exit 165, turning north on **Highway 64.** The road cuts through open prairie scattered with one-seed junipers, where you might glimpse a herd of elk or pronghorn. After passing through Valle (at about 40 miles) look for Red Butte to the northeast. Straight ahead, the canyon is barely

recognizable, a dark line on the horizon. This is a good route if you neglected to make reservations: You'll be passing several campgrounds and motels between Williams, **Valle,** and **Tusayan,** and some may have vacancies even during busy summer months. Most visitors experience their first canyon panorama at Mather Point, four miles past the South Entrance Station. A couple of miles farther along, historic Grand Canyon Village is tucked in a forest of ponderosa pine along the rim.

FROM FLAGSTAFF
Travelers bound for the South Rim from Flagstaff have three options. In addition to the Williams route, they can reach the South Entrance station via **U.S. 180** northwest or drive to the East Entrance. At 78 miles, U.S. 180 is the shortest route from Flagstaff to the canyon, and it's also very scenic, skirting just west of the San Francisco Peaks through a forest of ponderosa pine and aspen before cutting across a juniper woodland. Coconino National Forest offers numerous possibilities for side trips, including a back-road drive through Hart Prairie's aspen groves or a ride up the chairlift to the Arizona Snowbowl. As U.S. 180 swings west toward Valle, the road passes close to Red Mountain, an extinct volcano and fascinating geology hike. At Valle, turn north (right) on **Highway 64** for the remaining 20 miles to Grand Canyon.

East Entrance
FROM FLAGSTAFF
The park's quieter East Entrance is 89 miles north of Flagstaff, a scenic route with fascinating side trips for those interested in archaeology, geology, or Native American art. As you leave Flagstaff on **U.S. 89,** Elden Mountain

---

Previous: the Grand Canyon Visitor Center at the South Rim; the historic train depot at Grand Canyon Village.

and the San Francisco Peaks rise on the left. Cinder cones east of the road indicate the region's volcanic past. (You can make a looping 36-mile side-trip through Sunset Crater Volcano National Monument and Wupatki National Monument, which preserves several major prehistoric ruins.) U.S. 89 continues north through the Coconino National Forest and the Navajo Reservation, skirting the edge of the Painted Desert, marked by softly rounded low hills of the colorful Chinle Formation, until it reaches the junction with **Highway 64.**

FROM PAGE

If you're driving to the East Entrance from Page (about 110 miles), take **U.S. 89** south toward Cameron. Turn west (right) on **Highway 64** and travel 30 miles to the Grand Canyon's East Entrance. One mile north of the U.S. 89-Highway 64 junction, you can visit the Cameron Trading Post, a worthy side trip. Along Highway 64, stop for views of the Little Colorado River Gorge at the scenic overlook, where Navajo artisans sell jewelry, pottery, and other items. Desert View, one of the South Rim's highest overlooks, is just beyond the East Entrance. Here you'll find a seasonal campground, a general store, a gift shop and snack bar, restrooms, and the remarkable Watchtower, a Mary Colter landmark. It's another 23 miles to Grand Canyon Village.

North Entrance

Only 1 in 10 canyon visitors makes it to the North Rim (open May 15-Oct. 15). All routes to the North Rim converge at Jacob Lake, 30 miles from the park's North Entrance Station on **Highway 67.** From the entrance station, it's another 14 miles to the lodge at Bright Angel Point. Highway 67 is one of the loveliest drives in Arizona, through grassy meadows edged by hills with ponderosa pine, fir, spruce, and aspen.

FROM PAGE

From Page, travelers have two choices for reaching the North Rim. For the Kanab route (about 155 miles), head north on **U.S. 89,** then turn south on **U.S. 89A** and drive to Jacob Lake. For the Marble Canyon route (123 miles), take **U.S. 89** south, turning west (right) on U.S. 89A and continuing to Jacob Lake.

FROM THE SOUTH RIM

To get here from Grand Canyon Village on the South Rim (215 miles), take **Highway 64** (also known as Desert View Drive) east to **U.S. 89** (60 miles). If you haven't already explored the East Rim's overlooks and attractions, be sure to allow extra time for the drive.

Turn north on U.S. 89 and drive about 60 miles, turning west (left) on **U.S. 89A,** crossing the Colorado River over Navajo Bridge. The highway climbs the Kaibab Plateau toward Jacob Lake, where you can stop at the Kaibab Plateau Visitor Center, operated by the U.S. Forest Service and Grand Canyon Association, or grab a bite to eat before continuing to the park.

FROM PHOENIX

Phoenix and its surrounding communities, known as the Valley of the Sun, is about 230 miles south of Grand Canyon in Arizona's central desert.

Car

To get to the **South Rim** from Phoenix, a drive of about four to five hours, take I-10 west through downtown, then I-17 north to Flagstaff. From Flagstaff, drivers can choose between I-40 west to Williams, U.S. 180 northwest to Valle, or U.S. 89 toward the park's east entrance.

Airport

Phoenix Sky Harbor International Airport (PHX, 3400 E. Sky Harbor Blvd., 602/273-3300, http://skyharbor.com) is served by more than a dozen commercial carriers, including Air Canada, Alaska Airlines, British Airways, Delta, Frontier, JetBlue, Southwest, Sun Country, United, and American, which offers connections to Flagstaff's Pulliam

Airport (FLG). Sky Harbor has three terminals for commercial flights. Ground transportation options—hotel vans, taxis, light rail, and intercity shuttles—are located at each terminal's baggage claim area.

Train

Amtrak (800/872-7245, www.amtrak.com) is connected to Sky Harbor Airport, the Greyhound Station, and the Metro Center Transit Station via Amtrak's Thruway bus system. Both Amtrak's southernmost route, the *Sunset Limited,* and its *Texas Eagle* line stop at Maricopa, a town about 30 miles south of Phoenix. You'll need to arrange another form of transportation to get the rest of the way to Phoenix.

Bus and Shuttles

Greyhound (2115 E. Buckeye Rd., Phoenix, 602/389-4200 or 800/231-2222, www.greyhound.com) makes daily trips from Phoenix to Flagstaff, where you can make connections to Williams or Grand Canyon. The Greyhound station, open 24 hours daily, is near the Phoenix airport.

Arizona Shuttle (800/888-2749, www.arizonashuttle.com) makes several trips a day from Sky Harbor Airport or the Metro Center Transit Station (9451 N. Metro Pkwy. W., Phoenix) to Flagstaff. From Flagstaff, they provide shuttles to Williams and Grand Canyon Village. **Grand Canyon Shuttles** (888/215-3105, www.grandcanyonshuttles.com) offers charter service from Phoenix and other Arizona cities.

Tours

Open Road Tours (602/997-6474 or 855/563-8830, www.openroadtoursusa.com) has a single-day tour to Grand Canyon and Sedona as well as several multiday canyon tours with options for adding a smooth-water float or a ride on the Grand Canyon Railway.

Car Rental

Most national car-rental agencies have service desks at the **Sky Harbor's Rental Car Center** (1805 E. Sky Harbor Circle S., 602/683-3741). To get to the Rental Car Center, look for the rental-car shuttle outside your terminal's baggage claim area. All rental-car agencies use the same shuttle system. A handful of rental agencies don't have service desks in the Rental Car Center; they offer van service to their off-site locations from the center.

RV Rental

Cruise America (800/671-8042, www.cruiseamerica.com) has offices in Mesa. Another option with a Mesa location is **RV Rental Outlet** (480/461-0023 or 877/554-4108, www.rvrentaloutlet.com). **Ultimate RV Rentals** (www.ultimatervrentals.com) represents a network of companies and individual RV owners who rent their rigs to travelers.

Equipment Rental

REI (www.rei.com) has two stores in the Phoenix area. The Tempe location (1405 W. Southern Ave., 480/967-5494, 9am-9pm Mon.-Fri., 9am-7pm Sat., 9am-6pm Sun.) rents gear, including sleeping bags and snowshoes.

Food and Accommodations

Those planning to spend some time in the Valley of the Sun have plenty of accommodation choices. Rates are slashed May to mid-September, when the desert is sizzling hot. If you're planning to catch a Diamondbacks or a Suns game, stay in Phoenix's renewed downtown, which has risen from urban decay like, well, the proverbial phoenix. Neighboring Scottsdale boasts dude ranches, spas, and golf kingdoms like the Phoenician and Westin Kierland. Near the airport, Tempe is home to Arizona State University. Local dining highlights include Mexican cuisine, brewpubs, and pizza. Try:

- **La Santisima** (1919 N. 16th St., Phoenix, 602/254-6330, www.lasantisimagourmet.com)

- **Barrio Café** (2814 N. 16th St., Phoenix, 602/636-0240, www.barriocafe.com)

- **Pizzeria Bianco** (623 E. Adams St.,

Phoenix, 602/258-8300, www.pizzeriabianco.com)

- **Four Peaks Brewing Company** (1340 E. 8th St., Tempe, 480/303-9967, www.fourpeaks.com)

- **Hotel San Carlos** (202 N. Central Ave., Phoenix, 602/253-4121, www.hotelsancarlos.com)

- **Sheraton Phoenix Downtown** (340 N. 3rd St., Phoenix 602/262-2500, www.sheratonphoenixdowntown.com)

- **Phoenician Resort & Spa** (6000 E. Camelback Rd., Scottsdale, 480/941-8200, www.thephoenician.com)

- **Westin Kierland Resort & Spa** (6902 E. Greenway Pkwy., Scottsdale, 480/624-1000, www.kierlandresort.com)

FROM LAS VEGAS

Las Vegas is a convenient launching point for a Grand Canyon trip, easily reached by air from most U.S. cities, with a number of tour and travel options for getting to the canyon.

Car

It's 280 miles (4.5 hours) from Las Vegas to the South Rim. Take **U.S. 93** south to **I-40,** then take I-40 east to Williams, Arizona. Turn north on **Highway 64** and drive 60 miles to the South Rim.

It's about 270 miles (4 hours) from Vegas to the North Rim: Take **I-15** north for 128 miles to St. George, Utah. Just past St. George, take **Highway 9** east 10 miles to **Highway 59.** Continue east on Highway 59 for 32 miles. The highway number changes at the Utah-Arizona border, becoming **Highway 389.** Continue east another 33 miles to Fredonia and turn east on **U.S. 89A** for 30 miles to Jacob Lake. Turn south on **Highway 67** for 43 miles to the North Rim.

Airports

McCarran International Airport (LAS, 5757 Wayne Newton Blvd., 702/261-5211, www.mccarran.com), the primary commercial airport for Las Vegas, is located a few miles outside city limits in Clark County. More than 20 commercial carriers land here, including Aeroméxico, Air Canada, Alaska, American, British Airways, Delta, JetBlue, Southwest, Sun Country, United, and Virgin Atlantic. Most international airlines use Terminal 3.

At Terminal 1, look for ground transportation near the baggage claim area: Taxis are on the east, outside doors 1 to 4; limos and

Las Vegas is only a few hours from Grand Canyon.

shuttles are on the west, outside doors 7 to 13. At Terminal 3, taxis and limos are on the east and west sides of the building on Level Zero. A public bus stop is located outside Level Zero of Terminal 1. At Terminal 3, the bus stop is on the second level across from door 44.

North Las Vegas Airport (VGT, 2370 Airport Dr., 701/261-3801, www.vgt.aero) serves private aircraft, as well as many of the scenic airlines that fly tours to Grand Canyon. The airport is three miles northwest of downtown off Rancho Drive, between I-15 and U.S. 95.

Bus
Greyhound (200 S. Main St., Las Vegas, 702/383-9792 or 800/231-2222, www.greyhound.com) has connections to Las Vegas from locations nationwide. The bus station is open 24 hours daily.

Train
Though passenger trains do not travel to or from Las Vegas, **Amtrak** (800/872-7245) has a Thruway Service bus that can take passengers from McCarran International Airport to the train depot in Kingman, Arizona. From here, the Southwest Chief route connects to Williams and, ultimately, the Grand Canyon Railway.

Tours and Shuttles
Tour choices are plentiful and competitively priced, with daily departures and bus tours starting under $100 pp.

Papillon Helicopters (702/736-7243 or 888/635-7272, www.papillon.com) has air and ground tours to the South Rim and Grand Canyon West, as does **Sightseeing Tours Unlimited** (702/471-7155 or 800/377-2003, www.sightseeingtourslv.com), **Gray Line** (800/472-9546, www.graylinelasvegas.com), and **Best Tours** (866/828-1608, www.besttourslv.com).

St. George Shuttle (435/628-8320 or 800/933-8320, www.stgshuttle.com) offers charter service from McCarran Airport to the South Rim (year-round) and North Rim (spring-fall). **Grand Canyon Shuttles** (888/215-3105, www.grandcanyonshuttles.com) also offers charter service from Las Vegas.

Car Rental
McCarran International Airport's **Rent-A-Car Center** (7135 Gillespie St., 702/261-6001, near I-15 and I-215) hosts many national car-rental agencies. To get to the Rent-A-Car Center from Terminal 1, find door 10 or 11 near the baggage claim area and wait outside. Shuttles arrive every five minutes. At Terminal 3, shuttles to the Rent-A-Car Center depart from west doors 51 to 54 and east doors 55 to 58.

Hertz (800/654-3131) and Enterprise (800/736-8222) rent cars at the North Las Vegas Airport.

RV Rental
Bates International (800/732-2283, www.batesintl.com) is headquartered in Las Vegas. **Cruise America** (800/671-8042, www.cruiseamerica.com), **Sahara RV Center** (877/748-6494, www.sahararv.com), and several other RV rental agencies have offices here.

Equipment Rental
An hour south in Boulder City, **Desert Adventures** (1647-A Nevada Hwy., 702/293-5026, www.kayaklasvegas.com) has a wide selection of gear.

Food and Accommodations
You can choose among major hotel chains and accommodations convenient to the airport or the highway, but if you want the full Vegas experience, head for the Strip and its casino hotels. And while there's some great food along the Strip, culinary adventurers should explore Chinatown or downtown.

- **Carson Kitchen** (124 S. 6th St., 702/473-9523, www.carsonkitchen.com)

- **Pizza Rock** (201 N. 3rd St., 702/385-0838, www.pizzarocklasvegas.com)

- **La Comida** (100 6th St., 702/463-9900, www.lacomidalv.com)

- **Raku** (5030 W. Spring Mountain Rd., #2, 702/367-3511, www.raku-grill.com)

- **Stratosphere** (2000 Las Vegas Blvd. S., 800/998-6937, www.stratospherehotel.com)

- **Circus Circus** (2880 Las Vegas Blvd. S., 800/634-3450, www.circuscircus.com)

- **Flamingo** (3555 Las Vegas Blvd. S., 702/733-3111, www.flamingolasvegas.com)

- **Caesars Palace** (3570 Las Vegas Blvd. S., 702/731-7110, www.caesarspalace.com)

- **Bellagio** (3600 Las Vegas Blvd. S., 888/987-6667, www.bellagio.com)

- **New York-New York** (3790 Las Vegas Blvd. S., 866-815-4365, www.newyorknewyork.com)

- **Excalibur** (3850 S. Las Vegas Blvd. S., 800/879-1379, www.excalibur.com)

Getting Around

DRIVING

For the most part, driving in Grand Canyon National Park is easy—so easy that it can lead to complacency. Be aware that the park's semiarid climate and high elevations mean that both desert and mountain driving conditions apply. And because of Grand Canyon's remote location, if your car breaks down, help is sometimes a long way away.

Prepare for your trip with a maintenance check. Be sure your tires, including the spare, are in good condition. Check to see that your tool kit is complete, and that your motor-oil grade is appropriate for the season. Pack jumper cables, plenty of water, and a flashlight. If you're traveling in winter, add a shovel and warm clothing to your roadside emergency kit. The **Arizona Emergency Information Network** (www.ein.az.gov) has driving tips, suggested emergency items, bulletins about weather and fire, and real-time updates about emergency conditions.

A disproportionately large number of Arizonans drive white cars and trucks, and you'll soon stop wondering why. During the summer, a window shade can help keep your car's interior temperatures from reaching volcanic heights. If your car has leather seats, drape them with light-colored towels to keep them from getting hot or sticky. And if you wouldn't put it in an oven, don't leave it on the car seat: This includes your favorite CD, a chocolate bar, or the family dog.

Road and Weather Conditions

Check road conditions before driving to the canyon, especially if you are traveling during winter. At high altitude, weather can change quickly and vary dramatically, even over a relatively short distance. For example, on a June trip to the North Rim, you could be traveling through desert temperatures in House Rock Valley, then climb the Kaibab Plateau and find it snowing in Jacob Lake, 30 miles away. Late-summer thunderstorms are also highly localized, and flash floods can occur miles away from a storm cell.

Road conditions are available from:

- **Arizona Department of Transportation** (dial 511 or 888/411-7623, www.az511.gov)

- **California Department of Transportation** (dial 511 or 800/427-7623, quickmap.dot.ca.gov)

- **Nevada Department of Transportation** (dial 511 or 877/687-6237, nvroads.com)

- **Utah Department of Transportation** (dial 511 or 866/511-8824, www.udottraffic.utah.gov)

Weather conditions are available from:

- **Grand Canyon National Park** (928/638-7888, www.nps.gov/grca)

- **National Weather Service** (www.wrh.noaa.gov)

- **North Rim Visitor Center** (928/638-9875)
- **Kaibab Plateau Visitor Center** (928/643-7298)

Backcountry Driving

If you plan to visit the canyon's more remote overlooks, such as **Point Sublime** or **Toroweap,** fill your gas tank, pack plenty of water, double-check your spare, and inquire about road conditions before setting out. It's also a good idea to let someone know your itinerary. You'll need a high-clearance 4WD vehicle to negotiate the rough road to Point Sublime. For Toroweap, you'll need high-clearance for the last seven miles and the campground. The National Park Service warns that 25 percent of visitors driving to Toroweap get a flat tire (sometimes more than one), and that towing services to this remote area can cost as much as $2,000. Cell-phone service here is spotty, and there are few residents or travelers in this area.

Good maps are essential for backcountry travel. Many forest roads are suitable for passenger vehicles, but surfaces vary. If you are driving on forest roads on the Kaibab Plateau, keep in mind that road conditions usually downgrade as you approach the canyon rim. A wide gravel road suitable for passenger cars might end up as a two-track with rocks, ruts, and a high center, so narrow and tree-lined that it's difficult to turn around. Forest Service maps indicate surface types and help you make sense of what can be a confusing maze of fire roads.

On forest and Bureau of Land Management roads, muddy conditions can last into late spring, especially on the North Rim's Kaibab Plateau. Think twice before continuing down a soggy two-track. Even a 4WD vehicle can get hopelessly mired. Besides, "mudding" damages roads, creating ruts that harden and persist until the next rain, and causing erosion along roadsides when vehicles skirt wet spots by driving around them. Muddy conditions also occur after summer thunderstorms. Be wary of stream crossings in lower areas, such as on the Marble Platform. Flash flooding can turn a dry wash into a dangerous stream.

SHUTTLES AND TOURS
Shuttles

The South Rim has a free shuttle system that covers the Grand Canyon Village area year-round and Hermit Road from March through November. Shuttle buses stop at parking lots, lodges, visitor centers, and overlooks. The South Rim pocket map and guide includes color-coded route information. Detailed seasonal schedules can be found on the park's website (http://go.nps.gov/gc_shuttle).

Grand Canyon Shuttles (888/215-3105, www.grandcanyonshuttles.com) offers charter service from Phoenix, Las Vegas, and other cities as well as between the North and South Rims. From spring through fall, the **Trans-Canyon Shuttle** (928/638-2820 or 877/638-2820, www.trans-canyonshuttle.com) offers scheduled departures daily between the North and South Rims, a trip of 4.5 hours. One-way trips are $90 pp, and reservations are required.

Bus Tours

Xanterra Parks & Resorts (928/638-2631 or 888/297-2757, www.grandcanyonlodges.com) offers year-round guided motor coach tours along the South Rim. Options include sunrise or sunset tours as well as scenic drives along Hermit Road and Desert View Drive. Stop at the transportation desk in Bright Angel Lodge or Maswik Lodge for more information.

Train Tours

Grand Canyon Railway (800/843-8724, www.thetrain.com) offers four classes of passenger service from Williams to Grand Canyon's South Rim. The route passes through ponderosa pine forest, piñon-juniper woodland, and open prairie. Although you won't get canyon views from the train, you can sign up for a package tour that combines the train ride with lodging and guided rim tours.

River Trips

For the most complete inner canyon

experience, reserve a white-water rafting trip lasting 3 to 18 days. More than a dozen concessionaires and guides lead commercial rafting tours in Grand Canyon. Outside the park, smooth-water floats from Glen Canyon Dam to Lees Ferry make a pleasant, 15-mile tour lasting a half-day or all day. Contact **Canyon Discovery** (888/522-6244, www.raftthecanyon.com) or visit the transportation desk in Bright Angel Lodge or Maswik Lodge to make arrangements.

Horse and Mule Tours

On the South Rim, **Xanterra Parks & Resorts** (303/297-2757 or 888/297-2757) offers two options for mule rides into the canyon: a three-hour ride along the rim, or overnight rides with a stay at Phantom Ranch. Reservations can be made up to 13 months in advance, although last-minute cancellations are possible, particularly during the winter.

On the North Rim, **Grand Canyon Trail Rides** (435/679-8665, www.canyonrides.com) offers one-hour rides along the rim and half-day trips along the rim or partway down the North Kaibab Trail.

Horseback tours in Kaibab National Forest travel on dirt roads and trails near the park. **Apache Stables** (928/638-2891, www.apachestables.com) offers horseback tours and wagon rides near the South Rim, while **Allen's Guided Tours** (435/644-8150 or 435/689-1660) leads horseback trips near Jacob Lake and the North Rim.

RV
South Rim

If you won't be camping in your RV, park it and take advantage of the park's free shuttle system to get around Grand Canyon Village. You'll find spaces large enough for RVs just past the South Entrance Station at Parking Lot 1. This lot is between the visitor center and the Mather Point overlook. If you wish to park closer to the lodges in Grand Canyon Village, continue to the **Backcountry Information Center** (south of Maswik Lodge), where Lot D also has RV-size spaces.

If you're camping, make reservations well in advance. Inside the park, only the South Rim's **Trailer Village** (928/638-1006 or 877/404-4611, www.visitgrandcanyon.com) has RV sites with full hookups for vehicles up to 50 feet long. Showers and laundry are available at the Camper Services building near Mather Campground. You can also camp at Mather Campground, although there are no hookups, and vehicle length is limited to 30 feet. Very few sites at first-come, first-served. Desert View Campground can accommodate RVs, and there are no hookups. The South Rim's disposal station is located next to Mather Campground. Limited repairs are available at the Grand Canyon Village garage; the nearest RV repair services are in Williams or Flagstaff.

Outside the park in Tusayan, **Grand Canyon Camper Village** (928/638-2887, www.grandcanyoncampervillage.com) has 250 RV sites with hookups. The campground also has coin-operated showers and laundry, a store, a playground, restrooms, and a dumpsite. Several restaurants and a grocery store are within walking distance. A couple of miles south of Tusayan, **Ten X Campground** (877/444-6777, www.recreation.gov, May-Sept.) has pull-through sites. RVs up to 30 feet long can be accommodated, although there are no hookups.

Farther south in Valle, **Bedrock City** (928/635-2600, www.bedrockaz.com, Feb.-Nov.) has RV sites with hookups and a nearby grocery, diner, gift shop, game room, laundry, and showers.

Thirty miles east of the park's East Entrance, **Cameron Trading Post RV Park** (928/679-2231 or 800/338-7385, www.camerontradingpost.com) has RV sites with full hookups. The RV park is adjacent to historic and modern trading posts, a convenience store, and a restaurant.

North Rim

Inside the park, the **North Rim Campground** (877/444-6777, www.recreation.gov, May 15-Oct. 15) can accommodate

RVs up to 40 feet long. There are no hookups, but there's a dump station within the campground.

Outside the park, **Kaibab National Forest** (928/643-7395, www.fs.usda.gov/kaibab) operates seasonal **DeMotte Campground** (18 miles north of the rim) and **Jacob Lake Campground** (45 miles north of the rim). Both campgrounds can accommodate small motor homes; neither has hookups. Sites are available May 14 to October 15 by reservation (877/444-6777, www.recreation.gov). Just south of Jacob Lake, **Kaibab Camper Village** (928/643-7804 or 800/525-0924, 928/526-0924 off-season, http://kaibab-campervillage.com, May 15-Oct. 15) has 62 RV sites with full hookups.

For RV repairs, you'll need to drive to Page or Kanab. Limited repairs are available at the Chevron near the park's North Rim Campground and in Jacob Lake.

BICYCLE
Inside the Park

Bicycles are allowed on all paved and dirt roads on the South Rim and North Rim. However, many park roads are narrow and curving, and traffic is heavy, especially on summer weekends. Wear a helmet and bright colors, use hand signals, and ride single file in the same direction as traffic. In Arizona, bikes are subject to the same traffic rules as automobiles. The South Rim's free shuttle buses will accommodate bikes.

All hiking trails inside the park are off-limits to bicycles, with two exceptions. On the North Rim, cyclists can use the **Bridle Path.** On the South Rim, the **Greenway** is open to bicycles. The Greenway is a paved walking and cycling path that connects the Grand Canyon Visitor Center and plaza to the village, Hermits Rest, and Yaki Point. Car-free campsites are available for cyclists at both North and South Rim campgrounds.

Outside the Park

In **Kaibab National Forest** (www.fs.usda.gov/kaibab), dirt and gravel forest roads offer miles of shady, traffic-free rides for mountain bikers, some with canyon views. Near the North Rim, **Forest Roads 610** and **611** take you to the edge of the Kaibab Plateau for views of the eastern canyon and Marble Platform, with links to a 22-mile section of

Bike tours and rentals are available at the South Rim's Bright Angel Bicycles.

the **Arizona Trail.** Just a few miles from the South Rim, forest roads travel to historic Hull Cabin and the **Grandview Lookout Tower,** with distant canyon views from the Coconino Rim.

For more information about biking in Kaibab National Forest near the South Rim, contact the **Tusayan Ranger District** (928/638-2443). For rides near the North Rim, contact the **Kaibab Plateau Visitor Center** (928/643-7298) in Jacob Lake.

MOTORCYCLE

Spring and **autumn,** between winter snowstorms and the blazing summer sun, are the best times for motorcycle touring in the Grand Canyon area. Watch out for late-summer thunderstorms, which can spout hail and lightning July to mid-September, mostly during the afternoon. Arizona law requires helmets for riders younger than 18 and eye protection for drivers of motorcycles without windshields.

Be visible: Traffic around Grand Canyon Village is heavy, with lots of distractions, and the long, open, straight stretch on Highway 64 from Williams to Grand Canyon is notorious for inattentive drivers. Stick to walking and shuttle buses in the South Rim's congested village area, and save the bike for Desert View Drive.

If you like to keep a close watch on your ride, note that Maswik and Yavapai Lodges are most likely to have parking spaces near your room. Mather, Desert View, and the North Rim Campgrounds all allow motorcycles.

Route 66 towns near Grand Canyon, including Williams, Flagstaff, and Kingman, are popular with bikers, and if you need repairs or gear, these are your best bet.

Recreation

The majority of Grand Canyon visitors stay for only a few hours, rarely getting closer to the canyon than peering over its rim. But the best way to experience the canyon's vast reaches is to venture within them. Exploration has its risks: sheer cliff edges, hyperthermia or hypothermia (depending on the season), dehydration, rock falls, lightning strikes, flash floods, drowning, and unpleasant critter encounters. Park rangers rescue an average of 400 people in the canyon's backcountry each year. Most have failed to prepare adequately or have overestimated their abilities. But if you've done your homework, the canyon will reward you with inspiring views that change at every turn in the trail, and up-close encounters with geology, history, and desert life.

DAY HIKING

If you've never hiked before, don't let that stop you from hiking at Grand Canyon. Yes, the canyon is intimidating, but a **guided ranger walk** or a **rim hike** is a great way to get your feet dusty. If you're a hiker but you've never hiked Grand Canyon before, start with one of the popular, maintained, and patrolled trails in the central corridor of the canyon: **Bright Angel, South Kaibab,** or **North Kaibab Trails.**

Sufficient water and sun protection are critical. So is determining the "point of must return." Hiking guidebooks, park rangers, and even the kiosks in the plaza outside the South Rim's Grand Canyon Visitor Center can help you choose an appropriate day-hike destination. Keep in mind that it will take you roughly twice as long to hike back up to the rim as it did to hike down.

You don't need a permit for a day hike, but it's a good idea to pick up an informative brochure, available by donation from one of the metal trailside containers near the North Rim's Bright Angel Point, Walhalla Glades, and Widforss Trail, and at points along the Rim Trail on the South Rim. The Grand Canyon Association (GCA) publishes

Your Public Lands

Close to 60 percent of land in Arizona is held by federal or state government. Recreation opportunities and regulations vary among land managers. Geocaching, for example, is strictly prohibited in national parks but may be okay in certain national forest areas. For information and permits, contact the appropriate agency.

Grand Canyon National Park is administered by the **National Park Service** (www.nps.gov), a division of the U.S. Department of the Interior. The Park Service's mission is to preserve and protect.

National forest lands are monitored by the U.S. Department of Agriculture, with a mandate to manage timber, game, grazing, minerals, and other resources, which may include scenery and historic structures or artifacts. **Kaibab National Forest** (www.fs.usda.gov/kaibab) borders Grand Canyon National Park on the north and south. **Coconino National Forest** (www.fs.usda.gov/kaibab) surrounds the Flagstaff area.

The **Bureau of Land Management** (BLM, www.blm.gov), another agency within the Department of the Interior, is charged with sustaining the health, diversity, and productivity of public land in its jurisdiction. In Arizona, the BLM administers 12.2 million acres, including Grand Canyon-Parashant National Monument.

Wilderness areas (www.wilderness.net) have high levels of protection. Motorized and mechanized uses, including mountain bikes, are prohibited. Several wilderness areas surround the national park, including the Saddle Mountain and Kanab Creek Wilderness Areas that straddle the Kaibab Plateau.

Reservations (877/444-6777, www.recreation.gov) for **campgrounds** and cabins operated by federal agencies can be made by telephone or online. Recreational access to particularly sensitive locations, including parts of the Paria Canyon-Vermilion Cliffs Wilderness Area, may be on a lottery basis.

inexpensive booklets for a number of trails, including the Bright Angel, South Kaibab, and Hermit Trails, available at visitor centers and GCA bookstores. Learning a little bit about geology, plants, animals, and history before or during your hike will add to your experience.

Trail Etiquette

Be respectful of other hikers by doing your part to maintain natural quiet. Don't throw things into the canyon, a highly dangerous impulse. The traditional rule of the trail is to yield to hikers going uphill, but use common sense. Sometimes uphill hikers welcome a break, and sometimes they'll want you just to get out of their way. Always yield to mules by stepping off the trail on the inside. Bikes yield to hikers and equestrians.

Many Grand Canyon trails are historic and even prehistoric, used by pioneers and ancients. Structures, rock art, artifacts like pottery shards and lithic scatters, and less

obvious evidence like roasting pits, are fascinating reminders that humans have traveled the canyon for millennia. Treat these reminders as though you were in an outdoor museum—feel free to look, but leave them in place. Even the thin layer of oils on your fingertips can damage rock art. Federal and state laws protect all archaeological and historic sites, including artifacts, on federal lands. Violators are subject to fines and imprisonment. If you witness theft or vandalism, contact the park's **Silent Witness Program** (928/638-7767).

Help prevent erosion by staying on trails. Don't shortcut switchbacks. Watch for **cryptobiotic soils**—lumpy, grayish-black crusts that protect soil by retaining moisture and preventing wind erosion. "Crypto" is a symbiotic community of bacteria, lichens, and mosses. It takes decades to form and only a footstep to destroy.

For your own safety and for the health

of the animals, do not disturb or feed wildlife. Pack out all trash, including food scraps. If you see a condor, mountain lion, or feral burro, report the sighting to a ranger.

BACKPACKING

The same safety issues that concern day hikers are magnified for backpackers, and careful preparation—beginning with a **permit application**—is a must. Most canyon backpackers train for a trip, acclimating to elevation, distance, terrain, and load with aerobic conditioning, strength training, and endurance work. Attitude is as important as physical condition: being able to focus and concentrate, setting and achieving goals, and keeping a positive outlook.

Planning requires attention to detail, from packing enough of the right kind of food to researching water availability along your route. Good maps and trail guides can help you locate routes and water sources. Online resources managed by **Grand Canyon Hikers and Backpackers Association** (www.gchba.org) are especially helpful.

Aside from clothing, personal items, a tent (optional in summer), and a sleeping bag and pad, things to pack include: water, a filtration system, iodine tablets, electrolyte replacement, a backpacking stove (though in the summer, you may wish to pack foods that don't require cooking), matches, hand sanitizer, animal-proof food storage containers, a pocketknife, a flashlight or headlamp, sun protection, a first aid kit (including blister treatment), extra socks, a signaling device (a mirror or a whistle), and a repair kit (duct tape, safety pins, needle and thread).

BACKCOUNTRY PERMITS

Some 40,000 people camp in Grand Canyon's backcountry each year. In an effort to keep this wilderness as wild as possible, Grand Canyon National Park has instituted a **permit** system limiting the number and location of campsites. The park grants 50 to 100 percent of permit requests, depending on the season. The park's website has printable **Backcountry Permit Request Forms** (www.nps.gov/grca/planyourvisit.backcountry-permit.htm). Fees are $10 per permit plus $8 pp per night if you are camping below the rim, or $8 per group if you are camping above the rim.

Three popular trails (Bright Angel, South Kaibab, and North Kaibab) meet in the canyon's central corridor, where campgrounds book quickly. May and June, despite upward-creeping temperatures, are the most popular months to hike; and the odds of landing a permit decrease for these months, especially for large groups (only a handful of campsites are large enough to accommodate groups of 7 to 11).

When to Apply

The sooner you submit your completed form, the more likely you are to get your chosen dates and location. The quickest requests to be considered are written permit requests received **by fax.** Written permit requests can be made on the first day of the month up to four months prior to your starting month (a.k.a. "fourth month out"). For example, if you want to start your backpacking trip on May 5, you can send or fax your permit request on January 1. For a start date of October 31, submit a permit application on June 1.

How to Apply

In order to complete a permit request, you'll first need to establish an itinerary. Take advantage of the park's *Trip Planner*—available **online, in person, or by mail** (Backcountry Information Center/GCNP, P.O. Box 129, Grand Canyon, AZ 86023, www.nps.gov/grca), as well as the information available on the park's website detailing use areas, camp types, and stay limits. Permit requests must include the trip leader's contact information and credit-card information, group size, license plate numbers of cars to be left at the trailhead, and an itinerary showing dates and use areas for each night of the trip.

WRITTEN APPLICATIONS

All written applications received by 5pm on the first day of the fourth month out are ordered randomly by computer. In other words, all first-day applications have an equal shot, no matter how or when they came in. (This helps keep the fax lines from combusting at 12:01am on day 1.) Mail-in requests must be postmarked no earlier than the first day of the initial month, which means they'll be later than the applications received by fax or hand-delivered. Requests made by phone or email are not accepted.

The park responds to all written requests by U.S. mail. Allow a minimum of three weeks for the response. Your credit card will be charged up to the amount specified on your application. If you cancel a permit up to four days in advance of your start date, you'll receive a credit that you can apply to a future hike (valid for one year), minus a $10 cancellation fee. Written applications should be faxed or mailed.

- **Fax** application to: 928/638-2125.

- **Mail** application to: Grand Canyon Permits Office, National Park Service, 1824 S. Thompson St., Suite 201, Flagstaff, AZ 86001.

IN-PERSON APPLICATIONS

Alternatively, you can make an in-person verbal request at a backcountry office beginning the first day of the *third* month prior to your starting month. For a start date of September 15, for example, you can apply in person on June 1. If you walk into a backcountry office with an application for a date three months to three weeks before your start date, your application will be considered immediately, before any mailed or faxed requests received that day. After 21 days before a proposed start date, only in-person requests are considered. In-person applications are accepted at:

- **Backcountry Information Center** (928/638-7875, 8am-noon and 1pm-5pm

daily year-round), located on Center Road behind Maswik Lodge on the South Rim

- **North Rim Backcountry Office** (8am-noon and 1pm-5pm daily mid-May-mid-Oct.), located in the Administration Building near the campground

Last-Minute Permits

If your written application is denied, you can try to get a last-minute permit—**no more than one day prior to the start of your hike**—for one or two consecutive nights at a corridor campground (Indian Garden, Bright Angel, or Cottonwood Camp). Roughly 10 to 15 percent of early permits are cancelled, so even during popular seasons, last-minute permits, though rare, are possible. You must apply for last-minute permits **in person at a backcountry office.**

If no permits are available upon your arrival at the backcountry office, you can request a **waitlist number** for the next day. Return to the backcountry office at 8am the next morning and wait for them to call your number. If available permits have all been issued by the time your number is called, you can add your name to the next day's waiting list (and repeat as necessary). As permits are granted each day, you will move up on the waiting list.

Your chances for a last-minute permit are also good if you are interested in (and prepared for) a remote trip to locations in the eastern or western canyon. Though it's always better to apply for permits in advance, you can check availability at the **ranger stations at Lees Ferry, Tuweep, or Meadview.** Because the ranger may be gone on patrol when you arrive, it's good to have a Plan B, such as a day hike or scenic drive. But if your timing (and your credit card) is good, you could be tucking into your sleeping bag along Tuckup Trail or exploring a tributary on your way to a Marble Canyon beach camp.

Once you're on the trail, keep your permit in a visible location, such as attached to the outside of your trip leader's pack. In camp, the

Hiking Heroes

If Grand Canyon had a Hiking Hall of Fame, its founding members would surely include the pioneering Kolb brothers. In later decades, prolific hikers have inspired others with their accomplishments and stories. **Harvey Butchart** (1907-2002), a Northern Arizona University (NAU) math professor, hiked some 15,000 miles in Grand Canyon, making daring loops, bushwhacks, and first ascents—including some escapades today's park rangers would beg you not to try. His personal hiking log, preserved in NAU's Cline Library, is 1,000 pages long. Butchart continued to hike Grand Canyon until his 80th year.

   Colin Fletcher (1922-2007) made the first recorded through-hike of the inner canyon within park boundaries. He backpacked across the Esplanade and Tonto Platform for two months in 1963, describing his trip in *The Man Who Walked through Time*, a book as much about the inner journey of canyon hiking as it is about the route through the canyon's heart.

   Only a couple dozen hikers have hiked the entire length of Grand Canyon, including **Pete McBride** and **Kevin Fedarko,** who set out in 2015 to raise awareness about environmental threats. They section-hiked more than 650 miles, documenting the journey on film and in reports published by *National Geographic* (www.nationalgeographic.com).

permit must be in plain view, such as attached to a tent, so that patrolling backcountry rangers can check it.

Leave No Trace Principles

To protect the canyon and respect other backcountry users, all backpackers should practice Leave No Trace ethics:

- Stay on trails and camp in designated areas. Don't trench, dig, or rearrange Mother Nature to build a tent site—use an established site.

- Open fires are not allowed in the backcountry. Use a backpacking stove or bring food that doesn't require cooking.

- Pack out all trash. Leave campsites in the same condition as you found them (or better). Even the tiniest crumbs can attract rodents and ants.

- Discard dishwater at least 200 feet from small water sources, and strain food particles from the dishwater.

- Use biodegradable soap. Do not contaminate water pockets or small streams, which

may be needed by wildlife or other backpackers. If you are camped at the Colorado River, discard strained dishwater or urinate into the water—the river's volume is adequate for dilution.

- Bury solid human waste 200 feet from all water sources (including dry washes), camps, and trails. Dig a cat hole at least 4-6 inches deep. Look for organic soil; do not use sand or dunes. Pack out used toilet paper. The park is studying the use of "wag bags" in some backcountry areas, and waste disposal guidelines will likely be updated in the future.

FISHING

To fish inside the park, you'll need an Arizona fishing license, available at the South Rim's General Store. If you're traveling to the North Rim, you can stop and pick up a license at Jacob Lake Inn or Marble Canyon Lodge, not far from Lees Ferry, a popular fly-fishing area. For more information, contact the **Arizona Game & Fish Department** (602/942-3000, www.azgfd.gov) before your trip.

Travel Tips

WHAT TO TAKE

No matter what season you visit, you'll want to bring a **refillable water bottle** and protection from wind and sun. Weather conditions can change quickly. Layering is the best strategy to help you shift from chilly mornings to sunny afternoons. Pack for your activities: broken-in boots for a hike, a small flashlight for camping or for walking around Grand Canyon Village at night, a waterproof jacket if you're visiting during the summer monsoon.

What you won't need at Grand Canyon is a tie or dressy heels. As long as you stow away the backpack and put on a pair of clean jeans and a nice shirt, you'll pass—even at El Tovar, the canyon's swankiest restaurant.

TIME ZONE

If you're traveling to Grand Canyon from another state, be aware that Arizona stays on **Mountain Standard Time** year-round. With the exception of the Navajo Reservation, Arizona does not observe daylight saving time. That means if you're arriving from New Mexico for a summer vacation at Grand Canyon and stopping to visit Hopi and Navajo towns en route, you'll be changing time zones at least twice. (Newer residents consider it confusing, but after an appropriate period of adjustment, most Arizonans are grateful for an early sunset on hot summer days.)

LAWS AND REGULATIONS

As in all 50 states, legal drinking age in Arizona is 21, and **alcohol** is banned from most of the state's Native American reservations. Though cell phone use while driving hasn't been restricted statewide, several localities (including Coconino County) prohibit talking on the phone or texting behind the wheel.

Arizona's strict Smoke-Free Act prohibits its **smoking** in most public indoor spaces, including bars. The act doesn't apply to

Fill up at a water station before starting a hike.

businesses on Native American reservations, however, which establish their own regulations. Seasonal fire restrictions may include smoking bans in neighboring forests.

The use of **drones** (UAVs or unmanned aircraft) is prohibited in Grand Canyon National Park and all other national parks.

INTERNATIONAL TRAVELERS
Visas and Passports

Most international visitors need a passport and a visa to enter the United States. A nonimmigrant visa allows you to travel to a U.S. port of entry for the purpose stated on the visa and request permission to enter the country from the immigration inspector on duty. If the officer grants permission, a passport is required to enter the United States. Visas are waived for 38 countries, including France, Italy, Germany, Japan, and the United Kingdom. If you enter the United States without a visa, an individual machine-readable passport is required. Check with your home country's foreign ministry about obtaining a passport or visa, or to learn more about visa and passport requirements, visit the U.S. Department of State's website (http://travel.state.gov).

Air Travel

If you will be traveling within the United States on a commercial airline, be aware that carry-on regulations are subject to change. Generally, you can carry on personal toiletries in containers of three ounces or less, grouped together in a clear, quart-size, zip-top plastic bag. Many items, including mace or pepper spray, are prohibited. For more information about current travel regulations on domestic airlines, visit the Transportation Security Administration website (www.tsa. gov). Security checkpoint wait times vary by location, time of day, and day of the week. Contact your airline and airport for recommended arrival times.

Money

Major credit cards and traveler's checks are accepted almost everywhere. Before you leave on your trip, be sure your credit card and bank card have PINs (personal identification numbers) that will work overseas. Also check with your bank and credit card companies about transaction fees or foreign exchange fees. You may be able to avoid ATM fees by using your debit card to obtain cash at banks and grocery stores. ATM availability is limited inside the park, and you should exchange foreign currency for U.S. dollars before traveling to Grand Canyon. Most large U.S. banks offer exchange services; so do Sky Harbor (Phoenix) and McCarran (Las Vegas) Airports.

Tipping

At restaurants, it's standard to tip 15 to 20 percent on the total before taxes, depending on the quality of service. If you are dining in a group of six or more, a gratuity may be automatically added to the bill. (If so, this must be clearly stated on the menu or on the bill.) A minimum tip should be $1, even if you've ordered something less than $5. If you are ordering counter service, such as at a coffee bar or deli, you may see a tip jar near the cash register. In this case, tips are appreciated, especially if you've made a special request or substitution, but not required. Tipping at a bar is customarily $1 or $2 per drink or 5 to 20 percent of the total bill. (People often tip ahead on the first drink to encourage attentive service.) For baggage handling, tip $1 to $2 per bag. Leave $2 to $3 per day in your hotel room for housekeeping service. A room-service bill may or may not include a gratuity. Check to see if the gratuity has been included; if not, tip the waiter. Tip commercial tour guides 15 to 20 percent.

TRAVELING WITH CHILDREN
Ranger and Naturalist Programs

Most of the park's free ranger programs are suitable for kids, and any ranger program fulfills the activity requirement for the Junior Ranger Program. Check at visitor centers or online (http://go.nps.gov/gc_programs) for current offerings. Children must be supervised and accompanied by a parent.

Naturalists with the **Grand Canyon Field Institute** (GCFI, 866/471-4435, www.grandcanyon.org/fieldinstitute) hold single-day family programs combining history and hiking. Private, customized outings are also available.

Junior Ranger Program

The park's Junior Ranger Program is free, and it's a good way to keep kids focused as they participate in hikes or activities to earn a certificate and badge. Five different awards and program levels target age groups from 4 to 14. Required activities include at least one ranger program. On the South Rim, you can pick up a *Junior Ranger Activity Booklet* at the Grand Canyon Visitor Center, Park Headquarters, Verkamps Visitor Center, or Tusayan Museum. On the North Rim, Junior Ranger booklets are available at the North Rim Visitor Center. There's also a Junior Ranger program specifically for Phantom Ranch.

Trails

Many canyon trails have fine day-hike destinations suitable for kids, but if trails leading into the canyon are too steep for your parental peace of mind, stick to gentler trails above the rim. You'll find many opportunities to introduce your kids to nature: wildlife viewing, fire ecology, and identifying birds or wildflowers. (Remember: It's illegal to pick plants or collect seeds within the park.) If you'd rather turn the nature talk over to an expert, rangers guide short hikes several times a day on both rims. Ask about family-friendly ranger programs, such as the daily fossil walk (1 mile round trip). Other suggestions include:

South Rim: Trail of Time is perfect for geology buffs. Some paved portions of the Rim Trail are manageable for strollers.

North Rim: The Uncle Jim, Transept, Cliff Springs, and Widforss Trails follow the rim or head through the forest and are especially good choices for hiking with kids ages four and older.

Trains, Planes, Mules, and Boats

On the South Rim, the **Grand Canyon Railway** (928/635-2461, 928/773-0147, or 800/843-8724) has daily departures between Williams and Grand Canyon Depot. Most

Kids will enjoy mule tours.

air-tour companies offer discounts for children on scenic flights and on tour packages combining flights with land tours or boat trips. **Mule trips** (888/297-2757) to Phantom Ranch or along the rim don't have an age limit but require that all riders be at least 4 feet, 7 inches tall. Children ages 15 and younger must be accompanied by an adult on mule trips.

On the North Rim, hour-long **mule tours** (435/679-8665) are suitable for kids as young as seven years old. Wagon rides and horseback tours are offered by concessionaires in neighboring **Kaibab National Forest** (North Rim, 435/644-8150; South Rim, 928/638-2891 or 928/638-3105). **Colorado River Discovery** (928/645-9175 or 888/522-6644, www.raftthecanyon.com) leads half-day motorized, smooth-water floats from Glen Canyon Dam to Lees Ferry, suitable for children as young as four years old.

TRAVELING WITH PETS

Pets are permitted in developed areas of the park, including campgrounds, but must be leashed at all times and cannot be left unattended; a violation can cost $500. Among park lodges, only **Yavapai Lodge** (877/404-4611, www.visitgrandcanyon.com) has pet-friendly rooms. Pets are not permitted on shuttle buses or on hiking trails below the rim. The only exceptions are service animals. If you want to take a service animal below the rim, check with the **Backcountry Information Center** (South Rim 928/638-2125; North Rim 928/638-7868). At the South Rim, you can walk your pet on a leash on paved sections of the **Rim Trail.** On the North Rim, leashed pets are allowed on the **Bridle Path.**

If Rover loves to go hiking with you, inquire about trails in **Kaibab National Forest** (North Rim, 435/644-8150; South Rim, 928/638-2891 or 928/638-3105). Outside the park on the North Rim, **Kaibab Lodge** (928/638-2389) has a few pet-friendly rooms and offers a pet-sitting service for guests.

Never leave an animal alone inside a vehicle, even with the windows rolled down a few inches. During much of the year, Arizona's intense sunshine can heat up the interior of a car to 130-180°F in a matter of minutes.

Boarding Services

When visiting the South Rim, you can board your dog or cat for the day or overnight at the **kennel** (928/638-0534, 7:30am-5pm daily), located off Rowe Well Road west of Maswik Lodge. Reservations are recommended, and proof of vaccination is required. You can make arrangements to pick up your pet later than 5pm by calling 928/638-2631. There are no kennel services on the North Rim, but guests at **Kaibab Lodge** (928/638-2389) can arrange for pet-sitting.

An alternative is to board your pet outside the park in Williams, 60 miles south of the South Rim. Grand Canyon Railway's **Pet Resort** (800/843-8724) is available to the general public.

SENIOR TRAVELERS

The **America the Beautiful Senior Pass** (http://store.usgs.gov, $10) is a lifetime interagency pass for U.S. citizens age 62 and older, providing access at no charge to all federal recreation fee sites. It must be obtained in person at the park with proof of age, such as a driver's license, or in advance by mail ($10 processing fee). The pass admits up to three accompanying adult passengers in a noncommercial vehicle. In addition, pass holders receive a 50 percent discount on other park fees, such as for campsites in national park campgrounds. Senior discounts may or may not be offered by park concessionaires (but it never hurts to ask).

TRAVELERS WITH DISABILITIES

Many of the park's facilities were designed before ADA standards were established. Because of steps and narrow doorways, some of the park's historic buildings and cabins are only partly accessible, but most lodges have a number of accessible rooms, and several overlooks have wheelchair access. Restrooms vary in ease of use, but many are accessible. **Bright Angel Bicycles** (928/814-8704, www.bike-grandcanyon.com) rents wheelchairs on the South Rim. On the North Rim, wheelchairs are available for short-term loan at the visitor center.

For specific information about entryways, parking, grade, restrooms, and other details for attractions and facilities on the North and South Rims, refer to the park's *Accessibility Guide* (www.nps.gov/grca), available at park entrance stations and at Grand Canyon Visitor Center.

America the Beautiful Access Pass

The **America the Beautiful Access Pass** (http://store.usgs.gov, free) is an interagency pass for legally blind or permanently disabled U.S. citizens, good at all fee-based federal recreation sites. The Access Pass must be obtained in person at the park, with accompanying documentation such as a physician's statement, a document issued by a federal agency (such as the Veterans Administration or Social Security Administration), or by a state agency such as a vocational rehabilitation center. The pass admits the pass holder and up to three adult passengers in a noncommercial vehicle. The pass also provides a 50 percent discount on many park-based fees, such as campground stays.

Parking and Shuttles

If you are traveling at the South Rim in your own vehicle, you can ask for an **Accessibility Pass** at entrance stations, park lodges, or visitor centers. The pass, placed on the dashboard of your vehicle, allows access to some areas that are closed to general traffic, such as Yaki Point.

All park shuttle buses are accessible to wheelchairs smaller than 30 inches wide by 48 inches long. Most motorized scooters won't fit. Trained service animals are allowed on shuttles.

Accommodations and Campgrounds

Most park lodges on the South Rim have a number of accessible guest rooms. Shower chairs and TDD phones are available on request. Contact **Xanterra Parks & Resorts** (303/297-2757 or 888/297-2757, www.grand-canyonlodges.com) for information and reservations. The South Rim's **Mather Campground** (800/365-2267, www.recreation.gov) has accessible campsites. Request an accessible site when making your reservation and confirm accessibility when you register at the campground. The South Rim's Camper Services building has a shower-restroom accessible to wheelchairs; an on-site attendant has the key.

The North Rim's **Grand Canyon Lodge** (888/386-4383, www.foreverlodging.com) has a few cabins that are minimally accessible. Cabins are scattered through the forest, with steep, narrow, and rough sidewalks and stairways. The **North Rim Campground** (800/365-2267, www.recreation.gov) has designated sites with accessible picnic tables. These are linked to the showers and restrooms by a level, paved trail, and roll-in showers are available.

Trails

Gentle trails are available on either rim of the canyon. Along the South Rim, portions of the **Rim Trail** are paved and fairly level, particularly the two-mile section between Bright Angel Lodge and Mather Point. The North Rim's **Bridle Path** has a hard surface and is fairly level between Grand Canyon Lodge and the campground entrance (one mile). Trails below either rim are steep, with uneven surfaces and dangerous drop-offs. If you wish to take a service animal on hiking trails, arrangements can be made at the **Backcountry Information Center** (928/638-7875) in Grand Canyon Village near Maswik Lodge, or the North Rim's **Backcountry Office** (928/638-7868), located along the service road north of the campground entrance.

Ranger Programs and Tours

Many ranger programs are accessible; some are adapted for the visually impaired. With advance notice, bus tours offered by Xanterra Parks & Resorts can accommodate wheelchairs. Even mule tours may be accessible under some circumstances. Call the transportation desk at **Bright Angel Lodge** (928/638-2631) for advance tour reservations. For white-water river trips, contact individual outfitters and guides about accessibility. **Colorado River Discovery** (928/645-9175 or 888/522-6644, www.raftthecanyon.com) offers smooth-water floats from Glen Canyon Dam to Lees Ferry, appropriate for passengers with mobility or sensory disabilities.

Health and Safety

HOSPITALS AND CLINICS

For emergencies, call 911 (or 9-911 if you are calling from a room in one of the park lodges). Emergency phones at ranger stations connect directly to the park switchboard and do not require coins. Your cell phone isn't likely to get a signal inside the canyon. River guides carry satellite phones and are trained to assist in emergencies. Rangers and clinic staff handle emergencies on the South Rim, where a **walk-in clinic** (928/638-2551) is open all year. You can fill prescriptions here, but only with a handwritten order from your doctor. Flagstaff Medical Center is about 90 minutes from the South Rim by car.

The North Rim is more remote, and park rangers have first-aid certification or EMT training. The nearest small hospitals are in Page (130 miles) or Kanab, Utah (82 miles). Air transport to Flagstaff Medical Center is possible from either rim.

ALTITUDE

Elevations range 6,600 to 7,400 feet along the South Rim and 8,200 to 8,800 feet on the North Rim, high enough to affect many flatlanders, especially those with existing health problems. Signs of **altitude sickness** are headache, weakness, fatigue, shortness of breath, and dizziness. **Dehydration** is often a factor, so drink plenty of water. Taking a day or two to acclimate before hiking helps, as does slowing your pace and taking rest breaks. **Smoke** from wildfires or prescribed burns can also affect many individuals; check the park website (www.nps.gov/grca) for alerts.

FALLS

Every year, falls at Grand Canyon result in injuries and one to three deaths. Many of the victims were trying to get a photograph or scrambling around on rocks outside guardrails. Keep a close watch on kids (and a closer watch on your husband or boyfriend—most victims are young men). Stay behind fences and barriers and be cautious near the rim: Even large rocks can break loose, icy patches are common in the winter, and sand or small rocks make surfaces slippery any time of year. If you're hiking, don't cut switchbacks or go off trail, and step to the inside of the trail and wait for mules to pass. The canyon's terrain is rugged, and it's a long way down.

HEAT-RELATED ILLNESSES

High altitude, dry air, and hot summer temperatures multiply the effects of the sun. Below the rim, the canyon's rocky walls hold heat and reflect the sun's rays. Extreme inner canyon heat catches many people unprepared, and heat-related conditions are common. Protect yourself from sunburn by wearing a wide-brimmed hat, UV lenses, sunscreen or long sleeves, and lip balm. Above all, drink plenty of water.

Because the hot, dry air quickly dries perspiration, hikers may not realize how much moisture they are losing from sweat—up

Overlooks may be icy in winter.

to two quarts of water every hour. Rangers along the Bright Angel Trail treat as many as 20 cases of **heat exhaustion** daily during summer months. Symptoms are pallor, nausea, headache, cramps, and cool, moist skin.

Left untreated, heat exhaustion can lead to **heatstroke,** a life-threatening emergency. The face becomes flushed and the skin dry. The pulse is weak and rapid. The body's ability to regulate temperature is overwhelmed, and body temperature goes up, leading to mental confusion and eventual unconsciousness.

Hyponatremia (water intoxication) can look like heat exhaustion, with cramping, clamminess, headache, and nausea. But this serious condition is the result of drinking too much water without replacing electrolytes, leading to low concentrations of sodium in the blood. Like heatstroke, hyponatremia can lead to altered mental states and rapid pulse, and it too can be deadly.

To prevent heat-related illnesses, drink plenty of water and balance water intake by eating salty snacks or using electrolyte-replacement powders, gels, or drinks. Keep cool, resting in the shade and hiking within your abilities. If your hiking companion's mental state becomes altered, get immediate help. If you suspect heatstroke, cool the victim immediately by pouring water on his or her skin, clothing, and hair.

HYPOTHERMIA

With so many dire warnings about dehydration and heat, it's easy to overlook hypothermia as a danger. Exposure to cold and wet conditions can lead to the point where the body can't warm itself. Symptoms are the "umbles": mumbling, grumbling, stumbling, fumbling. If you're hiking during the winter, wear fleece rather than denim or heavy cotton, and pack a Thermos with a hot drink. Treat hypothermia with dry clothing, warm liquids, and protection from the elements.

DROWNING

Do not hike in tributary canyons when flash floods are a possibility, particularly during the late-summer thunderstorm season. Boaters should always wear a personal flotation device (PFD) or life jacket. The park service frowns on packrafting and limits packrafters to no more than five river miles per backcountry permit.

Don't Feed the Animals

No matter how much they ask, do not feed them.

Don't feed canyon critters, deliberately or inadvertently.

Feeding wildlife is not only illegal (with fines for violators), but also unethical and even danger-ous. Human food can damage animals' digestive systems. Wild creatures can become dependent on handouts, lose their ability to fend for themselves, and lose their caution around humans. Many cases of animals becoming aggressive toward people have been documented at Grand Canyon.

On some popular trails, squirrels and other rodents rip into your pack if you set it down even for a few seconds. This may seem relatively harmless, but a damaged pack is a hassle, and losing part of your well-planned food supply is worse. In riparian areas, particularly around Phantom Ranch, skunks and raccoons also make unwelcome nighttime visits.

Rabies and bubonic plague outbreaks aren't uncommon in Arizona, and a case of tick-borne relapsing fever (TBRF) was reported in 2015. Hantavirus, while less common, is deadly. If you think food has been contaminated, wrap it up and pack it out.

Here are some tips for keeping your food safe:

- Secure your food first when you make camp.

- Use the park's food storage boxes where available.

- Bring 20-30 feet of rope to hang packs. Be warned though that inner-canyon ringtails can outwit the most elaborate defenses in search of food.

- Store edibles inside containers, such as an ammo can or sacks made with lightweight polymer, steel mesh, or some other material strong enough to thwart sharp little teeth.

Colorado River currents are swift, with bone-chillingly cold water and dangerous rocks and rapids. To protect beaches from ammonia buildup, campers and river runners urinate in the river or in the wet sand at the water's edge. This can be a tricky proposition in the middle of the night when it's dark and you're sleepy. Carry a flashlight or headlamp, and be cautious on wet rocks.

BITES AND STINGS

The canyon is home to several biting insects, as well as several species of rodents and rattlesnakes. If you are allergic to beestings or insect bites, carry an EpiPen and be sure your hiking companions know how to use it. Prevent bites by watching where you place your hands and feet. Shake out clothing and bedding. Don't feed or pester wildlife. Although snakebites are rare, they are almost always the result of people trying to handle snakes. Deer, bighorn sheep, coyotes, lizards, and squirrels have bitten people offering them handouts.

Rabies and plague aren't uncommon in Arizona. Never handle a bat; if you see one during the day, it is likely infected with rabies. Keep your food supply secured when you are in camp: Ringtails, rodents, and ravens can get into packs even when they are hanging; use animal-proof containers. Hantavirus, a deadly respiratory illness, can be transmitted by inhaling dust from rodent waste. If you discover that your plastic bag of gorp has been chewed into, pack it out with the rest of your trash.

Some hikers feel safer carrying a bite extractor, which works for removing poison or stingers from insect bites as well as for snakebite venom. Any animal bite should be checked by a physician and monitored for signs of infection.

Resources

Suggested Reading

Thousands of books have been written about Grand Canyon, from scientific studies to thrilling adventure stories. The titles listed below are a mere sampling of helpful, fascinating, and educational canyon lore.

Human History and Archaeology

Anderson, Michael F. *Along the Rim*. Grand Canyon, AZ: Grand Canyon Association, 2001. This 72-page booklet provides a concise history of Grand Canyon Village and 22 overlooks along Hermit Road and Desert View Drive, making it an excellent take-along resource for a driving tour.

Coder, Christopher M. *An Introduction to Grand Canyon Prehistory*. Grand Canyon, AZ: Grand Canyon Association, 2000. The author provides a concise but comprehensive description of 12,000 years of human life in Grand Canyon.

Grattan, Virginia L. *Mary Colter: Builder Upon the Red Earth*. Grand Canyon, AZ: Grand Canyon Association, 2007. An excellent biography of eccentric and talented Mary Elizabeth Jane Colter, who designed the South Rim's most intriguing buildings.

Geology and Natural History

Alden, Peter et al. *National Audubon Society Field Guide to the Southwestern States*. New York: Alfred A. Knopf, 1999. With color photos and charts to help identify plants, animals, constellations, and landforms, this guide makes a good companion for a trip around the region.

Blakely, Ron, and Wayne Ranney. *Ancient Landscapes of the Colorado Plateau*. Grand Canyon, AZ: Grand Canyon Association, 2008. If you've ever wished you could travel back in time to see what the Grand Canyon area looked like millions of years ago, this book will take you there.

Kavanaugh, James, and Raymond Leung. *Field Guide to the Grand Canyon*. Phoenix: Waterford Press, 2001. This laminated and folded brochure is a pocket-size introduction to the canyon's most common plants and animals.

Lamb, Susan. *Grand Canyon: The Vault of Heaven*. Grand Canyon, AZ: Grand Canyon Association, 1999. This gorgeously photographed, oversize book is still the finest all-around book about Grand Canyon's human and natural history.

Ranney, Wayne. *Carving Grand Canyon*. Grand Canyon, AZ: Grand Canyon Association, 2012. Excellent illustrations and clear writing make this geological history easy for laypeople to understand.

Hiking and Recreation

Abbot, Lon, and Terri Cook. *Hiking the Grand Canyon's Geology*. Seattle: The

Mountaineers, 2004. Day-hiking and backpacking suggestions include step-by-step geologic information illustrated with helpful diagrams and photography.

Adkison, Ben. *Hiking Grand Canyon National Park*. Guilford, CT: Globe Pequot Press, 2016. This thorough hiking guide includes detailed trail information, maps, trail profiles, and color photos. Hikes are suggested by difficulty and experience levels, from family day hikes to challenging backpack routes.

Annerino, John. *Hiking the Grand Canyon*. New York: Skyhorse, 2017. A guide to 100 of the canyon's maintained trails, unmaintained trails, and unofficial routes, including insider tips on campsites, weather, and gear.

Belknap, Buzz. *Grand Canyon River Guide*. Boulder City, NV: Westwater Books, 2014. This waterproof guide's 120 pages include a sequence of river maps showing rapids, topography detail, and sights.

Lane, Brian. *Hikernut's Grand Canyon Companion*. Woodstock, VT: Countryman Press, 2013. For anyone planning to day hike or backpack the canyon's corridor trails—Bright Angel, South Kaibab, or North Kaibab—this 96-page book is an excellent resource. Detailed trail descriptions, maps, color photographs, and a gear list are particularly helpful for novice backpackers.

Martin, Tom. *Day Hikes from the River*. Flagstaff, AZ: Vishnu Temple Press, 2010. A hiking guide written from the perspective of the river, this book is indispensable for those on private boat trips. Information includes tips on where and how to tie in, campsites, topographic map sections, and detailed descriptions of 100 hikes.

Martin, Tom, and Duwain Whitis. *Guide to the Colorado River in Grand Canyon*. Flagstaff, AZ: Vishnu Temple Press, 2013. Campsites, rapids, natural history, and points of interest are included in this waterproof, mile-by-mile river guide. Maps include topographical detail, making this an excellent resource for river runners.

Various authors. *Grand Canyon Trail Guides*. Grand Canyon, AZ: Grand Canyon Association, 2005-2011. These 26- to 46-page pocket-size booklets cover Bright Angel, Grandview, Havasu, Hermit, North Kaibab, South Kaibab, and other trails. Cultural and natural history information is included with trail descriptions and maps—real bargains for under $5. Several are available as electronic downloads.

Good Reads

Dimock, Brad. *Sunk Without a Sound: The Tragic Colorado River Honeymoon of Glen and Bessie Hyde*. Flagstaff, AZ: Fretwater Press, 2001. This fascinating book recounts one of Grand Canyon's most enigmatic river expeditions, the honeymoon voyage of the Hydes, who entered the canyon in 1928 and never returned.

Dutton, Clarence. *Tertiary History of the Grand Cañon District*. Tucson: University of Arizona Press, 2001. This classic, first published in 1882, makes poetry of geology, and the illustrations by William Henry Holmes and Thomas Moran are breathtaking.

Fletcher, Colin. *The Man Who Walked through Time*. New York: Vintage, 1989. A classic adventure narrative that describes Fletcher's trek through the length of Grand Canyon. Inspiring and evocative, his account remains as fresh today as when it was written.

Ghiglieri, Michael, and Tom Martin. *Over the Edge: Death in Grand Canyon*. Flagstaff, AZ: Puma Press, 2012. A pair of guides and medical experts recount the stories of those who met their deaths in Grand Canyon. This 586-page book is not only a page-turner but also helpful in preparing for a successful canyon journey.

Powell, John Wesley. *The Exploration of the Colorado River and Its Canyons.* New York: Penguin, 2003. First published in 1872, Powell's expedition report combines adventure, geology, and anthropology with stirring accounts of canyon scenes.

Stegner, Wallace. *Beyond the Hundredth Meridian: John Wesley Powell and the Second Opening of the West.* New York: Penguin, 1992. One of the West's most influential authors outlines John Wesley Powell's life and sets the stage for contemporary environmental issues.

Maps

Black, Bronze. *Grand Canyon Map and Guide.* Flagstaff, AZ: Dragon Creek Publishing, 2008. A river guide and geologist created this artistic map chock-full of cultural and natural history, trail information, fun facts, and geologic details.

Kaibab National Forest. *North Kaibab Ranger District.* U.S. Department of Agriculture, U.S. Forest Service, 2003. For those who plan on back-road touring in the aspen and pine forests of the Kaibab Plateau, this map is essential, showing forest roads, road types, distances, trails, and wilderness boundaries.

Schulte, Kent. *Grand Canyon Trail Map.* Boulder, CO: Sky Terrain, 2016. An easy-to-read 1:40,000 topographic map that includes trails and backcountry-use areas from Desert View to Point Sublime. Trail descriptions and profiles are also included. It's an excellent map for backpackers and hikers, although Bass and Thunder River Trails are off the map.

Trails Illustrated. *Grand Canyon National Park #261.* Evergreen, CO: National Geographic Society, 2010. A 1:35,000 topographic map that details central Grand Canyon, including trails, roads, and the most developed areas of the park.

USGS Quadrangles. *United States Geological Survey.* For an extended backcountry trip, the most detailed map (or maps) is the 7.5-minute 1:24,000 quadrangle matching your route. You can find USGS quads in Flagstaff's numerous gear stores, at the Navajo Bridge Interpretive Center, or order them directly from USGS (888/275-8747, http://store.usgs.gov).

Internet Resources

Grand Canyon
Grand Canyon National Park
www.nps.gov/grca
The park's official website is an excellent resource for anyone planning a canyon trip. Information includes downloads, maps, permit applications, and details about hiking, sightseeing, campgrounds, the latest weather, and much, much more.

Campground Reservations
www.recreation.gov
Sure, you can make campground reservations here, but this site also has travel-planning suggestions and helpful links.

Grand Canyon Association (GCA)
www.grandcanyon.org
The GCA, a nonprofit organization founded in 1932, uses money from sales to support Grand Canyon National Park programs and publications. GCA stores at Grand Canyon do double duty as information centers, and the online shop has a fine selection of books and maps. Members receive discounts on purchases.

Grand Canyon Field Institute

www.grandcanyon.org/fieldinstitute

Grand Canyon Field Institute (GCFI) offers learning-based programs that incorporate day-hiking, backpacking, and camping with expert guides. Programs are discounted for GCA members.

Grand Canyon Hikers and Backpackers Association

www.gchba.org

A dedicated group of backcountry enthusiasts share their Grand Canyon trail-savvy on this website. Find out more about water sources, read trip notes about unusual destinations, or make plans to join a service project.

Grand Canyon Private Boaters Association

www.gcpba.org

Experienced river runners share information in this online community, focusing on issues affecting Grand Canyon boating and posting announcements about permits, river flows, and current conditions.

Grand Canyon Trust

www.grandcanyontrust.org

The Trust advocates collaborative, practical solutions to challenges facing the Colorado Plateau and Grand Canyon, focusing on air quality, energy, forest health, water, and other topics. Staff, members, and volunteers participate in single- and multiple-day trips that might involve habitat restoration, trail maintenance, or helping to harvest indigenous crops.

Beyond the Boundaries

Arizona Trail Association

www.aztrail.org

The Arizona Trail, more than 800 miles long, crosses the state from Utah to Mexico. Hikers, bicyclists, and equestrians can access sections of the trail on Grand Canyon's North and South Rims. The website lists travel resources and features an interactive map.

Bureau of Land Management (BLM)

www.blm.gov/az

Unpaved BLM roads travel 4,000 miles through rugged country in the Arizona Strip for remote camping, hiking, canyoneering, and sightseeing. For more information about the Paria Canyon-Vermilion Cliffs Wilderness Area or Grand Canyon-Parashant National Monument, start with the BLM's Arizona page.

Glen Canyon National Recreation Area

www.nps.gov/glca

Learn more about boating, fishing, hiking, canyoneering, and sightseeing opportunities on Lake Powell and its surrounding canyon country.

Glen Canyon Natural History Association

www.glencanyonnha.org

This nonprofit organization supports programs and publications for Glen Canyon National Recreation Area, Glen Canyon Dam, Rainbow Bridge National Monument, and Grand Staircase-Escalante National Monument. The site includes travel information and an online store with maps, books, and more.

Havasupai Nation

http://itcaonline.com

Includes a brief history of the Havasupai people and information for planning a trip to Havasu Canyon. To learn more about the Havasupai people, visit Arizona State University's online history class (http://grand-canyonhistory.clas.asu.edu) or read the classic *People of the Blue Water* by Flora Gregg Iliff.

Hopi Nation

www.experiencehopi.com

Learn about culture, sightseeing, and guide services for visiting the Hopi Mesas and villages. The nation's official website (www.hopi-nsn.gov) has recent news releases and information about Hopi government.

Hualapai Nation

www.grandcanyonwest.com

Start here to make reservations for the Hualapai Nation's Grand Canyon West attractions, including the Skywalk. The nation's official website (www.hualapai-nsn.gov) includes information about Hualapai history, government, and economy.

Kaibab National Forest

www.fs.usda.gov/kaibab
Find out about current conditions, camping, hiking, and sightseeing in the North Kaibab, Tusayan, and Williams districts of the forest. Order maps or download them for a fee using Avenza's app (www.avenzamaps.com), accessible offline.

Navajo Nation

www.navajonationparks.org
Learn more about visiting the Navajo Nation, including permits and fee schedules for camping and hiking on Navajo lands. For information on the Navajo people, visit the Navajo Nation's official website (www.navajo-nsn.gov).

Southwest Deserts

www.desertusa.com
Desert USA celebrates the people, places, and natural history of the Southwest's deserts. Check here for up-to-the-minute posts and links for wildflowers in bloom, current water levels at Lake Powell, and more.

Gateways

Flagstaff

www.flagstaffarizona.org
Find out more about attractions, accommodations, and self-guided tours for northern Arizona's largest mountain town.

Coconino National Forest

www.fs.usda.gov/coconino
This website has info about current conditions, camping, hiking, and driving on the Flagstaff Ranger District and other areas of the Colorado Plateau.

Museum of Northern Arizona (MNA)

www.musnaz.org

Located in Flagstaff, MNA has been interpreting and preserving the cultural and natural history of the Colorado Plateau since 1928. Visit the website to find out more about current exhibitions, events, and programs.

Kanab, Utah

www.visitsouthernutah.com
Kanab is a convenient base for exploring national parks and monuments in southern Utah and northern Arizona. You'll find lodging, dining, tours, recreation, and other travel information on this site.

Page

www.visitpagelakepowell.com
This site has information about staying and playing in Page, Lake Powell, and Glen Canyon National Recreation Area.

Williams

www.experiencewilliams.com
Find information on local attractions along Route 66, lodging and dining options, and community events.

Arizona

Arizona Office of Tourism

www.visitarizona.com
Arizona's signature sites and experiences are highlighted, with suggested itineraries and links to tours, lodging, and dining.

Arizona Highways Magazine

www.arizonahighways.com
This website is companion to the venerable magazine published by the Arizona Department of Transportation. Find out more about the state's most beautiful places or hit 'em with your best shots for Photo of the Day.

Hit the Trail

www.hitthetrail.com
Photographers, geologists, historians, and former park rangers contribute to this site, a handy compilation of travel tips for Grand Canyon and Sedona, including links to trail descriptions and current road conditions.

Index

List of Maps

Photo Credits

Title page photo: Grand Canyon starry night © Bristlecone Media; page 4 an aspen leaf in fall USDA Forest Service, Southwestern Region, Coconino National Forest, Brienne Magee; page 5 (top) pottery sherds found in Kaibab National Forest, USDA Forest Service, Southwestern Region, Kaibab National Forest, (bottom) elk © Salvatore Conte | Dreamstime.com; page 6 (top left) © Richard Mayer, (top right) © geordankeller/123rf.com, (bottom) © Kathleen Bryant; page 7 (top) © Scott Griessel/123rf.com, (bottom left) USDA Forest Service, Southwestern Region, Kaibab National Forest, (bottom right) NPS photo by Erin Whittaker; page 8 © Don Fink/123rf.com; page 9 (top) NPS photo by Michael Quinn, (bottom left) © Richard Mayer, (bottom right) © Kathleen Bryant; page 11 (top) NPS photo by Michael Quinn, (bottom) © Reinhardt | Dreamstime.com; page 12 (top) NPS photo by Michael Quinn, (bottom) © Varina Patel/123rf.com; page 13 NPS photo by Michael Quinn; page 14 © Flagstaff CVB; page 15 NPS photo by Michael Quinn; page 16 NPS photo by Michael Quinn; page 18 © Kathleen Bryant; page 19 NPS photo by W. Tyson Joye; page 20 © Natalia Bratslavsky | Dreamstime.com; page 21 (top and bottom) NPS photo by Michael Quinn; page 22 (top) NPS photo by Michael Quinn, (bottom) © Kathleen Bryant; page 23 © Kathleen Bryant; page 24 NPS photo by Michael Quinn; page 25 NPS photo by Mark Lellouch; page 26 NPS photo by Michael Quinn; page 27 NPS photo by Michael Quinn; page 28 © Ruben Martinez Barricarte | Dreamstime.com; page 29 (top) © Kathleen Bryant, (bottom) NPS photo by Michael Quinn; page 31 NPS photo by Erin Whittaker; page 35 NPS photo by Michael Quinn; page 40 © Richard Mayer; page 42 © Grand Canyon National Park Museum Collection; page 43 © Kathleen Bryant; page 46 © Kathleen Bryant; page 47 (top) NPS photo by Erin Whittaker, (bottom) © Kathleen Bryant; page 52 NPS photo; page 53 © Richard Mayer; page 55 (top) NPS photo by Michael Quinn, (bottom) © Kathleen Bryant; page 56 NPS photoby Michael Quinn; page 57 © Kathleen Bryant; page 61 NPS photo by Michael Quinn; page 65 © Kathleen Bryant; page 66 © Kathleen Bryant; page 75 © Kathleen Bryant; page 77 NPS photo by Michael Quinn; page 78 © Richard Mayer; page 82 © Kathleen Bryant; page 90 (top) NPS photo by Michael Quinn, (bottom) © Kathleen Bryant; page 91 NPS photo by Allyson Mathis; page 93 © Arlene Hochman Waller | Dreamstime.com; page 96 NPS photo by Michael Quinn; page 97 © Kathleen Bryant; page 101 © Kathleen Bryant; page 102 (top and bottom) © Kathleen Bryant; page 103 © Kathleen Bryant; page 106 © Kathleen Bryant; page 107 NPS photo by Michael Quinn; page 111 NPS photo by Michael Quinn; page 112 © Kathleen Bryant; page 118 © Kathleen Bryant; page 120 © Kathleen Bryant; page 122 © Kathleen Bryant; page 123 NPS photo; page 127 NPS photo by Michael Quinn; page 128 (top) NPS photo by Mark Lellouch, (bottom) NPS photo by Michael Quinn; page 129 NPS photo by Erin Whittaker; page 135 NPS photo by Michael Quinn; page 137 © Kathleen Bryant; page 138 © Katheen Bryant; page 139 NPS photo by Kristen M. Caldon; page 144 © Kathleen Bryant; page 146 © Kathleen Bryant; page 148 NPS photo by Michael Quinn; page 149 © Kathleen Bryant; page 151 (top and bottom) NPS photo by Erin Whittaker; page 153 © NPS collection; page 159 NPS photo/Michael Quinn; page 160 © Kathleen Bryant; page 162 © Kathleen Bryant; page 164 (top) USDA Forest Service, Southwestern Region, Kaibab National Forest, (bottom) © Kathleen Bryant; page 165 © Alberto Loyo/123rf.com; page 168 © Kathleen Bryant; page 169 © Chris Hill/123rf.com; page 174 © Kathleen Bryant; page 176 © jabiru/123rf.com; page 180 © Kathleen Bryant; page 182 © Kathleen Bryant; page 184 © Kathleen Bryant; page 185 © Richard Mayer; page 188 © Richard Mayer; page 190 © Kathleen Bryant; page 194 NPS Photo by Michael Quinn; page 198 USDA Forest Service, Southwestern Region, Kaibab National Forest, Dyan Bone; page 200 USDA Forest Service, Southwestern Region, Kaibab National Forest, Dyan Bone; page 201 USDA Forest Service, Southwestern Region, Kaibab National Forest; page 202 (top) © Flagstaff CVB, (bottom) © Josemaria Toscano/123RF; page 203 © Visions of America LLC/123rf.com; page 208 © Kathleen Bryant; page 209 © Kathleen Bryant; page 210 © Kathleen Bryant; page 211 USDA Forest Service, Southwestern Region, Coconino National Forest, Tyler Finvold; page 212 © Kathleen Bryant; page 218 © Kathleen Bryant; page 220 (top) © Kathleen Bryant, (bottom) Richard Mayer; page 221 © Richard Mayer; page 224 © U.S. Forest Service, Southwestern Region, Kaibab National Forest; page 227 © USGS photo from Grand Canyon

Also Available

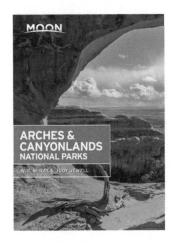

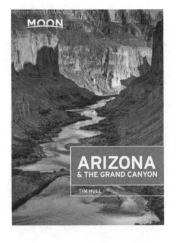

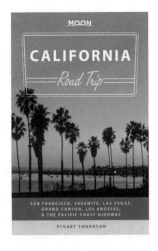

MAP SYMBOLS

≡≡≡	Expressway	○	City/Town	✈	Airport	⚲	Golf Course
≡≡≡	Primary Road	◉	State Capital	✗	Airfield	🅿	Parking Area
	Secondary Road	⊛	National Capital	▲	Mountain	≞	Archaeological Site
- - -	Unpaved Road	★	Point of Interest	✦	Unique Natural Feature	⬗	Church
—	Feature Trail	•	Accommodation			🯄	Gas Station
- - -	Other Trail			⚘	Waterfall		
....	Ferry	▾	Restaurant/Bar	⚑	Park	⬯	Glacier
≡≡≡	Pedestrian Walkway	■	Other Location	⬙	Trailhead	▨	Mangrove
▥▥▥	Stairs	Λ	Campground	⚐	Skiing Area	⬯	Reef
						⬯	Swamp

CONVERSION TABLES

°C = (°F − 32) / 1.8
°F = (°C x 1.8) + 32
1 inch = 2.54 centimeters (cm)
1 foot = 0.304 meters (m)
1 yard = 0.914 meters
1 mile = 1.6093 kilometers (km)
1 km = 0.6214 miles
1 fathom = 1.8288 m
1 chain = 20.1168 m
1 furlong = 201.168 m
1 acre = 0.4047 hectares
1 sq km = 100 hectares
1 sq mile = 2.59 square km
1 ounce = 28.35 grams
1 pound = 0.4536 kilograms
1 short ton = 0.90718 metric ton
1 short ton = 2,000 pounds
1 long ton = 1.016 metric tons
1 long ton = 2,240 pounds
1 metric ton = 1,000 kilograms
1 quart = 0.94635 liters
1 US gallon = 3.7854 liters
1 Imperial gallon = 4.5459 liters
1 nautical mile = 1.852 km

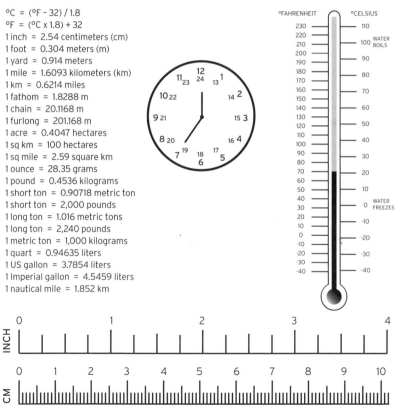

MOON GRAND CANYON

Avalon Travel
Hachette Book Group
1700 Fourth Street
Berkeley, CA 94710, USA
www.moon.com

Editor: Rachel Feldman
Series Manager: Sabrina Young
Copy Editor: Christopher Church
Production and Graphics Coordinator:
  Elizabeth Jang
Cover Design: Faceout Studios, Charles Brock
Moon Logo: Tim McGrath
Map Editor: Mike Morgenfeld
Cartographers: Brian Shotwell, Lohnes+Wright
Indexer: Greg Jewett

ISBN-13: 978-1-63121-565-0

Printing History
1st Edition — 1999
7th Edition — October 2017
5 4 3 2 1

Text © 2017 by Kathleen Bryant.
Maps © 2017 by Avalon Travel.
Some photos and illustrations are used by permission and are the property of the original copyright owners.

Front cover photo: full moon over Grand Canyon © nobleIMAGES / Alamy Stock Photo

Back cover photo: detail of interior Desert View Watchtower mural; NPS photo by Michael Quinn

Printed in Canada by Friesens

Avalon Travel is a division of Hachette Book Group, Inc. Moon and the Moon logo are trademarks of Hachette Book Group, Inc. All other marks and logos depicted are the property of the original owners.